P9-CRA-764

THE AMERICAN AGE

Other Books by Walter LaFeber:

The American Search for Opportunity, 1865–1913
Inevitable Revolutions: The United States in Central America, *2nd edition*
The Panama Canal: The Crisis in Historical Perspective, *2nd edition*
The Third Cold War
The American Century: A History of the United States since the 1890's (with Richard Polenberg and Nancy Woloch), *4th edition*
America, Russia, and the Cold War, 1945–1992
John Quincy Adams and American Continental Empire
The New Empire: An Interpretation of American Expansion, 1860–1898

THE AMERICAN AGE

United States Foreign Policy at Home and Abroad

WALTER LAFEBER

Second Edition

Volume I · To 1920

W · W · NORTON & COMPANY · NEW YORK · LONDON

The text of this book is composed in Linotype Walbaum,
with display type set in Walbaum.
Composition and manufacturing by The Maple-Vail Book Manufacturing Group.
Book design by Antonina Krass

Second Edition

Library of Congress Cataloging in Publication Data
LaFeber, Walter.
The American age : United States foreign policy at home and abroad /
Walter LaFeber. — 2nd ed.
p. cm.
Includes bibliographical references and index.
1. United States—Foreign relations. I. Title.
E183.7.L27 1994
327.73—dc20 93-14460

One Vol: ISBN 0-393-96474-4 (pa)
Vol 1: ISBN 0-393-96475-2 (pa)
Vol 2: ISBN 0-393-96476-0 (pa)

W. W. Norton & Company, Inc., 500 Fifth Avenue, New York, N.Y. 10110
W. W. Norton & Company Ltd., 10 Coptic Street, London WC1A 1PU

1 2 3 4 5 6 7 8 9 0

This book is dedicated to Michael Kammen, Larry Moore, Mary Beth Norton, Richard Polenberg, and Joel Silbey for being, over the years, friends, colleagues, and co-teachers of the U.S. Survey Course.

Contents

9 | Wilsonians, Revolutions, and War (1913–1917) 269

10 | Victors without Peace (1917–1920) 302

List of Maps

Preface to the Second Edition

Since the first edition of this book appeared in 1989, we and our world have gone through changes that are not merely memorable, but historic—the kinds of changes that occur only several times a century. Because of these transformations, and also because this book was fortunate in the kind of interest shown by teachers and scholarly reviewers, this new edition analyzes the 1989–1993 watershed in some detail while strengthening the features that students and teachers found useful in the first edition.

Four additions are especially important:

- The end of the Soviet empire, the U.S. response as the sole remaining superpower, and Bill Clinton's election are discussed not only from the American perspective, but, at the appropriate points, from other perspectives as well.
- The pre-1900 sections have been enlarged. *The American Age* was written especially for courses in the post-1914 history of U.S. foreign relations. It has been a pleasant surprise to learn that pre-1900 material is receiving increased attention in classrooms, and that teachers have found the book's early chapters useful—but they want more detail. So new discussions, and graphics, have been added especially on the Jeffersonian era, the 1830s–1840s, and 1890s. (Perhaps one reason for the interest in the pre–World War I era is that it so eerily, and sometimes frighteningly, resembles the 1989–1993 years with their ethnic violence, disruptions in the Balkans and eastern Europe, the rise of a vigorous Japan and a united Germany, and the appearance of radically new—and politically disruptive—technology and communications.)
- Materials have been used from newly opened files and fresh research to rewrite the book's sections on the outbreak of the cold war, the

causes of the Korean War, the Cuban missile crisis, and President Richard Nixon's policies and personality.
- Additional references are made to motion pictures and television, and new graphics of films have been used. Readers liked the book's use of these references, and the new material has been added in the belief that films do reflect large concerns of Americans and their foreign policies. (Sometimes, as is noted in the text, this reflection is badly distorted and dangerously misleading, even while being influential.) Television has increasingly shaped U.S. foreign-policy choices, not least in the Central American upheavals, the Persian Gulf War, and Somalia.

Virtually every chapter has had revisions and/or additions. All the bibliographies, especially the General Bibliography at the end of the book, are updated. For those interested in a more specific listing, the following are some of the topics discussed on the new pages: the beginnings of the secretary of state's office; Daniel Webster's Whig policies; the *Caroline* and *Creole* affairs, and the Maine boundary dispute; women's key role in the anti-imperialist movement after 1898; a new interpretation that frames the 1880s to 1913 era; the 1900–1913 revolutionary outbreaks in Latin America and Asia, with attention to the Chinese upheaval; the role of motion pictures in the 1915–1917 debates and again (with *Sergeant York*) in 1941; Truman's decisions to use the atomic bomb and to delay before accepting Japan's surrender; newly opened Soviet materials giving Moscow's perspective on the Marshall Plan and the Klaus Fuchs spy case; Stalin's and Mao's roles in the Korean War; John F. Kennedy's approach to the possibility of bombing China's nuclear facilities; Kennedy's views on Vietnam and the views of Oliver Stone's film, *JFK;* the post-1948 roots of U.S. policies on South Africa; the Chilean crises of 1973 and the film *Missing;* Reagan, Gorbachev, and breakthrough agreements; the end of the cold war, a growing disorder, and David Lynch's world on television and in films, 1989–1993.

In addition to the friends thanked in the Acknowledgments of the first edition, I am greatly indebted to Robert Beisner, Barton Bernstein, Tim Borstelmann, Philip Brenner, Kenton Clymer, Warren Cohen, Michael Doyle, Robert Hannigan, Alan Kraut, Fumiaki Kubo, Julius Milmeister, Martin Sklar, and Evan Stewart, as well as several outside readers, who provided criticism and materials for this edition. I am especially grateful to Steve Forman, History Editor of W. W. Norton's College Division, to Bonnie Hall and Kate Brewster, editorial assistants, and to a most helpful copy editor, Sandy Lifland, all of whom improved this edition considerably; and to long-time friends Ed Barber and Gerry McCauley. Lizann Rogovoy and Bob Rouse provided indispensable research help. Above all, I thank the students and teachers, as well as the general readers, who have used *The American Age* and found it helpful in understanding United States foreign policy.

Walter LaFeber
Spring 1993

Preface to the First Edition

This book has been written to provide a relatively brief (and, I hope, readable) overview of post-1750 U.S. foreign relations. Chapters' lengths increase markedly after 1890. The pre-1890 sections, however, include the material needed to understand the first century of those foreign relations; all or part of those chapters can be used as introductory assignments in a one-semester post-1890 class.

The title is taken seriously. As Professor Thomas A. Bailey once observed, the United States was a world power at the birth of its independence in 1776. Then, if not before, the American age began because the country already ranked with the great European nations in terms of territory, population, economic strength, and natural resources, not to mention ambition. This survey tries to develop several themes that tie 250 years together, make sense of them, and give students and teachers starting points for discussion. The most obvious theme is the landed and commercial expansion that drove the nation outward between 1750 and the 1940s. Then, resembling other living things that age, the country's power began a relative decline after the mid-1950s. Americans have yet to understand and come to terms with the causes and consequences of that decline, although presidents from Kennedy through Reagan have, in varying ways, shaped their policies so that the country could adjust to this new world.

The book's second theme is the steady centralization of power at home, especially in the executive branch of government after 1890. This centralization occurred not merely because of the normal quest of human beings for power, but also because the foreign policies that Americans have desired since the nineteenth century are most effectively carried out by a strong presidency. There are no recurring cycles in this book, only the long rise and the relative decline of U.S. power, and the steady accretion of authority by presidents because of the way

Americans have wanted to exercise that power. U.S. diplomatic history has often been written as if constitutional questions ceased to be important after 1865; this volume tries in small part to rectify that neglect.

A third theme is "isolationism," which means in U.S. history not withdrawal from world affairs (a people does not conquer a continent and become the world's greatest power by withdrawal or by assuming it enjoys "free security"), but maintaining a maximum amount of freedom of action. Americans who have professed to believe in individualism at home not surprisingly have often professed the same abroad.

A fourth theme is the importance of the transitional 1850-to-1914 era, a time when Americans' attitudes toward democracy, the Monroe Doctrine, the Constitution, and, especially, revolution underwent profound change and ushered in modern U.S. foreign policy. It is perhaps the great irony—and dilemma—of the nation's experience that it became a great power and wanted either to preserve the political *status quo* or only gradually to effect change precisely when the world began to erupt in revolution. This book tries to note some of the results of that irony and dilemma.

Finally, in the belief that how Americans act at home reveals much about how they act abroad, the analysis often focuses on domestic events (including films and sports). Social and diplomatic history have too seldom been wedded; parts of this account attempt in a minor way to start, at least, the courtship.

THE AMERICAN AGE

If I should not be thought too presumptuous I would beg leave to add what is my idea of the qualifications necessary for an American foreign minister in general. . . .

In the first place, he should have an education in classical learning and in the knowledge of general history, ancient and modern, and particularly the history of France, England, Holland, and America. He should be well versed in the principles of ethics, of the law of nature and nations, of legislation and government, of the Civil Roman law, of the laws of England and the United States, of the public law of Europe and in the letters, memoirs, and histories of those great men who have heretofore shone in the diplomatic order and conducted the affairs of nations and the world. He should be of an age to possess a maturity of judgment, arising from experience in business. He should be active, attentive, and industrious, and, above all, he should possess an upright heart and an independent spirit, and should be one who decidedly makes the interest of his country, not the policy of any other nation nor his own private ambition or interest, or those of his family, friends, and connexions, the rule of his conduct.

—John Adams (1783)

Domestic issues can only lose elections, but foreign policy issues can kill us all.

—President John F. Kennedy (1962)

1

The Roots of American Foreign Policy (1492–1789)

The Beginnings: Gold, God, and Paradise

William Seward, a fascinating scholar and New York backroom politician as well as Abraham Lincoln's secretary of state during the Civil War, once called the story of American development "the most important secular event in the history of the human race."[1] Seward might well have been correct. Americans, however, have viewed their secular, or more earthly, successes (such as making money) as part of a higher purpose. This view goes back to the origins of their country. Portuguese explorer Vasco da Gama needed few words to explain why a new world was discovered in the late fifteenth century: "We come in search of Christians and spices."

Mission and money or, as some historians prefer to phrase it, idealism and self-interest have for nearly five hundred years been the reasons Americans have given for their successes. From their beginnings, they have justified developing a continent and then much of the globe simply by saying they were spreading the principles of civilization as well as making profit. They have had no problem seeing their prosperity—indeed, their rise from a sparsely settled continent to the world's superpower—as part of a Higher Purpose or, as it was known during much of their history, a Manifest Destiny.

The most spectacular chance taker of his time said it directly. "Gold is most excellent, Gold is treasure," Christopher Columbus observed, "and he who possesses it does all he wishes to in this world, and succeeds in helping souls into paradise." Columbus was the original self-made man in America. As historian Edward Bourne observes: "His hopes, his illusions, his vanity and love of money, his devotion to by-gone ideals, his keen and sensitive observation of the natural world, his lack of practical power in dealing with literary evidence, his practical abilities as a navigator, his tenacity of purpose and boldness of execution, his lack of fidelity as a husband and a lover, his family pride,"[2] all mark Columbus as an appropriate figure to start the story of America's place in the world.

Columbus is also a useful symbol and starting point in American foreign policy for another reason: he founded empires by going westward. Again, nature, perhaps even the supernatural, seemed to be guiding Americans. They simply had to follow the sun. "We held it ever certain," the explorer Cabeza de Vaca declared in 1535, "that going toward the sunset we would find what we desired." Two centuries later, George Berkeley captured this vision in his famous poem that has the line "Westward the course of empire takes its way."

ON THE PROSPECT OF PLANTING ARTS
AND LEARNING IN AMERICA

The Muse, disgusted at an age and clime
Barren of every glorious theme,
In distant lands now waits a better time,
Producing subjects worthy fame:

In happy climes where from the genial sun
And virgin earth such scenes ensue,
The force of art by nature seems outdone,
And fancied beauties by the true:

In happy climes, the seat of innocence,
Where nature guides and virtue rules,
Where men shall not impose for truth and sense
The pedantry of courts and schools:

There shall be sung another golden age,
The rise of empire and of arts,
The good and great inspiring epic rage,
The wisest heads and noblest hearts.

Not such as Europe breeds in her decay;
  Such as she bred when fresh and young,
When heavenly flame did animate her clay,
  By future poets shall be sung.

Westward the course of empire takes its way;
  The four first acts already past,
A fifth shall close the drama with the day;
  Time's noblest offspring is the last.

Berkeley set out a great theme in Americans' foreign policy as they settled a continent by crossing from the Atlantic to the Pacific, moved across the Pacific Ocean to become a great world power for the first time in 1900, and then fought three major wars on the Asian mainland in the twentieth century. This westward movement has shaped much of the nation's best literature (the novels of Mark Twain and Willa Cather, and Robert Penn Warren's *All the King's Men* come to mind), as it has U.S. foreign policy.

Another key theme of American diplomacy also appeared during the era of discovery: the country's prosperity and success, sometimes its very existence, have depended on events thousands of miles away. The birth of Americans as a separate people came out of fourteenth- and fifteenth-century events. Religious crusades, scientific discoveries, attempts to find new routes to Asia so expensive Italian middlemen could be avoided—all led Portugal and Spain to undertake the expeditions that climaxed in the discovery of the New World. The Spanish finally built a three-century-old empire because they had succeeded in consolidating power at home (sometimes brutally, as expelling or enslaving Moors and some 100,000 Jews who would not join the Roman Catholic church) and seizing the money needed to pay for Columbus's voyages. This centralized power then set about discovering and colonizing parts of North America and most of South America, exploring the Pacific, circling the globe, and introducing the first black slaves into the New World as early as 1502, a full century before the British brought such slaves to their colonies. Aside from their "Christianizing" the New World's inhabitants, Spain so violently extracted gold and valuable minerals that Native Americans ("Indians") and black slaves who worked in the mines died in large numbers.

The political events in Spain and the economic opportunities in America combined to revolutionize world trade. From their beginnings, Americans formed part of a world economic system. Nor could they successfully isolate themselves from the upheavals of Europe. On the other hand, they also were pivotal in reshaping the globe's politics and economics. Their wealth and labor allowed Spain and then England and Holland to replace Italian and German cities as the world's trade centers. Furs, tobacco, sugar, and fish from North America replaced Asia's spices as the most valuable products in Europe's trade.

There is also another theme that links the five hundred years of America's relations with the rest of the world: the effect on those relations of new technology and scientific discoveries. Columbus depended on fresh calculations that indicated the world was round, not flat. He proved those calculations correct by using the latest compasses, astrolabe, and elaborate tables that measured longitude. From these first voyages of discovery through the Yankee clipper ship that conquered world trade, the Colt .44 revolver that conquered the West, the airplane that conquered distance, the atomic bomb, and the multistage rocket that conquered space, American foreign policy cannot be understood apart from the technology that transformed the world and made diplomacy ever more complex—and dangerous. Those technological conquests also help us to understand why Americans have too often believed that crises in foreign affairs might well be solved through new scientific breakthroughs.

The early quests for wealth, personal salvation, westward empire, control of the world's centers of political and economic power, and supremacy in technology led to both the settlement of America and its rise as the globe's superpower.

The City on a Hill—and on the Water

Throughout the 1500s, England watched Spain and Portugal explore the New World. But the British also shared in the profits by looting Spanish ships that carried precious metals back to Europe. England's settlements, however, failed disastrously until 1606–1607, when a group of wealthy investors established Jamestown, Virginia. Jamestown's founding and survival could be traced to its economic role in international trade. The founders were looking for the river system that supposedly provided entry into the fabled markets of Asia. They hoped that the James River might be such a system. Some 10,000 miles short of their goal, the settlers quickly discovered that they had to find an export crop to pay for their food and other imports from the home country. They tried silk and sassafras, but unfortunately neither was habit-forming. Then John Rolfe experimented in 1612 with Indian tobacco. In 1614, two barrels of cured tobacco left for England. Four years later, tobacco was a rage in Europe. Virginia shipped nearly 50,000 pounds abroad annually. The "hellish, devilish, and damned tobacco," as English critics called it, provided the settlement's lifeline to the world.[3]

Thus, hardly had America been settled than it transformed Europe's trade and personal habits. But tobacco also forced Virginia's foreign relations into surprising avenues. As growers discovered the profitability of importing black slaves to tend the fields, new trade routes extended southward to Africa. Westward the Virginians began seizing fresh land to replace the soil worn out by as few as three tobacco crops. The "hellish" weed had both locked America into Africa's history and had driven the settlers westward toward the sun—and the Native Americans.

To the north, another group of English men and women settled at Massachusetts Bay in 1630. Their leader, John Winthrop, uttered words that resounded nearly four hundred years later, when he urged the devout separatists: "We must consider that we shall be as a city upon a hill, the eyes of all people are upon us." Those are among the most famous words in American history and have been quoted repeatedly—from the founders in the 1780s to President Ronald Reagan in the 1980s—to define the U.S. mission in the world. Much less quoted are Winthrop's warnings in that famous utterance. "The care of the public must oversway all private respects," and "Wee must be knitt together in this work as one man." Or again: "Wee [should] be willing to abridge ourselves of superfluities for the supply of others' necessities."[4] Those words have been less popular in American history.

Indeed, from the start, the opportunities of foreign trade and landed expansion destroyed Winthrop's hope that "the city upon a hill" would be "knitt together . . . as one man." The city on a hill was actually a city on an ocean.[5] It had open to it world trade, especially the export of the famous Boston cod, which was exploited by adventurous individualists who cared more about profit margins than about Puritan restraints. From the start, fish were vital to American foreign relations because they brought in much-needed hard money (gold and silver) from Europe. The fisheries of the North Atlantic were the equivalent of the gold mines in South America—and the fish even reproduced. Moreover, one devout observer wrote at the time of settlement that the fisheries were so bleak that sailors would be tempted by neither "wine nor women."[6] It seemed a perfect combination of gold and God. No wonder that, as we shall see, three generations of the famous Adams family of Massachusetts devoted much of their distinguished diplomatic careers to keeping the fisheries in American hands. But the fisheries and other trade also shaped early foreign relations in another way: New Englanders invested their growing profits in western lands and thus pushed settlement toward the sunset until it collided with Native Americans and with Frenchmen who were settling Canada and exploring the Great Lakes region.

These first American foreign relations did nothing less than change American society. As one scholar has noted, the possibility of making fortunes in overseas trade and western territories made settlers "more interested in saving dollars than souls, more concerned with good land than compact villages, more excited about individual wealth than group welfare."[7] From their beginnings, Americans have never been able to separate their foreign relations from the way they carry on their lives at home.

The First Americans

The settlers did not discover a vacant East Coast. For the next 350 years they did not move over an empty continent. A central theme of American diplomatic history must be the clash between the European settlers and the Native Americans between 1620 and 1890. That clash led the settlers to fight wars of conquest, create a unique military machine to wage war, and nearly exterminate the Indian tribes.

Probably 8.5 to 10 million Native Americans populated all of North America in 1492. The first American immigrants had arrived well before the Europeans—in about 30,000 B.C. With as many as 600 different societies and over 200 languages, they had developed complex civilizations that carefully preserved—even as they lived from—the rivers, woods, land, and wild animals. By the time settlements of whites appeared in Virginia and Massachusetts, many Native Americans had already disappeared because of lack of immunity to the explorers' diseases, especially smallpox and measles which ravaged many tribes.

At the beginning of settlement, the Indians provided the food and agricultural know-how that allowed many of the whites to survive. But the Native Americans gradually began to fear the Europeans' growing numbers and different culture. Moreover, they were inflamed by internal divisions and fears of neighboring tribes. In 1622, on Good Friday, the Powhatans suddenly attacked and destroyed one-quarter of Virginia's white population. Thus began a series of wars between whites and Native Americans that soaked the rest of colonial history in blood. With British help and at great cost, the settlers not only won most of the conflicts, but virtually wiped out such tribes as the powerful Pequots in New England. The Indians had long been independent, were deeply divided among themselves, and could not cooperate in waging war. Some were easily bought off with money or European goods. Many even served as guides or raiders for the whites against other tribes. Although usually superior fighters individually, Native Americans did not fight for long periods with the intensity of the whites, nor—although they were highly skilled in making weapons—did they learn in the early decades how to make gunpowder.[8]

The settlers quickly drew several lessons from these seventeenth-century encounters. They developed a racism that provided an excuse to remove or kill Indians who blocked landed expansion. Native American cultures were not individualistic, Christian, or even monotheistic. It was, therefore, easy for the great Puritan divine, Cotton Mather, to believe that "Probably the Devil decoyed" the Indians to America "in hopes that the gospel of the Lord Jesus Christ would never come here to destroy or disturb his absolute empire over them."[9] The "noble savage" idea fascinated those in faraway British and French coffee shops, but it never interested American leaders such as Mather. The whites also learned that exploiting the environment—that is, destroying woods and killing large numbers of fur-bearing animals—not only was profitable for their overseas trade, but severely weakened the Native Americans. As colonial population grew, so many animals were killed and so many fields were cleared that the climate in North America changed.[10]

Finally, the settlers discovered from the Indian wars that they had to break with the European tradition of a professional army. Instead, they gave weapons to all able-bodied male settlers, who farmed part-time and fought part-time. Thus was born the militia system that formed the backbone for the American military over the next several centuries. Thus were also born the tactics for "Indian fighting"—guerrilla-type warfare instead of the traditional European armies-in-mass that slaughtered each other on open battlefields. These new tactics shaped U.S. military strategy in wars from the American Revolution through the interventions in the Caribbean–Central American region in the 1920s.

The American "Multiplication Table" and the European Power Struggle

The settlers sharply honed those military tactics in the century before 1776. The Indian wars diminished slightly by 1700, but the colonials then turned their rifles on other Europeans. From the beginning of their history, Americans lived not in any splendid isolation, far from the turmoil and corruption of the Europe many had hoped to escape. They instead had to live in settlements that were surrounded by great and ambitious European powers. France controlled the St. Lawrence River region through eastern Canada and down the Great Lakes to the Mississippi River. The French explorer La Salle had claimed Louisiana (that is, nearly all the vast lands whose rivers emptied into the Mississippi) as early as 1682. To the south, Spain moved out of Florida and consolidated its hold on the Caribbean region.

Perhaps the three great empires (British, French, and Spanish) might have lived at peace in the New World through much of the eighteenth century except for an incredible development: the American "multiplication table." This "table" referred to the high birth rate of colonials that produced families of five to ten children even as infant mortality rates dropped. The term itself was coined much later, in the 1840s by Representative Andrew Kennedy of Indiana. Kennedy told the House of Representatives that "our people are spreading out with the aid of the American multiplication table." He elaborated: "Go to the West and see a young man with his mate of eighteen; after a lapse of thirty years, visit him again, and instead of two, you will find twenty-two. That is what I call the American multiplication table."[11]

One result of the American "multiplication table" was almost continual war with France and Spain between 1689 and 1763. These struggles in the New World formed part of a larger European conflict among the three great imperial nations. But the wars also showed how Americans—whether they liked it or not—were part of European power politics even as they moved into the forests and fertile lands beyond the Appalachian Mountains. They could not separate their destiny from the destiny of those they had left behind in Europe. Their own imperial ambitions were not small. In 1745, William Shirley, the restless, imaginative governor of Massachusetts, captured the French fortress at Louisbourg in eastern Canada. He then set his sights on conquering the rest of Canada and all the French holdings in the Mississippi region. London officials, however, infuriated Shirley by making peace with the French (those hated Roman Catholics to the north) and restoring Louisbourg as part of an overall peace settlement.

Shirley and other colonial leaders impatiently waited for another opportunity they knew would soon arise. In the early 1750s, it happened. British settlers established forts in the central part of present-day Ohio. In 1752, the French retaliated by seizing a key fortress in the region. England's Indian allies swung over to support the French.

Benjamin Franklin (1706–1790), man of the world and Pennsylvania politician, colonial postmaster general, author of wise advice for a growing nation in Poor Richard's Almanack, *and member of the Continental Congress and the 1787 Constitutional Convention. He was also the original U.S. diplomat who combined worldly knowledge with the ability to play the New World "primitive" to charm both the salons as well as the foreign ministry in Paris in order to negotiate the crucial alliance with France.*

The Native Americans were coming to see that the French, who wanted the Indians' trade and Roman Catholic souls but not their territory, posed less danger than did the land-hungry British settlers. Virginia sent out a twenty-one-year-old surveyor-soldier, George Washington, to negotiate with the French. When talks failed, Washington attacked the French around the key strategic position of present-day Pittsburgh. Thus began the Seven Years' War—or the Great War for Empire, as it later became known. The struggle transformed the political face of North America and led directly to the American Revolution.

Benjamin Franklin and the Problems of a Rising People

The conflict also brought Benjamin Franklin to the world stage. The first American diplomat, Franklin's life illustrated the ambition and intelligence of the settlers. His career also demonstrated how Americans created a landed empire, then broke with England so that they could themselves run and profit from that empire.

Born in 1706 as the tenth child of Josiah and Abiah Folger Franklin in Boston, Franklin, at the age of seventeen, fought with his family and moved to Philadelphia. There he became a printer, accumulating both personal wealth (especially with his *Poor Richard's Almanack*) and political power. Franklin paraded as an ordinary man, but his travels and contacts with leading figures in colonial life gave him unique knowledge about America. He set up profitable printing companies in Antigua, Connecticut, and New York. In that sense, Franklin was perhaps America's first multinational corporation.

In 1751, Franklin, drawing on his research and knowledge of colonial life, published a pamphlet that remains crucial for understanding American foreign policy. *Observations Concerning the Increase of Mankind* began with careful calculations showing that Americans were doubling their population approximately every twenty years. This unbelievable figure, Franklin argued, had far-reaching consequences. First, it meant that additional land would soon be needed for settlement or else the colonies would be dammed up and become stagnant. Second, it meant that Britain should help find the land because Britain's manufacturers and merchants would enjoy a most profitable market in the new settlements. Finally, it became apparent that finding the necessary room meant war against the French and their Indian allies.[12] Franklin seemed to welcome that conclusion.

In his 1751 pamphlet, Franklin thus helped explain the causes of both the Great War for Empire and the American Revolution. When the struggle began in 1754, Franklin immediately focused on the problem that henceforth haunted American officials: How could they govern the tremendous expanse of land they hoped to conquer? He answered with the Albany Plan of 1754, a scheme that concentrated power in a central colonial agency that could effectively deal with Native Americans and fight the French. Neither the British Crown nor the thirteen colonial governments, however, would surrender power to the agency, so Franklin's idea died. It was thirty-three years ahead of its time and the Constitutional Convention.

In 1757, the Pennsylvanian sailed to London to serve as the colony's official representative. British military victories over France led to heated discussions over peace terms. The major question was whether London should take the rich French sugar island of Guadeloupe in the Caribbean or the largely empty expanse of Canada. Franklin had no doubt. Using his 1751 pamphlet as a weapon, he argued that the population explosion and the resulting sales for British manufacturers dictated seizing Canada. But his argument did not go unchallenged. A British pamphleteer, William Burke, warned that if Franklin's advice were followed and the French were expelled, the Americans would rush into the vast region and become uncontrollable. Burke also touched a nerve that remained sensitive for the next two hundred years of American diplomacy. Noting Franklin's argument that "security" required removing the French from Canada, Burke argued that "to desire the enemy's whole country on no other principle but that otherwise you cannot secure your own, is turning the idea of mere defense into the most dangerous of all principles. It is leaving no medium between safety and conquest. It is to suppose yourself never safe, whilst your neighbor enjoys any security."[13]

Franklin won the argument. In 1763, the British took Canada and all the land that stretched southward and westward to the Mississippi River. Spain, a French ally, received Louisiana territory from Paris in return for agreeing to an immediate peace. The Spanish gave East and West Florida to England in exchange for Cuba, which the British navy had seized. France's long career as a New World power was over. But Burke had the last word: "What the consequences will be to have a numerous, hardy, independent people [loose in the Canadian wilderness]" he left to the reader's imagination.

Humiliated French officials plotted revenge for their losses in 1763. Delighted colonials prepared to find their fortunes by following the sun.

The Road to Revolution (1763–1775)

But the colonials instead crashed into boundaries set by the British Empire. The empire's theory had for a century been "mercantilist"—that is, Great Britain had the right to operate the colonies for its own profit; in return, London protected the colonials from outsiders. Such was the theory. In reality, the colonials acted independently and largely protected themselves. By 1700, probably half of Boston's trade was illegal because it was with the French West Indies instead of with British merchants, as London's mercantile laws required. Few in London or Boston cared. Profits from the French trade went to London to pay for British goods. Prime Minister Sir Robert Walpole nicely, if insensitively, described colonial policy before the 1754 war as "Let sleeping dogs lie." But the dogs did not sleep. Merchants, settlers, and colonial legislators did as they pleased until they came to believe that they were the equal of London's Parliament in running colonial affairs.

From 1763 to 1765, Parliament decided to pay for the costs of the 1754–1763 war by taxing the colonies. London merchants, moreover, demanded that the illegal trade with France be stopped. The Stamp Act, taxing colonial newspapers and mail, raised the revenue. Other acts clamped down on smuggling. Americans responded with the revolutionary doctrine that they had been self-governing since the first

North America, during the war of 1754 to 1763 (The Great War for Empire), after the British drove the French from Canada and as the thirteen colonies started down the road to revolution.

settlements and that, consequently, Parliament had no right to regulate each colony's trade. Americans refused to import British goods. London officials dismissed the claim of self-government. They and the British merchants, however, could not dismiss the nonimportation policy. As trade declined, Parliament finally repealed most of the 1764–1765 acts. But it then tried to raise revenue more subtly—such as imposing a tax on tea. In late 1773, the colonials, led by a deeply religious revolutionary, Samuel Adams, dumped large amounts of tea in

Boston Harbor. The infuriated British lashed back with the Intolerable Acts (as the colonials termed them) of 1774: Boston port was closed, political power in Massachusetts was largely switched from the colonials to appointed British officials, and—in a related move that made Protestant land speculators of Massachusetts and Virginia furious—Canada's boundaries were extended to the Ohio River. The colonials could no longer follow the sun without running into the Roman Catholic Canadians who were now loyal to Great Britain.

Colonial legislatures convened a Continental Congress to discuss retaliation. Americans had suddenly learned that their foreign policy and individual freedoms were closely related. London's claim to regulate foreign trade struck at the heart of their political independence, which they had long taken for granted. The *Georgia Gazette* urged support in the South for the far-off Bostonians in 1774 by arguing that if the British claim to "have a right or power to put a duty on my tea," they "have an equal right to put a duty on my bread, and why not on my breath, why not on my daylight and smoke, why not on everything?"[14] The South also shared another grievance with the North. In 1763, the British had declared a "Proclamation Line" that prohibited colonials from settling west of the Appalachian Mountains. The purpose was to regulate settlement and avoid Indian wars. Treaties with Native Americans allowed some expansion after 1770, but the Quebec Act closed the door again in 1774. The door closed, moreover, just as frustrated Americans were turning westward to find the trade and profit that the British denied them in the French West Indies.

Colonial leaders concluded that they could no longer find help in London. British politics changed rapidly in the 1760s as new factions, created in part from profits from the colonies, moved to control Parliament. London's politics, as Franklin described it from the scene, were most corrupt: "This whole venal nation is now at market," he wrote in 1768.[15] Decent colonials had little hope for relief from such an indecent system. Such sentiments were returned by Londoners, who considered the colonials grasping and ungrateful. As England's most famous literary figure put it, "Sir, [Americans] are a race of convicts and ought to be thankful for anything we allow them short of hanging." Dr. Samuel Johnson continued: "You know I am willing to love all mankind, except an American."[16]

The links of British colonial policy were now being pulled apart from both sides of the Atlantic. Foreign-policy issues (trade, westward expansion) were in the middle of this pulling and hauling.

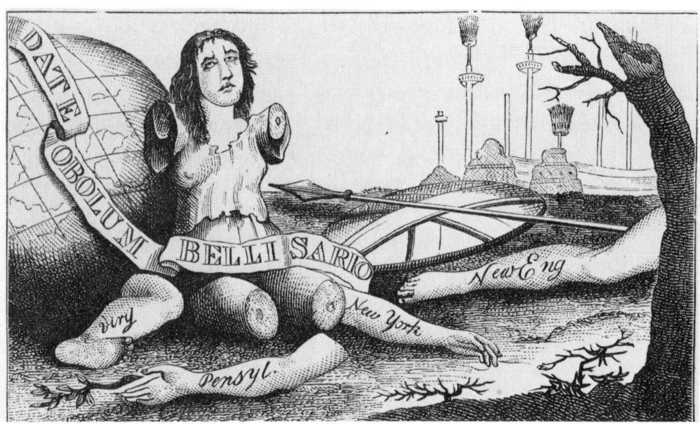

This 1774 cartoon of a woeful Great Britain, shorn of her badly needed colonial limbs, was by Benjamin Franklin. In addition to his other many talents, Franklin was one of the first important American political cartoonists. His view of the former British Empire (two years before the Revolution actually began) is indicated by the "Date Obolum Bellisario"—or "Give a Farthing to Belisarius," who was a general in Ancient Rome after the Roman Empire collapsed.

THE FOREIGN POLICY OF INDEPENDENCE (1776)

By early 1776, many of the 2.5 million white Americans thought of themselves as a separate people. As early as ten years before, a shrewd British observer told his nephew in North America that "you [in the colonies] wish to be an Empire by itself."[17] But revolution against the world's greatest power was not trivial. According to one British legal source, a convicted traitor was to be hanged and taken down while alive, then his entrails were to be removed and burned, his head to be chopped off, and his body divided into four parts.[18]

Despite the long shadows of British gallows, the First Continental Congress met in September 1774 to bring together twelve colonies and discuss the Intolerable Acts. The delegates pledged not to import or consume British goods until the acts were repealed. But the British were now determined to enforce their own law. They also ordered their troops to seize the powder and arms of the colonials at Concord, Massachusetts. On April 19, 1775, British forces and American militia clashed at Lexington and Concord. A Second Continental Congress, more radical than the first, convened. It learned that early military operations had gone badly. But Franklin, ever upbeat, urged his fellow rebels to consider the glories of the American "multiplication table":

"Britain, at the expense of three millions [pounds], has killed 150 Yankees this campaign, which is twenty thousand pounds a head. During the same time 60,000 children have been born in America."[19]

The rebels nevertheless rapidly needed other kinds of help as well. The Congress established a five-member Secret Committee of Correspondence to find allies abroad. Independence required an active, successful foreign policy. The committee marked the beginning of the later Department of State. Its members included Franklin and John Jay of New York. The committee sent three agents abroad to seek help, including the first official U.S. diplomat, Silas Deane of Connecticut, who was to sound out the French foreign minister, Charles Gravier, Count de Vergennes, about political aid and arms purchases. France had already decided to make a secret loan of $2 million to the colonials. Vergennes, who had been thirsting for revenge against the British since France's 1763 defeat, sent a secret agent to contact rebel leaders in late 1775, then moved to isolate Great Britain by forming alliances with Spain, Austria, and Prussia. The Dutch, whose ambitious traders clashed with British naval power, also helped by sending gunpowder and rifles badly needed by the colonial militias.

The Congress meanwhile decided to invade and annex Canada. It was one of the more amazing and disastrous decisions in American diplomatic history. Many colonials had lusted after Canada, and a number wanted to teach Roman Catholics a lesson. Resources for the invasion were scarce, but as Richard Henry Lee of Virginia put it in late 1775, "We must have that country with us this winter cost what it will."[20] The Congress, whose members had long damned Canadians, now switched tactics and begged the "fellow sufferers" to join the Revolution. When the Canadians refused, General Richard Montgomery's army moved from upper New York toward Montreal. Another force, commanded by General Benedict Arnold, marched on Quebec. Neither army reached its objective. Winter weather forced Montgomery's "half-naked" troops to retreat and join Arnold. Montgomery died, and Arnold was wounded in a brave but useless attack on Quebec on New Year's Eve. Arnold later distinguished himself in October 1776 by brilliantly blocking the British invasion from Canada. It was a significant but anticlimactic victory, given the original American desire of annexing their "fellow sufferers" in Canada.

Defeats in the north and second thoughts in the Congress threatened the Revolution. Then, in January 1776, appeared *Common Sense*, an incendiary, skillfully written pamphlet by Thomas Paine, whom Franklin had sent to America after Paine was fired from the British

Thomas Paine (1737–1809), born in England and author of Common Sense, *the incendiary pamphlet that helped push Americans to revolution. After serving as secretary of the Committee on Foreign Affairs, Paine moved to France, where he defended the French Revolution. He then returned to the United States but made the mistakes of attacking organized religion and criticizing George Washington. He lived out his life in poverty.*

government for demanding higher wages. *Common Sense* revitalized the revolutionary cause. Moreover, it directly stated themes that dominated U.S. foreign policy over much of the next two hundred years. Paine attacked the British king, George III, as an "ass" and disdained remaining subject to Great Britain: "There is something absurd, in supposing a continent to be perpetually governed by an island. In no instance hath nature made the satellite larger than its primary planet." The new United States had a higher calling: "The cause of America is in a great measure the cause of all mankind." As historian Reginald Horsman notes, Paine helped Americans "convince themselves that what was good for America was good for the world."[21]

How did Paine plan to achieve independence? By using trade as a diplomatic lever. Thus appeared one of the assumptions in U.S. history that Great Britain (and later Russia, Japan, Communist China, Cuba, and South Africa) could be tamed because, as Paine phrased it, American products "are the necessaries of life, and will always have a market while eating is the custom of Europe." Victory, moreover, could be won without political alliances. Because all Europe needed U.S. goods, "we ought to form no partial connection with any part of it. It is the true interest of America to steer clear of European contentions." Paine thus made a famous statement of U.S. "isolationism"—that Americans should maintain maximum freedom of action to protect their interests, which were distinct from, and purer than, Europe's.

Paine's pamphlet was electrifying not because it said much that was new, but because he so skillfully expressed the views of many revolutionaries. The timing was perfect. It appeared as the Congress faced its most fateful decisions on independence. Moreover, in those days Americans read. Literacy rates ran as high as 95 percent among white males in some states and was probably the highest in the world. (In the 1980s, by comparison, the United States ranked forty-ninth among 158 nations in rate of literacy.[22]) The 500,000 copies of *Common Sense* printed in 1776 are equivalent to 25 million copies in the 1990s, given the difference in population size. High literacy and a successful (and orderly) revolution coincided in American history.

French help, Paine's writing, and Britain's inability to score crushing military victories finally gave the Congress the courage to open American ports in April 1776 to the entire world. America had broken free of British mercantile laws. Two months later, Richard Henry Lee resolved that "these United Colonies are, and of right ought to be, free and independent states." He then proposed the necessary measure for independence: "That it is expedient forthwith to take the most effectual measures for forming foreign alliances." On July 2, the Congress accepted Thomas Jefferson's draft of the Declaration of Independence, but only after it was heavily rewritten. Even then, John Dickinson of Pennsylvania launched an attack to defeat the Declaration. He warned that Americans could never conquer and govern an empire that stretched beyond the Appalachian Mountains. He feared that the country would come apart in twenty or thirty years and believed that the Hudson River was "a proper boundary" for America's western limit. He warned that if Americans allied with France to win that empire, they would only exchange British for even more intolerable French masters.[23] Dickinson's arguments were prophetic, but Lee and John Adams had the votes. The United States declared its independence.

The French Trap

Two weeks later, John Adams gave the Congress his draft of a Model Treaty for alliances. It repeated some of Paine's principles but translated them into diplomatic tactics that shaped U.S. foreign policy long after 1776:

> What Connection may We safely form with [France]? 1st. No Political Connection. Submit to none of her Authority—receive no Governors, or officers from her. 2nd. No Military Connection. Receive no troops from her. 3rd. Only a Commercial Connection, i.e., make a Treaty to receive

> her Ships into our Ports. Let her engage to receive our Ships into her Ports—furnish Us with Arms, Cannon, Salt, Petre, Powder, Duck, Steel.[24]

Adams thus expected France to provide full economic aid and wage war with Great Britain in return for no political payoff except the possible breakup of the British Empire. He also expected France to treat Americans as commercial equals and help them conquer parts of North America, including the rich fisheries of Newfoundland, while France kept its hands off North American territory.[25] Congress accepted Adams's dreams. It was doubtful that France would accept. The doubt grew as Lord Howe's British troops won a major victory on Long Island that nearly destroyed the American army under the command of General George Washington. U.S. trade slowed, tobacco piled up on southern docks. New England fishermen could not ply their trade because of British warships.

In late December 1776, a frightened Congress remodeled the Model Treaty. It offered France islands in the West Indies. If the French brought into the war their Spanish allies, Spain (which most Americans despised because it was Roman Catholic as well as in control of the immense empire of Louisiana) could have the Floridas. Americans prepared to pay a price, even bargain away some of their possible empire, for help in obtaining independence. Paine's and Adams's belief in the power of mere commercial ties had been proven wrong. The Congress dispatched Franklin to France, John Adams to Holland, and John Jay to Spain to obtain alliances and money.

In France, Franklin described himself as "very plainly dress'd" among "the Powder'd Heads of Paris." He was, however, hardly the "noble savage" he liked to portray. In historian Tadashi Aruga's words, the shrewd Franklin did nothing less than "call in the Old World to liberate the New World from the Old World."[26] The word *diplomacy* comes from the Greek word for a message that is folded so that its contents cannot be read. In that sense, Franklin superbly practiced diplomacy, for the "noble savage" was more devious and sophisticated than he seemed. The French once even caught him trying to collect one loan from them twice. The twentieth-century poet, William Carlos Williams, summarized Franklin's achievements by writing, "He played with lightning and the French Court."[27] Franklin did so, moreover, despite his age (he was seventy-two in 1778); difficult ocean voyages; a bad case of gout; the desertion of his beloved son, William, to Great Britain; and a private secretary (Edward Bancroft) who, unknown to Franklin, was a British spy.

When the Philadelphian landed in Paris late in 1776, the cause seemed lost. British armies were poised to take Philadelphia and Albany, while the U.S. Treasury was nearly empty. Franklin's great test arose in late 1777, when news arrived of the U.S. victory in October over General John Burgoyne's British army at Saratoga, New York. The French became worried, moreover, when British officials approached Franklin about possible reconciliation, talks that the American imaginatively enlarged upon for his French friends. Vergennes decided it was time to make a formal treaty. He and Franklin signed the deal on February 6, 1778. The commercial provisions provided for reciprocity, much as Adams's Model Treaty had requested. But the political provisions did not resemble Adams's scheme. Each nation pledged military cooperation. The United States had to guarantee French control of certain West Indian islands and promise not to sign a separate peace with the British. The Americans even had to pledge to remain France's partner "forever." Franklin had nevertheless played it well. "My dear papa," a beautiful French woman wrote him, why do people criticize "the sweet habit I have taken of sitting on your lap, and your habit of soliciting from me what I always refuse?" But Franklin had also been using the wife to form a friendship with her husband—who became a key agent for selling weapons to Washington's armies.[28]

No sooner did France promise to help, however, than Vergennes instructed his agents in the New World to keep the United States as small and weak as possible. If the Americans grew powerful, he feared, they would conquer the West Indies, then "advance to the Southern Continent of America . . . and in the end not leave a foot of that Hemisphere in the possession of any European power."[29] He had, moreover, finally convinced Spain to join the war effort. The Spanish cared most about reconquering Gibraltar from the British and seizing more land in the New World—not about helping Americans become independent. Thus, France held contradictory treaty obligations: to the Americans to fight until independence was won, but to the Spanish to fight until Gibraltar was won.

When Jay arrived in Madrid to obtain more Spanish help, he was snubbed and infuriated. Spain's officials had no desire to create an independent American giant on the boundaries of their New World empire. Adams fared better in Holland. He received financial and commercial help—indeed, so much that the British finally turned and destroyed much of Holland's fleet while sacking valuable Dutch islands in the West Indies. After those disasters, Dutch help was necessarily limited.

John Jay (1745–1829), a well-to-do gentleman lawyer in New York, was U.S. minister to Spain when he helped negotiate the 1783 peace treaty with Great Britain. For that he was honored, but was damned and hanged in effigy when he negotiated another treaty with the British twelve years later.

By 1779–1780, the Continental Congress seemed to be a slave to Vergennes. Its sad state was not due solely to the number of American politicians on the French payroll—although in Lawrence Kaplan's words, that payroll "was long, illustrious, and well-padded"[30]—but because U.S. survival seemed to depend on French help. The currency was so worthless that Washington complained "that a wagon-load of money will scarcely purchase a wagon-load of provisions." For a moment, the Congress hoped to get help from Catherine the Great of Russia. She worked with Vergennes to set up a League of Armed Neutrality to lay low England's commercial power. But she did so for Russian, not American, interests—she hated revolutionaries. When Francis Dana arrived as the first U.S. minister to Russia in 1781, he found the reception as frigid and desolate as the Russian winter. After two years of failure, Dana finally trudged back home.

But the news reaching the Congress was not all bad. Americans helped themselves in 1778–1779, when George Rogers Clark and his Kentucky militia braved a Midwest winter to surprise and capture key British posts in Wabash River country (the later states of Indiana and Illinois). The United States then signed its first treaty with an Indian tribe, the Delaware, who promised to help U.S. forces. In western New York, General John Sullivan attacked Indians who, with British aid, had massacred several settlements of whites. In 1779, Sullivan's troops virtually destroyed the great Iroquois nation that comprised many tribes. These victories, especially Clark's, helped establish the U.S. claim to the transappalachian West that the British, to the surprise of many, recognized in the 1783 peace treaty.

In the East, Washington's armies marked time in 1779–1780. The

Chronology: 1774–1778	
September 1774	First Continental Congress meets; twelve colonies represented.
October 1774	Colonies protest Quebec Act by pledging not to import British goods.
May 1775	Second Continental Congress meets; more radical membership than First.
August 1775	King George III declares colonies in rebellion.
November 1775	Secret Committees of Correspondence established.
December 1775	French secret agent arrives in America as King George III cuts off all trade into the colonies.
Winter 1775–1776	American attempt to conquer Canada fails disastrously.
January 1776	Thomas Paine publishes *Common Sense*.
March 1776	Continental Congress sends Silas Deane to France.
April 1776	Continental Congress opens American ports to the world.
May 1776	King Louis XVI of France accepts Vergennes's argument to aid Americans.
June 1776	Richard Henry Lee proposes resolutions to declare independence, form a confederation, and make foreign alliances.
July 2, 1776	Continental Congress accepts Declaration of Independence.
July 18, 1776	John Adams presents Model Treaty.
August 1776	General Howe leads British army into New York.
December 1776	Continental Congress revises Model Treaty's provisions; Benjamin Franklin arrives in France as U.S. representative.
December 1777	News of U.S. victory at Saratoga in October arrives in Paris.
December 1777–January 1778	British approach Franklin to discuss reconciliation.
February 6, 1778	U.S. and France sign treaties of alliance in Paris.

British decided to concentrate their forces in the South, where the largest number of pro-British Americans (the Loyalists) lived. The growing threat to the South between 1779 and 1781 led frightened Virginians to strengthen the new nation's government by ceding to it lands north of the Ohio River claimed by Virginia. Since 1776, the states had haggled bitterly over the question of western lands. Some of the landless states refused to ratify the Articles of Confederation, which formed the national government, until the wealthier landed states, such as Virginia, gave up their western claims. Now the logjam was broken, and all thirteen states prepared to join hands under a common constitution. But even under the Articles, the government would have little real power. Most important, the critical right to tax and regulate commerce remained in the hands of each state. The currency's value continued to sink.

In 1780, a nervous Congress instructed Franklin to surrender U.S. rights to the Mississippi River, if necessary, to obtain quick French and Spanish help. Jay, whose short-fused temper had already exploded in his dealings with the Spanish, and Franklin refused to follow instructions. The visionary but pragmatic Pennsylvanian wrote that he would rather buy more U.S. rights to the Mississippi, even at "a great price . . . than sell a Drop of its Waters. A Neighbour might as well ask me to sell my Street Door."[31]

After months of U.S. begging, the French fitted out 6 ships and 5,000 troops for warfare. This fleet was large enough to help save the colonies, but not large enough to conquer more land for the Americans. Before the French fleet could arrive in mid-1780, the British won a major battle at Charleston and prepared to move north to trap Washington's forces. But British General Lord Cornwallis's troops suffered heavy losses at the hands of Generals Nathanael Greene and Daniel Morgan at Guilford Courthouse, North Carolina, on March 15, 1781. Cornwallis withdrew to Yorktown, Virginia, to await orders for marching north. Washington's troops and the French army of Comte de Rochambeau had planned to attack New York, but when the French fleet drove British ships from Yorktown, the two commanders swung south and defeated Cornwallis's bottled-up forces on October 19, 1781.

Yorktown was the Revolution's decisive campaign. In the months that followed, a new British government under Lord Shelburne came to power. Shelburne reversed London's position of not recognizing American independence. He shrewdly understood that granting independence did not mean U.S. dependence on France. To the contrary, the double bait of independence and British trade could lure Americans back under England's control. For his part, Franklin initially demanded that, in return for peace, the British give the United States most of their holdings in North America, including Canada. Shelburne abruptly dismissed that demand, and the two sides sat down to hammer out more realistic terms. The boundaries of an independent United States were to be the Great Lakes on the North, the Mississippi on the west, and the thirty-first parallel on the south. Americans received rights to fish the rich Newfoundland banks. In return, the United States promised not to hinder the British from collecting millions of dollars of debts owed by colonials to London and Scottish merchants, and to help restore the property of perhaps 200,000 Loyalists who had left the country to join the British side. The Mississippi was to be open to both the British and Americans.

The U.S. negotiators (Franklin, Jay, Adams, and Henry Laurens) agreed to the terms on November 30, 1782. The first three negotiators (especially Jay) handled the talks, and their major problem was whether to obey the Congress's instructions to deal away the Mississippi, if necessary. Another complication was the promise of 1778 not to make peace without Vergennes's participation. Franklin had no intention of obeying such instructions and promises. And when he asked for Jay's opinion, the angry New Yorker said that if they conflicted with U.S. interests, "I would break them like this"—and he snapped the stem of his clay pipe.[32] Vergennes, who actually had little choice in the matter, allowed the talks to go on because they gave him an excuse not to prolong the war simply for Spain's sake. The Spanish were insisting on fighting until they regained Gibraltar. A major British naval victory finally destroyed that dream, and Spain—bought off by the promise that it could have the Louisiana Territory—allowed Vergennes to make peace.

Bittersweet Results of Peace

That the Americans ended the conflict with their independence and a large landed territory is remarkable. That they did so with so little bloodshed and class conflict is astonishing. Unlike the great revolutions that later struck France, Mexico, China, and Russia, the American Revolution did not become radical and kill off the class that started the revolt. John Adams led the revolutionaries in 1776 and insisted that maintaining order would be "the most difficult and dangerous Part" for Americans in "this Mighty Contest."[33] Adams and his colleagues, however, maintained not only order, but, remarkably, their own political power.

In this sense, the American Revolution was not revolutionary at all. Instead, it was the first modern anticolonial war. With rich opportunities for landed settlement and money-making, and having decades of experience in the art of self-government, Americans just wanted the

British to get out of the way. The legacy of this experience turned out to be momentous for U.S. foreign policy. Henceforth, Americans smiled on anticolonial wars but frowned on revolution—unless it resembled their own. Given their own unique history, no other revolution could be the same.

To the Constitution: "What Will Render Us Respectable Abroad?"

In September 1783, Franklin penned the famous phrase "There never was a good war or a bad peace."[34] But having won independence through war by 1783, Americans nearly lost it in peacetime within three years. Shelburne had been correct: the United States needed British markets and goods. Lord Sheffield's widely read pamphlet of 1784, *Observations on the Commerce of the United States*, laid out British policy. Because the United States depended on British trade, Sheffield argued, London could demand tough terms. It especially could do so because under the Articles of Confederation, the thirteen states were too weak and decentralized to fight back with a united policy. Parliament consequently decreed that U.S. ships could not trade with the British West Indies, certain goods could be carried only on British ships, and Canadian-U.S. trade would be severely limited. John Adams angrily condemned Parliament as "a parcel of sots" for passing such rules, but the British were succeeding in making Americans into mere providers of raw materials for British factories and then buyers of the finished British goods carried on British ships.

In 1783, the United States bought three times the amount of goods from the British that it sold to them. Prices fell, money grew scarce. Depression rocked the country between 1783 and 1786. Unpaid, disgruntled soldiers threatened rebellion until Washington personally intervened in 1783 with a resounding speech that condemned anyone "who wickedly attempts to open the floodgates of civil discord and deluge our rising empire in blood."[35] Searching desperately for economic help, the United States signed commercial treaties with France, Holland, Sweden, Prussia, and Morocco, but even combined they could not equal England's ability to provide markets and capital. In 1784, Boston investors fitted out the *Empress of China* for the first U.S. venture to exploit the legendary markets of Asia. It was a scene that would be repeated in such later postwar depressions as the 1820s, 1840s, 1890s,

The United States in 1783, newly independent but surrounded by the navies and landed possessions of the great European powers.

and 1970s. Discovering the huge demand for ginseng, which the Chinese considered a stimulant for sexual activity, the first U.S. voyages carried over the herb, brought back tea, and made enormous profits. But the narrow, undeveloped China market—whose trade the Chinese tightly regulated so that they endured only slight personal contact with those they called the less civilized "New People"—could not replace British purchases.

The only solution was a unified, strong U.S. government able to discriminate against British goods and ships until London officials would open the West Indies and allow U.S. ships more rights. But such discrimination was impossible under the Articles of Confederation, which gave each state the right to control its own commerce. The British simply played off state against state.

This foreign-policy failure soon produced political crisis. In frontier Massachusetts, money virtually disappeared. Debtors, threatened with the loss of their land, organized under Daniel Shays to gain control of the courts through military force. The Massachusetts governor managed to put down Shays's Rebellion in 1786, but the effects of this near-revolution rippled as far away as Virginia. Washington, Jefferson (now U.S. minister to France), and James Madison all viewed Shays as the dangerous product of a bankrupt foreign policy. Other sections of the West seemed almost out of control as war veterans and other settlers rushed into the Ohio River territory. In 1779, Kentucky had about 200 white settlers. Six years later it contained 30,000. These Americans needed money and credit. They also needed protection against both Indians and the Spanish agents who sought to seduce them into Spain's empire—an empire that encircled Kentucky from the Mississippi around to the Floridas. George Washington visited the West, then warned that "the western settlers . . . stand as it were upon a pivot; the touch of a feather would turn them any way."[36] The individual states, however, could not coordinate an effective policy to deal with the Indians and Spain. In the background loomed British power. London officials refused to evacuate the northwest forts at Niagara, Detroit, and Oswego until the Americans settled their pre-1776 debt. British agents exploited the fur trade and encouraged Native Americans to drive back the settlers.

Washington's "rising empire" was fragmenting. The danger reached a peak when, in 1784, the Spanish sealed the Mississippi trade at New Orleans. Americans in Kentucky country suddenly faced the choice of losing their trade or joining the Spanish Empire. Spain then sent the smooth Don Diego de Gardoqui to strike a deal with the U.S. secretary of foreign affairs, John Jay. Spain knew that Americans needed markets and specie (gold and silver). Gardoqui offered new trade opportunities in Spain and its Canary Islands in return for Spanish control of the Mississippi for thirty years. An agonized Jay decided to accept. He concluded that Americans needed markets immediately. Anyway, he reasoned, the American multiplication table would soon swarm over the river to take possession of the trans-Mississippi. But Jay had chosen eastern merchant interests over western landed-commercial interests. The West rose in fury. The Congress accepted the Jay-Gardoqui Treaty 7 states to 5, but under the Articles of Confederation, 9 states were

James Madison (1751–1836), born in Virginia, educated at Princeton, deeply schooled in both the politics of a new nation and the political theory of the Western world. As the "Father of the Constitution," a founder of the American political party system, secretary of state between 1801 and 1809, and then president (1809–1817), the soft-spoken Virginian was perhaps the country's greatest political thinker, but also one of its least successful presidents.

needed to ratify a treaty. Thus, the West and South effectively blocked it. Westerners threatened to join the British in Canada and then, they warned the Congress, "Farewell, *a long farewell* to all *your* boasted greatness, [for we] will be able to conquer you."[37]

Jay and other nationalists tried to amend the Articles to give the Congress new power to deal with Spain, but under the Articles of Confederation any amendments required unanimous consent of the states. One state (usually Rhode Island or New York, whose trade prospered) could block Jay. In Virginia, Madison grew concerned about the growing crisis. Thirty-five years old in 1786, educated at Princeton (where he finished in three years by sleeping only two to five hours a night), and a young but powerful member of the Congress in 1781–1782, Madison knew intimately both national politics and political theory. Indeed, he remains the best and most influential political theorist the United States has produced. By late 1786, he had reached certain conclusions with which such friends as Washington, Jefferson, Jay, and Alexander Hamilton of New York agreed.

How, Madison asked, could America hope to survive? Only by having the power to retaliate against England and Spain. How could such power be obtained? "Only by harmony in the measures of the States," Madison responded. How could such harmony be obtained? Only by allowing a "reasonable majority" of states to make policy for all, instead of allowing a single state (such as Rhode Island) to block effective action. As Madison summarized the problem, "In fact most of our political evils may be traced to our commercial ones, as most of our moral [evils can be traced] to our political."[38] Radical change was needed. Madison and his friends led a drive to have the states meet in Philadelphia.

Publicly, they indicated that they only intended to amend the Articles. But in reality, they intended to establish a new form of government, one that would allow the United States to survive in the brutal world of clashing empires.

The "Grand Machine" of the Constitution

During six months of secret debate in an intensely hot Philadelphia summer, the convention's delegates wrote a constitution that transformed the nation's ability to handle foreign-policy problems. First, under Madison's urging, the delegates gave Congress the power to regulate trade and pass commercial measures by a mere majority vote (not the two-thirds required by the Articles). Southerners, afraid that the more populous North could outvote and thus control their tobacco and cotton trade, fought the proposal. Madison observed "that the real difference of interests lay not between the large and small but between the N[orthern] and Southn. States. The institution of slavery and its consequences formed the line" between the two sections.[39] In one of the convention's major compromises, the South agreed that a mere majority vote could pass trade measures; in return, the North accepted the continuation of the slave trade until at least 1808.

Second, treaties with other nations could be made lawful when the president proposed them and "two-thirds of the Senators present concur." This provision not only protected the South and West against another Jay-Gardoqui treaty, but it also created a stronger central government because only the senators "present" had to agree. States could no longer threaten to kill treaties simply by not attending Congress, as some did before 1787. This provision also applied to treaties made with Indian tribes, whom the whites usually considered separate nations.

Third, a single-person executive, the president, was created. It had no counterpart in the Articles of Confederation. Congress, however, had the ultimate power: the appropriation of funds for the executive's use. The executive was to be "Commander in Chief of the Army and Navy," could negotiate treaties for Senate consideration, and might nominate ambassadors and "other public Ministers" with "the advice and consent" of the Senate. The Constitution thus established a new agency to conduct day-to-day foreign policy.

Fourth, Congress received an amazing series of powers that it could exercise through a mere majority vote. Congress, not the states, could now "regulate Commerce with foreign Nations, and among the several

States, and with the Indian Tribes." It could do so, moreover, through its new "Power To lay and collect Taxes, Duties, Imposts and Excises." Of equal importance, the convention, acting on Madison's proposal, gave Congress the sole power to "declare" war. The 1787 convention clearly did not want the president to have the power to "make" war without Congress "declaring" it first. As Jefferson later observed, it was only right that the power to involve the nation in conflict should be taken from those in the executive "who are to spend" and given to those in Congress "who are to pay." The delegates, moreover, viewed the president's right to repel sudden attacks as only a necessary exception to the general rule.[40]

Congress received the power to rule all territory outside state control. In another meeting also held in 1787, members of the old Confederation Congress drew up the Ordinance of 1787 that specified a three-stage process through which a territory (such as Kentucky or Ohio in the 1780s) would have to pass to become a state. To ensure that the frontiersmen and -women behaved themselves, the ordinance gave Congress virtual dictatorial power in the first stage so that the territory could be run as a colony. After 1787, a new Congress had the money and ability to operate the ordinance and keep the restless West under control. Overall, the founders clearly wanted Congress to make general laws and rules for foreign policy. The president was to carry out these measures and conduct detailed diplomacy.

Finally, Madison provided a brilliant political theory on which these powers rested. He argued that the national government could be given great powers to defend the United States against other empires (such as the British and Spanish), but also protect individual freedom within America. This seemingly impossible job could be done, he believed, by placing checks and balances within the government itself. As he nicely phrased it, "Ambition must be made to counter ambition." Thus, the states retained significant authority to counter the national government. Thus, three branches of the federal government—the executive, Congress, and the Supreme Court—checked each other. Thus, the two parts of Congress itself, the House and the Senate, checked one another. With these devices and the vast powers in the hands of the new government, Madison felt that he and the other founders had solved a 2,500-year-old problem that the greatest minds—Aristotle, Montesquieu, Hume—had believed could not be solved: how to maintain a just and democratic system over an area as vast as the United States. Aristotle and the others had feared that selfish, individual interests would tear apart a large empire and lead to either anarchy or dictatorship.

Madison disagreed. He believed that dangerous "factions" could be neutralized by spreading them across a vast territory and then having the new government—with its federalism and its checks and balances—rule the territory.[41] Madison thus reversed the beliefs that had governed political theory. In doing so, he explained the new constitutional system and justified the creation of a new American Empire stretching over vast distances.

Great Losers: The Antifederalists

The detailed proceedings of the Constitutional Convention remained secret until the 1830s, but Madison publicly outlined his reasoning that undergirded the new government in *The Federalist*, a series of eighty-five essays, written with Jay and Hamilton and published anonymously in 1787–1788. The essays were needed because "Antifederalists" were determined to kill the Constitution in the ratifying conventions that each state convened to accept or reject the document.

The Antifederalists powerfully argued that Aristotle was right: republics must be small so that rulers and other dangerous factions could be closely watched. Other critics warned that the president would be of "the most dangerous kind too—an *elective* King." Elbridge Gerry of Massachusetts had quit the convention in disgust because he feared the new Congress could "raise armies and money without limit." Such power would ruin the people's liberties. Gerry was furious that Madison and Hamilton had succeeded in creating such centralized power and then had the nerve to call themselves "Federalists." Gerry suggested it would be more accurate to call the two sides "rats and anti-rats."[42]

The pivotal battle occurred in Virginia, where Madison's group opposed Governor Patrick Henry's. Head of a strong state machine, Henry did not want to surrender his powers. He was a talented politician and orator. (A poll in 1958 revealed that Henry's "Give me liberty or give me death" had become the second best-known quote in American history. Only "Come up and see me sometime," seductively uttered by movie actress Mae West, was more famous.)[43] Henry charged that the new government would sell out the transappalachian region, suppress liberty within the states, glorify the few who controlled the national government, and destroy the Articles of Confederation, which had pulled the country through the war. Madison responded that the Articles made up a "contemptible system," disdained by the world's powers. He then struck at the core of the problem: Americans had to govern themselves better at home so that they could protect themselves abroad. Madison summarized this in a classic phrase: "Does [Henry] distinguish between what will render us secure and happy at home, and what will render us respectable abroad? If we be free and happy at home, we shall be respectable abroad."[44]

Successful foreign policy, Madison argued, grew from the inside out. But Americans could survive as a people only if they could effectively fight the other great world empires. The United States has never been isolated or outside the world's political struggles. It was born in the middle of those conflicts, and its great problem was—and has always been—how to survive those struggles while maintaining individual liberty at home. Madison believed that he and his colleagues had gone far in solving that central problem. They devised a system that Franklin termed "the grand machine." Madison defeated Henry in the Virginia ratifying convention because of the promise of that "machine," because George Washington threw his great prestige back of the Constitution, and because the Federalists shrewdly agreed to add a bill of rights that would explicitly protect certain personal and state rights.

The Antifederalists lost the argument. They nevertheless raised the pivotal questions that plagued Americans over the next two hundred years. The more immediate problem, however, was to see whether the "machine" would work and the "course of empire" continue to move westward.

Notes

1. William H. Seward, *Life and Public Services of John Quincy Adams* (Auburn, N.Y., 1849), p. 362.
2. Edward G. Bourne, *Spain in America, 1450–1580* (New York, 1904), pp. 82–88.
3. D. A. Farnie, "The Commercial Empire of the Atlantic, 1607–1783," *The Economic History Review*, 2d ser., 15 (December 1962): 205–208.
4. The quote and useful analysis are in Samuel Eliot Morison, *Builders of the Bay Colony* (Boston, 1930), pp. 73–74.
5. Daniel Boorstin, *The Americans: The National Experience* (New York, 1965), p. 3.
6. Louis B. Wright, *The Dream of Prosperity in Colonial America* (New York, 1965), pp. 27–29.
7. Harold U. Faulkner, *Economic History of the United States* (New York, 1937), p. 93.
8. Allan R. Millett and Peter Maslowski, *For the Common Defense: A Military History of the United States of America* (New York, 1984), pp. 2, 9–18.

9. William T. Hagan, *The Indian in American History* (Washington, D.C., 1971), p. 8; Frederic E. Hoxie, "The Indians versus the Textbooks," *American Historical Association Perspectives* 23 (April 1985): 18–22.
10. Pauline Maier, "Second Thoughts on Our First Century," *New York Times Book Review*, 7 July 1985, p. 20.
11. Thomas R. Hietala, *Manifest Design: Anxious Aggrandizement in Late Jacksonian America* (Ithaca, N.Y., 1985), p. 111; an earlier citation is in Thomas A. Bailey's *A Diplomatic History of the American People*, 7th ed. (New York, 1964), p. 224.
12. Benjamin Franklin, *Observations Concerning the Increase of Mankind* . . . , in *The Papers of Benjamin Franklin*, ed. Leonard W. Labaree *et al.* (New Haven, 1959–), IV, pp. 233–234.
13. Franklin's Canada pamphlet is in *The Writings of Benjamin Franklin*, ed. Albert Henry Smyth, 10 vols. (New York, 1905), IV, pp. 55–57; Burke's argument can be found in Gerald Stourzh, *Benjamin Franklin and American Foreign Policy* (Chicago, 1954), pp. 70–74.
14. *New York Times*, 4 July 1976, p. F2; a key analysis of Sam Adams and these events is in William Appleman Williams, *The Contours of American History* (Cleveland, 1961), p. 112.
15. Benjamin Franklin to William Franklin, 13 March 1768, in *The Writings*, ed. Smyth, V, p. 117. A fine analysis of this crucial change in British politics is in Michael Kammen, *Rope of Sand* (Ithaca, N.Y., 1968), esp. pp. 314–318.
16. *Boswell's Life of Johnson*, ed. R. W. Chapman (New York, 1953), pp. 590, 876, 946.
17. Richard Van Alstyne, *Empire and Independence* (New York, 1976), p. 28.
18. Curtis P. Nettels, "The Origins of the Union and of the States," *Proceedings of the Massachusetts Historical Society* 72 (1957–1960), p. 71.
19. Benjamin Franklin to Joseph Priestly, October 1775, in *The Writings*, ed. Smyth, VI, p. 430.
20. Richard Henry Lee to George Washington, 26 September 1775 and 22 October 1775, in *The Letters of Richard Henry Lee*, ed. James C. Ballagh, 2 vols. (New York, 1911–1914), esp. I, p. 153.
21. Reginald Horsman, *The Diplomacy of the New Republic, 1776–1815* (Arlington Heights, Ill., 1985), p. 7; Thomas Paine, *Common Sense* (New York, 1942), pp. 23, 26–27, 31–32.
22. See Neil Postman's review of Jonathan Kozol's *Illiterate America* in *Washington Post Book World*, 31 March 1985, p. 5.
23. J. H. Powell, ed., "Speech of John Dickinson," *Pennsylvania Magazine of History and Biography* 65 (October 1941): 458–481.
24. John Adams, *Diary and Autobiography*, ed. Lyman H. Butterfield *et al.*, 4 vols. (Cambridge, Mass., 1961), II, p. 236.
25. Worthington C. Ford, ed., *Journals of the Continental Congress* (Washington, D.C., 1906), V, pp. 768–778.
26. Tadashi Aruga, "Revolutionary Diplomacy and the Franco-American Treaties of 1778," *Japanese Journal of American Studies* no. 2 (1985): 60. The Franklin quotes are in Benjamin Franklin to Mrs. Thompson, 8 February 1777, in *The Writings*, ed. Smyth, VII, p. 26.
27. William Carlos Williams, *In the American Grain* (New York, 1957), p. 153.
28. Recounted in *New York Times*, 3 January 1987, p. 11; the "forever" clause and the

treaties themselves are conveniently found in *The Record of American Diplomacy*, ed. Ruhl J. Bartlett, 4th ed. (New York, 1964), pp. 24–27.

29. Van Alstyne, pp. 92–93.
30. *The American Revolution and "A Candid World,"* ed. Lawrence Kaplan (Kent, Ohio, 1977), p. 141.
31. Benjamin Franklin to John Jay, 2 October 1780, in *The Writings*, ed. Smyth, VIII, pp. 143–144.
32. Robert Calhoon, *Revolutionary America: An Interpretive Overview* (New York, 1976), p. 153.
33. John R. Howe, *The Changing Political Thought of John Adams* (Princeton, 1966), pp. 8–9.
34. Benjamin Franklin to Josiah Quincy, 11 September 1783, in *The Writings*, ed. Smyth, IX, p. 96.
35. Richard Van Alstyne, *The Rising American Empire* (Chicago, 1960), esp. pp. 1–20.
36. Merrill Jensen, *The New Nation* (New York, 1950), p. 171. The best overview now is Frederick W. Marks III, *Independence on Trial: Foreign Affairs and the Making of the Constitution* (Baton Rouge, 1973, 1986).
37. *The Revolutionary Diplomatic Correspondence of the United States*, ed. Francis Wharton, 6 vols. (Washington, D.C., 1889), VI, pp. 223–224.
38. James Madison to James Monroe, 7 August 1785, in *The Writings of James Madison*, ed. Gaillard Hunt, 9 vols. (New York, 1901), II, pp. 155–157, 228–229; Irving Brant, *James Madison*, 6 vols. (Indianapolis, 1944–1961), III, pp. 55–56.
39. *The Records of the Federal Convention of 1787*, ed. Max Farrand, 4 vols. (New Haven, 1937), II, pp. 9–10. I am greatly indebted here to Professor Diane Clemens of the University of California, Berkeley, who is preparing a major monograph (to be published by Oxford University Press) on executive powers.
40. Abraham Sofaer, *War, Foreign Affairs, and Constitutional Power* (Cambridge, Mass., 1976), pp. 31–32.
41. *The Federalist*, ed. Clinton Rossiter (New York, 1961), p. 325; Sofaer, pp. 42–43.
42. Merrill Jensen, *The American Revolution within America* (New York, 1974), pp. 213–214; *The Anti-Federalist Papers*, ed. Morton Borden (East Lansing, Mich., 1965), esp. pp. 27–28, 37–39, 213; *Records of the Federal Convention*, ed. Farrand, II, p. 633.
43. Bernard Mayo, *Myths and Men* (Athens, Ga., 1959), pp. 1–24, has the poll and a good analysis of Henry.
44. *The Writings of James Madison*, ed. Hunt, V, p. 146.

For Further Reading

Most of the bibliographical references given in these sections specify post-1980 publications. For pre-1981 materials, no textbook can hope to compare with *Guide to American Foreign Relations since 1700*, ed. Richard Dean Burns (1983), which, with three indexes and more than 1,200 pages of references, is the necessary starting place for any student who wants to read more on the first three centuries of U.S. foreign policy. See also the notes to this chapter and the General Bibliography at the end of this book.

A stimulating account, much influenced by the U.S. experience in Vietnam during the 1960s and the 1970s, is Robert W. Tucker and David C. Hendrickson, *The Fall of the First British Empire: Origins of the War of American Independence* (1982), which should be used with Alison Gilbert Olson, *Making The Empire Work: London and American Interest Groups 1690–1790* (1992). Of special importance on the development of the American view of empire are Douglas Edward Leach, *Roots of Conflict: British Armed Forces and Colonial Americans, 1677–1763* (1966), and Francis Jennings, *Empire of Fortune* (1988), on the Seven Years' War. For a "realist" perspective, see the readable essays in Norman Graebner, *Foundations of American Foreign Policy* (1986), especially those on Franklin and Adams. Jonathan Dull has written on the first American diplomat in "Benjamin Franklin and the Nature of American Diplomacy," *International History Review* 5 (August 1983) and in "Franklin the Diplomat: The French Mission," *Transactions of the American Philosophical Society* 72, pt. 1 (1982) and has examined the larger picture in *A Diplomacy of the American Revolution* (1985). A fascinating account of Silas Deane's escapades is in James West Davidson and Mark H. Lytle, *After the Fact* (1982), and of an opponent of the Declaration of Independence in Milton E. Flower, *John Dickinson* (1983), while Louis W. Potts delves into U.S.-French diplomacy in *Arthur Lee: A Virtuous Revolutionary* (1981), and Lynne Withey presents a fresh perspective on the Revolution and its diplomacy in *Dearest Friend: A Life of Abigail Adams* (1981), as does Edith B. Gelles, *Portia: The World of Abigail Adams* (1992).

Encounters with Native Americans are covered in important essays in *The American Indian and the Problem of History*, ed. Calvin Martin (1986), from the Indians' viewpoint. Superb accounts have opened new perspectives on the military experience: *Arms at Rest*, ed. Joan R. Challinor and Robert L. Beisner (1987), especially the essays by Harold D. Langley and James A. Field, Jr., on the pre-1815 years; *Arms and Independence*, ed. Ronald Hoffman and Peter J. Albert (1984), especially the Royster, Higgenbotham, and Buel essays on foreign-policy aspects; Reginald C. Stuart, *War and American Thought: From the Revolution to the Monroe Doctrine* (1982); and Lawrence D. Cress, "Republican Liberty and National Security: American Military Policy as an Ideological Problem, 1783 to 1789," *William and Mary Quarterly* 38 (January 1981). George Washington deserves a special place: Don Higginbotham's excellent *George Washington and the American Military Tradition* (1985); Edmund S. Morgan's succinct *The Genius of George Washington* (1980); and *The Papers of George Washington: Revolutionary War Series*, Vol. I: *June–September 1775*, ed. Philander D. Chase (1985), with more volumes scheduled to appear soon.

Special topics are well handled in *Diplomacy and Revolution: The Franco-American Alliance of 1778*, ed. Ronald Hoffman and Peter J. Albert (1981); Lawrence S. Kaplan, "The Treaty of Paris, 1783: A Historiographical Challenge," *International History Review* 5 (August 1983); and the key sources in *The United States and Russia: The Beginning of Relations, 1765–1815*, ed. Nina N. Bashkina, Nikolai N. Bolkhovitinov, *et al.* (1980). On the years 1783 to 1789, begin with Frederick W. Marks III, *Independence on Trial*, 2d ed. (1986), which sees foreign policy as the major reason for the 1787 convention. Note *Beyond Confederation: Origins of the Constitution and American National Identity*, ed. Richard Beeman, Stephen Botein, and Edward C. Carter II (1987). A deserved examination of the "losers" is given in *The Anti-Federalist: An Abridgment of the Seven-Volume Set of the Complete Anti-Federalist*, ed. Herbert J. Storing (1985), and of the "winners" in *The Papers of James Madison*, ed. Robert A. Rutland *et al.* (1973, 1975), whose volumes are now up to the 1793–1795 years. Marks, *Independence on Trial*, has a useful bibliography on the foreign-policy implications of the decisions leading to the adoption of the Constitution. See also the important perspective in Jonathan Marshall, "Empire or Liberty: The Antifederalists and Foreign Policy, 1787–1788," *Journal of Libertarian Studies* 4 (Summer 1980).

2

A Second Struggle for Independence and Union (1789–1815)

Liberty and Empires

Americans were doubly blessed at the time of their independence. They had before them a vast, fertile territory that strained even the pioneers' wild imagination. A Pennsylvanian proudly wrote that the trees were taller, the soil richer than anywhere else in the world, while the Mississippi was "the prince of rivers, in comparison of whom the Nile is but a rivulet, and the Danube a mere ditch."[1] But Americans were also given a unique federal form of government by founders who were unique. The generation that gave Americans their independence and Constitution was the only generation in U.S. history that combined the nation's political leaders and its intellectual leaders in the same people.[2] The theoretical and the practical met, fortunately for Americans, at the moment their Constitution was written.

But even James Madison, the "father of the Constitution," as he later became known, was unsure whether the first government under the new laws could survive. "We are in a wilderness without a single footstep to guide us," he wrote to Jefferson in 1789. Madison quickly learned that the survival of individual freedom at home was related to the course of policy abroad. As he observed in the late 1790s, "The management of foreign relations appears to be the most susceptible of abuse of all the trusts committed to government."[3] Between 1789 and 1814, the United States struggled both to survive within the world of

Thomas Jefferson (1743–1826) wrote the original draft of the Declaration of Independence, served as governor of Virginia and U.S. minister to France, became the nation's first secretary of state under the new Constitution, and, as president, bought the Louisiana Purchase in 1803. He hoped to obtain the rest of North America in 1812, when he unfortunately thought that conquering Canada would be a mere matter of marching.

the titanic Napoleonic Wars, and to keep alive the union that had been formed in 1787–1788.

There was irony here. The person who was to run foreign policy for the new system was originally entitled "secretary for foreign affairs," but it turned out that the official seemed to have so little to do in the late 1780s that the job was renamed "secretary of state" and given the responsibility of guarding the nation's Great Seal, publishing laws, and taking the census. Thomas Jefferson thought so little of the position that he wanted to remain in Paris rather than join Washington's cabinet. But the Virginian finally accepted the post that paid $3,500 annually and had a staff of five for copying and translating messages. The War and Treasury departments were much larger and also worked in rather stately buildings, while the original State Department building was a small house on Broadway in New York City, where Washington's first government gathered before moving to Philadelphia in 1790.[4] But the irony was that the State Department, for all its lack of glamor, was to be the very center of the debate over the next quarter-century on whether the new nation, surrounded by great empires, could conduct a foreign policy that would allow the survival of the constitutional experiment. As was to be the case so often over the next several centuries, American domestic politics were crucial, but foreign policies involved matters of life and death.

The Framework: The United States (1789–1814)

When John Quincy Adams traveled as U.S. minister to Prussia in the mid-1790s, he had to wait outside the Berlin city gates while an officer tried to discover if a place called the United States actually existed. No such uncertainty was found in the Western Hemisphere. With astounding speed, Americans moved to conquer the land and commerce of the New World. The "multiplication table" continued to double the population approximately every twenty-two years. In Connecticut (the seedbed for populating much of New York and the Midwest), couples could brag of a dozen children, five times that number of grandchildren, and two hundred to three hundred great-grandchildren.[5] In the South, onrushing population put great pressure on Native Americans and the relatively few Spaniards who tried to hold on to the vast territories of Florida and the trans-Mississippi.

Not only the Constitution, but literature and technology shaped the nation. Noah Webster, an ardent nationalist (and Federalist), wrote his famous speller, reader, and dictionary to make Americans aware and proud of their distinct language, as well as to make them literate. Soon after the steam engine began to revolutionize British industries, it started replacing animal and human muscle in America. John Fitch may have been ugly, bad-mannered, and a wife deserter, but he also ran a newly invented steamboat on the river in Philadelphia, where the founders could see it in 1787. By 1790, the vessel was coming into regular use. Three years later, Eli Whitney perfected the cotton gin, which separated fiber from seed with such speed that the new machine fastened a cotton culture on the South. Cotton exports rocketed from 2 million pounds in 1794 to 18 million pounds in 1800 to 128 million pounds by 1820.[6] In 1798, Whitney devised the radical process of making rifles rapidly and cheaply out of interchangeable parts in an assembly-line process. American expansion was increasingly linked to its people's genius for machinery and technology.

Native Americans felt the brunt of this expansionism. Since many had fought alongside the British between 1775 and 1782, the settlers had no qualms about pushing them aside after the Revolution. The Indians fought effectively against the badly organized Americans. The new Constitution, however, gave the government the needed authority to raise armies, oversee settlement, and make treaties with the tribes. With this new power came a new philosophy: instead of being destroyed, the Indians were to be "civilized" and made to act like white farmers.

Thomas Jefferson best exemplified this approach. As president in 1808, he told a group of Indians that they should become small capitalist landowners. Then "you will mix with us by marriage. Your blood will run in our veins and will spread with us over this great land." If they did not follow his advice, Jefferson later commented, the alternative was not pretty: "They will relapse into barbarism and misery . . . and we shall be obliged to drive them, with the beasts of the forests into the Stony [Rocky] Mountains."[7]

The region between the Appalachian Mountains and the Mississippi (an area bordering the British Empire on the north and the Spanish Empire on the south and west) was becoming extremely productive, politically complex, and quickly populated. By 1795, Tennessee exported cast iron as well as whiskey and bacon. The West was not being filled by idyllic, self-sufficient Daniel Boones, but by settlers whose multiplying commercial interests produced so many farm and manufacturing goods that they thought of themselves as part of an international trading network. As the new Constitution took effect, moreover, Europe lost much of its ability to feed itself. The quarter-century agony of the French Revolution and Napoleonic Wars began. U.S. farm prices rose as foreign markets blotted up American cotton, tobacco, grain, meat, and fish. In the North as well as in the plantation South, as a Philadelphia orator put it, "the Star-bespangled Genius of America . . . points to agriculture as the stable Foundation of this rising mighty Empire."[8]

U.S. exports leaped from $19 million in 1791 to $108 million in 1807. But the country remained a debtor as imports shot up from $19 million in 1791 to $138 million in 1807. The debt was often paid for by the success of U.S. merchants and shipowners. They not only carried American trade, but the trade of others—especially the commerce generated by the rich British and French West Indies. As the European wars grew bloodier, this trade grew greater and the U.S. traders grew richer even as they became in reality parts of the British or French empires rather than the American system. As these traders came to care more about European than U.S. interests, they caused major problems for Washington officials between 1805 and 1814. Indeed, some northeastern merchants almost destroyed the new Union in 1814. But in the earlier years, they acted as a cutting edge for the expansion of American power in some unusual places. For example, they helped undermine Spain's control of Latin America by dominating the Spanish-American carrying trade.

The Yankees also targeted Russia's colonies in Alaska and the present American Northwest until they monopolized the rich fur trade between Alaska and China. That trade produced as much as 500 percent annual profit. In historian Howard Kushner's words, the supposedly Russian-controlled areas actually "depended on Yankee traders" for both supplies and exports.[9] The Russian tsar Alexander I tried to retaliate by giving a trading monopoly to John Jacob Astor's American fur company, which, the tsar hoped, would undercut other Americans and allow him to control Astor. Alexander next sent a mission into California to take over the San Francisco region so food from the area could replace supplies provided by Americans. Neither policy worked. By 1820, the Yankees were handsomely, if illegally, growing rich from the Russian Empire. A Bostonian, Captain Robert Gray, in 1792 found the magnificent river that he named after his ship, the *Columbia.* Gray's discovery gave the United States strong claim to the vast Oregon territory. Other American traders exploited the coasts for furs and, in three-year expeditions, grew rich selling them to China. They sometimes stopped for rest in Hawaii, thus giving them an early interest in those strategic islands as well. Before it was ten years old, the new United States was becoming a power in the Pacific region.

Americans also were proving that they could govern their growing continental empire. Shays-type rebellions were no longer to be tolerated. When William Blount (a leading politician in Tennessee) and James Wilkinson (a well-known scoundrel and schemer) renewed earlier plots to sell parts of the new West to Spain, Washington used his power simply to buy Blount and Wilkinson by giving them political jobs and military commissions. Washington became the central figure who held together the nation's domestic and foreign affairs. The first president set many of the precedents that later chief executives had to follow. He had "neither the quickness nor the brilliance of genius," the British minister reported to London, perhaps because of "his natural shyness and reserve." But, the minister granted, the president had "sound sense and . . . excellent judgement."[10] Jefferson noted that Washington was tall, "his deportment easy, erect, and noble; the best horseman of his age."[11] His long military career, the leadership of the revolutionary forces, and his service as chair of the Constitutional Convention gave him unequaled experience. He knew the West intimately, largely as a result of his own extensive land speculation. The first president believed that the Constitution's success depended not only on its words, but on its citizens' character. "A good general government," he wrote to one of his several intimate women admirers, "without good morals and good habits, will not make us a happy People."[12]

Jefferson agreed about the need for good morals, but he had fewer doubts than Washington. In designing a national seal, Jefferson suggested that it show the children of Israel led by a pillar of light from the heavens. He was confident that Americans were the new chosen people of God. Returning from France in 1790 to become the first secretary of state under the Constitution, his confidence was put to the test.

Chosen People, the British Empire, and the French Revolution

Washington understood his most important foreign-policy problem: "That we avoid errors in our system of policy respecting Great Britain."[13] The British continued to hold forts on U.S. territory and encouraged Indians to oppose American settlement. London also tightened its control on U.S. trade. To break that control, Madison rose in the first session of the First Congress to propose a series of measures that would utilize the new powers of the Constitution as a club to smash the British hold. His approach was direct: threaten other nations with commercial retaliation unless they treated American trade fairly. As the Virginian phrased it, "We possess natural advantages which no other nation does; we can, therefore, with justice, stipulate for a reciprocity in commerce. The way to obtain this is by discrimination."[14] Congress passed bills levying tonnage duties eight times higher on foreign vessels than on U.S. ships in American ports, and also imposed import taxes on foreign goods entering the country. Americans wanted freer trade, but they were prepared to play rough mercantilist trading games if necessary.

Madison nevertheless wanted more. He sought to favor French trade (because France bought more than it sold to Americans) and discriminate against the British. His proposals quickly encountered opposition from Secretary of the Treasury Alexander Hamilton. The illegitimate son of a Scottish merchant, at twenty Hamilton had been a brilliant pamphleteer for the Revolution and at twenty-six a hero at Yorktown. After practicing law and marrying into a powerful New York family, he had joined Madison to push through the Constitution. Only thirty-four in 1789 (Madison was thirty-eight), Hamilton split with the Virginian and Jefferson over foreign policy. The Treasury secretary put together a program that gave the new nation sound, centralized finances. His program promised to pay the large national debt and to establish a national bank to oversee the country's economy. But these schemes required a great deal of money, and those sums had to come from land sales or import taxes on goods that were mostly British. Hamilton, therefore, feared any measure that threatened Great Britain and that might lead to a cutting off of British capital or, worse, another devastating conflict. Thus, he opposed Madison's every attempt to get tough with the British. He even worked secretly with the British minister to undercut Madison's influence.

Jefferson and Madison were furious. Hamilton is "panic-struck if we refuse our breeches to every kick which Gr. Brit. may choose to give us," Jefferson fumed.[15] Nor did it lessen the Virginians' fear when Jefferson told Hamilton that the leading men in history were Francis Bacon, Isaac Newton, and John Locke, only to have the secretary of the Treasury reply dryly that he personally preferred Caesar.

In 1790, a cabinet crisis erupted when Spanish naval officers stupidly seized British ships in Nootka Sound off the northwest coast. London quickly planned to retaliate by marching troops from Canada to conquer Spanish lands along the Caribbean, a march that would take the troops through the Mississippi Valley. The British could end by surrounding the new nation on all four sides. Jefferson advised Washington that the British must never be allowed to make that march. Hamilton, however, warned that nothing should be done to alienate Great Britain, and, he added, it would help to have the Spanish thrown off the continent. Before Washington had to take action, however, the Spanish wisely apologized for the ship seizures, and the crisis passed.

It was quickly replaced by an even graver problem. In 1789, the French Revolution had begun. By 1793, it became an international struggle as France declared war on England, Holland, and Austria. Jefferson sympathized with the French. They seemed to be following the example of 1776. Madison was less starry-eyed about the upheaval, but for his own reasons he also favored the French. A great opportunity opened for U.S. commerce. As Jefferson phrased it, the United States wanted no part of the Europeans' problems except "we have only to pray that their soldiers may eat a great deal."[16] Hamilton agreed.

But the two men sharply divided over U.S. obligations to France under the 1778 alliance, a pact that remained in effect between the two nations, even though the 1778 governments had changed. Hamilton argued that U.S. national interests rose above any vague obligations under the treaty. Washington took his advice and issued a Neutrality Proclamation. Madison blasted the president's announcement for disregarding U.S. "duties to France," ignoring "the cause of liberty," and—of special concern—exercising a power that Madison believed belonged to Congress: the power to declare neutrality could also decide whether and against whom the United States might declare war.[17] But Washington stuck to his policy and established a constitutional precedent that claimed important power for the president. Nor did it help Jefferson when a new French minister, Edmond Charles Genêt, arrived and immediately began breaking U.S. laws by fitting out French privateers in U.S. ports to seize British ships. He then enlisted American boys to fight in France. Washington refused to deal with "Citizen" Genêt. As the Frenchman grew unpopular, Jefferson "saw the necessity of quitting a wreck which could not but sink all who should cling to it."

The French Revolution soon got out of hand. Dr. J. I. Guillotin's device for separating heads from bodies worked more frequently until King Louis XVI became a victim. After Genêt's supporters in Paris fell to a more radical faction, even he recoiled at the thought of returning. (He married into a wealthy American family and lived in the United States for the rest of his life.) Jefferson was sickened. The French were not following the moderate example of 1776. Two centuries later, one can see that the French Revolution, not the American, was more the model for such great upheavals as those in Russia, China, Iran, and Vietnam. As the British foreign minister Lord Grenville sniffed to an American in 1798, "None but Englishmen and their Descendents know how to make a Revolution." That belief became a central assumption in U.S. diplomacy.

In 1793–1794, Madison pushed his campaign to destroy British control of U.S. commerce. He received help from the British themselves in late 1793, when they seized 250 U.S. vessels that were carrying goods between France and the West Indies. Madison arose in the House of Representatives in March 1794 and bitterly attacked the action. He observed that the British sold the United States twice as much as they bought, while the French bought seven times more than they sold to the United States. It was time to cut British trade and shipping until London officials treated Americans fairly. Madison gained support from many who were outraged by the ship seizures. As Hamilton's program seemed about to collapse, the Treasury secretary brilliantly gained time and undercut Madison by convincing Washington to send Chief Justice John Jay to London to negotiate a settlement in order to avert possible war with the British.

A Turn: From Jay to X Y Z

Jay had one high card to play: he could threaten to join the new League of Armed Neutrality formed by several European nations to check British naval power. Hamilton, however, undercut his own diplomat by secretly telling London that the United States had no intention of joining the league. This deviousness left Jay to sign a treaty that sharply limited U.S.–West Indian trade. The pact gave Americans nothing on the issues of neutral rights (such as the valued U.S. principle that "free ships make free goods"), or impressment (the hated British practice of seizing their own—and sometimes American—citizens from U.S. ships on the grounds that they had deserted His Majesty's fleet). The British repeated their 1783 pledge that the Mississippi was opened to both nations. On the other hand, the British did agree to leave the northwest forts, and they opened Great Britain and the British East Indies to U.S. merchants. American trade with Asia consequently boomed. By 1801, Yankee ships carried 70 percent of all foreign trade with India.

But even this opportunity did not stop anti-Jay riots from erupting throughout the East. Mobs in Philadelphia threatened Vice-President John Adams's house and stoned the windows of the British minister's office. Americans were incensed at the limits placed on the West Indies trade. Westerners threatened to leave the Union if the British used the treaty to try to control the Mississippi. Madison was deeply angered. He argued that the House of Representatives had an equal right with the Senate to act on the treaty because the House had to appropriate money to put treaties into effect. Washington set another crucial constitutional precedent by invoking executive privilege and refusing to release the documents of the Jay mission. Then he denied that anything more than a two-thirds vote of the Senate was needed to ratify treaties. The president faced down the House, but his growing concern was over those he called "the restless and impetuous spirits of Kentucky," who threatened in the West to take matters into their own hands.

Since 1789, he had tried to protect the settlers from Indian attacks that were at least winked at by the British. In 1791, about a hundred miles north of Cincinnati, the Miami chief Little Turtle inflicted one of the worst defeats in history on a U.S. military force. Nine hundred whites were killed. The rest broke and ran. In 1793–1794, Washington finally placed General "Mad Anthony" Wayne in command of 3,000 men. After careful preparation, Wayne defeated the Shawnee in 1794 at the Battle of Fallen Timbers in the Ohio territory. The general leveled every Indian settlement he could reach, built forts (including Fort Wayne, now in Indiana), and opened the region to settlement.

Washington then enjoyed another well-timed success. The Spanish had joined Great Britain against France in 1793, but within a year they were ready to rejoin their traditional ally in Paris. To do so, however, created the danger that the British would retaliate by sweeping down on Spanish possessions in America. Those possessions were indeed already slipping away. Several years earlier, Spain had tried to seduce American settlers by encouraging them to settle in the Floridas. Jefferson was elated that the doors would be open: "We may complain of this seduction of our inhabitants just enough to make [the Spanish] believe it very wise policy for them & confirm them in it."[18] By 1794, Spain had lost control of most of those settlers and much of the Indian trade. When Madrid ordered the situation to be brought under control, a beleaguered Spanish official responded: "You cannot lock up an open field." Beset in both Europe and America, the Spanish were ready to talk. Washington sent Thomas Pinckney to Madrid. In late 1795, he signed a pact that pledged mutual cooperation to stop Indian attacks in the South and, most important, to open Spanish-held New Orleans to tax-free use for three years to the hundreds of thousands of Americans whose prosperity now depended on Mississippi trade.

The Pinckney Treaty was a godsend to Washington. In it, Spain promised the West the use of the Mississippi just as the Jay Treaty gave the East's merchants peace with the British fleet. Moreover, those who continued to oppose the Jay Treaty in Congress were quickly sobered by threats of losing the Union. New Jersey, for one, said it would dissociate itself from the South if the Jay pact were not ratified. As one Federalist wrote, "The conversation of a separation is taking place in almost every company."[19] Washington also threw his immense prestige behind Jay's agreement. The Senate barely accepted it by a 20-to-10 vote. Madison complained that "banks, the British merchants, the insurance companies" had won through bribery and threats. More accurately, however, the new nation had been saved in 1795–1796 by "Mad Anthony" Wayne, Pinckney, and Washington.

Americans now made a major turn. U.S.-British relations rapidly improved, while the French—embittered that the United States would accept the Jay Treaty but not honor the 1778 alliance—turned against Washington's administration. The French minister to Philadelphia, Pierre Adet, first tried to block the Jay Treaty, then worked vigorously to have Jefferson win the 1796 presidential election over Federalist candidate John Adams. That interference influenced Washington to

John Adams (1735–1826) was dour, brilliant, a leader of the revolutionary movement, and a co-negotiator of the 1783 peace treaty. The nation's first vice-president, then president (1797–1801), he demonstrated courage and skill in making peace instead of war with France in 1799–1800 and, as a result, decisively lost re-election in 1800.

issue (in a newspaper) his Farewell Address that warned Americans against tying themselves to tł fortunes of any "foreign influence." In words that have not lost their importance nearly two hundred years later, the president observed that "the nation which indulges toward another an habitual hatred or an habitual fondness is in some degree a slave." If such "slavery" could be avoided, he held out a magnificent vision: the growth of their power until Americans could virtually do whatever they wished. The Farewell Address remains significant because it argued that if Americans were restrained in the 1790s, they would have to suffer few restraints later. Of equal importance, the Farewell Address remains the major statement of the need for American freedom of action, a central theme in the first two centuries of U.S. foreign policy.[20]

Adams won the election, but Jefferson's triumph would have produced much the same foreign policy, Adet believed:

> [Jefferson, Adet reported to Paris,] seeks to draw near to us because he fears us less than England; but tomorrow he might change his opinion about us if England should cease to inspire his fear. . . . Jefferson, I say, is an American, and as such, he cannot sincerely be our friend. An American is the born enemy of all the peoples of Europe.[21]

John Adams led a rapidly developing but still primitive country—so primitive that when his wife Abigail took a coach from Philadelphia to join him in the new capital city of Washington, she became lost in the wilderness south of Baltimore. "You find nothing but a forest and woods on the way," she complained. But the city's location revealed great insight into the country's future, because it had been placed on the Potomac River in the belief that the waterway was to become a major route westward.[22]

With usual American sensitivity to events beyond the mountains, Adams quickly heard of Spanish and French plots to win over the distant settlements. George Rogers Clark, hero of the American Revolution, even became involved in some of the schemes, despite—or because of—a severe drinking problem. The president seized the initiative by sending three diplomats to France for talks. They were to terminate the 1778 alliance, make the French promise to behave in the West, and win France's recognition of wide-ranging U.S. trading rights. Three French agents, code-named "X," "Y," and "Z," countered with simpler proposals: Adams must apologize for his past criticism of the French, then give Paris a large loan as well as a $250,000 bribe to grease the negotiations. They also expected help in the ongoing war against the British. An astounded Adams broke off the talks. The cry was born, "Millions for Defense, but not one Cent for Tribute!"

The president had to fight a two-front struggle. An "undeclared war" broke out with France, which seized more U.S. ships between 1797 and 1800 than did the greater British fleet. On the home front, Hamilton, now a powerful lawyer in New York City, worked through his informants in Adams's cabinet to seize the opportunity and strike at the crumbling Spanish Empire in the South and West—preferably with British help. Adams and Hamilton, despite being fellow Federalists, had become bitter political enemies. Their personalities clashed, and the president strongly disagreed with Hamilton's pro-British views. Closer to Madison on the trade question, Adams wanted a vigorous, independent U.S. commerce. He called Hamilton "the bastard brat of a Scots peddler." Hamilton, in turn, had tried to block Adams's victory in 1796. Now Hamilton not only hoped to break ties with France, but personally to lead an army that would conquer the Floridas and trans-Mississippi—and even "take a squint at Mexico." Adams, who knew about Hamilton's admiration for Caesar, concluded that "this man is stark mad or I am."

Meanwhile, the Federalists pushed the Alien and Sedition Acts through Congress. These measures gave the government power to arrest aliens as well as newspaper editors who were suspected of being pro-French. In reality, the Federalists used the acts to persecute Jeffersonians. Not for the last time in American history was the threat of conflict abroad used to justify a witch hunt at home. Jefferson and Madison responded with resolutions passed in the Virginia and Kentucky state legislatures. These measures defied the two acts and implied that disunion would occur if the Federalists did not retreat.

The danger thus arose of both a full-scale war with France and a constitutional crisis at home. Adams commissioned three fighting ships and established the United States Navy Department to oversee operations. George Logan, a Pennsylvania Quaker, took it upon himself to sail to France and work out a peace settlement. His mission failed, and the Federalists passed the Logan Act, which made it illegal for any private citizen to negotiate with a foreign government. (In the 1960s through 1980s, the government threatened to invoke the law—for example, against actress Jane Fonda, who traveled to Vietnam—but the law was not applied.)

As U.S.-French relations reached a critical point, Adams took a politically dangerous but statesmanlike step. He overruled Hamilton and dispatched a peace mission to Paris. The president believed that France posed less of a danger ("There is no more prospect of seeing a French army here, than there is in heaven," Adams thought) than did Hamilton. Adams worried more about the probability of becoming involved in the Napoleonic Wars and the possibility of a severed Union. The French were now ready to deal. They needed U.S. trade, especially after the British fleet had nearly destroyed their navy. The Convention of 1800 ended the 1778 alliance. In return, the United States agreed to assume claims against France (although these were never fully honored). Each side agreed to grant the other most-favored-nation rights in trade and—not surprisingly—declared that neutrals (such as the United States) should have extensive rights to trade during wartime.

The United States thus ended the last European alliance it would have for nearly a century and a half. The experience had been bitter. The costs even touched the possibility of disunion. In 1801, Jefferson recalled how the western and eastern states had preserved the new constitutional system by balancing each other in the Jay Treaty and undeclared war crises. He concluded that those experiences provided "a new proof of the falsehood of Montesquieu's doctrine, that a republic can be preserved in only a small territory. The reverse is the truth. Had our territory been even a third only of what it is, we were gone."[23]

Jefferson and Louisiana

To the astonishment of many, the United States managed a peaceful transition of power in the 1800 election from Adams's Federalists to

"The Providential Detection" is a superb American graphic drawn for the bitter 1800 election fight by an artist who clearly hated Jefferson and his supposed ties to revolutionary France. As the Virginian kneels at the burning altar of French "despotism," a powerful (and beautifully sketched) American eagle stops Jefferson from throwing the Constitution into the flames. Note the all-seeing eye (in the upper right corner) watching out for the United States.

Jefferson's Republicans. The campaign had been brutal. The pro-Adams president of Yale, Timothy Dwight, warned that if Jefferson won, "we may see the Bible cast into a bonfire, the vessels of the sacramental supper borne by an ass in public procession," and "our wives and daughters the victims of legal prostitution." The reality was less exciting. Historian William Stinchcombe has noted that Adams was actually beaten by the backlash against the Federalist war scare—"the greatly increased defense spending, particularly on the army, and the notorious Alien and Sedition Acts," which Jefferson turned to his political advantage. The news of peace with France arrived too late to save Adams. In any case, years later he wrote that "I desire no other inscription on my gravestone than: 'here lies John Adams, who took upon himself the responsibility of peace with France in 1800.' " The new president moved quickly to build a consensus. "We are all Republicans, we are all Federalists," he declared in his 1801 inaugural address.[24]

He appointed his close friend James Madison secretary of state. Their foreign-policy assumptions were few but direct. As Jefferson wrote in 1801, American expansion should be thought of as virtually unlimited:

> However our present situation may restrain us within our own limits, it is impossible not to look forward to distant times, when our rapid multiplication will expand itself beyond those limits, and cover the whole northern, if not the southern continent, with a people speaking the same language, governed in similar forms, and by similar laws; nor can we contemplate with satisfaction blot or mixture on that surface.[25]

To achieve these goals, Americans had to protect their freedom of action: "Peace, commerce, and honest friendship with all nations, entangling alliances with none," as he announced in his inaugural address. In a rephrase of Paine's *Common Sense* and Washington's Farewell Address, Jefferson told a friend that "we have a perfect horror of everything connecting ourselves with the politics of Europe," but because Americans are "daily growing stronger," if they can have a few more years to build their power, they can tell others how the United States must be treated, "and we will say it."[26] Power abroad, as Madison had told Patrick Henry in 1788 (see p. 35), depended on effective rule at home. In this sense, Jefferson became the first chief executive to manage Congress through well-disciplined party leaders who followed the president's wishes. His foreign policies were often effective because he was able to whip Congress into line to support them. Jefferson successfully centralized power in the new Executive Mansion.[27]

Nor was Jefferson reluctant to build and use military power. However, he kept a sense of proportion. He never believed that the young United States could build a navy to challenge the British fleet, but he built a small flotilla of gunboats to fight the Barbary States between 1801 and 1805. Operating out of the North African Islamic states of Tripoli, Algiers, Tunis, and Morocco, the raiders demanded large tributes from ships plying the Mediterranean or the ships would be seized and sailors brutalized. Washington and Adams had paid tribute to these robbers. Jefferson refused and sent four warships to protect U.S. commerce. One ship ran aground, and Tripoli seized the crew. It was the first overseas hostage crisis in American history.

Jefferson went to war. Scoring several sensational victories on both sea and land, the president nevertheless had to pay $60,000 to obtain Tripoli's pledge not to capture other U.S. ships. During the War of 1812, the plundering of U.S. ships began again, but in 1815 President Madison dispatched a small fleet that forced the Barbary States to retreat. The U.S. Navy then leased a port on the island of Majorca in the Mediterranean so it could move quickly against future plundering. The American war with Barbary, however, was over.[28]

These characteristics of Jefferson's foreign policy—expansionism, freedom of action, centralization of power, and the willingness to use force in selected situations—appeared in his greatest triumph, the purchase of Louisiana in 1803. But the affair could have been a diplomatic catastrophe. Jefferson and Madison found themselves facing a crisis in 1801 when they learned that the weakened Spanish had finally

Toussaint L'Ouverture (1743–1803), the black revolutionary who led the fight to drive the French from Haiti, inadvertently helped the United States to purchase the Louisiana Territory from France.

surrendered to Napoleon's demands and sold him the Louisiana Territory. His war with Great Britain had stopped (temporarily, it soon turned out), and Napoleon turned to developing a New World empire. He especially wanted to find a food supply in Louisiana for the black slaves who produced highly profitable sugar crops in Haiti and Santo Domingo. In 1802, the crisis intensified when Spanish officials (who still controlled New Orleans) suddenly shut off the Mississippi to U.S. trade. Madison had long understood that whoever controlled that great river controlled the rapidly multiplying Americans settling in the West: "The Mississippi is to them everything," he wrote privately in late 1802. "It is the Hudson, the Delaware, the Potomac, and all the navigable rivers of the Atlantic States formed into one stream."[29]

In 1802, Jefferson and Madison devised a brilliant series of policies that finally forced Napoleon to sell not only New Orleans (the primary American objective), but most of the immense area between the Mississippi and the Rocky Mountains. First, Madison sent secret help to black revolutionaries, led by Toussaint L'Ouverture, who were fighting to overthrow French rule in Haiti. The secretary of state knew that without the sugar island of which Haiti was a part, Napoleon would not need Louisiana as a granary. The French finally captured Toussaint. But his followers fought on, and their successes—together with malaria, which devastated the French troops—led Napoleon to blurt out in frustration in early 1803, "Damn sugar, damn coffee, damn colonies."

Second, Jefferson used his Indian policy to pressure the French. Having long hoped to "civilize" the Native Americans, Jefferson suddenly ordered the removal of tribes into the trans-Mississippi region. This order forced Napoleon to worry about them, while turning the Midwest into a secure all-white base from which Jefferson could attack New Orleans. The greatest historian of the Jeffersonian era, Henry Adams, graphically summarized the effect on the Native Americans: "No acid ever worked more mechanically on a vegetable fibre than the white man acted on the Indian. As the line of American settlements approached, the nearest Indian tribes withered away."[30] Some tribes, however, finally fought bitterly in 1810–1811 before retreating.

Third, the president obtained authority from Congress to build 15 gunboats and raise 80,000 men for an assault on the lower Mississippi. Napoleon learned of this in early April 1803, just as he was pondering the failure of a large French force to sail to the New World because a late winter had frozen over European ports. Since Jefferson had sent James Monroe and Edward Livingston to purchase New Orleans and the Floridas for $10 million, they were in Paris (where Livingston was the U.S. minister) when Napoleon decided to unload all of his mainland holdings. About to start the war against Great Britain once more, he needed freedom from New World malaria, slave revolts, and possible war with the United States, as well as the money the sale would bring. He asked, and Jefferson finally agreed to pay, $15 million for all of Louisiana. Luck had helped give Jefferson and Madison the opportunity, but they had seized upon it to double the size of the United States.[31]

But the crisis was not over. Nothing in the Constitution provided for such an acquisition. When Louisiana developed into numerous new states, the balance of political power and the nature of American society could be radically changed. Federalists in New England were especially fearful. "We rush like a comet into infinite space," proclaimed Fisher Ames of Massachusetts. "Our country is too big for union, too sordid for patriotism, too democratic for liberty." Ames and other Federalists began planning to pull New England out of the Union. They apparently received encouragement from, of all people, Aaron Burr, vice-president of the United States. By 1803–1804, Burr and Jefferson had become bitter political enemies. The Ames Federalists, however, remained a small, if dangerous, minority. More representative was his-

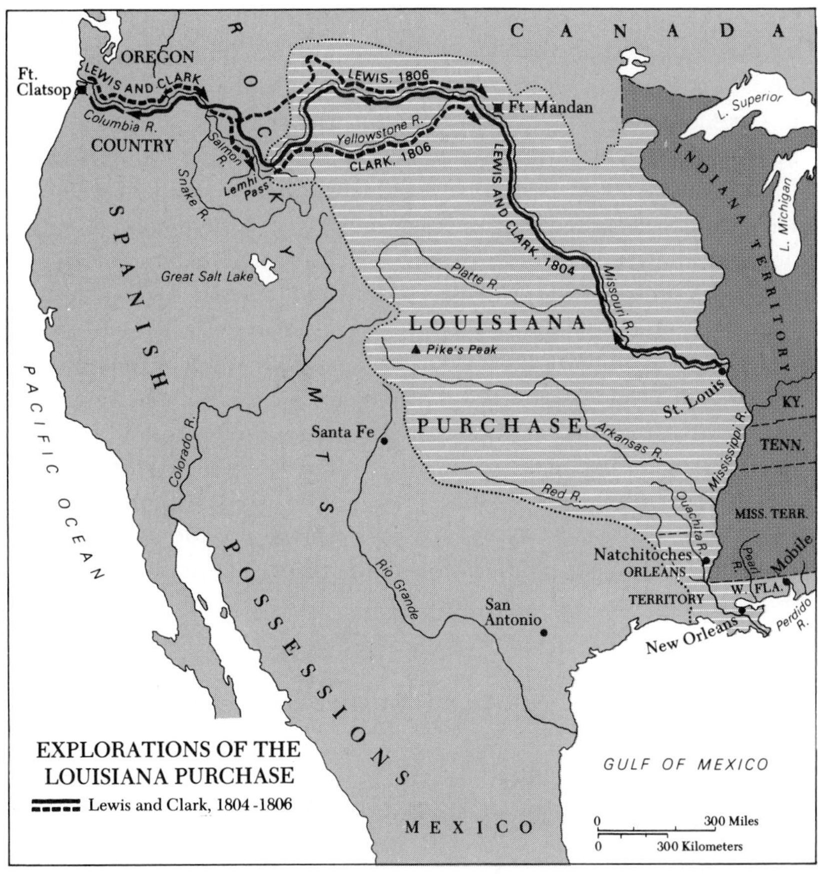

The Louisiana Purchase of 1803 doubled the size of the United States and later provided thirteen of the fifty states. The map also shows exploration that led to further settlement and expansion. When Napoleon sold the territory and was told that the boundaries were vague, he observed, correctly, that he supposed the Americans would make the most of vague territorial claims.

torian David Ramsay's oration of 1804 on the theme "What territory can be too large for a people, who multiply with such unequalled rapidity?"[32]

With that kind of support, Jefferson construed the Constitution liberally and assumed the United States could acquire and rule large new areas. He received backing from Gouverneur Morris, who had written a draft of the Constitution for the convention's debates in 1787. Morris pointed to Article IV, Section 3: "New States may be admitted . . . into this Union. . . . The Congress shall have Power to dispose of and make all needful Rules and Regulations respecting the Territory or other

Property belonging to the United States." In 1803, Morris added, "I always thought that when we should acquire Canada and Louisiana it would be proper to govern them as provinces and allow them no voice in our Councils."[33] Jefferson followed Morris's advice. He had little hope that the Indians, French, Spaniards, Creoles, and runaway Americans who had fled to New Orleans (often to escape a U.S. jail) were capable of self-government. Consequently, he obtained legislation that allowed him to rule Louisiana as a virtual dictator until it was peopled by responsible Anglo-Saxons. Meanwhile, order and security were to be maintained through force, if necessary.[34]

Thus, strong national power secured Louisiana. But arguments over who was to exert this power did lead to civil war in 1861, although not in the way Ames had envisioned. Meanwhile, Jefferson and Madison so disregarded Federalist fears that from 1804 to 1806 they tried through diplomacy, bribery, and covert pressures to pry the Floridas out of Spanish hands. These efforts stalled, especially as the two men suddenly faced a major conflict with the British Empire on the Atlantic sea lanes.

The Second War for Independence and Union

In 1805, prospering U.S. trade with both warring nations, Great Britain and France, came under attack from British author Sir James Stephen, who, in his *War in Disguise; or, The Frauds of the Neutral Flags*, argued that England should use its naval superiority to stop U.S. trade that aided Napoleon. That same year, British courts issued the *Essex* decision. It declared illegal and subject to seizure those U.S. ships that picked up goods in the French West Indies, off-loaded them briefly in the United States so that they would appear to be American goods, and then carried them to France. As the British began seizing U.S. ships, Napoleon retaliated by announcing a blockade of Great Britain, a blockade he could not enforce. Any ship entering European ports after stops in England, he declared, would be seized.

After "fattening upon the follies" of the Old World, as Jefferson had phrased it, Americans were becoming victims trapped between the two European giants. In a brilliant pamphlet of 1806, Madison attacked the new British regulations and warned that "all history" proved that war results from "commercial rivalships" of nations. He and Jefferson tried to counter not with military force, but with a Nonimportation Act of 1806 that threatened to exclude imports, especially British, until the Europeans promised to respect U.S. neutral rights. In compiling the list of excluded goods, however, the two men made a frightening discovery: Americans were more dependent on British textiles, iron, and steel than the British were on American goods. Jefferson believed that he could not afford to exclude those badly needed products. U.S. economic power was turning out to be quite different than Paine, Madison, and others had assumed it would be.

While he delayed putting the Nonimportation Act into effect, Jefferson confronted a more immediate problem. Great Britain had intensified its impressment searches of deserters from its fleet. Tens of thousands of British sailors had escaped from the poor pay, unspeakable food and conditions, and brutality (lashings were frequent) at a moment when England was locked into a battle to the death with Napoleon. A large number—perhaps as many as eight out of every ten men seized—were Americans who were then impressed into the dangers of British service. In June 1807, a British warship, the *Leopard*, boarded the U.S. ship *Chesapeake* just ten miles off Chesapeake Bay, killed three Americans, wounded eighteen, then carried off four men, of whom only one was a British citizen. Americans demanded revenge. At this moment, Jefferson could have taken a near-united nation into war against Great Britain. He realized, however, his relative military weakness and believed that economic pressure could force the British to behave. In November 1807, London announced orders in council tightening control over neutral shipping. Napoleon responded with a similar decree affecting ships dealing with the British.

When the president raised the possibility of war, his able secretary of the Treasury Albert Gallatin warned that the British could "land at Annapolis, march to [Washington]," and return to England before Jefferson could even raise a militia to fight. Meanwhile, as Federalist senator John Quincy Adams noted, the British orders struck "at the very root of our independence."[35] Jefferson finally responded with an Embargo Act that closed U.S. ports and made exports illegal. Unintentionally, the president helped the British, who could handle their own commerce, by cutting off French trade. He also infuriated American merchants and producers of exports, whose survival depended on trade. When smuggling intensified, Jefferson made arbitrary arrests and seizures of goods. As historian Burton Spivak argues, Jefferson faced a terrible choice between his belief in democratic ideals and his belief in the commercial destiny of Americans.[36] The president's political party as well as his ideals were threatened. In 1808, Madison won the Executive Mansion, but the Federalists, using the embargo as a whip against him, tripled their 1804 electoral vote.

Leaving office in early 1809, Jefferson proudly told his successor that, with Louisiana and after Florida, Cuba, and Canada were annexed, the United States would be "such an empire for liberty as [the world] has never surveyed since the creation; and I am persuaded no constitution was ever before so well calculated as ours for extensive empire and self-government."[37] Both his vision and his confidence in the Constitution, however, were to be tested in the next five years.

Jefferson, under strong congressional pressure, was forced to end the embargo as he left office. Congress replaced it with the Nonintercourse Act of 1809 that prohibited both British and French ships and goods from U.S. ports but pledged to restore normal commerce with any country that repealed its restrictions on American trade. When this measure brought no good result, Congress, in 1810, passed Macon's Bill Number 2, which reopened U.S. ports to all peaceful commerce but promised commercial nonintercourse against one country (for example, Great Britain), if the other (France) repealed its anti-U.S. trade laws. It was a law heaven-sent to a manipulator like Napoleon. He declared the restrictions lifted, then added conditions that meant that they were not lifted at all. A desperate, if suspicious, Madison foolishly accepted the emperor's assurance and cut off trade with England in early 1811. The British were furious, Madison humiliated, once Napoleon's scheme became clear. U.S. economic pressures were not working.

As early as 1809, the president had wondered whether war might be the only real alternative; by 1811, it was his firm conviction. He was not alone. The South and West were emerging from a severe three-year economic depression caused, in the view of the brilliant young South Carolina congressman John Calhoun, not by Madison's actions, but by "foreign injustice" committed by the British, who aimed to enslave Americans again into a "colonial state." The sharp decline of southern cotton exports from 93 million pounds in 1809 to 62 million pounds in 1811 allowed Calhoun to conclude that if the British continued to control U.S. trade, "the independence of this nation is lost. . . . This is the second struggle for our liberty."[38] The young Speaker of the House of Representatives in 1811–1812, Henry Clay of Kentucky, loudly agreed. Born in Virginia, trained in the law as well as in the dueling ritual and the gambling and drinking halls of frontier Kentucky, the tall, dynamic thirty-four-year-old Clay was rightly described by one political oppo-

Henry Clay (1777–1852) was born in Virginia and became a plantation owner in Kentucky. A power in the House of Representatives (1811–1825), he led the war hawks into the War of 1812. Later, as a U.S. senator, he championed commercial expansion and, as "the Great Pacificator," helped craft the compromises of 1820 and 1850 that temporarily preserved the Union from the strain of expansionism.

nent as "bold, aspiring, presumptuous, with a rough overbearing eloquence."[39] Running the House with a firm hand and working closely with Madison, Clay and Calhoun led a group of "War Hawks" elected in 1810 who were determined to force the British to behave.

Their determination turned to fury when news arrived in Washington during late November 1811 that a battle with Indians at Tippecanoe in Indiana territory resulted in the deaths of sixty-eight white men, including some well known to Clay and other war hawks. Evidence also arrived that the British had incited the Indians.[40] War hawks wore black armbands and charged London with "inciting the savages to murder." In truth, territorial governor William Henry Harrison's sharp practices had cheated the Native Americans of most of Indiana for a few dollars. Led by two great leaders, Tecumseh (a statesman and orator who preached that all land belonged to all Indians) and his brother Tenskwatawa the Prophet, the Native Americans had warned Harrison that they wanted no part of the white man's version of private property. "Sell a country!" Tecumseh exclaimed. "Why not sell the air, the clouds and the great sea, as well as the earth? Did not the Great Spirit make them all for the use of his children?"[41] Tecumseh hoped to avoid war—at least until he organized tribes as far south as Florida. But when Harrison marched close to the Prophet's town, the Winnebago tribe attacked. Suffering fewer casualties than Harrison's forces, the Native Americans nevertheless retreated, meanwhile scalping isolated white settlers on the way.

The war hawks and Madison prepared for battle. The president took the opportunity to order a secret operation to seize West Florida from

Tecumseh (1768–1813), a Shawnee leader who tried to stop the expansionism of the whites by allying Indian tribes from the Great Lakes to Florida. When the War of 1812 erupted, he fought with the British and was killed at the Battle of the Thames in Canada during the autumn of 1813.

the Spanish. He organized a coup, after which the plotters asked for U.S. annexation. The president nicely reasoned that the seizure was necessary to prevent the British from taking the area first. West Florida formally became a part of the Union in 1811. Madison then tried to repeat the operation in East Florida. That attempt, however, became an embarrassment when his secret agents botched the scheme. The president and Congress nevertheless declared in 1811 that henceforth they would not tolerate the transfer of New World territory owned by a foreign power to another foreign country. This "nontransfer principle" later became a part of the Monroe Doctrine.

Madison next named fellow Virginian James Monroe, who had close ties with the West, to replace Robert Smith as secretary of state. Smith, a Marylander, came from a mercantile group that hated Madison's economic policies. Moving toward war, the president then proposed to build a larger navy. But that measure lost 62 to 59 in the House. Clay and Calhoun voted for it, but every westerner except Clay voted "nay" on the grounds that the bill would, in the words of a Kentucky journal, "give an overwhelming influence to the commercial interest" in eastern cities. It was an odd way to prepare for war against the world's greatest naval power. The West, however, along with Madison and Jefferson, thought that the war would actually be decided beyond the Appalachians, especially in an invasion of Canada.

On June 1, 1812, Madison sent his war message to Congress. He charged the British with impressment, spilling "American blood" within American territory (a reference to the *Chesapeake* affair), "pretended blockades" and orders in council that allowed the British to have "plundered" U.S. shipping, and the "warfare just renewed by the savages" in the West. In reality, since 1807, the British had seized only 389 U.S. ships, while Napoleon had taken at least 460. But those numbers did not move Madison. The British threatened U.S. interests globally because of their naval power, their avowed competition for markets in such newly opening areas as Latin America (a region now breaking away from Spain), and their ties to the Native Americans. The House voted for war 79 to 49, the Senate 19 to 13. Voting was along party lines. The pro-war vote stretched through all geographical sections, including the coastal cities, whose merchants worked closely with British mercantile interests. Some of these merchants apparently preferred war to continued halfway measures such as embargoes. (Moreover, once war began, many of them grew rich smuggling and supplying British forces.) There can be no doubt, however, that, in the words of historian Ronald Hatzenbuehler, it was Madison, Monroe, and Clay who were "primarily responsible for directing war preparations."[42]

In July 1812, Americans were stunned to learn that on June 16 the British had repealed their orders in council. An economic depression, demands from British merchants, and a change in government in London led to the repeal. Historians have since speculated whether, if a transatlantic telegraph had existed in 1812 to speed the news of the repeal, the war would have been avoided. Probably not, for the impressment and Indian issues remained. The opportunity to conquer Canada was irresistible. Madison refused to reconsider the war declaration. Since 1789, he had determined to free U.S. commerce from British control. Now he had a chance to do it.

From Near-Catastrophe to Near-Victory

No sane American hoped for victory on the high seas (the British fleet had three fighting *ships* for every U.S. *cannon*).[43] Instead, Madison hoped to take advantage of Great Britain's preoccupation with Napoleon and believed that Canada could be seized as a hostage (as well as turned into a future U.S. state).

However, when U.S. forces drove into Canada, they were met by determined resistance—which included many Loyalists who had left the United States during the Revolution—and suffered a series of humiliating defeats. Tecumseh, in late 1812, seized the opportunity to unite tribes and join the British to capture both Detroit and an entire

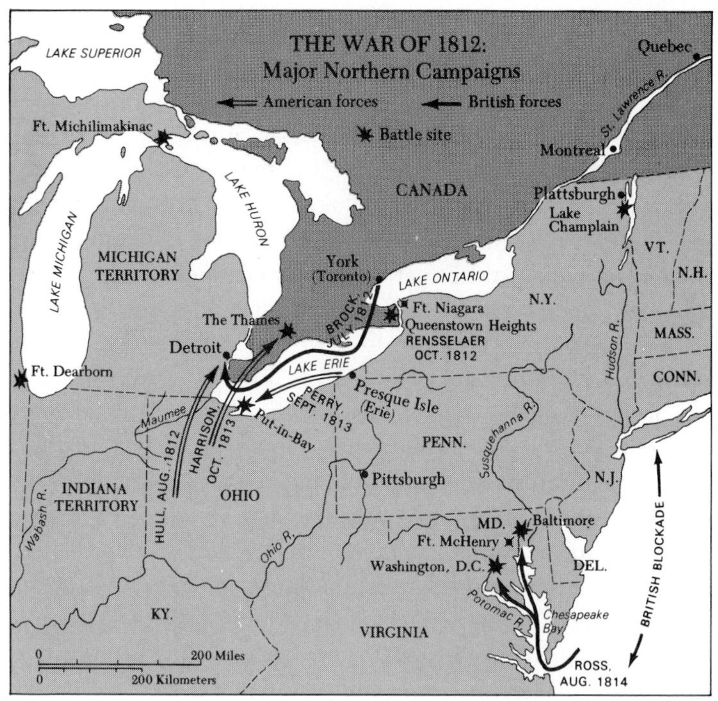

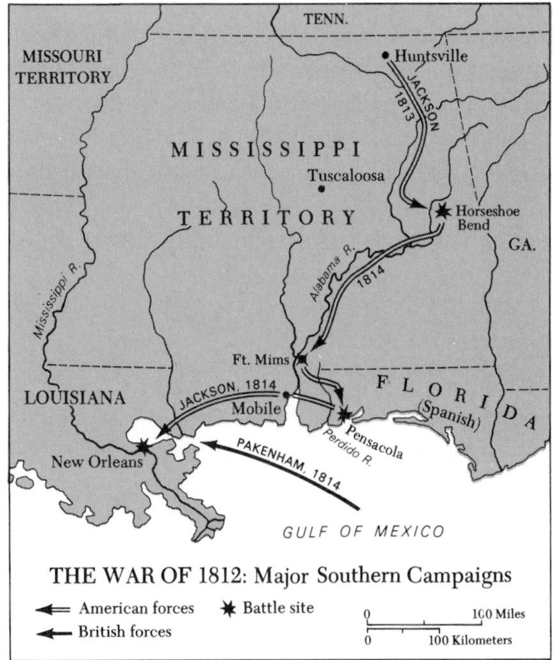

The War of 1812, which the United States lost on land but finally battled the British to a draw because of U.S. victories on the lakes and rivers.

American army. The Potawatomi tribe took the occasion to massacre everyone at Fort Dearborn (now Chicago). William Henry Harrison finally killed Tecumseh in 1813 after a series of brilliant U.S. naval victories on the Great Lakes sealed off British aid and isolated the Indian leader. Harrison held the Old Northwest, but Canada could not be conquered.

In the South, General Andrew Jackson of Tennessee, aided by Cherokees, defeated Creek Indians (the "Red Sticks") and then dictated a peace that opened much of Alabama to whites. Jackson was suddenly a national hero. He soon became a household word in January 1815, when his troops squashed a British invasion at the Battle of New Orleans. That triumph helped propel Jackson to the White House in 1828, although it occurred two weeks after the peace treaty was signed in Europe.

Otherwise, the war was notable because it nearly destroyed the new constitutional government. British ships controlled the coast. Their troops landed in Washington, burned the city in 1814, and forced James and Dolley Madison to escape into the hills across the Potomac River. Even Calhoun was dispirited: "Our executive officers are most incompetent men. . . . We are literally boren [*sic*] down under the effects of errors and mismanagement."[44] New England's (especially Boston's) merchants openly traded with, and loaned money to, Great Britain. In late 1814, some of these New Englanders met at Hartford, Connecticut, and threatened to leave the Union unless constitutional amendments gave them veto power over such issues as commercial questions and the admission of new western states into the Union. Only the peace treaty negotiated at Ghent, Belgium, in late 1814 ended this threat of possible secession.

Actually, within two weeks after war began, Madison had sought peace talks. By late 1813, the British were ready to deal: the wars with Napoleon seemed to be ending, so impressment could be stopped. London military officials had no stomach for dispatching the huge, costly force and fighting the long war required to conquer the United States. Sharp changes in Europe's diplomatic situation demanded British attention as well. As historian Donald Hickey summarizes, the British wanted peace because "of the lack of military progress in America [especially on the Great Lakes], unfavorable diplomatic developments in Europe, and domestic discontent over taxes."[45] The distinguished U.S. diplomatic team consisted of Henry Clay, John Quincy Adams, and Albert Gallatin (Jefferson's brilliant former secretary of the Treasury, who spent much of his time keeping peace between the ram-

As part of their major land offensive, the British landed in Maryland in August 1814, then marched on and burned the capital at Washington, D.C. President and Dolley Madison fled the city, and then a tornado hit the capital to complete the destruction. The British were finally beaten at Baltimore, and peace terms were signed in December 1814.

bunctious Clay and the dour Adams). They stopped a British demand for the annexation of Maine and parts of New York. The two sides then worked out the Treaty of Ghent (or the Peace of Christmas Eve). Both countries simply accepted the prewar territorial boundaries. Nothing was included about neutral rights.

Given the disastrous military situation around Washington and the disastrous political situation in New England, the United States won a remarkable diplomatic victory. The War of 1812 would be remembered less for Madison's embarrassed rush from a burning capital than for producing "The Star Spangled Banner," Uncle Sam (an actual person who provided supplies to beleaguered U.S. troops), and Jackson's postwar triumph at New Orleans. Because of the end of the Napoleonic Wars in Europe, impressment and orders in council no longer troubled relations. Hartford Federalists and their demands evaporated in the warm light of peace.

But it had been a brush with tragedy. The Jay Treaty, the X Y Z affair, the Alien and Sedition Acts, New England's anger over political power moving toward Louisiana, and Hartford's last-gasp attempt to remain within the rich British trading system even if it meant leaving the American one—all had threatened to destroy the Union. The nation had survived—if barely—and Americans were free for the first time since their independence forty years before to turn west and seize the incredible opportunities of a continental empire. It was to be a turn, however, that again nearly destroyed their Union in civil war.

Notes

1. Merrill Jensen, *The New Nation* (New York, 1950), pp. 88–92.
2. Edmund S. Morgan, "The American Revolution Considered as an Intellectual Movement," in *Paths of American Thought*, ed. Morton White and A. M. Schlesinger (Boston, 1963), pp. 32–33.
3. Richard B. Morris, *Seven Who Shaped Our Destiny* (New York, 1973), p. 1; Arthur M. Schlesinger, Jr., *The Imperial Presidency* (Boston, 1973), p. 15.
4. Bradford Perkins, *From Sea to Sea, 1776–1865*, in *The Cambridge History of U.S. Foreign Relations*, ed. Warren Cohen (New York, 1993), ch. III.
5. Rowland A. Berthoff, *An Unsettled People* (New York, 1971), pp. 136–137.
6. U.S. Bureau of the Census, *Historical Statistics of the United States: Colonial Times to 1957* (Washington, D.C., 1960), p. 547.
7. Reginald Horsman, "American Indian Policy and the Origins of Manifest Destiny," *University of Birmingham Historical Journal* 11, no. 2 (1968): 131–134.
8. Joyce Appleby, "Commercial Farming and the 'Agrarian Myth' in the Early Republic," *Journal of American History* 68 (March 1982): 840–841.
9. See Howard Kushner's review of N. N. Bashkina *et al.*, *The United States and Russia* in *Journal of American History* 68 (June 1981): 125; Irby C. Nichols, Jr., "The Russian Ukase and the Monroe Doctrine: A Re-evaluation," *Pacific Historical Review* 36 (February 1967): 13–26.
10. Bradford Perkins, *The First Rapprochement: England and the United States, 1795–1805* (Philadelphia, 1955), p. 24.
11. Saul Padover, *Jefferson* (New York, 1942), p. 182.
12. *Washington Post*, 22 February 1985, p. E1; Marcus Cunliffe, *George Washington, Man and Monument* (Boston, 1958), p. 129.
13. Arthur B. Darling, *Our Rising Empire, 1763–1803* (New Haven, 1940), p. 130.
14. Irving Brant, *James Madison*, 6 vols. (Indianapolis, 1944–1961), III, pp. 246–254.
15. William P. Cresson, *James Monroe* (Chapel Hill, N.C., 1946), pp. 120–121.
16. J. Fred Rippy and Angie Debo, *The Historical Background of the American Policy of Isolation* (Northampton, Mass., 1924), pp. 148–149.
17. Brant, III, pp. 375, 382.
18. Joseph E. Charles, *The Origins of the American Party System* (New York, 1961), p. 85.

19. *Ibid.*, p. 113.
20. Burton I. Kaufman, "Washington's Farewell Address: A Statement of Empire," in *Washington's Farewell Address: The View from the Twentieth Century*, ed. Burton I. Kaufman (Chicago, 1969), a fine selection; Victor Hugo Paltsits's *Washington's Farewell Address* (New York, 1935) remains the best study that includes the various drafts.
21. The quote and an analysis are in Samuel Flagg Bemis, "The Farewell Address: A Foreign Policy of Independence," *American Historical Review* 39 (January 1934): 267.
22. Alfred Kazin, "In Washington," *New York Review of Books*, 29 May 1986, pp. 11–12.
23. Thomas Jefferson to Nathaniel Niles, 22 March 1801, in *The Writings of Jefferson*, ed. Paul Leicester Ford, 10 vols. (New York, 1892–1899), IX, p. 221.
24. William Stinchcombe, *The XYZ Affair* (Westport, Conn., 1980), p. 129; Albert Jay Nock, *Jefferson* (Washington, D.C., 1926), pp. 237–239; Perkins, *From Sea to Sea*, ch. IV.
25. Thomas Jefferson to James Monroe, 24 November 1801, in *The Writings of Thomas Jefferson*, ed. Andrew A. Libscomb, 20 vols. (Washington, D.C., 1903), X, p. 296.
26. Thomas Jefferson to William Short, 3 October 1801, in *The Writings*, ed. Ford, VIII, p. 98.
27. Good discussions of Jefferson's use of presidential powers are Abraham D. Sofaer, *War, Foreign Affairs, and Constitutional Power: The Origins* (Cambridge, Mass., 1976), pp. 167–227, and Robert M. Johnstone, Jr., *Jefferson and the Presidency* (Ithaca, N.Y., 1978); on Madison's role, Richard E. Ellis, *The Jeffersonian Crisis* (New York, 1971), pp. 236–237.
28. An interesting post-1979 perspective is Forrest McDonald, "The Hostage Crisis of 1803," *Washington Post*, 20 May 1980, p. A19; also Reginald Horsman, *The Diplomacy of the New Republic, 1776–1815* (Arlington Heights, Ill., 1986), pp. 84–86.
29. James Madison to Thomas Pinckney, 27 November 1802, in *The Writings of James Madison*, ed. Gaillard Hunt, 9 vols. (New York, 1901), VI, p. 462.
30. Henry Adams, *History of the United States during the Administrations of Jefferson and Madison*, 9 vols. (New York, 1889–1891), VI, 69.
31. The best account is Alexander DeConde, *This Affair of Louisiana* (New York, 1976); see also E. Wilson Lyon, *Louisiana in French Diplomacy, 1759–1804* (Norman, Okla., 1934), pp. 195–202; James Madison to Edward Livingston, 18 January 1803, in *The Writings*, ed. Hunt, VII, p. 7.
32. William H. Goetzmann, *When the Eagle Screamed* (New York, 1966), p. 9; Julian P. Boyd, "Thomas Jefferson's 'Empire of Liberty,' " *Virginia Quarterly Review* 24 (Autumn 1948): 553.
33. Drew McCoy, *The Elusive Republic* (Chapel Hill, N.C., 1980), p. 203; Gouverneur Morris to Robert Livingston, 4 December 1803, quoted in *Congressional Record*, 55th Cong., 3d sess., 19 December 1898, p. 294.
34. James Madison to Robert R. Livingston, 31 January 1804, in *The Writings*, ed. Hunt, VII, pp. 114–116. Jefferson's constitutional problems set historical precedents and are examined in Walter LaFeber, "An Expansionist's Dilemma," *Constitution* 5 (Fall 1993):5–13.
35. Gilbert Chinard, *Thomas Jefferson . . .* (Boston, 1926), pp. 420–421.
36. Bradford Perkins, *Prologue to War: England and the United States, 1805–1812* (Berkeley, 1961), p. 77; Paul A. Varg, *Foreign Policies of the Founding Fathers* (East Lansing,

Mich., 1963), pp. 190–192; Burton Spivak's *Jefferson's English Crisis* (Charlottesville, Va., 1984) is a fine analysis.

37. Boyd's "Thomas Jefferson's 'Empire of Liberty' " gives the context.
38. John Calhoun's reply to John Randolph, 12 December 1811 and defense of 29 November, House Foreign Affairs Report, in *John Calhoun, Papers*, ed. Robert L. Meriwether (Columbia, S.C., 1959–), I, p. 83; Perkins, pp. 434–435; U.S. Bureau of the Census, *Historical Statistics of the United States* . . . , p. 547. Madison's aggressive policies were pushed by a small but powerful group labeled "the militants of 1809" by Reginald C. Stuart in his important article "James Madison and the Militants," *Diplomatic History* 6 (Spring 1982): 145–167.
39. Edmund Quincy, *Life of Josiah Quincy* (Boston, 1868), p. 255.
40. Henry Clay to ____, 18 June 1812, in *The Papers of Henry Clay*, ed. James F. Hopkins (Lexington, Ky., 1959–), I, p. 674.
41. Angie Debo, *A History of the Indians of the United States* (Norman, Okla., 1970), pp. 90–93.
42. Ronald L. Hatzenbuehler, "The War Hawks and the Question of Congressional Leadership in 1812," *Pacific Historical Review* 45 (February 1976): 1–22; the best book-length study on the subject is now J. C. A. Stagg, *Mr. Madison's War . . .* (Princeton, 1983).
43. Brant, VI, p. 39.
44. John Calhoun to Dr. James MacBride, 25 December 1812, in *Papers*, ed. Meriwether, I, p. 146.
45. Donald R. Hickey, "American Trade Restrictions during the War of 1812," *Journal of American History* 68 (December 1981): 517–538.

For Further Reading

In addition to the notes to this chapter, most of whose references are not repeated here, consult the General Bibliography at the end of this volume. For pre-1981 materials, one must examine *Guide to American Foreign Relations since 1700*, ed. Richard Dean Burns (1983). The best recent overview with excellent bibliography is Bradford Perkins, *From Sea to Sea, 1776–1865*, in *The Cambridge History of U.S. Foreign Relations*, ed. Warren Cohen (1993). A brilliant examination of the context is *Capitalism and a New Social Order: The Republican Vision of the 1790s* by Joyce Appleby (1984), especially important for commercial policies. Other accounts examining the framework of the era are *The American and European Revolutions, 1776–1848*, ed. Jaroslaw Pelenski (1980), conference papers on comparative aspects; Peggy K. Liss, *Atlantic Empires: The Network of Trade and Revolution 1713–1826* (1983), key on post-1800 Western Hemisphere relationships; Javier Cuenca Esteban, "Trends and Cycles in U.S. Trade with Spain and the Spanish Empire, 1790–1819," *Journal of Economic History* 44 (June 1984); Daniel C. Lang, *Foreign Policy in the Early Republic: The Law of Nations and the Balance of Power* (1986); Dorothy V. Jones, *License for Empire* (1982), beautifully arguing that post-1776 Indian policy was a form of "containment"; Reginald Horsman, *Race and Manifest Destiny: The Origins of American Racial Anglo-Saxonism* (1981), indispensable; Ralph Ketcham, *Presidents above Party: The First American Presidency, 1789–1829* (1984); and Steven Watts's superb *The Republic Reborn . . . 1790–1820* (1987).

For the 1790s specifically, a succinct treatment is Frank T. Reuter, *Trials and Triumphs: George Washington's Foreign Policy* (1982); Jacob E. Cooke's biography, *Alexander Hamilton* (1982); Paul D. Nelson, *Anthony Wayne: Soldier of the Early Republic* (1985), on both the military and Indian campaigns. Lawrence Kaplan is a leading scholar of the era, as is demonstrated in his *"Entangling Alliances with None": American Foreign Policy in the Age of Jefferson* (1987); and a useful essay is Burton Spivak, "Thomas Jefferson . . . ," in *Traditions and Values: American Diplomacy, 1790–1865*, ed. Norman Graebner (1985), as is Spencer C. Tucker, "Mr. Jefferson's Gunboat Navy," *American Neptune* 43 (April 1983). A new overview is Robert W. Tucker and David C. Hendrickson, *Empire of Liberty: The Statecraft of Thomas Jefferson* (1990). And for the most colorful—and dangerous—opponent to Jefferson, see *Political Correspondence and Public Papers of Aaron Burr*, ed. Mary-Jo Ryan and Joanne Wood Ryan, 2 vols. (1983). The 1807 debacle is examined in several centuries of context in Richard J. Ellings's *Embargoes and World Power* (1985), while Clifford L. Egan's *Neither Peace nor War; Franco-American Relations, 1803–1812* (1983) provides important counterpoint; J. C. A. Stagg, *Mr. Madison's War* (1983), superbly examines Canada and the West Indian trade as causes of the 1812 war, but within the entire 1783–1830 framework; Ronald L. Hatzenbuehler and Robert L. Ivie, *Congress Declares War* (1983), skillfully dissects congressional voting behavior; Robert Rutland, "James Madison . . . ," in *Traditions and Values*, ed. Graebner, is by a leading scholar who is also the lead editor of *The Papers of James Madison, Presidential Series* (1984–); C. Edward Skeen, *John Armstrong, Jr., 1758–1843* (1981), has important material on French diplomacy and the mismanagement of the 1812 war; Lawrence D. Cress, *Citizens in Arms* (1982), has written a superb social history of the 1812 conflict. An excellent account of expansionism is *Astoria and Empire* by James P. Ronda (1990), on the U.S.-British rivalry on the Pacific to 1812. For extensive recent sources, consult Dwight L. Smith *The War of 1812: An Annotated Bibliography* (1985).

3

The First, the Last: John Quincy Adams and the Monroe Doctrine (1815–1828)

Windmills, Clipper Ships, and Good Feelings

Soon after the peace of 1814, Lord Castlereagh, the British foreign minister, shrewdly observed that Americans won their wars not on the battlefield but "in the bedchamber." He could have made much the same observation about how Americans won much of the North American continent between 1815 and 1850. Freed of European quarrels for the first time in their history, Americans burst westward. Sixteen states existed in 1800, but there were twenty-four by 1824. As early as 1820, as many people lived in the new states formed after 1789 as had inhabited the original thirteen states before the Revolution. These new states formed the springboard for the drive across the continent.

The doubling of the population every twenty to twenty-five years fueled the search for new land, as did basic changes in the economy. Since their early history, Americans had prospered from the carrying and re-export trade—that is, carrying anyone's goods (not just American products) in the efficient ships that worked out of such ports as Salem, Boston, New York, Philadelphia, Alexandria, and Charleston. The profits had grown so fat in carrying British goods worldwide that between 1807 and 1814 some New England merchants cooperated more with London's laws than with Jefferson's and Madison's wishes. After 1815, these merchants began to disappear. With peace, British ships were free to carry British goods.

The U.S. merchant, moreover, found a more profitable investment in a new home-grown industrial complex. That complex remained in its infancy until the Civil War, but a major first step was taken in 1813–1815 when a group of wealthy merchants established the Waltham textile works. For the first time, this factory efficiently brought under one roof the various processes of spinning and weaving. Waltham's profits soon demonstrated that Americans could begin to compete with British manufacturers. But that success came much later. Between 1815 and 1819, the British dumped so many goods on the United States that Americans suffered a severe economic panic in 1819. New Englanders demanded a tariff wall to protect them from the dumping. By 1820, about $50 million was invested in U.S. manufacturing. (By 1860, that figure was to amount to $1 billion.)

These twists and turns of the 1815-to-1820 economy bankrupted many Americans, who then moved west to find their fortune. The country seemed to be in perpetual motion as people flooded over the Appalachians and the Mississippi. A German visitor wondered how Americans could survive while acting as if they were always "tied to the wing of a windmill." Events occurred so rapidly, he said, that "ten years in America are like a century in Spain."[1] One of those broken by the 1819 panic was Moses Austin, an Illinois lead miner. Austin decided to start anew by leading a small band of Americans into Mexico's province of Texas. Thus began the U.S. conquest of the region. Other victims of the economy turned farther west to search out land and trading opportunities in Oregon, although the 1837 depression sent the major flood of settlers into the Northwest. By 1825, American geography texts showed Texas already having closer ties with the United States than with Mexico. By 1834, a widely used geography primer already showed Texas, California, and Oregon as parts of the United States, even though they were not to be annexed for a decade or more.[2]

Not that everyone moving west had given up on the carrying trade. Indeed, the U.S. merchant fleet was entering its greatest era. These years ushered in the period of the magnificent Yankee clipper ship, admired on the world's oceans. As early as 1820, U.S. consuls watched over American interests in such exotic spots as French Mauritius, Java, the Philippines, and Hawaii. Treaties to protect Americans were signed in the 1820s with Tahiti and Hawaii. In the 1830s, the first official U.S. diplomat to Asia, Edmund Roberts, sailed west to the Far East and made treaties with Siam (later Thailand) and Zanzibar.[3] The U.S. ships that explored these corners of the globe carried not British (or French) goods, but American exports. They also transported to Europe the cotton and tobacco grown on the South's slave plantations. Cotton allowed Americans to dominate European markets and obtain the capital needed to buy new lands and build needed roads and canals. Between 1815 and 1860, cotton accounted for more than half the value of all U.S. exports. Its importance began to slide after 1840, when western grain crops started to capture foreign markets.[4] But by then, the system was fixed: the Northeast possessed much of the nation's capital, ships, and manufacturing, while the South was wedded to cotton and the slave labor that produced it.

Thus, precisely at the moment U.S. landed expansion accelerated westward, two systems—a northern free-labor industrial and commercial complex, and a southern slave-agricultural complex—began to struggle over which system would control the course of the nation's foreign policy. The struggle demonstrated again how domestic developments molded foreign policy, and how foreign policy, in turn, influenced the everyday lives of Americans—until the Civil War that the foreign policy helped bring about took 600,000 of those lives.

That horror was in the future. Between 1815 and 1825, optimism, not fear, guided U.S. expansion. For example, in an 1824 cabinet meeting, President James Monroe declared that he was afraid that the distant Oregon settlements would become a separate nation. Instantly, his secretary of state, John Quincy Adams, and secretary of war, John Calhoun, disagreed. Although Adams hated slavery and Calhoun justified it, both fully agreed, in Adams's words, that the Constitution's federal system "would be found practicable upon a territory as extensive as this continent."[5] Oregon might be three thousand miles away and claimed by the Russian and British empires, but these men had no doubt about the future. The nation was entering the 1815-to-1860 era of "manifest destiny"—that is, the belief that God had created North America for exactly the kind of white farmers and merchants that the American settlers happened to be.

They had such confidence despite (or was it because of?) the virtual disappearance of political parties by 1820. As the Federalists committed political suicide at the 1814 Hartford Convention, James Monroe managed to establish one major party, the Jeffersonian Democrat-Republican, that removed much of the two-party competition. The nation headed into the so-called "era of good feelings." The name was most misleading. Even if formal political-party competition had disappeared, factions and individuals attacked each other so bitterly inside Monroe's cabinet and in Congress that at times the government came to a halt. Monroe nevertheless bragged that with his one general party

John Quincy Adams (1767–1848) became the nation's greatest secretary of state because of his vast experience (minister to Russia, the Netherlands, and Prussia, as well as U.S. senator from Massachusetts), education, intelligence, and sense of history. He was also possessed by a discipline and an intensity that clearly appear in this photograph.

in control, the nation's government had "approached . . . perfection; that in respect to it we have no essential improvement to make."[6] Such beliefs also generated confidence in their manifest destiny as Americans moved west and across the oceans. The "era of good feelings" also made possible virtual miracles: the re-election of Monroe in 1820 to a second term with only one electoral vote opposing him, and—more significantly—the rise to power of John Quincy Adams.

ADAMS

The years 1816 to 1824 marked one of the most successful eras in American diplomatic history. Without doubt, John Quincy Adams remains the nation's greatest secretary of state because of his accomplishments during those years.

No one was ever better trained to guide the nation's foreign policy.

Born in 1767, he was the son of two of the most talented Americans, Abigail and John Adams. At the age of eleven, he traveled with his father to Europe and in his teens served as secretary to the first U.S. mission to Russia. Meanwhile, he mastered five languages, French literature, ancient as well as modern history, European and American theater, and began to learn the often-fatal intricacies of Europe's power politics. From both his father and mother, he inherited a strong American nationalism, intense suspicion of British politics, and stern Calvinist discipline. The nationalism appeared when he won election from Massachusetts to the U.S. Senate in 1802, after returning from serving as U.S. minister to the Netherlands and Berlin. Although representing a strong Federalist state, Adams supported Jefferson's and Madison's purchase of Louisiana and the embargo. For such political treason, the Federalists threw Adams out of office. Madison named him minister to Russia in 1809. In St. Petersburg, his dislike of Great Britain was not hidden. As an English observer vividly described Adams in 1812:

> Of all the men whom it was ever my lot to accost and to waste civilities upon, [Adams] was the most doggedly and systematically repulsive. With a vinegar aspect, cotton in his leathern ears, and hatred to England in his heart, he sat in the frivolous assemblies of Petersburg like a bull-dog among spaniels; and many were the times that I drew monosyllables and grim smiles from him and tried in vain to mitigate his venom.[7]

Adams's view of England was not in doubt, but his personality was more complex than this observer wanted to admit. Adams loved parties and was an expert on wines. He also loved the theater, so much so that at age fourteen he decided he must leave actresses alone if he were to discipline himself to be a statesman. In 1795, he had such a fine time in London that he wrote in his diary, "There is something so fascinating in the women I meet in this country that it is not well for me. I am obliged immediately to leave it."[8] At age thirty, he married the talented Louisa Catherine Johnson. Her spouse's dedication to protecting U.S. interests carried her into a special kind of hell. She suffered twelve pregnancies, with eight ending in miscarriages, as she followed her husband throughout Europe and the United States. Louisa buried their only daughter in Russia, where her husband took the family without consulting his wife.[9] One son later committed suicide.

Throughout, John Quincy Adams never doubted his country's destiny. In a cabinet meeting, one of Monroe's advisers declared that Americans must not be so openly ambitious, because the British were criticizing U.S. expansionism. Adams shot back that nothing should be done: "Nothing we could say or do would remove this impression until the world shall be familiarized with the idea of considering our proper dominion to be the continent of North America." It would only be a matter of time before the "law of nature" led to the annexation of Spain's holdings in the south, and Canada in the north. Until Europeans understood "that the United States and North America are identical," the secretary of state lectured the cabinet, any denial of U.S. ambition "will have no other effect than to convince them that we add to our ambition hypocrisy."[10]

He could utter such spread-eagle, manifest-destiny statements, but Adams never believed that Americans would always be on God's side regardless of what they did. When he heard that naval hero Stephen Decatur had cried the famous words "Our country, right or wrong," Adams disagreed. "May our country be always successful," his version went, "but whether successful or otherwise always right. I disclaim as unsound all patriotism incompatible with the principles of eternal justice."[11] His faith in "eternal justice" was strong, although Adams's religious beliefs were complex. He did believe that the Creator worked according to fixed, scientific laws and that with discipline and education these laws could be discovered. Thus, Adams arose each morning at 5:00 A.M. to read the Bible for an hour in the belief that because God had especially blessed the United States, the proper course of U.S. foreign policy could be discovered by studying God's word.[12] And, thus, he wrote the historic and still used *Report on Weights and Measures* that provided scientific standards for the use of—and to tie together—the continent. Adams wrote the *Report* during his busiest days as secretary of state by arising an hour or two earlier each morning—that is, 3:00 A.M.

Adams studied diplomacy as carefully as he studied his science and Latin. He understood the first principle: the greatest threat to the United States came from the British, for they occupied Canada, could control the seas, and were moving to dominate the newly independent Latin American states that were breaking away from Spain. But there was a second principle: if the British could be contained in Canada, over the long run the American "multiplication table" and U.S. commercial ambition would occupy and control the rest of the continent and, perhaps, such choice Latin American areas as Cuba. The key to his policy was containment, a policy famous in dealing with the Soviet Union after World War II, but which Adams brilliantly created to block the British 125 years earlier. A third principle was his understanding that the Americans and British had certain common interests that he could exploit. Most important was London's interest in having the Spanish Empire break up so that London merchants could develop Latin American markets. The United States also wanted Spain out of the New World. Thus, Adams saw that the powerful British fleet would actually protect U.S. interests by keeping Spain and other Old World powers out of Latin America—without Americans having to pay for it. To reap such benefits, however, he understood that Great Britain and the United States had to be at peace. It was a well-conceived diplomatic strategy that soon gained historic victories.

Setting the Stage

Adams helped ensure peace with Great Britain by overseeing two agreements, the first signed by Acting Secretary of State Richard Rush. The Rush-Bagot pact of 1817 was an executive agreement made between the U.S. and British governments that demilitarized the Great Lakes and helped prevent accidental clashes along the U.S.-Canadian border. Many Canadians were not pleased. Having been invaded twice by the United States within forty years, they preferred to keep their defenses fully armed. When they pulled their cannons off the Great Lakes, they nevertheless kept them aimed at the Americans. London officials, however, wanted no border outbreaks. They had enough problems in Europe and Latin America. Consequently, they sacrificed Canadian wishes to make a deal with the United States. It was not the last time they would sacrifice Canadian interests. The Rush-Bagot deal was historically important for another reason. Instead of submitting it to the Senate as a treaty that would require a two-thirds vote for ratification, Monroe put it into effect by merely announcing it to Congress in his annual message. The usual straight-arrow Monroe, however, knew he was stretching his constitutional powers, so he asked Congress whether the executive was constitutionally competent to put such a pact into effect. The Senate never gave a direct reply, but it did approve this "agreement" without voting on it as a treaty. Thus the major constitutional precedent was set that allowed presidents to make such agreements with other governments without asking for Senate ratification. By the mid-twentieth century, such "executive agreements" were to replace treaties as the most numerous form of agreements with other nations.[13]

A second historic pact with the British was the Convention of 1818.

Adams obtained the perpetual U.S. right to fish along the Newfoundland coast, settled outstanding disputes over slaves that the British had taken from southern states, and opened new opportunities for each nation in the other's commerce. More important, Adams established the forty-ninth parallel as the U.S.-Canadian boundary from Lake of the Woods to the Rockies. This boundary shut the British off from northern access to the Mississippi River. He thus unknowingly obtained most of the present states of Idaho, Montana, and North Dakota, as well as parts of the incredibly rich Mesabi iron-ore range that was to help create the U.S. steel industry sixty years later. Finally, and of equal importance, the convention provided that the disputed region of Oregon would remain "free and open" to both nations. Adams believed the provision would allow the American population explosion to seize Oregon peacefully.

He next tried to open the British West Indies to U.S. trade. After Adams threatened economic retaliation against London shipping, the British opened several ports. But Adams wanted more. He demanded that the British charge a U.S. ship no higher tariff than they charged their own vessels. That demand was too much. London officials closed the West Indies to teach Adams (now president) a lesson, and it was left to Adams's hated political opponent, Andrew Jackson, to use diplomatic politeness and regain access again in 1830.

The West Indies episode revealed Adams's belligerence and ambition. He assessed himself in 1817 as "a man of reserved, cold, austere, and forbidding manners; my political adversaries say a gloomy misanthropist, and my personal enemies, an unsocial savage." A friend was more complimentary: "Mr. Adams is in person short, thick, and fat . . . and neither very agreeable nor very repulsive. . . . He is regular in his habits, and moral and temperate in his life."[14] By 1821, Spanish officials doubtless thought Adams's own view was more accurate.

THE TRANSCONTINENTAL TREATY

With the British contained, Adams, in 1818, began negotiations to obtain East Florida from Spain. The Spanish Empire was gasping its last breath in most of Latin America, but its minister to Washington, Luís de Onís y Gonzalez, used every diplomatic trick he knew to stall the U.S. advance. "I have seen slippery diplomats . . . ," Adams complained, "but Onís is the first man I have ever met with who made it a point of honor to pass for more of a swindler than he was."[15]

Andrew Jackson (1767–1845) gave his name to an entire age (the Jacksonian Age of the 1820s to the 1850s) and, after becoming president in 1828, had a bitter personal feud with John Quincy Adams. But in 1818–1820, the two men were the perfect pair for American expansionism—General Jackson as the ruthless frontier fighter who seized key parts of Florida, Adams as the tough diplomat who parlayed Jackson's victory into a treaty that gave the United States not only Florida, but a continent.

In 1817–1818, drama in Florida radically changed the context of the Adams-Onís talks. Monroe had ordered General Andrew Jackson to the Florida border to stop attacks by the Seminole Indians on the advancing white settlements. Jackson, who was seldom moderate when dealing with Indians or the British, decided to attack the problem's root. He marched into East Florida, destroyed Indian villages, captured and promptly hanged two British citizens who he claimed were egging on the tribes against Americans, and took the region for the United States. Monroe and most of his cabinet were horrified. Hanging British citizens could cause the second burning of Washington in just five years. Adams alone defended Jackson. The secretary of state argued that London would not retaliate because the two British subjects were in the wrong. Besides, England wanted no war with the United States. Adams wrote a blistering public paper condemning the two victims and the Seminoles. As historian Richard Drinnon notes, the paper "was a virtuoso performance that added luster and reach to the theme of merciless savages and outside agitators."[16] Adams carried the day. The cabinet decided to support Jackson, who had become, after all, enormously popular for killing Englishmen and Indians at New Orleans and now East Florida.

Adams put it to Onís directly: if Spain did not give up Florida immediately, "Spain would not have the possession of Florida to give us." The British had refused to move against Jackson. The Spanish were isolated. The secretary of state now demanded more. Negotiating the 1818 convention had reopened Adams's long interest in Oregon and the Pacific coast. He asked for Spain's claims to that region. Onís

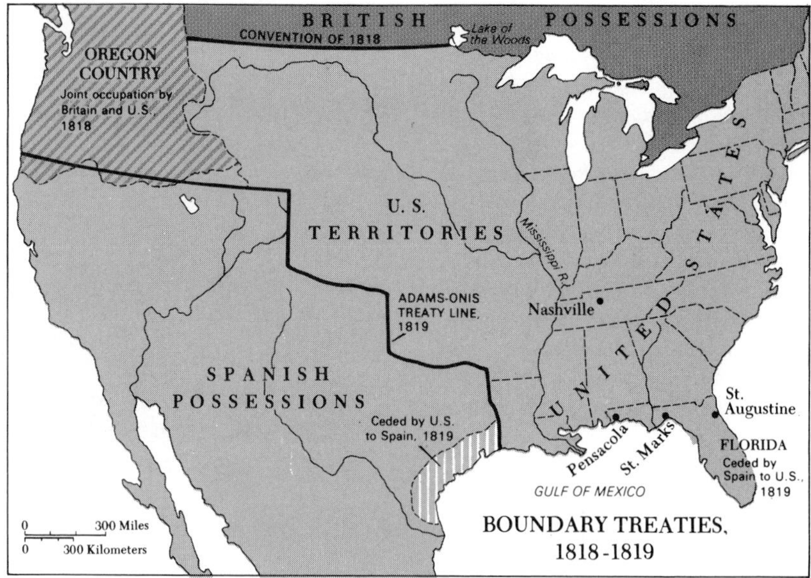

After three years of negotiations, Adams obtained a treaty continental in scope but whose boundaries turned out to be vague—so vague that Americans could later use them in the Texas region to make further landed claims.

responded by asking for Adams's promise not to recognize the Latin American nations that were rebelling against Spain, and for the U.S. recognition that Spain owned Texas. Adams flatly refused to make the promise. He also objected to giving up rights to Texas; but on this issue, the Monroe cabinet overruled him. Thus, the deal was struck: Spain turned over Florida and its rights to the Pacific coast in return for the United States dropping certain monetary claims against Spain and recognizing Spanish claims to Texas. For virtually no money and the surrender of no actual U.S. interest, Adams obtained all of Florida and the first U.S. formal rights to the Pacific coast. When the Senate finally ratified the Transcontinental Treaty in 1821, Adams bragged in his diary that he had first proposed the Pacific-coast part of the pact and had almost single-handedly carried the talks through to victory. The treaty, he observed, "forms a great epocha in our history."[17]

Opening "A Great Tragic Volume"—and July 4, 1821

It was ominous that at the same moment Adams was expanding the United States to the Caribbean in the south and to the Pacific in the west, he and the country suddenly had to confront the deadly issue of slavery. Adams quickly understood that it was the issue that could destroy the Union he was creating.

The struggle began in 1819, when Missouri applied for admission to the nation as a slave state. Northerners responded by proposing to exclude slavery from all the former Louisiana Purchase Territory, of which Missouri was a part. Southerners condemned the proposal for bottling up their own expansion of cotton lands. The slave system depended on continual expansion, not least because without the possibility of shipping young slaves west, southerners in the older states could find themselves (as one warned) "dammed up in a land of slaves." Congressional business stalled as the debate grew bitter. Adams initially paid little attention to it, but he came to see that slavery threatened the future of U.S. foreign policy. He had always believed that God intended Americans to rule all of North America as a land of freedom, but by 1820 he concluded, "The greatest danger of this Union was the overgrown extent of its territory, combining with the slavery question." Even Adams now wanted neither Texas nor Florida unless slavery was excluded from them. He understood earlier than most that

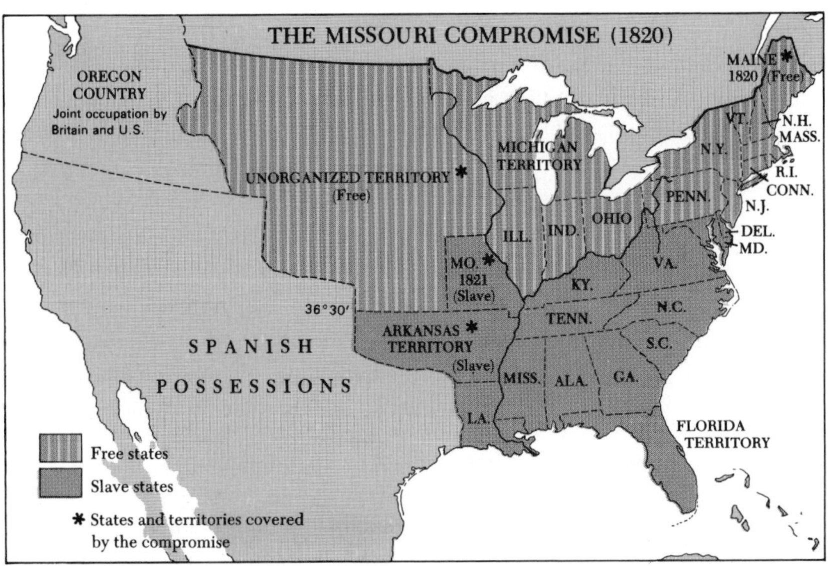

The furor and sectional bitterness that led to the great debate of 1819–1820 were not quieted by the 1820 Missouri Compromise, but only blunted until further expansion in the 1840s resurrected the issue of slave expansionism and led to the Civil War.

American expansion could no longer be discussed without having to decide whether slave or free states would benefit from expansion. In this respect, he confided to his diary, the Missouri debate "is a mere preamble—a title-page to a great tragic volume."[18] In 1820, Congress struck a compromise: Missouri entered as a slave state, Maine a free state—thus maintaining the balance—and slavery was prohibited in northern Louisiana Territory but allowed in the southern. Adams doubted that the compromise would settle the problem.

For the first time, Adams began seriously to wonder whether God was blessing or condemning the United States. He began rethinking his nation's and his own ambitions. Adams wanted quiet and no more debates over slavery. He certainly wanted no wars for conquest to the south that could enlarge slave territory and increase the power of the South. Adams's views clashed with those of Henry Clay, the powerful Kentucky senator who was openly challenging Adams and Jackson for the presidency in 1824. Clay pushed to recognize the new Latin American nations, regardless of relations with Spain. The Kentuckian even urged helping the revolutionaries "by all means short of actual war." Adams condemned immediate recognition. It could destroy his deal with Onís. He believed, moreover, that the United States had little in common with the monarchical Roman Catholic governments appearing to the south. Adams had no illusion they were following the example of 1776. The great South American liberator, Simón Bolívar, actually agreed with Adams. Bolívar admired how North Americans made their "weak and complicated" Constitution work. But he thought that applying the political, civil, and religious system of the "English-American" to the "Spanish-American" was an impossibility.[19]

Adams was especially afraid that any U.S. involvement, even in supposed wars for liberty and independence, could destroy the United States. In an address on July 4, 1821, Adams answered Clay by warning—in words that would be repeatedly quoted 150 years later by those opposing the U.S. war in Vietnam—about certain American commitments:

> Wherever the standard of freedom and independence has been or shall be unfurled, there will her [the United States'] heart, her benedictions, and her prayers be. But she goes not abroad in search of monsters to destroy. She is the well-wisher to the freedom and independence of all. She is the champion and vindicator only of her own. . . . She well knows that by once enlisting under other banners than her own, were they even the banners of foreign independence, she would involve herself beyond the power of extrication, in all the wars of interest and intrigue, of individual avarice,

> envy, and ambition, which assume the colors and usurp the standard of freedom. The fundamental maxims of her policy would insensibly change from *liberty* to *force*. . . . She might become the dictatress of the world. She would no longer be the ruler of her own spirit.[20]

Adams continued to oppose recognition of new Latin American nations, but in 1822 Monroe overruled him. The president wanted to reap the economic benefits of recognizing the new governments before the British. Adams gave in but made it clear that the United States recognized only governments that controlled their country and that promised to respect that country's international obligations (such as protecting U.S. citizens). No moral approval, he emphasized, was involved. Adams's recognition policy (which followed Jefferson's policy set in 1793) was followed by all future presidents until Woodrow Wilson changed it nearly ninety years later.

The Monroe Doctrine

In his annual message to Congress in December 1823, Monroe climaxed six years of successful foreign policy by announcing a historic set of principles. Later (after 1844) called "the Monroe Doctrine," the message was largely shaped by Adams. It summarized the secretary of state's containment policy in the Western Hemisphere. The message told Europeans to stay out of American developments, thus leaving the United States as potentially the strongest power in the hemisphere. Moreover, as Adams had long since realized, a delicious part of the policy was that the British, for their own interests, would actually keep other Europeans out of the New World while the United States developed its own strength.

The belief that the Americas were for Americans had deep roots. It at least went back to Paine's *Common Sense* (see p. 19). But more immediate events triggered the 1823 declaration. One was the rapid development of U.S. trade with Latin America that gave Washington officials good reason for preventing the reconquest of South America by Spain or her European friends, especially France and Russia. U.S. exports to Latin America rose from $6.7 million in 1816 to nearly $8 million in 1821, despite a slump caused by the 1819 economic panic. Latin America took 13 percent of U.S. exports, and if the Spanish could be kept out—and British economic competition cut out—the Southern

Hemisphere promised to be a rich market for North American producers.

In 1821, the problem of possible European intervention moved closer to home. The Russian tsar, Alexander I, notified the world that in order to protect his claims stretching from the Aleutians and Alaska down to San Francisco, all land north of 51 degrees latitude would be sealed off, and no non-Russian ship was to be allowed within 100 miles of the northwest coasts. The tsar thus directly excluded both U.S. claims to parts of the Northwest that Adams obtained from Spain, and the right of American merchants to trade in the vast region. The United States and Great Britain protested. Adams bluntly told the Russians in July 1823 that "the American continents are no longer subjects for *any* new European colonial establishments."[21] Nor would the secretary of state recognize the 100-mile limit. He passionately believed that U.S. merchants should be able to buy and sell wherever they wished. Adams condemned European colonialism not only because it politically sealed off pieces of land, but also because it closed down trade. He had already told the British government in late 1822 of his feelings about these central issues: "The whole system of modern colonization is an abuse of government and it is time that it should come to an end." He had aimed that barrage specifically against London's claim to Oregon.

These problems of trade and Russian-British ambitions arose in an explosive political atmosphere. In 1821, the Greeks had revolted against the brutalities of Turkish control. Americans jumped to the conclusion that it was 1776 again. They raised thousands of dollars (especially among idealistic college students who knew their Greek), and such names as Syracuse and Athens came into vogue as city names. Monroe searched for a way to help the Greeks but was cut short by Adams, who warned that it was a European quarrel over which the United States had no control. When Adams received a request for a personal contribution to help Greece, he flatly refused. Not only would such a contribution break U.S. neutrality, he replied, but "we had objects of distress to relieve at home more than sufficient to absorb all my capacities of contribution."[22] He was practicing what he had preached in his July 4, 1821, address.

The shrewd British foreign secretary, George Canning, carefully watched Adams's performance. Although he disliked being lectured about his country's colonialism, Canning understood that U.S. and British interests coincided. Both nations wanted Spain, France, and Russia out of the New World. British merchants were busily profiting from trade with the newly independent Latin Americans. Canning,

James Monroe (1758–1831), although president between 1817 and 1825, was not so much the author of the Monroe Doctrine (1823) as was his secretary of state, John Quincy Adams. But Monroe had been an early and a successful U.S. diplomat himself. The Virginian had helped negotiate the Louisiana Purchase while serving in Paris during 1803 and was Madison's secretary of state between 1811 and 1817 as well as secretary of war part of that time.

moreover, wanted the Quadruple Alliance, led by the tsar and including other European monarchies who opposed British foreign policies, to gain no dramatic victory by restoring Latin America to Spain. He, therefore, sent a most attractive offer to Adams: the United States could make a joint announcement with the world's greatest power, Great Britain, that no more colonial rule would be allowed in Latin America. Both nations would then show their own good faith by promising to take no more territory in the region.

Flattered, Monroe asked Jefferson and Madison for advice. Both former presidents recommended accepting Canning's offer. Adams, however, single-handedly stopped the move for the joint declaration. He saw that the second part of the deal (a mutual promise to take no more territory) would prevent the United States from someday annexing Texas and Cuba. He had no doubt that both areas were to become parts of his country, although not necessarily through armed conquest. As he instructed the U.S. minister to Spain in April 1823:

> There are laws of political as well of physical gravitation; and if an apple severed by the tempest from its native tree cannot choose but fall to the ground, Cuba, forcibly disjoined from its own unnatural connection with Spain, and incapable of self-support, can gravitate only towards the North American Union, which by the same law of nature cannot cast her off from its bosom.[23]

Nature's will, the secretary of state argued, must not be blocked by the pledge suggested by Canning. Adams, moreover, had long argued that any such deal was unnecessary because the British would keep out other Europeans anyway. Nor did he want to join the British so openly against Russia. It was in the U.S. interest to play off those two European powers in the Northwest, to neutralize both, and then to move in itself. Adams thus convinced Monroe to announce the policy by himself and maintain complete freedom of action: "It would be more candid, as well as more dignified . . . , than to come in as a cock-boat in the wake of the British man-of-war."[24]

In his annual address to Congress on December 2, 1823, the president announced the Monroe Doctrine's substance in three principles. First, he reviewed the exchanges with the tsar, exchanges which had been friendly. The Russians were willing to discuss their claims in the Northwest. Making no threats, Monroe issued the noncolonization principle that Adams had carefully crafted: "The American continents . . . are henceforth not to be considered as subjects for future colonization by any European powers." Historian Edward Crapol has discovered a letter of 1831 in which Adams stated that this principle was aimed not only at Russia, but was "a warning to Great Britain herself."[25] All the Europeans were to be contained—then expelled.

Next, Monroe discussed the Greek crisis, then used it to introduce the doctrine's second principle: the so-called two-spheres policy. But in declaring that the affairs of the Old and New Worlds should not become entangled (or what some historians have called a policy of "isolationism"), Monroe carefully chose his words: "In the wars of the European powers in matters relating to themselves we have never taken any part, nor does it comport with our policy to do so." The president—note—did not say that the United States would remain out of all foreign quarrels, only those involving "matters relating" solely to Europeans. He and Adams fully understood that as a budding world power, U.S. interests might have to become involved in European quarrels—as in 1812–1814.

Third, Monroe announced a general hands-off policy: "We should consider any attempt on [the Europeans'] part to extend their system to any portion of this hemisphere as dangerous to our peace and safety." The president quickly added that "with the existing colonies or dependencies of any European power we have not interfered and shall not interfere." But no further European expansion or influence could be tolerated. These phrases were directed against Spanish and French hopes of restoring Spain's influence in Latin America, but they could also be applied to British activities in the Northwest.

Although supposedly aimed at the Russians, the Spanish, and the

French, Adams's policies, in historian Ernest May's phrase, were "particularly hard on the British."[26] London officials posed the greatest threat to the United States, especially to continued American landed and commercial expansion. Monroe's 1823 message took that expansion for granted—indeed, it was viewed as a requirement for the country's survival. In a rephrase of Madison's argument in *The Federalist* Numbers 10 and 14 (see p. 34), Monroe recounted proudly the American population explosion and the creation of new states:

> It is manifest that by enlarging the basis of our system and increasing the number of States the system itself has been greatly strengthened in both its branches. Consolidation [that is, centralized government] and disunion have thereby been rendered equally impracticable. Each government [the states and the national], confiding in its own strength, has less to apprehend from the other.[27]

Adams must have read those words with mixed emotions. He fully understood after the Missouri Compromise debate of 1820 that continued expansion might not render disunion "impracticable," but instead bring on fresh threats of disunion.

The Monroe Doctrine set up the ground rules for the great game of empire that was to be played in the New World. European colonization was to stop, European influence to be contained. The Old World and the New World were to be increasingly separated, unless U.S. interests forced it to become involved in Old World struggles. Especially notable was the Adams-Monroe view of Latin American revolution. The two officials did not praise it for being in the U.S. tradition, for it was not. They nevertheless refused to interfere in those revolutions, nor did the two men hope to guide the outbreaks (or, as Adams put it in his 1821 speech, to go abroad "in search of monsters to destroy"). Monroe demanded that Europe follow this example.

Meanwhile, the Latin Americans were to be on their own. When they soon made five direct requests to Washington for U.S. guarantees of their independence, the North Americans refused to act. France sent a fleet to make demands of Haiti, and in 1833 the British seized the Malvinas (Falkland Islands) over Argentina's protests, but the United States did nothing. The Monroe Doctrine's importance for North America was immediate, especially in the Northwest; but for Latin America, its impact was to be felt in the more distant future.

It had been a remarkable eight years in American foreign policy: settlement of explosive Canadian boundary questions, the containment of the world's greatest power, annexing Florida, the first claims to the Pacific coast, and the announcement of the Monroe Doctrine principles. If he had not been overruled by the president, Adams might also have successfully laid claim to Texas, and not only annexed another empire, but averted the Texas question that helped push the United States into civil war. Remarkably, Adams had accomplished all this with brains, not brawn, for the United States military power paled in comparison with the British. Historian William Earl Weeks has noted that "the gap between relative power and relative accomplishment is the true measure of statesmanship. Surely no other statesman in American history accomplished as much as Adams did with so little economic and military power."[28]

GREAT LOSERS: ADAMS THE PRESIDENT

During the 1817–1825 "era of good feelings," Adams acted without having to worry too much about an opposing political party sniping at him. But an absence of parties did not mean an absence of politics. Quite the contrary. Without the controls and understood procedures of a political-party system, politics turned individualistic and vicious. As historian Joel Silbey has argued, the American democratic system worked best when two strong institutional political parties competed against each other in that system, and worked worst when those parties were weak.[29] The Monroe administration proved Silbey's argument. While Adams conducted his brilliant, lone-wolf diplomacy, Monroe accomplished little at home. Nor could the president control the personal ambitions and hatreds that tore his administration apart. Adams was even accused (falsely) of appearing in church barefoot and tieless.[30] (It was true, however, that the secretary of state regularly swam nude in the Potomac River.)

In this political confusion, Adams outmaneuvered three other opponents to win the presidency in 1824. Andrew Jackson obtained the largest number of popular votes, but because no candidate won a majority of electoral ballots the decision was thrown into the House of Representatives, as the Constitution provides. At a crucial moment, Henry Clay threw his support to Adams, who then triumphed. Clay's action was not unnatural: he disliked Jackson personally and agreed with Adams's strong nationalist program for creating roads, canals, and a higher tariff. The new president, however, then made Clay secretary of state. Jacksonians cried that they had been victimized by a "corrupt bargain." No such "bargain" has been documented by historians, but obviously Adams and Clay understood each other. The accusation, in any case, destroyed whatever chance the new president might have had to pass his political program or win re-election in 1828. Clay and Adams were ruthlessly attacked by the brilliant and eccentric John Randolph of Virginia, a long-time power in Congress. When Randolph called the two men a combination of "the puritan with the blackleg," Clay challenged him to a duel. In the famous encounter on the Virginia side of the Potomac in April 1826, Clay's second shot pierced Randolph's coat, while the Virginian fired in the air. (Critics claimed that Randolph took pains to wear an extra-large coat that day.) Randolph so hated Clay that when the Virginian died in 1833 he ordered that he be buried with his face to the West—so he could keep his eyes on Henry Clay.

With this kind of political dirt flying around him, Adams had little chance of realizing his great dream: uniting and developing the empire he had acquired as secretary of state. His presidency is important because it marked the last attempt by a chief executive to tie North and South together through a nationally supervised program of roads, tariffs, canals, and with such scientific projects as a national university, naval academy, and exploring expeditions. Adams saw what most failed to see: that the nation was sharply dividing along the lines of a free-labor, rapidly growing North and West that were commercial, wheat-growing, and increasingly industrial, and a slave South that was becoming locked into a one- or two-crop economy and could not keep up with the North's population gains. As he became president, however, Americans were fanning out across a continent, states were rewriting constitutions to decentralize and democratize their politics, and Jacksonians were accusing Adams of wanting to centralize power because "all Adamses are monarchists." Andrew Jackson rode this democratic wave into the presidency in 1828. Believing in the centralization of Madison, Hamilton, and John Adams, John Quincy Adams was, in this sense, the last important figure of the revolutionary generation. He was also largely isolated. Nor did his dislike of mass democracy and his lack of talent and sensitivity for public politics help him.

While he did uncomfortably live at the Executive Mansion, Adams's major foreign-policy problem arose in 1826, when delegates from newly independent Latin America planned to meet in Panama to discuss cooperation and mutual protection. They invited the United States to participate. At first, Adams was not enthusiastic. He feared the delegates wanted to involve the United States in their revolutions. When he was assured that the Panama congress planned to discuss other topics, the president agreed to send delegates, but only to work for more liberal trade, for an agreement to the noncolonization principle announced in the Monroe Doctrine, and—most interestingly—for the end of an "exclusive" (that is, Roman Catholic) church that he believed held back religious liberty. Secretary of State Clay, long an advocate of North-South cooperation, wanted to embody these principles in what he called "good neighborhood" treaties. The U.S. Congress, however, refused to appropriate money to send the two delegates. Southerners feared that Adams secretly planned to use the conference to oppose the slave trade and work with black revolutionaries in Haiti. Adams finally laid these worries to rest, but it was too late. While the debate roared on, one of the two delegates had died. The other never reached the meeting. The episode revealed not only the deep divisions between North and South America, but also within U.S. politics.[31]

In 1825–1827, Adams unsuccessfully attempted to acquire Texas. He believed that the area could be annexed as a free territory. Within ten years, as Texans became independent and slaveholding, Adams turned violently against any plans for annexation. In 1826, he also renewed the joint-occupation pledge with England in regard to Oregon territory. In doing so, he beat back proposals that would have surrendered U.S. claims to fine harbors in the present state of Washington. The renewal was Adams's only major achievement as president. The nation's greatest secretary of state, he was also one of its least successful presidents.

Defeated overwhelmingly in 1828, Adams despised his conqueror. When Adams's own alma mater gave Jackson an honorary degree in 1833, he refused to attend "to see my darling Harvard disgrace herself by conferring a Doctor's degree upon a barbarian and savage who could scarce spell his own name."[32] Adams at first decided to retire, "as much as a nun taking the veil." But he missed Washington and was determined to fight, alone if necessary, against the Jacksonians. Ralph Waldo Emerson caught him perfectly at this point: "He is no literary old gentleman, but a bruiser, and he loves the melee."[33] Elected by his home district in 1830, Adams spent the last seventeen years of his life in the House of Representatives fighting for the rights of free speech of antislave groups and working tirelessly against expansion of any slave territory. "Old Man Eloquent," as he was called, died on the floor of the House in 1848 as he attacked the U.S. attempt to conquer much of Mexico. He had long since concluded that because Jackson had defeated his national programs of 1825 to 1828, the Union was doomed to split between North and South.

Poet Walt Whitman wrote in 1848 that "John Quincy Adams was a virtuous man—a learned man—and had singularly enlarged diplomatic knowledge; but he was not a man of the People."[34] More than a century later, however, a superb historian of the era, Bradford Perkins, concluded that Adams's "new American generation vindicated the aspirations of their fathers in 1776."[35] No greater compliment could be paid to the statecraft of 1817 to 1828.

Notes

1. Marvin Meyers, *The Jacksonian Persuasion* (Stanford, 1957), pp. 122–127.
2. Laurence M. Hauptmann, "Westward the Course of Empire: Geography Schoolbooks and Manifest Destiny, 1783–1893," *The Historian* 40 (May 1978): 430–431.
3. William H. Goetzmann, *When the Eagle Screamed* (New York, 1966), pp. 95–96.
4. Douglass C. North, *Growth and Welfare in the American Past* (Englewood Cliffs, N.J., 1966), ch. VI.
5. *Memoirs of John Quincy Adams*, ed. Charles Francis Adams, 12 vols. (Philadelphia, 1874–1877), VI, pp. 250–251.
6. Richard Hofstadter, *The Idea of a Party System . . . 1780–1840* (Berkeley, 1969), pp. 192–197.
7. George Dangerfield, *The Era of Good Feelings* (New York, 1952), p. 7.
8. Samuel Flagg Bemis, *John Quincy Adams and the Foundations of American Foreign Policy* (New York, 1949), p. 8.
9. Jack Shepherd, *Cannibals of the Heart: A Personal Biography of Louisa Catherine and John Quincy Adams* (New York, 1981), is especially useful on this relationship.
10. *Memoirs of John Quincy Adams*, ed. Adams, IV, pp. 438–439.
11. John Quincy Adams to John Adams, 1 August 1816, in *The Writings of John Quincy Adams*, ed. Worthington C. Ford, 7 vols. (New York, 1913–1917), VI, p. 61.
12. Henry Adams, *The Degradation of the Democratic Dogma* (New York, 1919), pp. 28–31.
13. Frederick Merk, *The Oregon Question* (Cambridge, Mass., 1967), pp. 122–124; Bradford Perkins, *From Sea to Sea, 1776–1865*, in *The Cambridge History of U.S. Foreign Relations*, ed. Warren Cohen (New York, 1993), ch. III.
14. Quoted in *Writings of Adams*, ed. Ford, VI, p. 519n; Bemis, p. 253.
15. On Onís, 7 August 1821, in *Writings of Adams*, ed. Ford, VII, p. 167.
16. Richard Drinnon, *Facing West: The Metaphysics of Indian-Hating and Empire-Building* (Minneapolis, 1980), pp. 108–111.
17. *Memoirs of John Quincy Adams*, ed. Adams, IV, p. 275.
18. *Ibid.*, IV, pp. 502–503, 524–525, 530, 531; V, pp. 3–12, 68.
19. *Selected Writings of Bolívar, vol. I: 1810–1822*, ed. Harold A. Bierck, Jr. (New York, 1951), p. 179.
20. The text is in *John Quincy Adams and American Continental Empire*, ed. Walter LaFeber (Chicago, 1965), pp. 42–46. Italics in original.

21. *Memoirs of John Quincy Adams,* ed. Adams, VI, pp. 157, 163.
22. *Ibid.,* VI, pp. 324–325.
23. John Quincy Adams to Hugh Nelson, 28 April 1823, in *Writings of Adams,* ed. Ford, VII, pp. 372–373.
24. *Memoirs of John Quincy Adams,* ed. Adams, VI, p. 179.
25. Edward P. Crapol, "John Quincy Adams and the Monroe Doctrine: Some New Evidence," *Pacific Historical Review* 48 (August 1979): 414.
26. Ernest May, *The Making of the Monroe Doctrine* (Cambridge, Mass., 1975), pp. 181–182.
27. *A Compilation of the Messages and Papers of the Presidents, 1789–1897,* ed. James D. Richardson, 10 vols. (Washington, D.C., 1900), II, pp. 219–220.
28. William Earl Weeks, "New Directions in the Study of Early American Foreign Relations," *Diplomatic History* 17 (Winter 1993): 88–89; William Earl Weeks, *John Quincy Adams and American Global Empire* (Lexington, Ky., 1992), especially its discussion of the 1819–1821 treaty talks; Kenneth M. Coleman, "The Political Mythology of the Monroe Doctrine," in *Latin America, the United States and the Inter-American System,* ed. John D. Martz and Lars Schoultz (Boulder, Col., 1980), pp. 98–99. There is a good overview from the French perspective and an interesting thesis about the split between official and public opinion in Réne Rémond, *Les États-Unis devant l'opinion française, 1815–1852,* 2 vols. (Paris, 1962), II, pp. 606–611. For the quite different U.S. policy on the Malvinas in 1982, see p. 706.
29. Joel H. Silbey, *The Partisan Imperative* (New York, 1985 and 1987), especially chs. III and IV.
30. James Sterling Young, *The Washington Community* (New York, 1966), pp. 186–188, 236–238.
31. *Compilation of the Messages and Papers of the Presidents,* ed. Richardson, II, p. 319; an excellent survey is Andrew R. L. Clayton, "The Debate over the Panama Congress and the Origins of the Second American Party System," *The Historian* 47 (February 1985): 219–238; also Bemis, pp. 537–561.
32. Samuel Flagg Bemis, *John Quincy Adams and the Union* (New York, 1956), p. 250.
33. Gore Vidal, *Matters of Fact and of Fiction* (New York, 1979), p. 169.
34. Walt Whitman, *The People and John Quincy Adams* (Berkeley Heights, N.J., 1961), p. 17.
35. Bradford Perkins, *Castlereagh and Adams* (Berkeley, 1964), p. 347.

FOR FURTHER READING

Consult the notes to this chapter and the General Bibliography at the end of this book; most of those references are not repeated here. Most important, begin with *Guide to American Foreign Relations since 1700,* ed. Richard Dean Burns (1983), whose thoroughness in listing pre-1981 materials cannot be matched by any textbook.

In addition to the Weeks, Dangerfield, North, May, and—above all—Bemis and Perkins volumes listed in the notes, the following provide important interpretations and superb contexts for understanding this era of Adams: Ronald E. Seavoy, *The Origins of the American Business Corporation, 1784–1855* (1982), good on the interchange between economics and politics; the essays on the 1815-to-1861 era in William H. Becker and Samuel F. Wells, Jr., *Economics and World Power: An Assessment of American Diplomacy since 1789* (1984); Ralph Ketcham, *Presidents above Party* (1984), which discusses the political framework; and Peter D. Hall, *The Organization of American Culture, 1700–1900* (1982), which stresses how the northeastern elites maintained their power through the new corporation.

Harry Ammon, Monroe's leading biographer, summarizes his views in "James Monroe and the Persistence of Republican Virtue," in *Traditions and Values: American Diplomacy, 1790–1865*, ed. Norman Graebner (1985); and in the same volume Graebner analyzes "John Quincy Adams and the Federalist Tradition." The sad, sometimes comic, and most instructive story is told in Mary Hargreaves, *The Presidency of John Quincy Adams* (1985); while the key Latin American view is examined in David Bushnell, "Simon Bolívar and the United States: A Study in Ambivalence," *Air Force University Review* 37 (July–August 1986); and there is overlapping material on Adams's nemesis in John M. Belohlavek, *"Let the Eagle Soar!": The Foreign Policy of Andrew Jackson* (1985). Especially revealing is Vivien Green Fryd, *Art and Empire: The Politics of Ethnicity in the U.S. Capitol, 1815–1860* (1992).

4

The Amphibious Expansion of a Sixty-Five-Hundred-Thousand-Horsepower Steam Engine (1828–1850)

The Context: Manifest Destiny and Railroads in Russia

During the 1830s, increasing numbers of Americans moved into Texas and Oregon. In the 1840s, these two areas plus one-third of Mexico were annexed to the United States. The nation's territory increased by more than 50 percent to about three million square miles. At the same time, the amphibious Americans, who were moving on sea as well as land, sealed their first formal trade and diplomatic agreements with China. Henry David Thoreau, the philosopher of Walden Pond, observed Americans spreading out over continents and ocean as if "we have the Saint Vitus dance." Half a century later, at the height of British power, Lord Salisbury advised students who wished to understand England's history to use very large maps. The same advice could have been given in the 1830s and 1840s to observers of American history.

These decades mark the zenith of U.S. Manifest Destiny. The term appeared, appropriately, in mid-1845, when a Democratic editor, John

L. O'Sullivan of New York, summarized the feelings of most Americans: any European attempt to prevent the U.S. annexation of Texas was an act against God, for opposition might check "the fulfillment of our manifest destiny to overspread the continent allotted by Providence for the free development of our yearly multiplying millions."[1] Two years later, Secretary of the Treasury Robert J. Walker explained both history and the American future by declaring in a government report that "a higher than any earthly power" had guided American expansion and "still guards and directs our destiny, impels us onward, and has selected our great and happy country as a model and ultimate centre of attraction for all the nations of the world."[2]

But there also existed a darker side to Manifest Destiny. O'Sullivan's newspaper, the *Democratic Review*, warned in 1848 that Americans had no choice: "A State must always be on the increase or the decrease," for this was "the law of movement."[3] Expand or die became the shadowy underside of American thinking, especially as the population continued to double each generation and as millions of immigrants—including those driven out in the late 1840s by Irish famine and German revolutions—flooded into American cities. The threat perhaps appeared most dangerous to the South's slaveholders. They demanded more land to replace worn-out soil in southeastern states, to provide more room for blacks who were outnumbering whites in the older states, and to increase representation in Congress so that the South could breathlessly try to keep up with rampaging northern growth. O'Sullivan himself, although from the North, ended his career by supporting the South's attempts to seize new lands in the Caribbean. He finally declared himself proslavery, claimed that in the Civil War the South fought for "American liberty," and urged American blacks to erect a monument to the first slave trader.[4]

O'Sullivan and the other Manifest Destiny faithful believed that God had given them a special sign of His favor in the 1830s and 1840s. At the moment the United States grew by half, it also began to experience a transportation and communication revolution. That revolution enabled Americans to tie their vast land together with links undreamed of just a generation earlier. If Americans believed in the supernatural aspect of Manifest Destiny, they could also trust in the hard realities—the iron and steel—that made Manifest Destiny possible. Editor Thomas Ritchie noted in 1847 that James Madison had believed that the United States, under the new Constitution, could expand indefinitely, but not even Madison understood how new inventions made expansion possible. The railroad, new ships, the "magnetic telegraph had not entered into the dreams of the most enthusiastic philosophers." In 1844, just five days after a telegraph sent the first message, its inventor, Samuel F. B. Morse, received in Washington the news, via wireless from a partner in Baltimore, that James K. Polk had received the Democrats' presidential nomination. Polk's war with Mexico was the first American conflict covered by war correspondents. They used telegraph and pony express to speed reports published in the new "penny press" that quickly reached tens of millions of Americans.[5]

U.S. engineers even supervised 30,000 Russians building railroads in the tsar's empire. In 1847, an overinspired author prophesied the results when U.S. know-how encountered Europe's downtrodden:

> Who knows but in a few years the now Russian serf may stand a free man at his own cottage door, and as he beholds the locomotive fleeting past, will take off his cap . . . and bless God that the mechanics of Washington's land were permitted to scatter the seeds of social freedom in benighted Russia.[6]

Asa Whitney, who had made his fortune in the China trade, lobbied in the 1840s for a transcontinental American railroad that would attain two historic objectives at once: link together the sections of the United States and enable U.S. producers to ship their products cheaply so that they could capture Asian markets. The railroad, Whitney believed, would "revolutionize the entire commerce of the world; placing us directly in the centre of all." He preached that the American Empire need not go the way of all past empires that were now dust: "They had not the press, nor the compass, nor the steam-engine."[7] Whitney and other believers, led by Democratic senator Stephen A. Douglas from Illinois, soon obtained federal funds to build railways, but southerners—content with their waterways and fearful that the new iron horse would most benefit northern merchants—prevented building the transcontinental railway system until they left the Union in 1861.

The pull of Manifest Destiny and new technology was so strong that, O'Sullivan argued, Americans would never have to kill for conquest: "It will never be the forcible subjugator of other countries."[8] Poet Walt Whitman phrased it best as he caught the new power and confidence of an expanding, industrializing America:

> While the foreign press . . . is pouring out ridicule on this Republic and her chosen ones—Yankeedoodledom is going ahead with the resistless energy of a sixty-five-hundred-thousand-horsepower steam engine! It is

> carrying everything before it South and West, and may one day put the Canadas and Russian America in its fob pocket! Whether it does these things in a conventionally "genteel" style or not, isn't the thing: but that it will tenderly regard human life, property and rights, whatever step it takes, there is no doubt.[9]

John Winthrop's seventeenth-century dream of an American community of virtue was giving way to a fragmented, spread-out society that cared more about wealth than virtue and more for individual freedom than community. During this era, the acute French observer, Alexis de Tocqueville, studied America and coined the word "individualism" for the first time. Tocqueville feared that unless it were controlled, individualism would isolate Americans and lead to the destruction of their society and freedom.[10] The remarkable limited liability company, or the corporation, developed at this time. Many states happily issued charters to individuals, which gave them the right to raise money through public sale of stock to build railways, and telegraph and steamship lines.

Two forces tried to pull Americans back and keep them under some control. The first was a new political party system that grew from the grass roots in the 1820s and 1830s. It cut across state lines to bring Americans together.[11] The Democratic party of Jackson and Polk believed in a passive federal government that largely left the states and individuals to conduct their own affairs. The Democrats thus favored low tariffs, a decentralized Treasury system, and state-built internal improvements. In foreign policy, their party contained such ardent landed expansionists as Polk, Douglas, and Walker. It also included many who favored mercantile expansion, especially if it came at the expense of the British, whom the Democrats—notably the growing number of their Irish members—feared and despised. The Whig party leadership, on the other hand, tended to come from commercial, manufacturing, and wealthier slaveholding classes. These groups wanted government support as they tried to create an orderly, regulated society at home and to find more overseas markets. They worked for higher tariffs, and national banking and internal improvement systems. In foreign policy, Whigs lined up consistently against landed expansion. They were afraid that its inevitable warfare and unpredictability could pull apart American society. But they did favor mercantile expansion. Whigs feared any conflict with the British that might upset their trade routes.

Leading Whigs included Daniel Webster and Henry Clay. Webster embodied Whig foreign-policy principles in the 1840s. The political power of mercantile, industrializing Massachusetts, he also acted as the U.S. agent for the Baring Brothers banking house of London. The Barings financed much of the new U.S. merchant fleet and manufacturing complex. They had even lent the money for the Louisiana Purchase. Always in need of cash, Webster naturally wanted no wars with the British, nor did he and Clay want to lose the cotton markets and Whig votes in the South that might result from such a war. They led in forging political compromises, especially in 1850, that kept the Union together. Moreover, it was Webster who sent the historic U.S. mission to China in 1842–1844, which formally opened that country to Americans, and it was Webster who was responsible for opening Japan to the West in the 1850s. For all their caution, concern for pocketbook commercial issues, and desire for quiet, however, not even Whigs were immune to certain virulent forms of Manifest Destiny that were sweeping through the United States. They, like most Americans then and long after, strongly believed that Manifest Destiny would bring the blessings of American democracy to many other peoples. "Do we deceive ourselves," Webster proclaimed in 1832, "or is it true that at this moment that love of liberty and that understanding of its true principles which are flying over the whole earth, as on the wings of all the winds, are really and truly of American origin?"[12] Nature seemed to be spreading the "principles" of American democracy as nature's winds spread the smell of sweet blossoms.

Nature, however, received considerable help from an increasingly powerful presidency. The Jacksonian era's political system contributed much to the development of the modern presidency, especially as democracy spread and popular votes for the president gained importance over the old, elitist electoral-college system. Elections focused more and more on the presidential vote. A shrewd winner, in turn, could dominate both his party and Congress, especially on foreign-policy questions. Jackson and Polk, both masters of the new politics, became such powerful chief executives that they could ram through their foreign policies despite strong congressional opposition.

The U.S. system thus began to resemble an hourglass: large at the top with a strong presidency, large at the bottom with an expanding population and state powers, but narrow in the middle where congressional and federal powers were located. The question became whether that slim middle could hold the hourglass together, especially as expansionism and Manifest Destiny exerted tremendous pressure on the system.

Removing Native Americans

After the War of 1812, the government's policy toward the Indians changed for the worse. Jefferson had hoped that they could be turned into farmers and assimilated into white society. After 1815, Native Americans were not to be assimilated, but removed—if necessary, by force—to unwanted lands beyond the Mississippi. The warfare of 1811 to 1814 shaped the new policy, but so did the belief of Clay, Jackson, and others that Indians could not be "civilized." As Jackson declared in 1830, "What good man would prefer a country covered with forests and ranged by a few thousand savages to our extensive Republic, studded with cities, towns, and prosperous farms . . . , occupied by more than 12,000,000 happy people, and filled with all the blessings of liberty, civilization, and religion?"[13]

During the 1820s and 1830s, the five great Indian tribes in the South were forced to move westward. The Choctaws went into Oklahoma territory. After brief resistance, the Creeks' men were put in chains by Alabama forces and moved to Oklahoma with neither weapons nor cooking utensils. The Chickasaws moved out peacefully, but the Seminoles hid in the Florida Everglades until the U.S. Army used bloodhounds to track them down. Forty percent of the Seminole population died in that struggle and in the final march west.

Most notable was Cherokee resistance. The Cherokees lived, unluckily, in an area of Georgia where gold was discovered. In 1830, state authorities began evicting the Indians. Jackson fully supported Georgia. The Cherokees, however, took their case to the United States Supreme Court. In the famous *Cherokee Nation* decision of 1831, Chief Justice John Marshall ruled that an Indian tribe was not a "foreign state." But it was "a distinct political society," and tribes were "domestic dependent nations." The next year, the Court ruled that U.S. law and the Constitution, not state law, controlled Indian-white relations. Jackson, however, refused to carry out the decision. The president allegedly declared, "John Marshall has made his decision; now let him enforce it." Georgia, then the U.S. Army, arrested and sent the Indians on a terrifying forced march. One observer estimated that 4,000 of the 18,000 Cherokees forced out after 1835 died on the journey westward.[14]

In the North, the Native Americans were also driven across the Mississippi. After being cheated by a fraudulent treaty, the Sauk and Fox tribes fought back in the short-lived Black Hawk War of 1831–1832.

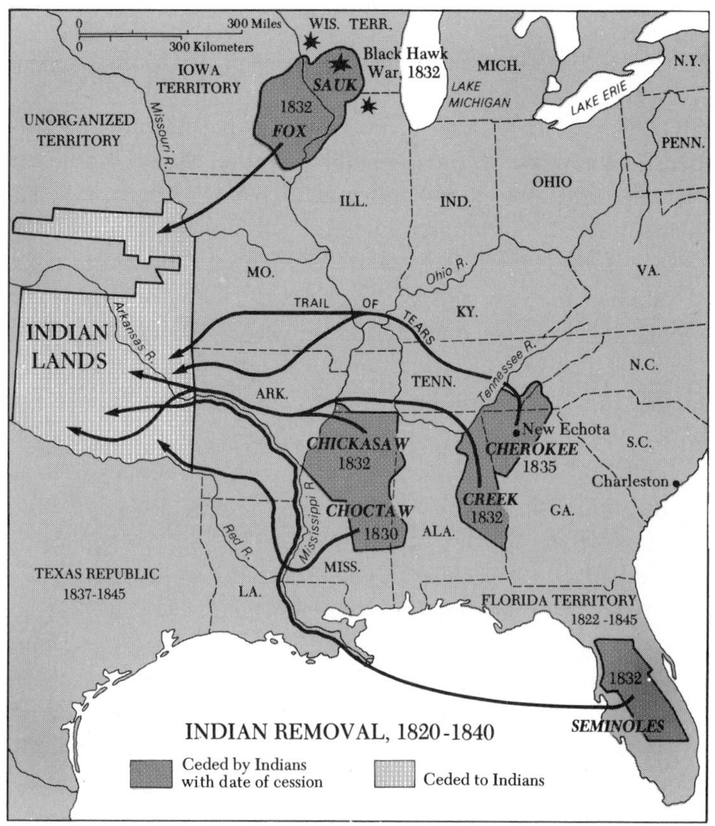

While the U.S. government steadily expanded the national boundaries after 1800, it also used force to remove large numbers of Native Americans from their lands. U.S. foreign policy and policy toward American Indians have been closely related.

That conflict is better remembered because of a young, nervous Illinois militiaman, Abraham Lincoln, who served patrol duty. Otherwise, the tribes moved out peacefully, if unwillingly. The removals confirmed the whites' view that the Indians were inferior, could be brutalized whenever necessary, and were not under the protection of the national government but were at the mercy of local authorities. These views could be transferred to other peoples. As the United States prepared to annex parts of Mexico, O'Sullivan's *Democratic Review* declared, "The Mexican race now see, in the fate of the aborigines of the north, their own inevitable destiny." The *New York Evening Post* neatly combined Manifest Destiny and Indian policy to justify the killing: "Providence has so ordained it. . . . The Mexicans are aboriginal

Indians, and they must share the destiny of their race."[15] The Indian removals and wars of the 1830s provided racial beliefs and battlefield experience that helped prepare Americans for their war of 1846–1848.

The Road to China

American expansion moved on both land and sea. It thus reflected the needs of both agrarians who sought new lands, and producers (both agrarian and industrial) and merchants who required foreign markets. U.S. officials had to take such needs into account. Polk, for example, carefully tried to balance his policies for landed and overseas expansion. Often the two nicely meshed, as in the drive for Oregon and California. But above all, the history of the 1830s and 1840s shows how Americans thought of Asia not as the Far East (which was a British term), but the Far West, the natural extension of their movement across the continent.

The maritime wing of U.S. expansionism rapidly gained momentum in the 1830s. In 1832, growing U.S. trade with the western Pacific led Jackson to send Edmund Roberts to make commercial treaties with Siam, Southeast Asia, and Japan. Roberts succeeded in Siam and Muscat, but failed at Hue—not the last time U.S. diplomacy was to have problems in the area later known as Vietnam. He died before reaching Japan. In 1839, President Martin Van Buren played to mercantile interests by ordering Captain Charles Wilkes to explore the Pacific. Wilkes gave the nation its first claim to Antarctica (which he was the first also to recognize as a separate continent) and the strategic port of Pago Pago in Samoa. As historian Thomas McCormick observes, the Wilkes mission of 1839–1842 helped make the United States "the most knowledgeable power in the world as far as the great Pacific basin was concerned."[16]

Americans also staked out claims to the way station of Hawaii. U.S. traders and missionaries had been settling on the beautiful islands for more than a generation. The settlements created replicas of Protestant Boston society, even to the extent of restricting native and Roman Catholic religious practices. When British and Canadian claims threatened the newcomers, President John Tyler publicly warned in December 1842 that non–United States governments were to keep their hands off the islands. It marked the first time that Hawaii was brought under a Monroe Doctrine–type of policy.

The double column of U.S. traders and missionaries also marched into the much larger arena of China during these years. The United States had no formal treaties with the Chinese but instead depended on, and cooperated with, British power—even to the point of working with English traders to develop the highly profitable opium traffic. Chinese called the Americans "second chop Englishmen."[17] U.S. exports of furs, ginseng, and—of all things—ice chopped from ponds around Boston were exchanged for imports of tea, hides, and gunnysacks. Nevertheless, of the fifty-five foreign firms in the great trading city of Canton in 1836, only nine were American. U.S. businessmen had difficulty understanding the Orient's customs. In one story, an ignorant trader learned to his distress that he was eating not a "quack quack," but a "bow-wow-wow."[18] Even missionaries, who adjusted to strange ways better than most merchants, met major problems. Between 1814, when the first Chinese was baptized in a Protestant ceremony, and 1839, the dozen Protestant missions (of which seven were American) each averaged less than one convert per year.[19]

Missionaries and traders alike began to push for formal U.S. treaties so that they could better compete for their China markets. Then, between 1839 and 1842, the Chinese and British engaged in the Opium War. The conflict resulted from European demands for continued use of Canton as part of the rich, illegal opium trade. When the British won those rights in the 1842 Treaty of Nanking, they also seized Hong Kong, opened four other Chinese ports to the West, and assumed power over China's ability to fix tariff and customs rates. The Americans now realized that they had to win equal trading privileges on their own.

Their new interest in Asia also resulted from internal U.S. pressure. The intense economic depression of 1837–1841 severely struck merchants and New England–southern textile manufacturers. In 1842, President Tyler flatly declared that "the greatest evil which we have to encounter is a surplus of production beyond the home demand, which seeks, and with difficulty finds, a partial market in other regions."[20] The president's Whig administration, led by Secretary of State Daniel Webster, appointed Caleb Cushing as the first U.S. minister to China. Cushing came from an old Massachusetts merchant family. Tyler's quaint personal letter to the emperor of China began: "I hope your health is good. . . . The Chinese are numerous. You have millions and millions of subjects. . . . The Chinese love to trade with our people, and to sell them tea and silk, for which our people pay silver, and sometimes other articles. But if the Chinese and the Americans will trade, there should be rules."

Webster then laid down the rules. These were incorporated in the

1844 Treaty of Wangxia (i.e., Wanghia). The United States received most-favored-nation status in China's trade—that is, it automatically received any trade rights the Chinese gave others (such as the British). Americans also received extraterritorial rights, meaning that all U.S. citizens and their property were to be free of Chinese law and instead regulated and protected by U.S. officials and law. The British and Americans congratulated themselves for forcing extraterritoriality out of the Chinese. In truth, the practice had begun with medieval China's decision to let foreign "barbarians" and their queer ways stay to themselves so that they would not disturb the superior Chinese civilization.

Americans, ignorant of that nation's traditions and convinced of their own unselfish desire to help the Chinese, entered into a "special relationship." That relationship rested for the next century on most-favored-nation and extraterritorial privileges. Later in the nineteenth century, it would become known as the "open door" and would be defined in the 1890s by Secretary of State John Hay as "a fair field and no favor" for all the nations involved in trying to exploit the China market. The open-door policy attempted to protect China from European or Japanese colonization so all of it would be open to U.S. traders. Americans soon prided themselves as being the only anti-imperialists who dealt with the Middle Kingdom. The Chinese quickly sensed this misplaced self-satisfaction. They played off Americans against the other foreign nations in an attempt to keep all of them at bay.

U.S. trade developed well after the Treaty of Wangxia. So did the work of Roman Catholic and Protestant missionaries. They became interpreters for U.S. diplomats and merchants, the cutting edge of American influence that penetrated the nation's interior, and, in all, the eyes and ears through which most Americans saw and heard about China. The emperor continued to fight Christianity. The vast and bloody Taiping Rebellion of 1850–1864, in which perhaps as many as 20 million people died, was aimed at destroying foreign influences as well as the Manchu dynasty. But the missionaries remained. They soon justified the use of force to bring the Chinese to God. One popular book, *Hand of God in American History*, argued that "war is the sledgehammer of Providence" to open China to "the family of nations and the benign influence of Christianity."[21] Thus, when France and Great Britain made war on China in 1857–1858 to obtain new trade rights, Americans refused to join the conflict. In 1858, however, they signed with China the Treaty of Tianjin (i.e., Tientsin) that gave them the spoils won by the Europeans. Nearly all of China was opened to U.S. trade, the emperor finally accepted Western diplomats at his capital of

Beijing (i.e., Peking), and he now had to tolerate openly the work of the missionaries. The Wangxia and Tianjin treaties formed the legal and diplomatic base on which U.S.-China relations rested for the next ninety years.

Texas, Maria Child, and James K. Polk

The Americans' movement into China between 1830 and 1860 coincided with their annexation of the immense Pacific-coast strip that stretched from Oregon territory to San Diego. China, like California and Oregon, formed part of the great westward movement that shaped and shook American society during the mid-nineteenth century. But it was the Texas question that triggered the U.S. seizure of the West Coast during the climactic years 1844 to 1848.

The three hundred American families led by Moses Austin into Texas during 1819–1821 had become 15,000 Americans by 1830. The Mexican province turned into another part of the American frontier as immigrants, lured by the possibility of obtaining 4,400 acres of land for a mere $200, flocked in to find their fortune. In addition to accepting Mexican citizenship, Mexico required the settlers to be Roman Catholic and have no slaves. The Americans ignored the last two rules. In 1830, Mexico City officials realized that Texas was being swamped by the multiplying Americans, some of whom ranked among the most uncontrollable gunslingers on the frontier. Santa Anna, who ruled Mexico, finally abolished all state legislatures, centralized power in Mexico City, and moved an army into Texas to control the settlers. Instead of obeying, the Texans replayed 1775–1776: they demanded full restoration of their rights, set up Committees of Correspondence to coordinate resistance, and finally, in 1836, declared their independence. Texas won a short, bloody war. The new government was helped by thousands of Americans who rushed in for glory, action, and land. Some of the emigrants died when the Texas garrison at the Alamo was wiped out in early 1836, but others helped win the pivotal battle of San Jacinto. Meanwhile, Stephen Austin, Moses' son, borrowed most of his funds from the United States to fight the war.

President Andrew Jackson soon recognized Texas independence. He wanted to annex the country, but he and his successor, Martin Van Buren, knew that the time was not ripe. Annexation could lead to an unpopular U.S. war with Mexico. Moreover, after the 1837 depression struck, Americans concentrated on their economic problems at home.

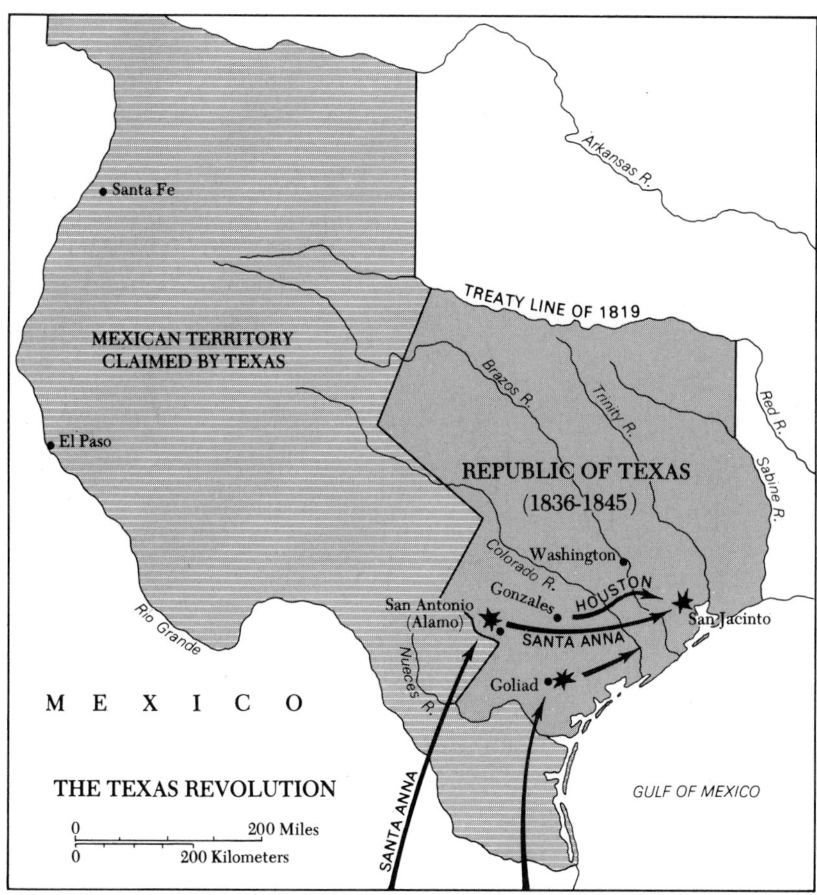

The Texas revolution of 1836 not only ended Mexico's rule of the region, but helped trigger the massive U.S. expansionism of the 1840s. Texas was independent between 1836 and 1845, when, amid bitter debate, it joined the Union as the twenty-eighth state.

Most important, any move to take Texas triggered a vicious debate within the United States. Annexation would mean that the South had a vast new area for slavery. John Quincy Adams led the opposition in Congress, but he enjoyed support from the rising antislave movement.

Anti-Texas voices reverberated throughout the North. None was clearer than Lydia Maria Child's. By the 1830s, this remarkable woman was a widely read novelist and publisher of the first children's magazine in the United States. She concluded that women's rights could be won only in a society that first repudiated black slavery. In 1833, she published *An Appeal in Favor of That Class of Americans Called Afri-*

Lydia Maria Child (1802–1880) was a pioneer in publishing and women's rights, then but made a special mark on U.S. diplomatic history as a vigorous opponent of American—especially slave—expansion.

cans, apparently the first book by a white American to call for immediate emancipation of the slaves. It also laid out the explosive argument that slaveowners controlled the U.S. government. The *Appeal* angered many of Child's readers and nearly bankrupted her. Child did not retreat. When the wife of a Virginia senator argued that southern women helped slave women, especially during childbirth, Child shot back that in the North, "after we have helped the mothers, *we do not sell the babies.*" In the words of historian Edward Crapol, "For more than forty years as writer, petitioner, organizer, pamphleteer, and editor, she fought slavery, sought racial and sexual equality, and decried [what she called] 'the insane rage for annexation in this country.' "[22] Child, Adams, and other antislave advocates stalled the Texas annexation movement until early 1844. Then, President Tyler and his new secretary of state, John Calhoun, pushed for a Senate vote on the issue. Calhoun publicly used proslavery arguments to justify annexation. Needing a two-thirds vote of approval, the treaty went down to an overwhelming 35-to-16 defeat in June 1844.

Within eleven months, however, the United States annexed Texas and was about to declare war on Mexico. The remarkable turnaround was brought about by James K. Polk. One of the most successful presidents in achieving his goals, especially in foreign policy, Polk is usually rated by historians as one of the half-dozen "great" presidents. Born in North Carolina in 1795, Polk soon moved to frontier Tennessee. When he was seventeen years old, Polk was strapped to a table, given a large amount of whiskey, and then suffered through a gallstone operation that broke his health. Unable to farm and fascinated by books, he went to the University of North Carolina, where he won honors in mathematics and classics. He studied law, entered politics, and was elected to the House of Representatives. Polk quickly made his reputation as a Jacksonian who opposed nearly everything John Quincy Adams stood for. The Tennessean attacked "consolidation" of government, ideas favoring national universities or internal improvements, "expensive and unnecessary foreign missions," and "European etiquette."[23] Polk showed little interest in political theory or history. Adams caustically remarked that Polk had "no wit, no literature . . . , no philosophy," but Adams had to grant that Polk possessed immense determination and will. He also was blessed with uncommon political instinct. His ability as an open-air orator won him the title "Napoleon of the stump." In 1839, he became governor of Tennessee. In 1841 and 1843, however, he was defeated in the governor's race. But in 1844, he was elected president of the United States.

That this first "dark horse" candidate in American history won the presidency owed much to Texas and the power of Manifest Destiny. As the Texas issue heated up in early 1844, the two leading presidential candidates, Democrat Martin Van Buren of New York and Whig Henry Clay of Kentucky, publicly declared they did not want to annex Texas. Both preferred the issue to die down so that they could discuss less dangerous, but politically attractive, issues such as tariff and banks. Polk, however, came out for annexation. Already close to Andrew Jackson, who, with his dying breath, now worked to take Texas, Polk won support from powerful politicians in the South and West who wanted a spread-eagle foreign policy. These operators manipulated the Democratic nominating convention's rules and, when it deadlocked,

James K. Polk (1795–1849) of Tennessee (shown in an early daguerrotype by Mathew Brady) is often considered one of the strongest of all presidents. Polk added more land to the nation than any president except Jefferson. But the Tennessean also presided over a disintegrating political party system that had helped hold the Union together, and his foreign policy was a cause of the Civil War.

pushed Polk forward as a compromise candidate. The nominee's platform called for strict construction of the Constitution, but also "the re-occupation of Oregon and the re-annexation of Texas at the earliest practicable period." (The "re-" prefixes alluded to the Democrats' mistaken claim that John Quincy Adams had happily given away U.S. claims to Texas and Oregon in the 1820s.) The 1844 campaign was close and bitterly fought. One Whig claimed that Polk's supporters called Whig candidate Clay such awful names that one could conclude "he was more suitable as a candidate for the penitentiary than President of the United States."[24] The Whigs returned the name-calling in kind, but Polk won by a paper-thin margin.

John Tyler, the outgoing president, decided to leave his mark on history by annexing Texas not through the usual constitutional method of a two-thirds Senate vote (which remained unobtainable), but through the unusual tactic of a joint resolution that required only a majority of the House and Senate. The House passed the measure. The Senate, however, balked when several powerful members feared that claims over the vague Texas-Mexico boundary would lead to war. Polk, preparing for his inauguration, won these key votes by apparently promising to send a mission to negotiate the boundary issue peacefully. The Senate then voted for annexation 27 to 25. Texas became part of the Union on December 29, 1845, as Tyler set a constitutional precedent by acquiring empire through a simple majority of both houses. But Polk then somehow neglected to settle the boundary issue. He instead attempted to use it and other claims to force Mexico to sell California. Although weak and divided, the Mexican government refused to deal on Polk's terms. Meanwhile, the new president alienated pivotal Democrats, including Van Buren, with his appointments and positions on domestic issues. Even Vice-President George Dallas became angry: Polk's "most devoted friends [complained] . . . with bitter grief and shame, of his crooked politics. His defeats, they said, gave them less pain than his intrigues."[25]

WEBSTER, POLK, AND LOOKING JOHN BULL IN THE EYE

After his election as president in 1968, Richard Nixon told his speechwriters to study James Polk's 1845 inaugural address, because the Tennessean, in Nixon's words, promised to be "president of all the people."[26] Regardless of their promises, however, both Polk and Nixon soon came to preside over a nation tragically divided by their foreign

Daniel Webster (1782–1852) was elected to Congress from New Hampshire at age twenty-nine, and in 1827 became a senator from Massachusetts. For the next quarter-century, he, along with Henry Clay, embodied Whig foreign policy that emphasized commercial expansion (especially in Asia); peace with Great Britain; and the 1850 Compromise that, temporarily saved the Union. Historian Kenneth Shewmaker concludes that the Webster-Ashburton Treaty of 1842 not only "possibly averted a third Anglo-American war, it laid the basis for a rapprochement with England that has endured to the present." (Daniel Webster: The Complete Man *[Hanover, N.H., 1990], p. xxiii.)*

policies. In Polk's case, that division began with Texas and nearly exploded into war with Great Britain over Oregon.

Polk's (and the Democratic party's) sometime recklessness in twisting the British Lion's tail can be better understood by comparing his policy with the Whig party's approach fashioned by Daniel Webster just a few years before in the early 1840s. A host of U.S.-British confrontations were erupting, but Webster—who, as a good Whig wanted peaceful commercial expansion, no clashes with the world's great economic power (Great Britain), and no jarring political debates that would threaten the Union—took a distinctly different approach to these confrontations than did Polk.

The crises began in 1837 when some Canadians rebelled against British rule. Ever willing to help their neighbors in such efforts, a few Americans used the vessel *Caroline* to send supplies to the small band of revolutionaries. Pro-British Canadians attacked the *Caroline* in U.S. waters, killed a U.S. citizen, and spectacularly sunk the boat in flames just above Niagara Falls. Outraged Americans south of the border prepared for war, in part by exhibiting in Buffalo, New York, the body of their slain countryman (his "pale forehead mangled by the pistol ball, and his locks matted with his blood!" according to one hard-breathing New York newspaper). President Martin Van Buren cooled passions by sending General Winfield Scott, who warned that any attack on Canada would have to be "over my body."

The issue festered for two years until 1840, when a Canadian, Alexander McLeod, made the serious mistake of drinking too much in a

Buffalo tavern and then bragging that he had done the killing in the *Caroline* raid. He was immediately jailed on charges of arson and murder. The British demanded McLeod's release on the grounds that he had not been near the *Caroline* and, anyway, the attack had been ordered by the government in Canada and was not the act of a single man. As New Yorkers (and other anti-British voices) angrily demanded McLeod's execution, Webster became secretary of state in early 1841. Publicly, Webster took a hard line. Privately, he worked with New York to free the prisoner before another clash broke out. The jury finally freed McLeod for the good reason that he had proven he had been miles away from the *Caroline* on the night of the attack. Webster and his good friend, Lord Ashburton, the British minister to the United States, then tied up loose ends. Ashburton essentially apologized for the *Caroline* attack, and Webster apologized for McLeod's long detention. The secretary of state also had Congress pass a law in 1842 that henceforth brought under federal (not state) jurisdiction any foreigners charged with criminal acts who were acting under orders of their government.

Having solved the international problems caused by drunkards in Buffalo, Webster and Ashburton then had to contend with a more serious crisis: slavery. In 1839, slaves aboard the Spanish slave ship, the *Amistad*, mutinied and tried to force their white captives to take them back to Africa. Instead, the whites steered the ship north until, finally, a U.S. ship captured the *Amistad* off Long Island. Abolitionists instantly demanded freedom for the Africans. In 1841 the Supreme Court indeed granted their freedom on the grounds that the *Amistad* had broken treaties between Great Britain and Spain that prohibited the slave trade. The Spanish, in turn, demanded indemnity in cash. Webster flatly refused, and the Africans returned to their home in 1842.

The slave-trade question refused to go away. In late 1841, slaves took over a U.S. ship, the *Creole*, sailing from Virginia to New Orleans, and piloted it to the British possession of Nassau. There officials freed the slaves on the grounds that the king had ended slavery in all his possessions a decade earlier. Webster bitterly opposed slavery, but as secretary of state he had to listen to southern slaveholders who warned that the *Creole* mutiny could not be allowed to stand without either punishment or indemnity (or, preferably, both). Again Webster and Ashburton worked out a solution. The British did not return the Africans, but they did promise no future interference with U.S. vessels driven into British ports by "accident or by violence." In 1853, a claims commission awarded the United States $110,000 for the property in humans lost in the *Creole* affair.

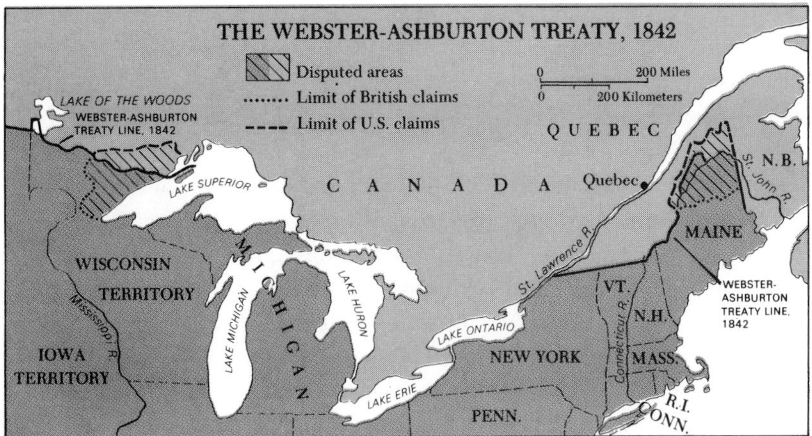

The Webster-Ashburton Treaty of 1842 settled the disputed boundaries of Maine (although not to the satisfaction of everyone in Maine) and gave the United States land between Lake Superior and Lake of the Woods, on which were later found the rich Mesabi iron deposits—a base for the nation's iron and steel industries several generations later.

Webster and Ashburton had narrowly avoided two potential catastrophes in the *Caroline* and *Creole* affairs. Perhaps their success was not too surprising since Ashburton had married an American woman and was head of the great banking institution, the House of Baring (his family name had been Alexander Baring), which poured money into U.S. investments—and which over the years had paid handsomely for legal advice from Daniel Webster. The two men understood each other perfectly. But that understanding was strained to a near-breaking point in the most dangerous U.S.-British problem of the early 1840s: an argument over the boundary between Maine and Canada. That boundary had been fuzzy ever since the 1783 peace treaty (see pp. 26–27) failed to make clear which country owned some 12,000 square miles of highly strategic and rich (especially because of lumber) territory. Webster secretly held two old maps that seemed to put most of the land inside Canada. He kept these from his good friend, Ashburton, while using secret funds controlled by President John Tyler to send an agent to Maine and explain to the local citizens why a compromise was necessary with the British. That compromise was worked out between Webster and Ashburton in July 1842. The sixty-seven-year-old British aristocrat was ready to deal—in part to escape the "oven," as he accurately called summertime Washington, D.C.

The United States received about 7,000 of the disputed 12,000 square miles, and also obtained territory in New York, Vermont, and in the Lake Superior region (an area soon discovered to have rich iron-ore deposits). Webster then told Ashburton of the old maps upholding much of the British claim. The minister was not unhappy; he valued good relations with the United States over the acreage (and Canadians) in question. But his British critics unleashed a blistering attack on Ashburton's diplomacy—only, in a melodramatic turn in a series of U.S.-British melodramas—to have *another* map suddenly turn up in London that upheld the most extreme U.S. claim to the territory. Thus, Ashburton's high reputation as a diplomat was preserved. So which of these various maps was correct? Which nation deserved some of the richest lumber and mineral resources in the Western Hemisphere? The answer, as historian Howard Jones suggests, is that "no map was both authentic and valid" because they either had not been used at Paris in 1783 or boundary questions had been delayed, to be decided later. But the Webster-Ashburton Treaty was both a tribute to the skill of the two negotiators and a signal that differences between Americans and the British no longer had to be resolved with war.[27]

Unfortunately, that historic lesson was almost lost on President Polk in 1845–1846. Granted, the stakes in his struggle with the British were enormous. The Oregon contest was fought over an empire that contained nearly half a million square miles—or an area larger than France, Germany, and Hungary combined. U.S. merchants dominated the region's commerce. Word had spread rapidly after one shipowner had traded several dollars of trinkets to Indians for $20,000 worth of otter pelts. The Native Americans soon called all white men "Bostons" because every white person seemed to come from the Massachusetts port.[28] Few permanent white settlers lived in Oregon by 1830, but that changed rapidly after missionaries came to believe that the Indians wanted to learn about Christianity. With Samuel Parker and the intrepid Marcus and Narcissa Whitman in the foreground, during 1835–1836 the missionaries followed a pathway along the Oregon Trail out of Independence, Missouri. They moved their wagon trains through plains and desert, across the Rockies, and then down into the lush Willamette Valley. The economic troubles of 1837–1841 also pushed out-of-luck farmers along the Oregon Trail. In 1845, some 3,000 Americans arrived in Oregon to double the white population. The new technologies, moreover, were now cutting distances. If you had represented Oregon in the U.S. Congress before the mid-1840s, you would have had to spend about twenty-five weeks going to Washington and another twenty-five weeks returning home, leaving about two weeks to spend in the capital. After the mid-1840s, the railroad, telegraph, and steamship rapidly reduced travel time.

At first, Polk handled the growing problem with the British over Oregon carefully and wisely. In mid-1845 he offered the king's minister to Washington, Richard Pakenham, a deal that divided the Oregon territory along the forty-ninth parallel. The proposal placed both banks of the Columbia River in U.S. territory, even though no American settlements existed north of the great waterway. Faced with a grave political crisis in London at that moment, the British government would probably have accepted Polk's offer just to resolve the distant Oregon question. But Pakenham foolishly rejected the deal without consulting London. Polk, angry and believing that the British had now put themselves at a disadvantage, then demanded all the land to the northernmost U.S. claim, 54°40′. The British flatly rejected the demand. They were not about to surrender much of their northwestern territory and virtually all of the region's best harbors.

Polk received vibrant support from Democrats in the Midwest, where land hunger and faith in God-directed expansionism was strongest. The cry of "Fifty-four forty or fight" soon resounded, encouraged by John L. O'Sullivan, who at this point coined the term "manifest destiny." Northern and many southern Whigs, however, wanted no war with their best customers in England. The U.S. Army, which numbered only 6,000 in 1830 (and one-quarter of those deserted within the year), had grown to 11,000 by the early 1840s, but it was both highly undependable and too small to fight the British Empire in such a faraway place. With Americans divided and his military unprepared, Polk nevertheless whipped up feelings over Oregon. In his annual message of December 1845, he resurrected the Monroe Doctrine (which had slept peacefully and largely forgotten since 1823). He used it to warn Great Britain that "no future European colony or dominion shall with our consent be planted or established on any part of the North American continent."

The president then urged Congress to terminate the 1827 joint-occupation agreement that had regulated Oregon affairs. When a timid congressman expressed the fear that this meant war, Polk retorted "that the only way to treat John Bull was to look him straight in the eye." Behind those overly defiant words was Polk's belief that the British needed U.S. trade—notably cotton (especially since the British Parliament was just then committing itself to a radically new free-trade policy). "We hold England by a cotton string," a Virginia Democrat bragged.[29]

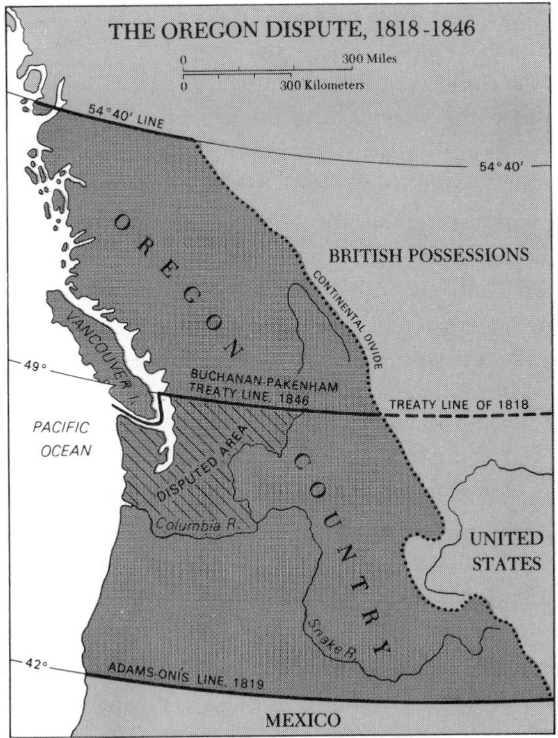

The disputed northwest region and the 1819 and 1846 settlements that preserved peace with Great Britain, and also preserved the U.S. hold on invaluable land and ports.

The "string" proved to be more fragile than John Bull's eye. The British told Polk that they would not retreat beyond the forty-ninth parallel. They next mobilized thirty warships for possible action. Polk, a devout Presbyterian who seldom conducted business on the Sabbath, quickly called a cabinet meeting on Sunday to discuss the crises. Already facing a war with Mexico, he decided to send the Oregon issue to the Senate for resolution. This decision shifted responsibility, and the president no doubt assumed that the Senate, with Webster (now returned to represent Massachusetts) and Calhoun in the lead, would accept the forty-ninth-parallel compromise. Webster gloated that the Oregon treaty reversed the Constitution's procedure: "Here is a treaty negotiated by the Senate, and only agreed to by the President." Polk had nevertheless turned possible war and his own humiliation into a victory. The United States obtained the Oregon territory, including both banks of the Columbia River. The agreement came none too soon, for the president had meanwhile maneuvered the country into war with Mexico.

The "Fire-Brand in the Body": The Mexican War and Slavery

In his inaugural address of 1845, Polk stressed that U.S. expansionism meant extending "the dominions of peace. . . . The world has nothing to fear from military ambition in our Government. . . . Our Government can not be otherwise than pacific." Within fifteen months, Polk took the country into a war for conquest. The reason was his determination to obtain California.

Americans had sailed along California's coast for generations. As early as 1829, they controlled its cattle-hide and provision exchanges as surely as they monopolized Russian America's trade to the north. Richard Henry Dana's famous account, *Two Years before the Mast,* popularized the romance of the California coast. By 1845, about a thousand Americans, many pushed out by the 1837 panic, had trekked across the continent to settle the region. There was, however, no popular cry to annex California in 1845. The settlers were outnumbered by at least 7,000 Spanish and Mexican natives. Most Americans knew or cared little about the area. The issue of California never arose in the 1844 presidential campaign. Only Polk seemed to care, but he cared a great deal.

An astute politician, the Tennessean wanted California not only for its land, but especially for its fine ports. Owning the harbors of San Francisco and San Diego could magnificently enhance the mushrooming U.S. trade in the Pacific and—as Polk fully appreciated—greatly please American merchants. The president, moreover, suspected that the British were using their financial control over Mexico's debt to force the Mexicans to sell, or at least to mortgage, their province of California to London financiers. It was for that reason, as he privately told a friend, that "in reasserting Mr. Monroe's doctrine [in the 1845 message] I had California and the fine bay of San Francisco as much in view as Oregon."[30]

In late 1845, Polk sent John Slidell (a U.S. congressman and influential lawyer from New Orleans) to make Mexico a series of offers, including one of $25 million and the U.S. assumption of its claims against the Mexicans in return for much of California, New Mexico

CHRONOLOGY, 1844–1848

June 1844	Secretary of State John Calhoun's treaty for annexing Texas overwhelmingly defeated 35–16 in Senate.
November 1844	James K. Polk wins presidential race over Henry Clay.
February 1845	Polk secretly makes deal with Senate leaders for Texas.
March 1, 1845	President John Tyler signs joint resolution to annex Texas.
March 4, 1845	Polk inaugurated.
July 1845	Polk proposes division of Oregon at 49°; British minister rejects proposal without submitting it to his superiors in London.
October 1845	Polk sends Thomas O. Larkin to stir up demands in California for annexation.
November 1845–March 1846	Polk sends John Slidell to Mexico to obtain California and New Mexico. Slidell mission fails.
December 1845	Polk revives Monroe Doctrine to demand the "whole" of Oregon.
January 1846	Polk sends General Zachary Taylor's troops into disputed territory of Rio Grande.
February 1846	Rise of "Manifest Destiny" and "Fifty-Four-Forty-or-Fight" cries in Congress over Oregon issue.
May 8, 1846	Polk learns of Slidell mission's failure; prepares for war.
May 9, 1846	Polk learns that Mexican forces attacked Taylor's troops in disputed territory.
May 11, 1846	Polk sends war message to Congress.
June 1846	Treaty with Great Britain to settle Oregon passes Senate.
July 1846	Walker tariff, lowering rates significantly, passes Congress.
August 8, 1846	David Wilmot proposes the Wilmot Proviso in House.
August 18, 1846	U.S. Army occupies Sante Fe.
February 1847	After bitter debate, House passes Wilmot Proviso; Senate kills it.
September 1847	General Winfield Scott's forces capture Mexico City.
January 1848	Discovery of gold sets off California gold rush.
February 1848	Nicholas Trist signs Treaty of Guadalupe Hidalgo to end war.
November 1848	Zachary Taylor wins presidency over two candidates of divided Democratic party.

territory, and the Rio Grande as the Texas-Mexico boundary. To the Mexico City government, this was but one more in a continual stream of political crises. It refused to deal with Slidell, nor could it have negotiated Polk's terms without falling from power. A change in early 1846 brought an even more ardent anti-U.S. regime into office. Polk turned to other alternatives. He had earlier instructed the U.S. consul in California, Thomas O. Larkin, to watch for both British activities and any opportunity to start a revolt against Mexican rule. Larkin could find no opportunity to play the role of Thomas Jefferson in California. But in June 1846, American settlers in the Sacramento area took advantage of the looming U.S.-Mexican war to declare their own independent "Bear Flag" state. The Republic of California survived less than a month, for, by July 1846, Polk was embarked on his main policy: conquest of all of California by force.

The president's policy was both simple and devious. He slowly squeezed Mexico militarily until it struck back. He then misrepresented the evidence for the attack to obtain Congress's declaration of war. In July 1845, ten months before war began, Polk instructed the U.S. military commander in Texas, Zachary Taylor, to move across the Nueces River into territory (between the Nueces and the Rio Grande) that was hotly disputed between Texas and Mexico. In January 1846, the president told Taylor to encamp on the Rio Grande itself. In April, the Mexican army demanded that Taylor move back. He responded by blockading the Mexicans and threatening them with starvation. On April 24, they tried to break the blockade, and blood was spilled. Back in Washington, Polk was becoming frustrated by Mexico's refusal to deal with Slidell. On May 9, he and his cabinet decided to settle the claims against Mexico and block British influence by declaring war. Later that day, Polk received word of the attack on Taylor's forces.

The president immediately sent a war message to Congress that was as historically inaccurate as it was politically potent. "The cup of forbearance had been exhausted" even before the news of the fighting arrived in Washington, Polk declared. "But now . . . Mexico . . . has invaded our territory and shed American blood upon the American soil." Doubting Whigs, even some Democrats, demanded evidence. The key documents, Polk's followers responded, were at the printer's and not available. Besides, they added, Congress should trust the president. The House of Representatives voted for war 174 to 14 (with John Quincy Adams in the small minority, as usual). In the Senate, John Calhoun—who now had acquired Texas for the South and wanted no war for Mexican territory that probably could not support slavery—and

E. W. Clay's 1846 cartoon is a classic example of good American graphic art as well as of rampant American Manifest Destiny and anti-British feelings in 1846. The "Union," or an early "Uncle Sam" figure, is cutting up Mexico for trying to steal his "boot" of Texas. Note the early "John Bull" figure of the British Empire fishing for all of Oregon while Uncle Sam's back is turned.

a few others tried to slow down the rush to battle. They failed. The war declaration passed 40 to 2, with Calhoun abstaining.[31]

Polk finally had his war, but he also faced a terrible dilemma. He had called the war merely a defensive response to a Mexican attack, but in reality he wanted a war for conquest. Such a war could require high and politically unpopular expenses, as well as a large army that would have to be paid for by an already suspicious Congress. He discovered, moreover, that his two top military commanders, Generals Winfield Scott and Zachary Taylor, were both Whigs. If they covered themselves with glory, they could become leading presidential nominees. Polk had already declared that he would not be a candidate in the 1848 race, but he coldly disliked Whigs (whom he often condemned as "Federalists") and especially feared Scott and Taylor.

The two generals made real the president's nightmare. Attacking across the Rio Grande, Taylor won a series of victories at Monterey and Buena Vista, although at Buena Vista, Taylor's 5,000 troops had been surprised by a 20,000-man Mexican force. At Monterey, the

Americans won despite the absence of one of their top officers, who had taken a strong laxative the night before. (Nevertheless, Congress later gave the officer a jeweled sword for his "gallantry at Monterey.")[32] Meanwhile, Scott landed at Vera Cruz in a brilliant amphibious operation, for which he had designed the first landing crafts in U.S. military history. He then began a march toward Mexico City that no less an authority than the Duke of Wellington (conqueror of Napoleon) said could not be done. In a careful campaign that kept his casualties low, Scott reached Mexico City in late summer 1847 and prepared to wait for the government's surrender. He had even avoided costly battles with the Mexican army in the hope that patience would bring about a political settlement.

Polk had neither the time nor the temperament for such a campaign. As soon as war was declared, he asked Congress for $2 million to purchase peace (and California) from Mexico. His request set off an

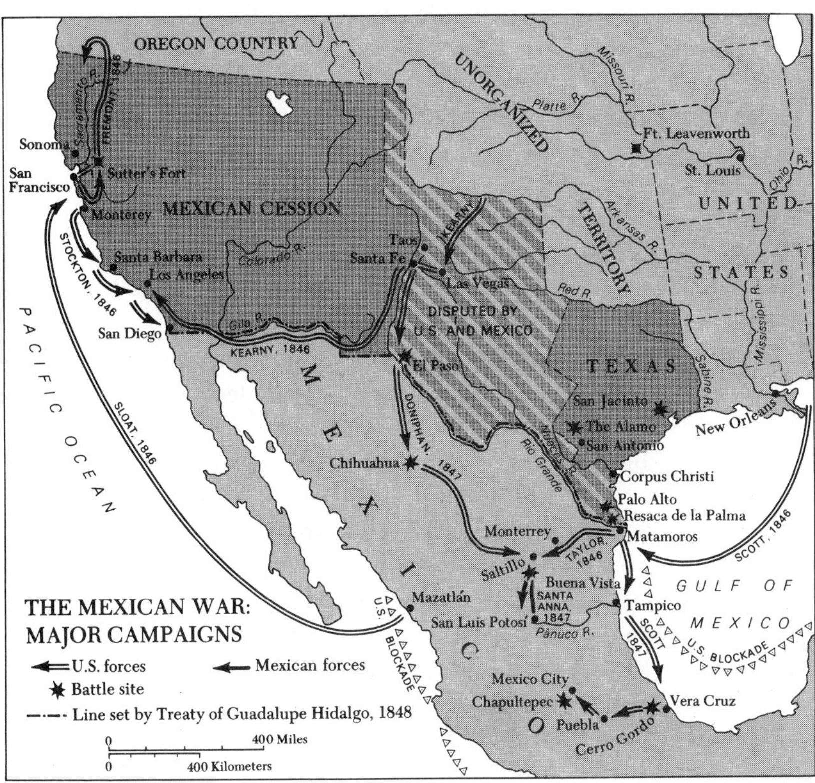

The U.S. war with Mexico (1846–1848) increased American territory by nearly 50 percent, gained valuable California ports, and helped lead to the Civil War.

explosion that reverberated for the next twenty years. When he asked Congress to legislate the funds, Democrats—who had become angered by Polk's political appointments and proslavery foreign policy in Texas—attached an amendment to the legislation that became known as the Wilmot Proviso. It was named after a Pennsylvania Democrat, David Wilmot, who belonged to Van Buren's Free Soil wing of the party. The proviso required that the money not be used to purchase any territory that would allow slavery. Democrats and Whigs from the South immediately condemned the measure. In the House vote, Polk's Democratic party splintered, but the proviso passed. Fifty-two northern free-state Democrats supported, and all fifty southern Democrats opposed, the measure. The Senate, where free- and slave-state representation was in balance, prevented the Wilmot Proviso from becoming law. Nevertheless, everyone involved understood that a political monster had appeared, one that could not be easily killed.

Polk could not understand what he had done. He denied that the great domestic issue had anything to do with foreign policy: slavery "was purely a domestic question" and "not a foreign question." In reality, of course, slavery had everything to do with foreign policy. Expansion, the central theme of the American experience since 1607, now raised the possibility of one side—either slave or nonslave—controlling vast new territories and, thus, soon controlling the government itself. Polk did see that "the slavery question . . . is a fire-brand in the body,"[33] but he also believed that because slavery could not exist on the poor soils of northern Mexico, Congress was raising the issue simply to embarrass him. The president proposed to settle the rising argument by extending the 1820 Missouri Compromise line of 36°30′ to the Pacific. But that compromise was no longer adequate. It could leave the vast Mexican territories south of the line open to slavery. Foreign policy and domestic concerns were so intertwined that each now threatened to strangle the other.

Congress quarreled and Democrats split while Whig generals triumphed. Those were not the results for which Polk had bargained. Despite the battlefield victories, however, Mexico refused to surrender. By the summer of 1847, even John L. O'Sullivan had doubts about Manifest Destiny: "I am afraid it was not God that got us into the war, but that He may get us out of it is the constant prayer of yours very truly."[34] The president finally decided to send Nicholas Trist to discuss peace with the Mexicans. A State Department clerk, Trist had mostly made his political fortune by marrying Thomas Jefferson's favorite granddaughter. He believed ardently in Manifest Destiny but now feared that the war threatened to destroy the Union. Trist wanted a quick peace. His early talks with Mexico, however, collapsed. Polk began to wonder whether Trist wanted peace so badly that he might even be willing to give up claims to much of California to achieve it. Almost as bad, the president learned that Trist and Scott had become fast friends. Polk told the diplomat to return immediately.

Mexico's refusal to surrender then produced another crisis for the president. An "All-Mexico" movement appeared. It demanded that U.S. claims and loss of life could only be satisfied by seizing the entire country. The movement had its most feverish supporters among northern Democrats, both among the sensationalistic press in cities such as New York and the agrarian–Manifest Destiny expansionists of the Midwest. Polk fueled the All-Mexico drive by leaving open the possibility of more war and more conquest if Mexico did not immediately give him what he wanted. As the All-Mexico mania intensified, however, Trist killed it in a single stroke. He ignored Polk's orders to return after he heard that Mexico might be prepared to discuss peace terms. Scott's plan to wait out his opponents had finally worked. Trist obtained all that Polk had originally demanded: California, New Mexico, and the Rio Grande boundary.

Infuriated that Trist had disobeyed his order to return, Polk nevertheless had little choice but to accept the peace treaty of Guadalupe Hidalgo. It was either accepting what he had initially wanted or facing a profound political crisis generated by the All-Mexico and Wilmot Proviso zealots. Polk chose peace. After all, as he told Congress on July 6, 1848, California and the New Mexico territory "constitute of themselves a country large enough for a great empire."

Two Near-Misses and a Near-Settlement

Polk had apparently learned little from the experience. His passion for expansion and his inability to understand the links between domestic and foreign policy forced him to face two more potential crises.

In April 1848, Yucatán—a province of Mexico—asked for U.S. aid against an Indian revolt. Yucatán also asked Spain and Great Britain for aid. Polk immediately requested permission from Congress to intervene. Waving once again the Monroe Doctrine, he warned that the United States would occupy Yucatán before allowing it to come under European influence. Americans were tired of hearing about Mexico, none more so than John Calhoun. The South Carolina sena-

John C. Calhoun (1782–1850) of South Carolina defended slavery and slave expansionism almost literally until his dying breath. But Calhoun disliked the War with Mexico and bitterly fought Polk's attempt to use the Monroe Doctrine as a tool to obtain more territory.

tor unleashed an attack on the request that not only finally killed the plan, but raised fundamental questions for Americans in the future.

Calhoun, who had been in Monroe's cabinet in 1823, denied that the original doctrine had anything to do with occupying such places as Mexico. It only said that North America would keep its hands off Latin American problems and expected Europeans to do the same. The South Carolinian observed that if the United States occupied Yucatán, a most dangerous precedent would be established: other Latin American countries (such as Yucatán) will have obtained the power "to make us a party to all their wars" on their terms and according to their own, not United States', interests. "We shall be forever involved in wars" to save Latin Americans from themselves, Calhoun warned. It was one of the most powerful attacks ever made on the Monroe Doctrine. Fortunately for both Polk and Calhoun, Yucatán resolved its problem, and Polk withdrew the request.[35]

Even though the debate had been an embarrassment, Polk next set his sights on Cuba. In May 1848, John L. O'Sullivan and Democratic senator Stephen A. Douglas from Illinois privately urged Polk to buy Cuba from Spain. Americans had long coveted the island. In 1848, moreover, France had freed its West Indian slaves. England had freed its bondsmen in 1833. Cuba now remained as the major slave society in the Caribbean. American slaveholders believed that the island had to be saved from the building pressure for emancipation. They were joined by northern merchants who profited from Cuban routes and even from the secret, but highly lucrative, trade in black men and women—a trade that had been outlawed forty years before. Cuba exemplified slavery at its worst. About 324,000 slaves and 425,000 whites lived on the island, bound together in a decaying and brutal system.

Polk nevertheless pushed for annexation. He believed that it would ease the fears of southerners who felt that they were becoming a minority section. The island, moreover, "would speedily be Americanized [with whites] as Louisiana had been," as Secretary of State James Buchanan phrased it. Perhaps nothing could have more aroused and divided American society in 1848 than a debate over Cuban annexation. Fortunately, Polk's plan never reached that point. Despite U.S. pressure, Spain refused to sell. Buchanan had used the occasion, however, to warn Spain that Cuba must never pass into the hands of any other power.

Polk's proposals on Yucatán and Cuba occurred amid a wild U.S. political scene. In mid-1848, the Democrats split. The regular party nominated Lewis Cass of Michigan, a zealot for Manifest Destiny who had fought to take Texas and opposed the Wilmot Proviso. Antislave Democrats quit the convention and nominated Martin Van Buren of New York on the Free Soil ticket. The Whigs countered with Zachary Taylor. The Mexican War hero was such a strong believer in traditional values that he acknowledged his nomination late because the notification letter arrived with postage due and he refused to pay it. After Taylor won and assumed the presidency, he moved to settle the central question of how to govern the vast territory conquered by Polk.

In one of the great debates in U.S. history, the Compromise of 1850 was hammered out in the Senate. A dying Calhoun warned that "the cords which bind these states together" were snapping under "the agitation of the slavery question." He intimated the need for constitutional amendments to protect the rights of slaveholders in the new territories. But the aged Henry Clay and Daniel Webster carried the day for the more moderate forces. They argued that local conditions and climate should settle the issue. The final compromise, therefore, brought in California as a free state (as its inhabitants desired). It allowed citizens in New Mexico and Utah territories to work out their own policy on the slave question. This approach became known as popular sovereignty. The slave trade (but not slavery) was finally abolished in the District of Columbia, where humans had been traded for cash and crops in the shadows of U.S. government buildings for half a century. In return, the federal government promised, in a Fugitive Slave Law, to help southerners capture and return runaway slaves. This "businessman's peace," as the compromise was called, postponed the war over the Union for ten years.

Manifest Destiny in Central America

The Senate also passed another historic measure in 1850: the Clayton-Bulwer Treaty gave Americans their first formal right to realize a dream of centuries—an isthmian canal in Central America to link the Atlantic and the Pacific. The treaty was an appropriate act with which to climax the U.S. trade and territorial conquest of the 1840s.

Until this time, Great Britain dominated Central American affairs. Growing U.S. interest in Asian trade, the annexation of Oregon and California, then the dramatic discovery of gold in California during 1848 transformed the Central American power balance. Adventurers and entrepreneurs from the United States profited from turning the region into a passageway for Americans who traveled from the East to the West Coast or to the far Pacific. Newly arrived Americans discovered that the British controlled several strategic areas on the Atlantic-coast side of a possible canal (the Mosquito Coast in Nicaragua, and Belize, bordered by Guatemala) and had been eying the Panamanian area of New Granada. U.S. diplomats neatly played on the fears of the Latin Americans to checkmate the British. The U.S. minister to New Granada, Benjamin Bidlack, signed a treaty in 1846 that gave the United States transit rights across Panama. In return, the United States guaranteed transit rights in the area for other parties. The Senate, realizing that this deal amounted to an entangling alliance, delayed ratification until 1848. The Bidlack pact enabled Americans to build the first transcontinental railway (of 48 miles) in Panama during the 1850s and provided the excuse, in 1903, for Theodore Roosevelt's seizure of Panama to build the present canal. Nicaragua and Honduras, also fearful of British imperialism, next signed treaties giving the United States transit rights. The Americans and British were on a collision course.

To avoid possible war, British minister Sir Henry Bulwer and Secretary of State John Clayton worked out a pact providing that (1) neither nation would build an isthmian canal in Central America without the consent or cooperation of the other, (2) neither would fortify or found new colonies in the area, and (3) if a canal were built, both powers would guarantee its neutrality. It was a handsome victory for Zachary Taylor's administration. The British had recognized the United

States as an equal in Central America. Whigs were delighted with both the isthmian rights and the dodging of war with Great Britain. Democrats, led by Stephen A. Douglas, not surprisingly condemned the treaty for compromising with the hated John Bull.

The Legacies of Manifest Destiny and James K. Polk

The importance of 1840s expansionism in American history goes far beyond the new influence in Central America or even the conquest of the million-square-mile empire in the West. Ralph Waldo Emerson compared the Mexican War to a dose of arsenic for the Union. The military hero of the Civil War, General Ulysses S. Grant, recalled in his memoirs that he had "bitterly opposed" invading Mexico and wanted to obtain the southwest territory through peaceful means. "The Southern rebellion [the Civil War] was largely the outgrowth of the Mexican War," Grant believed.[36] More than a century later, historian Thomas Hietala would look back over Polk's systematic expansionism and conclude that it "was not manifest destiny. It was manifest design."[37]

Polk also left another historic legacy. The way in which he led the United States into the Mexican War set precedents for later powerful chief executives—indeed, provided an early preview of the so-called "imperial presidency" of the twentieth century. Abraham Lincoln, then a young Illinois Whig strongly opposed to Polk's policies toward Mexico, attacked these new presidential powers in a now-famous letter written to a friend in 1848:

> Allow the President to invade a neighboring nation, whenever *he* shall deem it necessary to repel an invasion, and you allow him to do so, *whenever he may choose to say* he deems it necessary for such purpose—and you allow him to make war at pleasure. Study to see if you can fix *any limit* to his power in this respect, after you have given him so much as you propose. . . . You may say to him, "I see no probability of the British invading us" but he will say to you, "be silent; I see it, if you don't."
>
> The provision of the Constitution giving the war-making power to Congress, was dictated, as I understand it, by the following reasons. Kings had always been involving and impoverishing their people in wars, pretending generally, if not always, that the good of the people was the object. This, our Convention [of 1787] understood to be the most oppressive of all Kingly oppressions; and they resolved to so frame the Constitution that *no one* man should hold the power of bringing this oppression upon us.[38]

Polk never lived to see the Civil War that his own use of presidential power had helped bring about. As chief executive, he worked long hours to supervise every act of his administration. While other officers fled Washington's summer heat, the president remained. Polk grew to believe, moreover, that his administration was the victim of petty politics and the presidential ambitions of others. "I now predict that no President of the U.S. of either party will ever again be re-elected" to a second term, he said.[39] The self-discipline and the politics and passions of U.S. foreign policy killed him. Within four months of leaving the presidency, Polk died at the age of fifty-four.

NOTES

1. Julius W. Pratt, "The Ideology of American Expansion," in *Essays in Honor of William E. Dodd*, ed. Avery Craven (Chicago, 1935), p. 343.
2. *Ibid.*, p. 342.
3. Albert K. Weinberg, *Manifest Destiny* (Baltimore, 1935), pp. 192–223.
4. Arthur M. Schlesinger, Jr., *The Age of Jackson* (Boston, 1945), pp. 496–497.
5. The Ritchie quote is in Thomas R. Hietala, *Manifest Design: Anxious Aggrandizement in Late Jacksonian America* (Ithaca, 1985), p. 198; good background can be found in John Holenberg, *Foreign Correspondents: The Great Reporters and Their Times* (New York, 1964), pp. 28–29.
6. Leo Marx, *The Machine in the Garden* (New York, 1964), is a superb analysis.
7. Charles Vevier, "American Continentalism: An Idea of Expansion, 1845–1910," *American Historical Review* 65 (January 1960): 324–327, a small classic; Hietala, pp. 198–199.
8. Frederick Merk, *Manifest Destiny and Mission in American History: A Reinterpretation* (New York, 1963), pp. 107–108.
9. Walt Whitman, *The Gathering of the Forces*, 2 vols. (New York, 1920), I, pp. 32–33.
10. "What's So Bad about Feeling Good?" *Public Opinion* 8 (April/May 1985): 3, is an update and evaluation of Tocqueville's insight.
11. Joel H. Silbey, "The Election of 1836," in *History of American Presidential Elections, 1789–1968*, ed. Arthur M. Schlesinger, Jr., 4 vols. (New York, 1971), I, pp. 577–583, 598–599; *The American Party System*, ed. William N. Chambers and William Dean Burnham (New York, 1975), p. 112.
12. Robert W. Tucker and David C. Hendrickson, *The Imperial Temptation* (New York, 1992), p. 173.
13. Reginald Horsman, "American Indian Policy and the Origins of Manifest Destiny," *University of Birmingham Historical Journal* 11, no. 2 (1968): 138.
14. Angie Debo, *A History of the Indians of the United States* (Norman, Okla., 1970), pp. 101–111.

15. Pratt, p. 344.
16. Thomas McCormick, "Liberal Capitalism . . . ," in Lloyd Gardner *et al.*, *Creation of the American Empire*, 2d ed. (Chicago, 1976), pp. 120, 130.
17. Stuart C. Miller, "The American Trader's Image of China, 1785–1840," *Pacific Historical Review* 36 (November 1967): 381.
18. Mira Wilkins, *The Emergence of Multinational Enterprise: American Business Abroad from the Colonial Era to 1914* (Cambridge, Mass., 1970), p. 9; Miller, 384–385.
19. Peter W. Fay, "The Protestant Mission and the Opium War," *Pacific Historical Review* 40 (May 1971): 145–149.
20. Hietala, pp. 60–63.
21. John R. Bodo, *The Protestant Clergy and Public Issues, 1812–1848* (Princeton, 1954), pp. 230–231.
22. Edward P. Crapol, "Lydia Maria Child: Abolitionist Critic of American Foreign Policy," in *Women and American Foreign Policy*, ed. Edward P. Crapol (Westport, Conn., 1987), pp. 1–18, and Crapol's superb essay, "The Foreign Policy of Antislavery, 1833–1846," in *Redefining the Past: Essays in Diplomatic History in Honor of William Appleman Williams*, ed. Lloyd C. Gardner (Corvallis, Ore., 1986).
23. Charles G. Sellers, *James K. Polk, Jacksonian: 1795–1843* (Princeton, 1957), p. 112.
24. James T. Hathaway, *Incidents in the Campaign of 1844* (New Haven, 1905), p. 26.
25. Norman A. Graebner, "James K. Polk," in *America's Ten Greatest Presidents*, ed. Morton Borden (Chicago, 1961), p. 135.
26. William Safire, "Second Inaugural Address," *New York Times*, 14 January 1985, p. A19.
27. Howard Jones, "Daniel Webster, the Diplomatist," in *Daniel Webster: "The Completest Man,"* ed. Kenneth E. Shewmaker (Hanover, N.H., 1990), pp. 204–218, provides an especially good summary of these episodes; Howard Jones, *To the Webster-Ashburton Treaty; A Study in Anglo-American Relations, 1783–1843* (Chapel Hill, N.C., 1977), is excellent on the background and standard on the negotiations, especially pp. 88–102; Howard Jones, *Mutiny on the Amistad* (New York, 1987), tells the story of the mutiny by the slaves and negotiations for their freedom, especially pp. 204–219 on Webster.
28. Ray Allen Billington, *Westward Expansion* (New York, 1949), pp. 509–511.
29. *The Diary of James K. Polk during His Presidency*, ed. Milo M. Quaife, 4 vols. (Chicago, 1910), I, p. 155; Hietala, p. 74.
30. *Diary of Polk*, ed. Quaife, I, p. 71.
31. Charles Sellers, *James K. Polk, Continentalist: 1843–1846* (Princeton, 1966), pp. 416–421, has a good account of the debate and Polk's springing of the war declaration preamble on Congress.
32. *Parade Magazine*, 8 April 1984, p. 17.
33. *Diary of Polk*, ed. Quaife, II, pp. 289, 305.
34. Frederick Merk, *The Monroe Doctrine and American Expansion, 1843–1849* (New York, 1966), p. 253.
35. *Ibid.*, p. 231; Dexter Perkins, *The Monroe Doctrine, 1826–1867* (Baltimore, 1933), pp. 182–183.
36. Gore Vidal, *Matters of Fact and of Fiction* (New York, 1977), p. 179, for context.
37. Hietala, ch. II, has a good discussion.
38. *The Political Thought of Lincoln*, ed. Richard N. Current (Indianapolis, 1967), pp.

43–44. Lincoln, of course, used those presidential powers to the utmost just thirteen years later.
39. *Diary of Polk*, ed. Quaife, II, p. 314.

For Further Reading

Consult the notes of this chapter and the General Bibliography at the end of this book (most of whose references are not repeated below), but especially note *Guide to American Foreign Relations since 1700*, ed. Richard Dean Burns (1983), light-years ahead of anything else on pre-1981 sources and helpfully organized as well.

A sweeping cultural overview on Manifest Destiny is Vivien Green Fryd's *Art and Empire: Ethnicity in the U.S. Capitol, 1815–1860* (1992). The earlier years are covered in Robert Remini's prize-winning biography *Andrew Jackson and the Course of American Empire* (1981) and in John H. Schroeder's fine *Shaping a Maritime Empire* (1985), which covers the U.S. Navy's activities from the 1830s to the Civil War. Four superb books make westward expansion come alive: Sandra L. Myres, *Westering Women and the Frontier Experience, 1800–1915* (1982), and Annette Kolodny, *The Land before Her: Fantasy and Experience of the American Frontiers, 1630–1860* (1984), Julie Ray Jeffrey, *Converting the West: A Biography of Narcissa Whitman* (1991), which are vivid on the horrors that confronted women in the westward trek; and Bill Gilbert, *Westering Man: The Life of Joseph Walker* (1983).

The best and most complete overview remains David M. Pletcher, *The Diplomacy of Annexation: Texas, Oregon, and the Mexican War* (1973), with excellent sources noted; specific areas are well covered in Wilbur D. Jones, *The American Problem in British Diplomacy, 1841–1861* (1985); Michael H. Hunt's pathbreaking *The Making of a Special Relationship: The United States and China to 1914* (1983); Curtis T. Henson, Jr., *Commissioners and Commodores: The East India Squadron and American Diplomacy in China* (1982); and the readable Arthur P. Dudden, *The American Pacific* (1992); while key figures are analyzed in Frederic A. Greenhut, "Edmund Roberts: Early American Diplomat," *Manuscripts* 35 (Fall 1983), and in three superb works by Kenneth Shewmaker: "Daniel Webster and American Conservatism," in *Traditions and Values: American Diplomacy, 1790–1855*, ed. Norman Graebner (1985); "Forging the 'Great Chain': Daniel Webster and the Origins of American Foreign Policy toward East Asia and the Pacific, 1841–1852," *American Philosophical Society* 129 (September 1985); and *The Papers of Daniel Webster: Diplomatic Papers* (1983–   ), of which Shewmaker is chief editor. The South's leading figure tells his story in *The Papers of John C. Calhoun*, ed. Clyde N. Wilson *et al.* which, by 1991, had reached 1844 documents and Calhoun's more intense involvement in foreign policy; and John Niven, *John C. Calhoun and The Price of Union: A Biography* (1992). Deborah Pickman Clifford, *Crusader for Freedom: A Life of Lydia Maria Child* (1991), is an important biography.

On the Mexican War, aside from the Pletcher volume (and its bibliographical references) noted above, the following are important: Paul H. Bergeron, *The Presidency of James K. Polk* (1987); Carlos Bosch Garcia, "The Mexican War," in *Diplomatic Claims: Latin American Historians View the United States*, trans. and ed. Warren Dean (1985), an important Latin American perspective; Neal Harlow, *California Conquered: War and Peace on the Pacific, 1846–1850* (1982); Ernest M. Lander, Jr., *Reluctant Imperialists: Calhoun, the South Carolinians, and the Mexican War* (1984); four essays on the 1840s in *Foundations of American Foreign Policy*, ed. Norman Graebner (1986); and two works by Graebner himself: "The Mexican War: A Study in Causation," *Pacific Historical Review* 49 (August 1980), and the reprint of his 1955 book, *Empire on the Pacific* (1983), with an important interpretation and an updated bibliography.

Especially useful is Norman E. Tutorow, *The Mexican-American War, an Annotated Bibliography* (1981).

5

The Climax of Early U.S. Foreign Policy: The Civil War (1850–1865)

Foreign Policy as a Cause of the Civil War

American expansion accelerated after 1815. It seemed out of control by 1850. The new Democratic president, Franklin Pierce, candidly declared in his 1853 inaugural address that "my administration will not be controlled by any timid forebodings of evil from expansion." Pierce had been elected on a platform that embodied Manifest Destiny. It termed the Mexican War "just and necessary." George Sanders, a Kentucky politician, caught perfectly the spirit of the age: Americans "are booted and spurred, and are panting for conquest."[1]

The Civil War logically climaxed post-1815 expansionism and the fragmentation of the United States. But it was also part of larger changes in the Western world. Europe endured an era of revolution between 1789 and 1850. Modern industrial capitalism and middle-class society were born amid the rubble of old classes overwhelmed by the new forces. This birth, moreover, was made more painful because large numbers of common people became active political participants for the first time, both in the United States and in western Europe. Many of these people were also caught up in mass migrations that shocked and transformed many parts of the world.[2] The United States especially experienced the astonishing effects of the immigration. Between 1820 and 1840, about 700,000 newcomers entered the country; but between 1840 and 1860, some 4.2 million flooded over eastern cities and western lands. In Europe, communism first began to appear as a movement to be reckoned with; in the United States, the first important labor unions emerged. The United States could not escape the crosscurrents that rocked the Western world.

Amid this rapid change and the promise of indefinite expansion in the post-1815 era, two factions emerged in the United States to struggle over the question of who would control the foreign policies and benefit from the expansion. They were the same two that James Madison had observed were the main opponents in the 1787 Constitutional Convention: the slave and the nonslave states (see p. 32). Since 1787, the Union had been kept in precarious balance by equally dividing the new territories between the two. After 1850, however, the balance began to disappear when California entered the Union and the free states gained a majority in the U.S. Senate. The North, with its much larger population, already could control the House of Representatives. In addition, the North was becoming wealthier faster than the South. By 1859, the value of the former's manufacturing alone was ten times greater than that of the latter's cotton. People discussed King Cotton, but the real rulers were iron, leather, and wheat. Per-capita income in the industrial Northeast was double that of the South.

Power created power. Railroad mileage in New England and the Midwest outstripped the South's. Western farmers were linked to the Northeast's merchants by bands of iron. The new rail system neutralized the Mississippi and other north-south waterways. Chicago, nonexistent in 1800, became a railroad hub and saw its population jump from 30,000 in 1850 to 110,000 in 1860—an amount larger than the South's Charleston, Memphis, Mobile, and Atlanta combined. Southerners found themselves trapped in a one-crop slave economy. They were dependent on northeastern bankers and shippers. They were at the mercy of world cotton markets over which they had little control. They lived in the middle of a growing black population that had already set off slave revolts. They were unable to increase the number of white or immigrant inhabitants to keep pace with the North. And now they were in a minority in both houses of Congress.

These developments directly shaped U.S. foreign policy: southerners believed that the survival of their society relied on acquiring new land. Cuba and Central America were the areas most frequently targeted. Only expansion could give the South new soil to replace worn-out land in the older states. Only expansion could give southerners hope to bal-

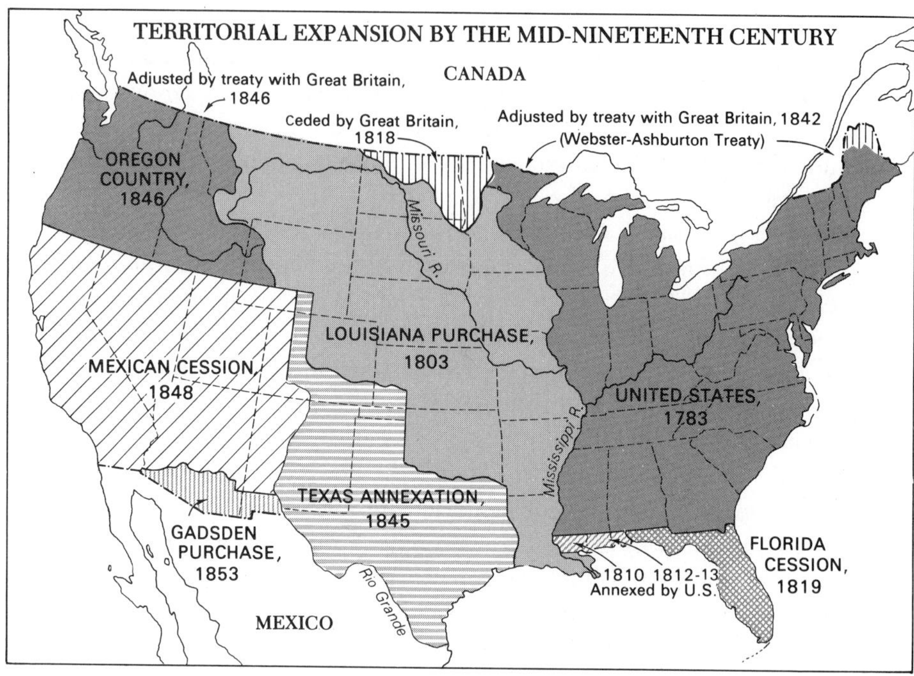

The United States in the 1850s, after expansion rounded out the continental boundaries and just before the Civil War nearly tore it in half.

ance once again the North's power in Congress. Northerners, for their part, had no intention of losing their newly found power. And northern farmers certainly had no intention of allowing the South to block them from settling their free-labor system in new territories.

In the 1850s, therefore, two explosive forces collided. A great debate erupted over the direction of American expansion. In 1860, the election of Abraham Lincoln (a free-soil Republican who gained fame and income as a sharp lawyer for the new railroads) convinced the South that it had finally lost control of U.S. foreign policy. It could no longer hope to obtain fresh lands for slavery, cotton, and political power. So the southerners left the Union. The bloodiest event in their history demonstrated how Americans could not escape the intimate relationship between their foreign and domestic affairs.

Young America: South, North, and at Home

More than a century later, it is difficult to recapture the ferocity, even violence, with which Americans conducted this foreign-policy debate in the 1850s. In the Democratic party, an extreme group, Young America, used popular racist arguments to put down those who urged restraint ("the old fogies") and instead insisted on "sympathy for the liberals of Europe, the expansion of the American republic southward and westward, and the grasping of the magnificent purse of the commerce of the Pacific." Young America's leading politician, Stephen A. Douglas of Illinois, believed his country too great to have silly "disputes about boundaries" or to "suffer mere 'red lines' on maps." Douglas and his friends condemned their "unnatural mother," Great Britain, for trying to contain U.S. expansion.[3] Young America's idea was to expand both north and south, then worry about the political problems later—although some, such as Douglas, believed that the problem of which section was to govern the newly acquired regions could be resolved through "popular sovereignty," that is, allowing the settlers to decide whether they wanted a slave or free society.

Young America was more than rhetoric and bombast. Its favorite presidential candidate in 1852, Franklin Pierce of New Hampshire, won the election and promptly gave diplomatic posts to the group's members. The appointments included minister to France (John Mason of Virginia) and minister to Spain (Pierre Soulé of Louisiana). Young America, however, then ran into a series of difficulties. Expanding southward meant dealing with black and other nonwhite races in Cuba and Latin America, an encounter that most Americans hoped to avoid. In 1854, for example, a crisis arose when Spain illegally seized a U.S. ship. Then rumors flew that the Spanish were about to free the slaves in Cuba. The Pierce administration used the opportunity to order Soulé

Franklin Pierce (1804–1869) from New Hampshire had never made a mark as a member of Congress or the Senate, and was even accused of being the sad "hero of many a well-fought bottle." But his expansionism, identification with the Young America movement, and hatred of abolitionists surprisingly gained him the Democratic party's nomination, then the presidency in 1853. Over the next four years, the expansionism of this untalented man further dragged the nation down the path toward civil war.

to buy Cuba for $130 million. If Spain refused, the minister was to plan "to detach" Cuba from Spain.

Soulé, Mason, and James Buchanan (U.S. minister to Great Britain) met in Ostend, Belgium, to coordinate their moves. The three were not the calmest of diplomats (Soulé had already shot the French minister in Madrid during a duel after someone in the French Embassy had publicly commented on Mrs. Soulé's breasts). The ministers now sent a secret message to Washington—the Ostend Manifesto—that urged "wresting Cuba from Spain" if the island could not be purchased. Both Europeans and northerners in the United States instantly condemned the "manifesto." Pierce beat a hasty retreat. The clumsiness of Young America deepened free-soilers' suspicions of a slave-power conspiracy to control U.S. foreign policy. The episode and the reaction to it also ruined any chance to annex Cuba during the 1850s.

Another setback to Young America occurred in the North. Few believed that Canada could simply be seized; after all, it was owned by the world's greatest power. But Canadians were growing restless under British rule. They especially wanted more trade with the growing market to their south. In 1854, the United States made a significant reciprocity agreement by signing the Marcy-Elgin Treaty. (Trade reciprocity means lowering U.S. tariffs to a nation in return for that country making reciprocal, or similar, concessions.) Young Americans viewed the treaty as a first step toward annexation of Canada. In reality, however, the pact helped quiet Canadian unrest. The British also promised Canada greater independence, and in 1867 Canada gained control over many of its own affairs.

Ardent expansionists suffered a major setback at home between 1854 and 1857. Douglas brought a bill before Congress to organize Nebraska Territory into two states, Kansas and Nebraska, where a key section of the proposed transcontinental railroad was to be built. Southerners refused to support Douglas unless the Missouri Compromise of 1820 (which prohibited slavery north of 36°30′) was explicitly repealed. Douglas successfully worked for the repeal of the prohibition. All of Kansas-Nebraska opened to slaveowners. Free-soilers were furious. They used the North's superiority in money and population to flood the region with antislave advocates. Violence erupted. As the southern part of the territory became known as "bleeding Kansas," free-soilers turned bitterly against Douglas and his idea of popular sovereignty. But so did many slaveholders who now realized that they could no longer compete with the North's power.

Both sides began to demand government guarantees and protection for their own cause. Popular sovereignty became discredited. When Douglas insisted on retaining the idea, southern Democrats, who wanted Washington to protect slavery in all territories, disavowed him. The Democratic party split in 1857–1858. An adhesive that had kept the Union together, the two-party system (which contained in each party both northerners and southerners), now became a three-party system: northern Democrats, southern states-rights Democrats, and the new Republican party. Political affiliations began to divide more and more along sectional lines.

No longer could Americans conquer new lands and assume that the question of who was to control the area could be worked out peacefully and democratically. Now foreign-policy expansionism could mean war at home in the form of a "bleeding Kansas." But Americans were not about to stop doing what they had been doing for centuries. They continued to try to carry out a vigorous expansionist foreign policy. Three case studies—the first involving Japan, the second revolving around the ambitions of William Henry Seward, and the third focusing on Central America—are especially revealing. The first two give a glimpse into the future. The third attempted to recreate a past that, as southerners and Young America boosters learned to their sorrow, was not to be repeated.

Whigs and Asia

In 1850, Millard Fillmore moved up to the presidency after Zachary Taylor's sudden death. Fillmore appointed Daniel Webster as secretary of state. The nation was still recovering from the bitter 1850 Compromise debate (see p. 123), and Webster set out to use bombastic pronouncements (but little action) on foreign policy as a means of making Americans proud and bringing them back together. A superb opportunity arose after Hungary revolted against Austria. Tsarist Russia, Austria's conservative ally, quickly smashed the rebellion and restored the monarchy. When Austria discovered that the United States had planned to recognize the revolutionaries, it shot off a strong protest to Washington. Webster responded with the so-called Hülsemann letter (sent to Austria's chargé in Washington, Chevalier Hülsemann) in which he told Austria in grand terms how Americans would support freedom anywhere they pleased. For good measure, Webster added that compared with the United States, Austria was nothing more than "a patch on the earth's surface." As historian Kenneth Shewmaker observes, the Hülsemann letter was a "classic example of tailoring foreign policy to the needs of domestic politics."[4]

Webster and the Whigs also stirred hearts when they loudly welcomed Louis Kossuth, the Hungarian revolutionary leader, to the United States in 1851. Kossuth, however, mistakenly believed that when Webster and other Americans praised his revolution, they also were offering to help it directly. No U.S. political leader, especially among Whigs, considered challenging the Russian use of force in Hungary. As historian Donald S. Spencer has shown, Young America Democrats more strongly supported Kossuth's cause than did the Whigs, but not even these Democrats offered their bodies to ensure that Hungary could enjoy the blessings of 1776.[5] The disillusioned Kossuth left the United States in 1852 virtually unnoticed.

Other than fine, if empty, declarations, the Whigs offered one other outlet for expansionist-minded Americans in the 1850s: the promise of new opportunities in Asia. China had been opened to Americans by the last Whig administration. Webster now focused on Japan. As the London *Times* understood, once Americans took San Francisco, "the course lies straight and obvious to Polynesia, the Philippines . . . and China, and it is not extravagant to suppose that the merchants of this future emporium may open the commerce of Japan."[6] The commerce had largely been closed to the West. U.S. businessmen, as well as politicians such as John Quincy Adams, had long believed that it was against the laws of nature for countries to close themselves off from commerce and "civilization." "We do not admit the right of a nation of people to exclude themselves and their country from intercourse with the rest of the world," declared a group of U.S. merchants who eyed the Japanese market.[7] Hating iron curtains and colonial powers that shut them out of some markets, Americans have long looked at trade as a natural and an inalienable right. Japan needed to be opened as well to protect shipwrecked U.S. sailors. They had often been brutally treated when washed up on Japanese shores.

But above all was the lure of profit—a profit that came from the new technology of steamships and the growing trade they carried to and from Asian ports. President Fillmore's May 10, 1851, letter to the Japanese emporor (a letter written by Webster) stressed the importance of this technology and trade in the opening of the historic relationship. Having acquired "the great countries of Oregon & California," Fillmore told the emporor, Americans with their new steamships can suddenly reach Japan "in less than twenty days. . . . Our object is friendly commercial intercourse, and nothing more. . . . Your empire has a great abundance of coal . . . which our Steamships, in going from California to China, must use." When Commodore Matthew C. Perry learned in 1852 that he was to head a mission to open Japan, he rushed up and down the Boston-Washington region to collect new American inventions and information from businesses so he could instruct the Japanese how to become industrialized. He later gave them their first telegraph as well as a miniature railroad that delighted Japanese officials who rode on it with gowns flying in the wind.[8]

Americans, however, also planned to "civilize" Japan. Until that happened, the Asians would resemble Native Americans who insisted on living outside the law. "You have to deal with barbarians as barbarians," a Whig senator from North Carolina declared, because Japan could not be expected to act like "the civilized portion of mankind." That view gained popularity after the Japanese acted rudely toward Perry during his first visit in 1853; but they then became cooperative a year later, when he returned with a much larger fleet. The U.S. secretary of the navy concluded that triumphs such as Perry's were "but an extension of popular virtue, republican simplicity and world-teaching example." A less enthusiastic senator from Florida, however, wondered whether Americans should only "take one continent at a time."[9]

The Japanese learned quickly. After intense internal debate, they followed the principle of jujitsu—that is, use the opponent's strength to control him. Soon after Perry departed, Japan set up an Institute for the Investigation of Barbarian Books so that it could learn how the West had become so strong technologically and militarily. On the other hand, Western philosophy and religion were clearly inferior and disruptive, so they were to be ignored.[10] By 1858, the Japanese willingly dealt with the American consul, Townsend Harris, more openly than they had with Perry. The 1858 treaty first opened five major ports to foreign trade and affirmed extraterritoriality rights. Diplomatic representatives were exchanged. In 1864, a small fleet of foreign warships, including a single U.S. vessel, shot their way back into Japan after foreigners were mistreated. But the Japanese adjusted rapidly. In 1868, the emperor returned to power. Under his rule the people resumed learning from foreigners while also playing them off against each other. The small, disciplined nation of islands learned the lessons so well that within a generation it challenged the West for supremacy on the Asian mainland.

Many Americans saw their successes in Japan as simply Manifest Destiny. A popular magazine caught the spirit and gave it proper historical perspective. "Twenty years ago the 'far west' was a fixed idea

Walt Whitman (1819–1892) of New York is perhaps the greatest American poet and is certainly one of the nation's most original voices. He explored especially what he termed "the new empire" of the mid-nineteenth century that reached across the continent and toward Asia.

resting upon a fixed extent of territory," the journal wrote in 1852. But now "President Fillmore finds a 'far west' on the isles of the Japanese Empire and on the shores of China."[11] Poet Walt Whitman best expressed the belief that although U.S. territorial expansion had hit the wall of the Pacific Ocean, that was no reason to stop expanding. As Whitman said in his 1860 poem "The New Empire" (written to celebrate the first visit of Japanese diplomats to New York City), the Pacific could become a vast highway that opened to Americans an incredible future.

> I chant the world on my Western Sea; . . .
> I chant the new empire, grander than any before—as in a vision it comes to me;
> I chant America, the Mistress—I chant a greater supremacy;
> I chant, projected, a thousand blooming cities yet, in time, on those groups of sea-islands;
> I chant commerce opening, the sleep of ages having done its work—races, reborn, refresh'd. . . .[12]

Seward: Prophet of U.S.-Russian Relations

No politician of the era better exemplified its spirit or more dominated its foreign policy than William Henry Seward of New York. "A slouching, slender figure; a head like a wise macaw, a beaked nose; shaggy eyebrows; unorderly hair and clothes; hoarse voice; offhand manner;

free talk, and perpetual cigar" was the firsthand description of Seward by Henry Adams.[13] Appearances could deceive. Despite the informality, Seward had one of the best-stocked minds of his time. His foreign policies, in the words of historian Ernest Paolino, "anticipated the direction of American foreign policy for the next generation and beyond."[14] Those policies arose from a deep, although not original, reading of history. As one of his biographers remarked, "He made the past his servant." When Seward first visited Washington in the 1840s, he was amazed at "how little study and how little learning men who have ambition on this great stage are content to arm themselves."[15]

A graduate of Union College in New York (at the age of nineteen in 1820), Seward was a lawyer and then the highly successful governor of New York before he entered the Senate as a Whig in 1849. He immediately opposed slave expansion. The New Yorker declared that "a higher law than the Constitution" should guide antislavery actions, a phrase that seemed to hint of revolution to many nonsoutherners as well as to slaveholders. By 1858, he warned of an "irrepressible conflict" that would continue until either slavery or freedom triumphed. These words did not come easily, for Seward, like his hero John Quincy Adams, believed in the nation's Manifest Destiny. But also like Adams, he opposed slave expansion so his own free-soil region could control the western lands—and Congress. Seward coveted Cuba, Central America, Mexico, and Canada. He even believed that, ultimately, so many Americans would live in the Southwest, the nation's capital should be moved from Washington to the Mississippi Valley—or perhaps even Mexico City. Realizing the political price of such expansion in the 1850s, however, he switched his expansionist enthusiasm to commerce and the Pacific trade.

Seward was the first U.S. official who developed a coherent Asian policy. It rested on a bedrock assumption: that the first step toward controlling Asia's markets required the spread of industry, railroads, and canals through the American heartland. "Open up a highway through your country, from New York to San Francisco," he proclaimed to the Senate in 1853. "Put your domain under cultivation and your ten thousand wheels of manufacture in motion. The nation that draws most materials and provisions from the earth, and fabricates the most, and sells the most of productions and fabrics to foreign nations, must be, and will be, the great power of the earth."[16] He was convinced that the Monroe Doctrine was already largely fulfilled. The United States was well on its way to dominating the Western Hemisphere. It was now "the Pacific Ocean . . . and the vast regions beyond" that were

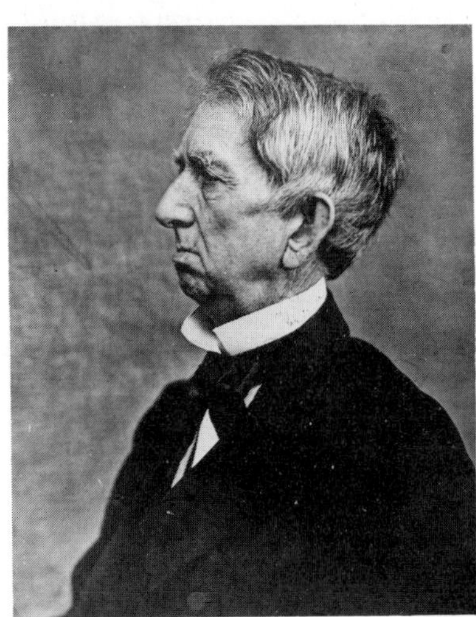

William Seward (1801–1872) had been a brilliant lawyer and governor of New York before moving to the U.S. Senate in 1849, where he became the leader of the Whig and, later, Republican parties. Lincoln defeated the outspoken antislave New Yorker for the White House, but Seward left his mark as the prophet (and later, between 1861 and 1869 when he served as secretary of state, as the diplomat) for American expansionism into the Caribbean and, especially, the vast Pacific Ocean regions.

to "become the chief theatre of events in the world's great hereafter."[17]

An ambitious politician, a student of history, Seward was also a Whig who urged the creation of a federal program of internal improvements (such as national railroads) so that future Americans could use the most efficient transportation. His radical antislave statements prevented him from capturing the Whig and then Republican party presidential nomination. But Abraham Lincoln appointed Seward to head the Department of State in 1861, and in that post the New Yorker was able to carry out some of his dreams. He worked out the tactics for protecting both U.S. interests and freedom of action in Asia. The tactics included working for the territorial integrity of all Asian nations (that is, not allowing Japanese or Europeans to colonize mainland markets). He aimed at avoiding any political alliances but cooperated with any nation that also wanted to maintain the open door.

Seward then drew a startling conclusion. The Americans' westward push put them on a collision course with Russia. He hoped that the meeting would be friendly. As secretary of state in 1861, he instructed the new U.S. minister to St. Petersburg, Cassius Clay of Kentucky, that "Russia, like the United States, is an improving and expanding empire. Its track is eastward while that of the United States is westward." Seward believed that "Russia and the United States may remain good friends until, each having made a circuit of half the globe in opposite directions, they shall meet and greet each other in the region [Asia] where civilization first began, and where, after so many ages, it has now become lethargic and helpless."[18]

Such a breathtaking perspective was not new. Thirty years before, Alexis de Tocqueville, the acute French visitor, had prophesied that Americans and Russians, although "their starting point is different and their courses are not the same," seemed "marked out by the will of heaven to sway the destinies of half the globe."[19] In 1856, Commodore Perry, fresh from his triumph in Japan, warned that American and Russian expansion would continue until "the Saxon and the Cossack will meet once more" in Asia. "Will it be friendship? I fear not! I think I see in the distance the giants that are growing up for that fierce and final encounter: In the progress of events that battle must sooner or later inevitably be fought."[20] Seward was perhaps more optimistic than Perry. More important, the New Yorker could help control the growing relationship with Russia because of his power as secretary of state. Before Seward could realize his plans in Asia, however, he had to face a crisis at home that arose out of slavery and three centuries of imperial dreams.

Central America and Cuba

An observer in the 1850s wondered why Americans fought each other so fiercely over such an issue as slavery in the desert regions of the southwest United States. It was a debate over "an imaginary Negro in an impossible place," this observer concluded. But he missed the context of the debate, for it occurred amid rampant expansionism. It seemed that it would be only a matter of time before regions north and south would fall to the irresistible magnet of U.S. Manifest Destiny.

In late 1853, the U.S. minister to Mexico, James Gadsden, following President Pierce's orders, approached Mexico to discuss the purchase of territory so that a U.S. railroad could have a clear southern route to the Pacific. The Mexican government, in need of money, agreed to sell a smaller area than Gadsden requested, some 45,000 square miles, in return for $15 million. The Gadsden Purchase ran into fierce antislave opposition in the Senate. The revised treaty then provided paying $10 million for 29,670 square miles, which included part of present-day Arizona and New Mexico. It marked the first time the Senate refused to accept land offered to it. Nevertheless, no one would have then guessed that the deal rounded out the boundaries of the continental United States. It marked the end of the conquest of an ocean-to-ocean empire.

At the time, however, it seemed one more step southward, with many more to follow. Just the first six months of 1854 exemplified how the aggressive Americans were on the move. During those months (the

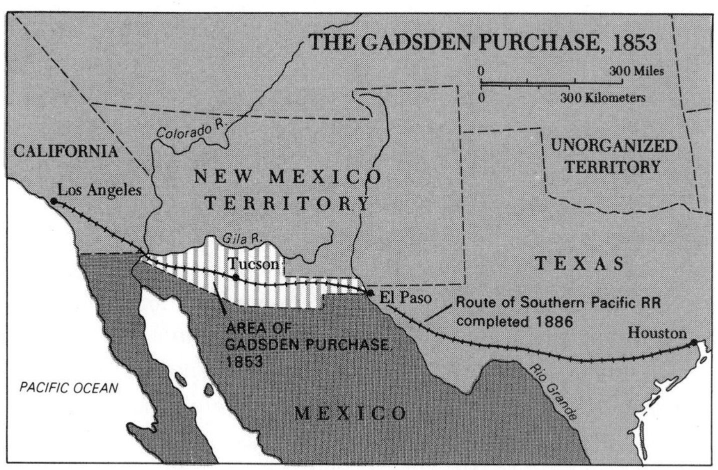

U.S. minister to Mexico, James Gadsden (a native of South Carolina) bought for $10 million what was finally an area of 29,670 square miles so that the southern states could have a transcontinental railway route. The Gadsden Purchase, accepted by the U.S. Senate despite violent northern opposition, rounded out the nation's continental boundaries in 1853–1854.

time when the bitter Kansas-Nebraska debates were shattering the Democratic party), Gadsden sent his treaty to the Senate; an American, William Walker, announced his plans to seize part of Mexico; the possibility of war with Spain over Cuba loomed; the Ostend Manifesto became public; the U.S. Navy shelled Nicaragua; and southerners launched new "filibustering" expeditions aimed at seizing Cuba and other Latin American territories for slavery.[21]

Americans seemed to be taking over Central America. Slaveholders hoped to acquire new territory and possibly even states. Merchants coveted control of the profitable, short isthmian passageways through Nicaragua and Panama that linked the two oceans. Even Republican free-soilers eyed Central America as the place in which free African Americans could be settled in a colonization scheme. Such resettlement would quiet the racial question at home—"Keep our Anglo-Saxon institutions as well as our Anglo-Saxon blood pure and uncontaminated," as a Republican declared—and would spread U.S. influence and values to Latin America.[22] The colonization plans finally collapsed because some Republicans did not want to lose cheap black labor. Moreover, the colonizers discovered that the cost and time needed to ship out all African Americans far exceeded the nation's available resources. In the 1850s, however, colonization remained a much-discussed solution to growing racial problems.

Nicaragua attracted special attention. The British had seized control of the eastern entry to a possible interocean canal route in the 1840s. One of the great U.S. adventurers, Cornelius Vanderbilt, appeared in 1848 to acquire from Nicaragua the right to monopolize transportation on the country's waters. U.S. power dramatically appeared in 1854. One of Vanderbilt's officials killed a Nicaraguan. Anti-American feelings ran high. The U.S. minister attempted to restore calm, only to have a bottle thrown at him. He asked Washington to teach the Nicaraguans a lesson. Commander George Nichols Hollins appeared at the Atlantic coast port of Greytown. Hollins demanded an apology and an indemnity from the Nicaraguans. The commander then loaded his ship's cannon and leveled the port's huts and buildings.

Hollins had scarcely sailed off before William Walker appeared. About five feet tall, very thin, a man consumed by the idealistic reform movements of the time (such as women's rights and the abolition of slavery), Walker had been a lawyer, then a journalist in New Orleans. By 1855, he had unsuccessfully tried to use a small private army to spread the blessings of democracy to parts of Mexico. Nicaraguan political factions asked him to help them fight their opponents. This "gray-eyed man of destiny," as he came to be known, assembled sixty men and, with Vanderbilt's help, conquered Nicaragua in 1855. The U.S. government moved to recognize Walker's regime officially. The self-styled disciple of democracy, however, made a fatal mistake. He allowed Nicaraguan land and mineral rights to be stolen by American business interests. Nicaraguans merely objected. Vanderbilt, whose interests were threatened, was not as passive. He set out to destroy Walker. The British gladly joined the crusade. In 1857, Walker fell. He could conquer Nicaragua but not Vanderbilt. The adventurer tried three more times to capture parts of Central America. In 1860, Honduran troops captured and shot him. The first U.S. clash with Nicaraguans had not been a happy occasion, as Nicaraguan school children forever after learned.

Cuba also became a target of U.S. expansionists. Southerners led the charge. "With Cuba and St. Domingo," the Charleston *Southern Standard* trumpeted, "we could control the productions of the tropics, and, with them, the commerce of the world, and with that, the power of the world."[23] A colorful and dangerous example of the South's determination was a secret society, the Knights of the Golden Circle, that pledged to extend slavery throughout the Gulf of Mexico. By 1860, the Knights claimed 65,000 members, three state governors, and several of President Buchanan's cabinet. But northerners also set their sights on the Caribbean. Some—particularly in New York City—especially desired Cuban trade. By 1855, U.S. commerce with the island had doubled in a decade until it was seven times greater than Great Britain's and even four times larger than Spain's—which owned Cuba. For their part, abolitionists wanted Cuba in order to open new markets for northern farmers and to end the slave trade in the region. The North's primary motive for coveting Cuba, however, was increased trade.

After the fiasco over the Ostend Manifesto in 1854, the issue died down, then revived with a rush in 1858. The Democratic party had suffered a severe blow. In 1857, the Supreme Court ruled in the *Dred Scott* decision that slavery could be taken into U.S. territories. (A territory was the stage just before a region reached statehood.) The Court added that the federal government had to protect the slaves, because they were property. Southern Democrats rejoiced. Northern Democrats, led by Stephen A. Douglas, opposed the Court's decision: they urged that the issue be settled in the territories through popular sovereignty. Southerners roundly condemned Douglas. Desperate Democratic leaders, led by inept, but expansion-minded President Buchanan, tried to use foreign policy to reunite the party. Polk's former secretary of the Treasury, Robert Walker, told the president: "Cuba! Cuba! (and Puerto Rico, if possible) should be the countersign of your administration, and it will close in a blaze of glory."[24]

Buchanan responded in 1858 by urging Congress to appropriate money to buy Cuba. Douglas and southerners came together to back the measure. But free-soilers blasted it. They were part of a rapidly growing Republican party that had come unexpectedly close to winning the presidency in 1856 and appeared to be in a position to take the House of Representatives in 1858. Seward, newly converted to the Republicans from the dying Whig party, helped lead the attack. In one of the more unique claims in American history, Seward announced that Cuba must some day become part of the United States because "every rock and every grain of sand in that island were drifted and washed out from American soil by the floods of the Mississippi, and the other estuaries of the Gulf of Mexico."[25] Some day—but not in 1858. The slave controversy, Seward believed, first had to be resolved. He received support from other Republicans, who argued that most Cubans were Roman Catholic and that the U.S. constitutional system could "only be maintained . . . on the principle of Protestant liberty."[26]

There was also the possible obstacle of the British fleet. London officials believed that Cuba would fall naturally into American laps, much as John Quincy Adams had predicted thirty-five years earlier. But they were determined not to allow the United States to conquer the island, because it would allow southern slave expansionists to threaten British holdings in the West Indies. In 1857, the British minister to Washington secretly suggested to London that Americans should have Cuba. His superiors replied that he must have lost his senses. Giving Cuba to the United States would resemble pleasing "an animal of Prey by giving him one of one's traveling companions. It would increase [the animal's] desire for similar food and spur him to obtain it."[27]

Out of the smoke and excitement of American expansionism in the 1850s, only the Gadsden Purchase actually emerged, although Cuba, Central America, Canada, and Hawaii were heatedly discussed. In 1859, the United States even made the McLane-Ocampo Treaty in which, in return for a $4 million loan, the Mexicans would give their neighbor extensive railroad routes and the right to intervene with force to provide police protection over all of Mexico. But the U.S. Senate rejected the deal; and in other questions as well, the antiexpansionists carried the day. These foreign-policy issues nevertheless shaped many of the great debates and hopes of the decade as well as intensified southern frustration and fears. Foreign-policy issues were a central cause of the Civil War, for, while relatively few Americans urged total abolition of slavery in all southern states, many determined never to allow slaveholders to establish their "peculiar institution" in the newly acquired territories. Nor were the southerners to be allowed to conquer new regions for their slave system. Foreign-policy issues had combined with domestic controversy to form the combustible mixture that blew the United States apart.

Lincoln and the Foreign-Policy Dreams of 1860–1861

The Cuban issue resembled a monster in a science-fiction story that repeatedly had knives driven through its heart but refused to die. Left for dead by Seward and other Republicans in Congress during 1859, the issue arose again a year later. This time Abraham Lincoln decided to kill it once and for all. His decision helped drive the South out of the Union.

Lincoln was a supreme politician who had carefully thought through the central problem of the relationship between foreign policy and slavery. Born in the slave state of Kentucky (and married into a slave-holding southern family), Lincoln moved to Indiana and then Illinois, where he ran successfully for office within seven months of his arrival. Only between 1849, when he returned to Illinois after serving a term in the U.S. House of Representatives, and 1854 did he not run for elected office. A lawyer for the new Illinois Central Railroad and a devout political follower of Henry Clay, Lincoln understood the industrializing corporate America that was transforming the nation's economy. As for slavery, he condemned all abolitionists "who would shiver into fragments the Union of these states" and "tear into tatters its now venerated Constitution." He also condemned, however, any measure that hinted of allowing slavery into the territories or newly acquired foreign areas. These lands were to be preserved for white men without slaves.

In 1858, Lincoln challenged Stephen A. Douglas in the Illinois Senate race. In their famous debates, Lincoln outlined his own views (expansion for none but free white men), then asked the "Little Giant" if he favored taking new territory regardless of how such a conquest might affect the slavery controversy. Douglas's amazing answer revealed his Young America expansionism:

> This is a young and growing nation. It swarms as often as a hive of bees, and . . . there must be hives in which they can gather and make their honey. . . . I tell you, increase, and multiply, and expand, is the law of this nation's existence. You cannot limit this great republic by mere boundary lines. . . . Any one of you gentlemen might as well say to a son twelve years old that he is big enough, and must not grow any larger, and in order to prevent his growth put a hoop around him to keep him to his present size. What would be the result? Either the hoop must burst . . . or the child must die. So it would be with this great nation.[28]

Lincoln barely lost the 1858 election. But by forcing Douglas to separate himself from many northern moderates and southern radicals, the loser became a national figure. In the 1860 Republican convention, he triumphed as a moderate over Seward. The 1860 election became a four-way race among Lincoln; Douglas, who gained the Democratic party nomination; John Bell of Tennessee, whose Constitutional Union party included remaining Whigs who hoped to find some compromise; and John Breckinridge of Kentucky, the nominee of the South's proslavery Democrats. Lincoln won a plurality of the popular vote and a majority of the electoral ballots to gain the presidency. The South prepared to secede. Congress met in short session during January–February 1861 to try to hold the Union together. John Crittenden of Kentucky fashioned a compromise that provided federal protection to slavery where it existed. Then, in the crucial clause, he proposed that "slavery or involuntary servitude" would be prohibited north of the old Missouri Compromise line of 36°30′ but protected in all territory "now held, or *hereafter acquired*" (italics added).

Lincoln flatly rejected the Crittenden Compromise. "A year will not pass till we shall have to take Cuba as a condition upon which [the South] will stay in the Union," he warned friends. "There is in my judgment but one compromise which would really settle the slavery question, and that would be a prohibition against acquiring any more territory."[29] With those words, Lincoln not only separated himself from Douglas's belief that the American "bees" had to have new "hives" from which to swarm. He temporarily stopped four centuries of Amer-

Abraham Lincoln (1809–1865) was considered a mere "prairie statesman" by leading Republicans. But he outmaneuvered them to win the presidency in 1860, then named some of them to his cabinet, where he could both watch and use them to restore the Union. Secretary of State Seward is seated in the right foreground. It took Seward awhile before he could accept his subordinate position.

ican territorial expansion. No American with his authority had ever taken such a position. Madison, Monroe, Polk, and Douglas, among many others, had argued that the preservation and prosperity of the American system depended on continued landed expansion. Lincoln took another tack. He believed that no expansion was preferable to expansion that enriched slavery and discriminated against freeholding whites.

The Crittenden Compromise never passed Congress. Lincoln took office in March 1861 as southern congressmen left Washington. The new cabinet debated the issue of trying to maintain the Union. The lead was taken by Secretary of State Seward, who had looked down on Lincoln as a "prairie statesman" and believed only he, Seward, could prevent a civil war. The New Yorker had urged compromise and moderation. He feared war. So did his supporters in the New York City mercantile community who acted as bankers and shippers for the great southern cotton crop. As early as January 1861, Seward thought he had hit upon a scheme to save the Union. As he privately told the British minister to Washington, he could unite America by declaring war against foreign powers who threatened to interfere with U.S. interests in the Caribbean. This scheme had one beneficial result. British officials decided to wait before trying to interfere in, or trying to gain benefits from, the growing sectional crisis.

But Lincoln continued to refuse to compromise on the territorial issue. The president then decided to force the question by overruling Seward and sending provisions to Fort Sumter, a Union-held island in Charleston Harbor. Lincoln's move would surely lead South Carolina to fire on the fort and start civil war. The desperate Seward then took a final gamble. On April 1, 1861, the secretary of state told Lincoln that Spain and France seemed to be threatening Santo Domingo and other areas in the Caribbean. Seward suggested that explanations be "demanded" from both European nations. If their answers were unsatisfactory, Lincoln should "convene Congress and declare war against them." Seward perhaps had in mind the conquest of Cuba. He then told the president that he (the secretary of state) should have all necessary power to conduct the diplomacy as well as the war that might result. Seward was convinced that the South would re-enter the Union to help fight such a conflict.[30]

Lincoln quietly buried the astonishing proposal. But Seward's idea was not new. He had been warning the British and others for months that a war for territorial expansion could resolve the domestic crisis. Americans, moreover, had gone to war in 1812 and 1846 to resolve internal as well as external problems. What was new in 1861 was Lincoln's determination not to use foreign policy as a salve for the temporary relief of the burning issue of slavery.

The Diplomacy of the Civil War

As the North's blue- and the South's gray-uniformed armies prepared for battle in the spring of 1861, their leaders prepared to battle for European support. The Confederate nation's president, Jefferson Davis of Mississippi, had extensive political connections. He had been a U.S. Army officer, then married Zachary Taylor's daughter against Taylor's wishes. Davis also was experienced; during the 1850s he had led the South's fight in the Senate for landed expansion. A moderate among the secessionists, Davis had not at first sought the presidency. His wife recalled that when he received the telegram notifying him of the election, "he looked so grieved that I feared some evil had befallen our family."[31] Davis knew that the North's larger population and greater resources could grind down the South unless he obtained European aid. Russia and France, however, might neutralize each other's help. The tsar's government favored the North because Russia might need Union ports and support in case of possible war with Great Britain. Louis-Napoléon's France had nearly 700,000 textile workers dependent on southern cotton. Napoleon, moreover, had imperial dreams of his own for Latin America. He hoped to divide and contain North American expansion southward.

The key to Europe's response was, therefore, Great Britain. Economically, it was divided in its sentiments. The country's gigantic textile industry imported 80 percent of its cotton from the South. But the 1860 bumper crop had provided British mills with a two-and-a-half-year supply of the fiber. That breathing space allowed England to develop alternative supplies in India and Egypt. Moreover, a historic turn in Anglo-American trade had occurred in the mid-1840s. Lower British tariffs combined with spectacular new U.S. wheat crops (brought about in large part by such new technology as the McCormick reaper) to make England increasingly dependent on North American grain. King Corn began to checkmate King Cotton. Poor European grain harvests in 1860, 1861, and 1862 helped Lincoln by enriching U.S. farmers, who were becoming so efficient that they could feed both the giant Union armies and hungry Europeans. The British, in turn, found a vast market in the booming North for their manufactures. As Seward privately observed in early 1861, his section provided the "chief consumption of European productions," and more than a southern rebellion would be needed to "change these great features of American commerce."[32]

Aside from these economic magnets, powerful British liberals favored the North's battle to end slavery, especially after Lincoln's Emancipation Proclamation in September 1862. Because of their own self-interest, the British did not support the South. Divided economic and political opinion did not allow London officials to form a strong, united position. War with the Union could gravely endanger British shipping and, of course, Canada. Intervention might play into the hands of Louis-Napoléon, of whom the British were deeply suspicious as he constantly begged them to take the lead in helping the South. Moreover, with the humiliating northern military defeat at the first and second battles of Bull Run (near Manassas, Virginia) during 1861–1862, many Europeans believed a Union defeat was only a matter of time.[33]

Especially important in the British calculation was the issue of precedent. In April 1861, Davis, who had virtually no navy, commissioned privateers (privately owned ships that operated like pirates in preying on northern merchantmen). Lincoln retaliated with a blockade of the South. That act trapped Lincoln, for a blockade indicated an actual state of war. He had previously insisted that the South was not in a state of war with the North, but only in a state of rebellion. If a state of war was recognized, it could allow Europeans to deal with both sides equally. In May, London declared its neutrality, an act that also recognized the South's belligerent status. Seward and Lincoln, who had warned Europeans against such action, were angered. Seward severely warned France not to deal further with the South, or he would cut off all food exports that Frenchmen were "likely to need most and soonest." (While the crisis was building, however, Seward maintained close personal relations with the French minister to Washington by sending him fine cigars.)

The secretary of state also drafted a tough, even threatening, note (Dispatch Number 10) to the British. Lincoln calmed down Seward's rhetoric, and the new U.S. minister to Great Britain, Charles Francis Adams (John Quincy's son), watered down the wording before giving it to the British government. Adams's intelligence, calmness, and well-timed toughness made him one of the most successful diplomats in American history. A single major mistake in London could have changed the course of the Civil War.

Adams and Seward especially appealed to precedent and British self-interest. When the U.S. government intercepted neutral vessels en route to a neutral port and searched them for contraband, it committed an act that the British had repeatedly committed from 1793 through 1812. The British now did not strongly object as Lincoln repeated their earlier acts. In both the Revolutionary War and the War of 1812, the United States had depended on privateering, much to British displeasure. When Lincoln declared the South's privateering illegal, the British, who had considered it illegal years earlier, happily agreed. Finally, London honored Lincoln's loose blockade (the North did not have the ships needed to throw a tight blockade around the South's 3,500-mile-long coastline) because the British had used such a blockade in the past and would no doubt need to use it in the future.

After mid-1861, Seward settled down to conduct such successful diplomacy that historians have ranked him as the second greatest secretary of state in American history, just behind Seward's idol, John Quincy Adams. The New Yorker met and mastered four spectacular tests. The first occurred in November 1861, when hot-tempered Captain Charles Wilkes of the Union's navy learned that two Confederate diplomats, John Slidell and James Mason, had sailed for London on the British ship *Trent.* Wilkes stopped the ship, seized Slidell and Mason, then allowed the vessel to continue. The British protested and dispatched an ultimatum for the release of the two men. Seward knew that Wilkes had acted illegally. The Confederates had to be freed. But northern feelings ran high. Wilkes became a hero. Seward decided to release Slidell and Mason but, in a brilliant note to Great Britain, argued that Wilkes had been in the right. The secretary of state next neatly expressed gratefulness to the British for finally recognizing that their own acts of impressment before 1812 had been wrong. Seward thus averted war with Great Britain while stroking northern feelings. Journalist Richard Henry Dana wrote, "Seward is not only right, but sublime."[34]

A second crisis occurred in 1862, during the worst Union military setbacks. In March, the Confederate ironclad *Virginia* (formerly the *Merrimac*) fought a more powerful Union warship, the *Monitor*, to a standstill. The battle marked the first time that armored naval vessels had fired on one another. The stand-off demonstrated that the Confederate navy might not be as weak as many had assumed. On land, General Robert E. Lee's forces scored such impressive victories that Seward refused to discuss the Union's humiliations in his diplomatic correspondence.[35] Europeans, led by France, threatened to intervene and mediate a peace. Seward wrote the tsar, who was friendly to the

Union's cause, that Europe could "commit no graver error" than to become involved in the war.[36] A similar but toned-down version of this message also went to London.

Union general George McClellan, who had been overly cautious in fighting Lee, dramatically stopped the South's advance at Antietam, Maryland, in September. Lincoln meanwhile gained support in late 1862 by issuing the Emancipation Proclamation that freed all slaves in areas controlled by the Confederacy. Over the winter and early spring of 1863, a bolder general, Ulysses S. Grant, took great risks but succeeded in cutting off the Confederate force at Vicksburg, Mississippi. Grant's victory split the Confederacy and gave Lincoln control of the lower Mississippi. The triumph occurred, moreover, at the same time (July 1863) that northern troops won a bloody but decisive victory at Gettysburg, Pennsylvania. Concern over European intervention quickly declined in the North. Seward's diplomacy had gained time until the Union's greater resources could be mobilized to wear down Lee's brilliantly directed but undermanned forces. The Union's victories, especially at Antietam, Lincoln's well-timed Emancipation Proclamation, and Adams's shrewd use of these events were critical in forcing the British to pull back from any thought of helping the South.

Seward and Adams faced a third crisis in 1862–1863, when the Confederacy contracted with a British firm, the Laird Brothers, to build several ships. Before Adams could stop the construction, the *Alabama* and *Florida* slipped out of the shipbuilding yards and began attacking northern commerce. Insurance costs in the North rose as merchant shipping sank. A greater danger appeared when Laird began building armored rams that could break the North's blockade and attack northern coastal cities. Adams warned the British foreign secretary, Lord Russell, that if the Laird rams sailed, "it would be superfluous in me to point out to your Lordship that this is war." Aware that allowing the ships to leave was both bad policy and bad law, Russell had already stopped their launching. After the war, the British realized that outfitting these vessels set bad precedent; if the British themselves became involved in a war, their enemy could contract with U.S. shipbuilders to build such ships. To remove the precedent and improve tattered Anglo-American relations, the British paid the United States $15.5 million in 1872 to settle the *Alabama* claims.

A fourth crisis occurred in Mexico. In 1855, Santa Anna, who had tormented and teased both Texans and James K. Polk, finally lost power in Mexico City. He was replaced by Benito Juárez, whose ardent nationalism led him to suspend debts owed to Europeans. In 1861, a joint Spanish, British, and French force appeared to collect the debts, but the first two nations stopped cooperating when they learned that the French intended to control all of Mexico. In 1863, Napoleon III found another tool to achieve his plans for seizing Mexico, establishing a vast New World empire, and finally blocking the expansion of North American Protestants. The tool was an Austrian archduke, Maximilian, who, with his beautiful wife, Carlotta, was persuaded by Louis-Napoléon to lead a French force into Mexico. Seward strongly protested the Austrian's establishment of a monarchy during 1864, but he could do little else. With Lee's surrender at Appomattox Courthouse in Virginia on April 9, 1865, however, a huge, seasoned Union army was suddenly available to move south. General Philip Sheridan, who had trapped Lee at the final battle, led 50,000 soldiers to the Mexican border. Then, Seward again demanded that Maximilian leave Mexico. He carefully never mentioned the Monroe Doctrine, which Europeans refused to recognize, and instead rested his case on U.S. security interests—and, of course, on Sheridan's troops. But Seward only had to wait and watch as Juárez's guerrillas destroyed Maximilian's depleted army. Louis-Napoléon, concerned about the rise to power of Germany in the center of Europe, lost interest in Mexico and reneged on his earlier pledge not to desert the hapless archduke. In June 1867, a Mexican firing squad ended Maximilian's dreams. Carlotta spent most of the next sixty years insane and rambling around Europe in search of help to revive her empire.

Union armies, overwhelming northern resources, Lincoln's shrewdness and determination, Seward's diplomacy, and Adams's skill won the war. Ninety years after an independent United States had set out to settle a continental empire, the territory had been obtained, but at the cost of a civil conflict that took 600,000 lives. With the continent conquered and the issue of slavery decided, a new era opened. A different nation and a different foreign policy emerged. In historian Thomas Schoonover's words, "dollars not dominion" were to spread America's blessings.[37]

Notes

1. Reginald Horsman, *Race and Manifest Destiny* (Cambridge, Mass., 1981), p. 228; David Potter, *The Impending Crisis, 1848–1861* (New York, 1976), pp. 181–182.

2. Eric Hobsbawm, "The Crisis of Capitalism in Historical Perspective," *Socialist Revolution* 6 (October–December 1976): 82–83. A superb analysis of this background is Kinley J. Brauer, "Diplomacy of American Expansionism," in *Economics and World Power . . .*, ed. William Becker and Samuel F. Wells, Jr. (New York, 1984), esp. pp. 56–58, 112–114.
3. Horsman, pp. 284–286.
4. Kenneth E. Shewmaker, "Daniel Webster and the Politics of Foreign Policy," *Journal of American History* 63 (September 1976): 314.
5. Donald S. Spencer, *Louis Kossuth and Young America* (Columbia, Mo., 1977), pp. 136–183.
6. David M. Pletcher, *The Diplomacy of Annexation: Texas, Oregon, and the Mexican War* (Columbia, Mo., 1973), p. 577.
7. Quoted in Akira Iriye, "America Faces a Revolutionary World," manuscript, in author's possession (1976), p. 2.
8. Eugene S. Ferguson, "The American-ness of American Technology," *Technology and Culture* 20 (January 1979): 18–19; Kenneth Shewmaker and Kenneth Stevens, eds., *The Papers of Daniel Webster. Diplomatic Papers, Volume 2, 1850–1852* (Hanover, N.H., 1987), pp. 255, 289.
9. William Neumann, "Religion, Morality, and Freedom: The Ideological Background of the Perry Expedition," *Pacific Historical Review* 23 (August 1954): 247–257.
10. John Paton Davies, "America and East Asia," *Foreign Affairs* 55 (January 1977): 368–394.
11. William Neumann, "Determinism, Destiny, and Myth in the American Image of China," in *Issues and Conflicts*, ed. George L. Anderson (Lawrence, Kan., 1959).
12. Walt Whitman, "A Broadway Pageant," in *Drum-Taps*, ed. F. DeWolfe Miller (Gainesville, Fla., 1959), pp. 62–64.
13. Henry Adams, *The Education of Henry Adams, an Autobiography* (Boston, 1918), p. 104.
14. Ernest N. Paolino, *The Foundations of the American Empire: William Henry Seward and U.S. Foreign Policy* (Ithaca, N.Y., 1973), p. 212.
15. Frederic Bancroft, *The Life of William H. Seward*, 2 vols. (New York, 1900), I, p. 153.
16. *Ibid.*, I, p. 469.
17. William H. Seward, *The Works of William H. Seward*, ed. George Baker, 5 vols. (Boston, 1853–1883), I, pp. 247–250.
18. *Ibid.*, V, p. 246.
19. Alexis de Tocqueville, *Democracy in America*, 2 vols. (New York, 1948), I, p. 434.
20. Hans Kohn, *American Nationalism, an Interpretive Essay* (New York, 1957), p. 175.
21. Potter, pp. 177–178.
22. Eric Foner, *Free Soil, Free Labor, Free Men* (New York, 1970), pp. 272–280.
23. Kohn, p. 117.
24. Bancroft, I, pp. 472–478.
25. Albert K. Weinberg, *Manifest Destiny* (Baltimore, 1940), p. 66.
26. Foner, p. 228.
27. Gavin B. Henderson, ed., "Southern Designs on Cuba, 1854–1857, and Some European Observations," *Journal of Southern History* 5 (August 1939): 385.
28. Harry Jaffa, *Crisis of the House Divided* (Seattle, 1973), p. 406.

29. David Potter, *Lincoln and His Party in the Secession Crisis* (New Haven, 1942), p. 223.
30. Bancroft, II, ch. 29. There are important comments and bibliography offered by Professors Kinley Brauer and Norman Ferris on Seward's proposal in *The Society for Historians of American Foreign Relations Newsletter* 13 (September 1982): 12–15.
31. Nathaniel W. Stephenson, "Jefferson Davis," in *Dictionary of American Biography*, ed. Allen Johnson and Dumas Malone, 21 vols. (New York, 1930–), V, p. 127.
32. Seward, V, pp. 210–211.
33. Brian Jenkins, *Britain and the War for the Union*, 2 vols. (Montreal, 1974–1980), II, pp. 61–105.
34. Foster Rhea Dulles, *Prelude to World Power: American Diplomatic History, 1860–1900* (New York, 1965), p. 11.
35. William H. Seward to Simon Cameron, 6 September 1862, Instructions, Russia, Record Group 59, National Archives, Washington, D.C.
36. Norman A. Graebner, "Northern Diplomacy and European Neutrality," in *Why the North Won the Civil War*, ed. David Donald (Baton Rouge, 1960), pp. 65–75.
37. T. D. Schoonover, *Dollars over Dominion* (Baton Rouge, 1978), p. 283.

For Further Reading

Consult the notes of this chapter and the General Bibliography at the end of this book; these materials are not repeated below. Above all, use the unparalleled *Guide to American Foreign Relations since 1700*, ed. Richard Dean Burns (1983), for pre-1981 materials. The following mostly deal with post-1981 publications. The best recent overview, with excellent bibliography is Bradford Perkins, *From Sea to Sea, 1776–1865*, in *The Cambridge History of U.S. Foreign Relations*, ed. Warren Cohen (1993).

K. Jack Bauer's *Zachary Taylor* (1985), sets the stage, especially with its examination of the 1850 debates that began under Taylor's presidency. Other major biographies are Larry Gara, *The Presidency of Franklin Pierce* (1991); and William C. Davis, *Jefferson Davis* (1991). The South's drive for expansion is interestingly and well told in Charles H. Brown, *Agents of Manifest Destiny* (1980), and Robert E. May, *John A. Quitman* (1985). The scene in the West and conflict with Native Americans can be explored in Robert M. Utley's *The Indian Frontier of the American West, 1846–1890* (1984), which also has a fine bibliography. James T. Wall, *Manifest Destiny Denied* (1982), is especially good on Nicaragua in the 1850s. Key is *The Papers of Daniel Webster: Diplomatic . . . 1850–1852*, ed. K. E. Shewmaker and K. R. Stevens (1987).

The entire era, and especially 1861–1868, is beautifully explored in James M. McPherson, *Ordeal by Fire: The Civil War and Reconstruction* (1982), with a superb bibliography. Herman Hattaway and Archer Jones, *How the North Won: A Military History of the Civil War* (1983), is detailed and focuses on Grant; Richard Current's *Speaking of Abraham Lincoln* (1983) is a series of important essays by a foremost Lincoln scholar; William Appleman Williams's *Empire as a Way of Life* (1980) is a stimulating analysis that is especially important for its original view of Lincoln. Also provocative and important are Norman Ferris, "William Seward and the Faith of a Nation," in *Tradi-*

tions and Values, ed. Norman Graebner (1985), and Gordon H. Warren, *Fountain of Discontent: The Trent Affair and the Freedom of the Seas* (1981). Warren F. Spencer has provided the definitive account on the title's subject and also much on the diplomacy in *The Confederate Navy in Europe* (1983), and interesting views by scholars in India are given in T. C. Bose's "The Diplomacy of the Civil War" and Dwijendra Tripathi's "Indian Cotton and Cotton Diplomacy," both in *American History by Indian Historians*, ed. Giri S. Dikshit, 2 vols. (1969), especially volume 2. On the Mexican crisis, the leading scholar is Thomas D. Schoonover, whose *Dollars over Dominion* (1978) should now be supplemented with his edition of *Mexican Lobby: Matías Romero in Washington, 1861–1867* (1986), a fascinating account of Washington politics during the Civil War as well as of U.S.-Mexican and U.S.-European relations. Another important foreign view is in Martin Crawford, *The Anglo-American Crisis of the Mid-Nineteenth Century: "The Times" of London and America, 1850–1862* (1987).

6

Laying the Foundations for "Superpowerdom" (1865–1896)

Legacies of the Civil War

Americans emerged from the dark shadows of the Civil War as a reluctantly united nation and, in the North, as a supremely confident people. Lincoln and Seward had exerted immense military power to force the South into unconditional surrender. At the same time, they had successfully managed the most delicate of foreign policies. These triumphs consolidated U.S. power and, in the words of historian David P. Crook, allowed the nation "to continue its headlong rush into superpowerdom."[1]

But something more than northern power triumphed. An incredible new industrial and communications complex also emerged from the conflict. This complex formed the launch pad for that "rush into superpowerdom" over the next thirty years. Many of the North's businesspeople had not wanted civil war, but once the South seceded, they moved quickly to pass probusiness legislation through Congress. They also took advantage of the nearly bottomless needs of the huge northern armies to make immense profits. When the North's humiliation at the first Battle of Bull Run in mid-1861 indicated that the war would be long, one northern financier confidently predicted a fortune for every person on Wall Street "who is not a natural idiot."[2] A young U.S. businessperson of 1860 lived in a nation that produced hardly any steel and little petroleum. Just forty years later, that person lived in the land that was the world's largest steel manufacturer and dominated the world's oil markets.

The Civil War provided the running start for such triumphs. Andrew Carnegie, the greatest iron and steel baron of the era, entered business during the war. Soon after oil pools were initially found in Pennsylvania during 1859, young John D. Rockefeller began combining his first five refineries during the Civil War. As early as 1865, oil ranked sixth on the list of U.S. exports. Rockefeller had begun the Standard Oil (later Exxon) global empire. The war spurred the same dramatic development in the businesses of carriages, sugar refining, and canning.

These businesses laid the foundations on which was built the world's economic superpower of the twentieth century. Such dominance resulted in part from considerable governmental aid. For example, Carnegie reaped huge profits partly because his steel business was protected against cheaper British steel by high tariff walls. From the 1840s until 1861, low tariffs had prevailed, but once the southerners left Washington, a series of tariff measures whipped through Congress. At first, the tariffs were to produce revenue to pay for the war effort, but by 1862, business lobbyists descended on the Capitol to bribe and cajole Congress into passing tariffs that protected their businesses from foreign competition. After the war, government expenses dropped, but the tariff walls remained high. By the 1890s, U.S. business had become so powerful that it could even vault over these walls to sell abroad and thus dominate world as well as American markets.

The manufacturers could move their goods on a rail system that had amounted to 31,000 miles in 1860, but 259,000 miles in 1900. Again, war and government action accelerated growth. In acts of 1862 and 1864, Congress gave railroad companies huge chunks of public land and easy credit to build transcontinental as well as shorter rail systems. By 1872, Washington had given private railroad builders 150 million acres, or an area equal to Maine, New Hampshire, Vermont, Massachusetts, Rhode Island, Connecticut, New York, and part of Pennsylvania combined. The Union Pacific Railroad doubled its original land grant by spending almost half a million dollars to bribe Congress. But few cared about the costs, either financial or moral. One industrialist pointed out the meaning of all this for U.S. foreign policy. Because of the vast rail system, he observed, "the drills and sheetings of Connecticut, Rhode Island, and Massachusetts and other manufacturers of the United States may be transported to China in thirty days; and the teas and rich silks of China, in exchange, come back to New Orleans, to Charleston, to Washington . . . to Boston in thirty days more."[3]

Despite the millions who served in the armies, labor remained cheap for the industrialists because of increased immigration. About 800,000 immigrants arrived between 1861 and 1865. Again, the government played a crucial role in helping private business. The 1864 contract labor law allowed business firms to send agents to Europe and Asia for laborers who were willing to sail to the New World. Seward had argued that Americans were happily following the example of other great empires: "The intermingling of races always was, and always will be, the chief element of civilization . . . [and] we emulate the sway of ancient Rome."[4] As secretary of state, Seward was able to encourage the entry of cheap Chinese labor to work on his favorite project, the transcontinental railroad. In 1868, he and Anson Burlingame (a former Massachusetts congressman and U.S. minister to China who now represented the Chinese government itself) wrote the so-called Burlingame Treaty that allowed the free immigration of each country's citizens.

With the cheap labor, great rail system, government grants, low taxes, and protected market, the number of industrial establishments rocketed upward some 80 percent during the 1860s until they hit 252,000. The number of industrial laborers soared 56 percent, to over 2 million. A new United States of factories and urban areas appeared. But despite the growing number of businesses, new concentrations of power also emerged. In key industries, giant corporations such as Standard Oil, Carnegie Steel, and Singer Sewing Machine began to swallow up small, individually owned businesses. The government gave corporations the right to raise large amounts of money through sale of stocks, but each investor had only limited liability if the business went sour. This almost magical power allowed a concentration of capital unimagined before the Civil War. As the *New York Commercial and Financial Chronicle* observed in 1866, "There is an increasing tendency in our capital to move in larger masses than formerly. Small business firms compete at more disadvantage with richer houses, and are gradually being absorbed into them."[5] These "larger masses" made the U.S. economy both highly efficient and a tough new competitor for the great banking and business combines of Europe. An industrializing America moved out to fight with the old giant empires in a prizefight ring that was global.

The Context of the Era: Triumph and Tragedy

The United States became a great world power between 1865 and 1900. It did so even as Americans endured severe economic depressions and

In 1901, the Minneapolis Tribune *cartoonist caught the U.S. confidence that Americans were about to replace Europeans as the great world trading power. That confidence had begun to appear a generation earlier as the incredibly productive U.S. industrial and agricultural complexes came to dominate world markets—even in the middle of one of the worst economic depressions in history.*

widespread violence at home. Charles Dickens's opening for his novel, *A Tale of Two Cities*, perfectly applied to the United States of the post–Civil War era: "It was the best of times, it was the worst of times." It was the best of times because of the growing internal market (U.S. population more than doubled to 71 million between 1860 and 1900), the near-tripling of wheat production, the eightfold increase in coal production, the fivefold rise in steel and rail manufacturing, and the gushing of oil production by some twenty times to 55 million barrels in 1898. Total exports of all goods jumped from $281 million to $1.2 billion between 1865 and 1898, while imports rose from $239 million to $616 million. U.S. iron and steel products moved up the export list rapidly to threaten the traditional leaders—cotton and wheat.[6] Americans thus challenged Europeans for the world markets for highly profitable processed goods.

Beginning in 1874, moreover, U.S. exports regularly exceeded imports to produce a favorable balance of trade. With few exceptions (as during the economic panic of 1893–1894), the efficient Americans continued to sell more than they bought abroad—until 1971, when their comparative efficiency plummeted and they returned to their unfavorable merchandise trade balances of a century earlier. The profits gained from these post-1874 trade balances created even more efficient machines at home and fresh U.S. investments overseas.

But it was also the worst of times. In 1873, financial panic struck the country. Americans settled into a twenty-three-year-long depression that, with only a few brief upturns in the 1880s and early 1890s, became one of the most tragic in their history. Some twenty-three years of "boom" were nearly hidden in twenty-three years of "bust." For the depression was caused by the same production of U.S. factories and farms that raised the nation to the top of the slippery pole of international economic competition. Americans produced far more than they could consume. Prices consequently fell. But the increasingly mechanized industries continued to churn out more goods. Finally, laborers were put out of work in growing numbers. Strikes and riots gripped Chicago, Brooklyn, San Francisco, Cleveland, and other large cities. A perceptive British observer, Goldwin Smith, declared that "the youth of the American Republic is over; maturity, with its burdens, its difficulties, and its anxieties, has come."[7]

But even worse lay ahead. Nearly 24,000 labor strikes hit the United States between 1881 and 1900. One evolved into the Haymarket Riot of 1886, in which both strikers and police were killed in Chicago. Four supposed "anarchists" were hanged; another committed suicide. In 1894, President Grover Cleveland sent federal troops into Chicago to break up a railroad strike that had paralyzed much of the city. Not coincidentally, in 1886, the term *capitalism* had entered the American vocabulary as meaning "the concentration of wealth in the hands of the few; the power or influence of large or concentrated capital."[8]

The United States thus became a great world power as its system came under harsh attack at home. But the system was under attack because its productivity was so stunningly successful. Even with the doubling of U.S. population, certain businesses needed more and more overseas markets. The new iron and steel industry exported 15 percent of its goods by the turn of the century, sewing-machine makers 25 percent, oil refiners 57 percent of their illuminating oil. Farmers depended on volatile, unpredictable foreign markets to take as much as one-quarter of their wheat production. Between 70 and 80 percent of the cotton crop went abroad. As Russian and Argentine wheat fields enlarged in the late nineteenth century, and Egyptian and Indian cotton competed in world markets, Americans found out the hard way

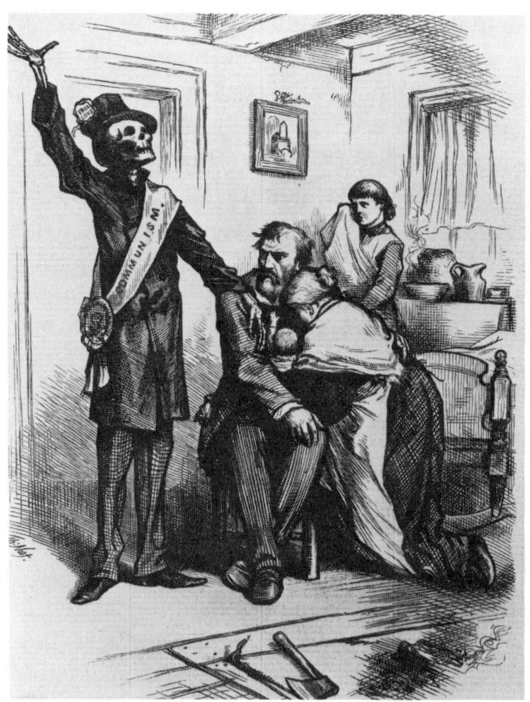

"Home, Sweet Home! There's no place like home!"
Destroyer of All: "Home ties are nothing. Family ties are nothing.
Everything that is—is nothing."

Thomas Nast did most of his drawings in the 1860s and 1870s, but he continues to rank as one of the greatest and most influential of political cartoonists. This powerful work of 1878 (just as Americans endured economic crises and a general labor strike) has two special characteristics: the depiction of a good American family trying to get along honestly, and the ghostly figure of "Communism" (with a "Free Love" button in his hat) cynically praising the home before he tries to destroy it. After the appearance of communism in the Paris Commune of 1871, most Americans hated the ideology and the social breakdown and violence associated with it. Anti-communism, as Nast shows, has deep roots in American society, especially during eras of great change.

how developments overseas directly affected their daily lives. Wheat prices received by U.S. farmers fell from $1.90 a bushel in 1860 to 57 cents in 1895. Cotton dropped below the 10-cents-a-pound break-even point to half that amount. Farmers went bankrupt, endured the agonies of moving west to find a new life, or moved their families into city tenements—all because they could not sell enough overseas.

These victims found little sympathy from their representatives in Washington. As the Civil War tariff and railway legislation vividly demonstrated, the political as well as economic system was coming under the control of the new corporate leaders. The officials who made foreign policy usually shared the views—and sometimes even the pocketbooks—of those who ruled the business community. Seward had observed that a political party was "in one sense a joint stock company in which those who contribute the most, direct the action and management of the concern." The politics were often not highly moral. But in terms of consolidating the power of the industrialists and others who shaped the new postwar United States, the politics were spectacularly effective. When Benjamin Harrison, a Republican, learned that he won the 1888 presidential election, he declared: "Providence has given us the victory." A Republican Pennsylvania political boss complained to a friend, "Think of the man. He ought to know that Providence hadn't a damn thing to do with it." Harrison "would never know how close a number of men were compelled to approach the gates of the penitentiary to make him President."[9]

The terrible shaking of the entire U.S. system between 1873 and 1897 even took some of the winners to the brink of a breakdown. John D. Rockefeller later recalled "how often I had not an unbroken night's sleep. . . . All the fortune I have made has not served to compensate for the anxiety of that period." Theodore Roosevelt, along with many others, turned for relief to "the strenuous life," as TR termed it in a famous speech of the 1890s. He urged Americans to "boldly face the life of strife" through "hard and dangerous endeavor. Oversentimentality, oversoftness . . . , and mushiness are the great danger of this age and this people," Roosevelt warned. "Unless we keep the barbarian virtues, gaining the civilized ones will be of little avail."[10] Americans took TR's advice and churned into furious activities during the 1880s and 1890s, especially in the new sports of baseball, football, and basketball. A rage for bicycle riding found men and women pedaling onto the roads. Indeed, a "new woman" appeared, one who rode bicycles, played tennis, and even attended golf clubs and racetracks. Bernarr MacFadden's *The Power and Beauty of Superb Womanhood* (1901) displayed exercises so women could have the "muscular strength" to equal the hyperactive American male.[11] Thus, many Americans found outlets in feverish activities at home—and overseas.

Much of their energy focused on finding overseas markets for the U.S. glut of goods. Business needed an efficient global foreign policy to match industry's efficient global sales networks. A leading manufacturer was quoted in 1885 as saying that business most of all needed "an intelligent and spirited foreign policy" that would "see to it" that enough overseas markets were obtained, even if the use of military force was necessary.[12] Some Americans disagreed. Led by William Jennings Bryan in the 1890s, these dissenters argued that prices and employment could be improved by coining more silver (and not just gold) so that more money would be in circulation. But even these silverites accepted the common view that more foreign markets were required. They only shrewdly added that by using more silver, Americans would be able to capture those markets in areas where silver was widely used—as in China and Latin America. When the silverites and Bryan went crashing down to defeat in the 1896 presidential election, the all-purpose solution of more overseas markets continued to dominate American thought. Four years before, in 1892, U.S. foreign trade had already exceeded that of every country in the world except Great Britain. But it was not enough.

Some businesses found a new way to capture overseas markets. In the 1880s, it became possible for the first time to speak of U.S. multinational corporations. Such leading companies as Singer Sewing Machine, McCormick farm machinery, Standard Oil, and Kodak Camera directly invested overseas so they could more easily sell their products abroad. The 1890s economic depression spurred this movement. Sherwin-Williams Paint almost literally made good on its slogan "We Cover the Earth." By 1890, worried European officials warned of an "American invasion" into their economies. Articles appeared with the titles "The Americanization of the World" and "The American Invaders" to discuss the new multinationals. The largest firms did not require government help. But smaller companies did need support from the State Department. Consequently, a revitalized U.S. Consular Service and such business groups as the National Association of Manufacturers (formed during the depths of the 1894–1895 depression) appeared to work for the ambitious multinational corporations.[13]

The largest firms often handled their own foreign policy. By the 1890s, for example, John D. Rockefeller's Standard Oil controlled 70 percent of the world's oil markets. It quadrupled its sales abroad during the 1880s. William Herbert Libby, who directed Rockefeller's overseas invasion, bragged that petroleum had "forced its way into more nooks and corners of civilized and uncivilized countries than any other product in history emanating from a single source." But the Russian oil industry, with financial support from the great Rothschild banking house of France, rose to challenge Standard Oil. Rockefeller successfully fought back. A U.S. State Department consul in the Russian oil-producing area carefully kept Standard up-to-date on the competition's movements. Rockefeller opened new refineries in central Europe. And Standard set up a subsidiary that specifically targeted its efforts to undercut Russian moves in western Europe and the Far East. Long before other Americans fought a cold war with Russia, Standard Oil executives were engaged in their own bitter conflict.[14]

A Chronology of Postwar Expansion: The Alaska Purchase and a Backlash

The U.S.-Russian confrontation, however, lay out of sight in a clouded future when Secretary of State Seward laid plans for an ambitious, post–Civil War foreign policy. Indeed, Russia, of all the major powers, seemed in 1865 to be the United States' best friend. Part of the tsar's fleet had made a dramatic, highly popular visit to the Union's ports during the Civil War—although Americans later learned (as Seward believed at the time) that the Russians actually cared less about the North's cause than finding refuge for their own ships in case of a war with the British. That war nearly occurred in the wake of a Polish uprising against Russia's rule in 1863. But Russian-American relations received a real boost in 1867, when the tsar decided to sell Alaska.

Alaska's fate had been decided by U.S. traders and merchants as early as the 1820s. By that date, the Russian Trading Company, charged with ruling and exploiting Alaska for the tsar, actually depended on U.S. sources—not Russian—for most of its necessities. By 1865–1866, the U.S. minister to St. Petersburg, Cassius Clay of Kentucky, pushed for Alaska as a route through which a U.S.-built telegraph line would link the two great countries. (The energetic fifty-six-year-old Clay worked for this project, that is, when he was not fighting off protective mothers of young girls he admired or when he was not challenging Russian nobles to duels with bowie knives.) The telegraph project was never completed, but Clay used information obtained from it to help persuade Russian officials to sell Alaska. Seward concluded the deal in Washington during March 1867. The United States agreed to buy the great expanse for $7.2 million.

But congressional opposition quickly arose. The price seemed extravagant for a frozen wasteland ("Walrussia" or "Seward's Ice Box," as Alaska became known). Seward and President Andrew Johnson, moreover, were hated by radical Republican leaders because the president wanted to bring the South back rapidly into the Union on easy terms. Seward finally triumphed for five major reasons. First, he and

OUR NEW SENATORS.

Seward's purchase of Alaska from Russia turned out to be one of the all-time real-estate bargains, but he was ridiculed in 1867. Here a cartoonist has Seward telling the Alaskan representative to "bring . . . Mr. Seal along with you [to Washington]."

the Republican Senate leader, Charles Sumner from Massachusetts, emphasized the rich Alaskan mineral and animal resources awaiting exploitation by ambitious Americans. Second, they and others stressed that the purchase meant that the United States would partially block Great Britain's and Canada's access to the Pacific—would "cage the British Lion on the Pacific Coast," in one congressman's words—and perhaps make the annexation of Canada easier. Third, Alaska and the Aleutian Islands would serve, in the phrase of Republican House leader Nathaniel P. Banks of Massachusetts, as the "drawbridge between America and Asia." The rich China and Japan trade could be reached and protected more easily by the great circle route passing from San Francisco to Alaska to Asian markets. Fourth, Russia was a good friend. By working with her, Americans could remove a possible future source of conflict and cooperate with the friend against their common enemy—Great Britain. Finally, when the House of Representatives hesitated to appropriate the $7.2 million, the Russian minister in Washington apparently distributed about $73,000 as bribes to grease the passage. Seward, moreover, had already run up the Stars and Stripes over Sitka, Alaska—which allowed one congressman to proclaim: "Shall that flag which waves so proudly there now be taken down? Palsied be the hand that would dare remove it."[15]

Seward thus added 586,000 square miles, or an area nearly two and a half times the size of Texas, to the Union. The editor of *U.S. Railroad and Mining Register* crowed that the purchase ensured American greatness in the Pacific. But more, he added, both Americans and Russians "believe that in time not far remote Washington and St. Petersburg will be the political poles of the earth. . . . Never was international friendship deeper than between America and Russia."[16] Little could the ecstatic editor imagine what lay ahead for that "friendship."

Nor, in the flush of victory, could Seward and other expansionists imagine that Alaska was to be the last U.S. landed conquest for more than a generation. Seward had been able to annex the Midway Islands (about 1,200 miles west of Hawaii) in 1867 for possible use as a way station and cable point in the Asia trade. But he failed in efforts to obtain bases in Santo Domingo, Haiti, the Central American isthmus (for a future ocean-to-ocean canal), Hawaii, Greenland, and the Danish West Indies (Denmark's Virgin Islands) in the Caribbean. Congress was more interested in questions of the South and newly freed blacks than in distant territories. Such bases, moreover, could cost money, and the nation already was burdened with a huge Civil War debt. The House of Representatives actually passed a resolution in late 1867 opposing "any further purchases of territory" because of the country's "financial condition." Many also believed the nation already had enough land. As the *Chicago Tribune* phrased it, in the vast western regions "we have already more territory than we can people in fifty years."[17]

Americans, for the first time in their history, even lost interest in immediately annexing Canada. Radical Irish-Americans—Fenians—hoped to free Ireland from British rule by moving out of Buffalo, New York, to attack Canadian territory and thus stir up a U.S.-British war. Even Seward, who long lusted after Canada, disavowed the Fenians' bloody raids. After the 1867 North America Act, in which England granted autonomy to the new Dominion of Canada, some disgruntled western Canadians rebelled against the new regime and flirted with the idea of attaching their region to the United States. But Washington officials had lost their passion for such a romance. Their attention turned inward and then focused on the critical problem of finding overseas markets for their overproductive farmers and industrialists.

A Chronology of Postwar Expansion: Winning the West

Americans obviously did not lose interest in foreign policy between the Civil War and the 1898 war. They only went about dealing with foreign policy differently. U.S. officials realized that they faced a new set of problems. The most immediate problem was settling the vast western territories that had been conquered since 1803. Such settlement was crucial for two reasons: to find new agricultural lands for the growing population and to develop the routes for the transcontinental railroads that would carry U.S. goods to Pacific ports, from which the goods could find markets in Asia.

But settlement meant that tribes of Indians had to be moved or destroyed. In this sense, the wars against the Native Americans between 1870 and 1890 marked the last step needed to unify and consolidate the United States before Americans could go abroad to become the superpower of the twentieth century. About 360,000 Indians lived west of the Mississippi in 1850. They included the powerful Sioux, Cheyennes, and Comanches. White and black Americans numbered about 20 million. In 1860, 1.5 million whites lived in the West, but by 1890

Between the Civil War and 1890, white Americans fought a seemingly continual war against the Indians to control land seized before 1848. Far from being a quiet period in American settlement, it was one of the most active—especially for the U.S. Army.

George Armstrong Custer (1839–1876) graduated at the bottom of his West Point class but fought bravely in the Civil War before leading two hundred of his troops into an Indian ambush in which he and his men were massacred. His name became synonymous with one of the few failures in nineteenth-century American expansion.

that number had multiplied six times. Native Americans had no idea that so many white people existed.

Many of the new settlers doubtless agreed with Theodore Roosevelt's view in his popular book, *The Winning of the West* (published in several volumes between 1889 and 1896), that "this great continent could not have been kept as nothing but a game preserve for squalid savages. . . . The man who puts the soil to use must of right dispossess the man who does not, or the world will come to a standstill."[18] In the early nineteenth century, Indians had been treated as "separate nations," but by 1871 Congress no longer viewed them as separate nations or made lasting treaties with them. Instead, U.S. officials simply passed laws to push Native Americans off desirable lands, created isolated reservations for the tribes, and—in the Supreme Court's words—saw the Indians not as "nations," but as "local dependent communities."

These views of Roosevelt and the government justified driving the Native Americans off their rich western lands. The victims not surprisingly struck back. Most notably they did so in 1876 at Little Bighorn in Montana, when 2,500 Sioux warriors, some with 16-shot repeating rifles, surrounded and slaughtered 260 men of George Custer's Seventh Cavalry. As later accounts described the horror, the cavalrymen were "bawling in terror, shooting themselves and each other." Then the "discovery of Custer's obliterated force: hills strewn with bloated pink, stripped, mutilated corpses and dead horses. Eyeballs and brains extracted and laid out on rocks, hearts impaled on poles."[19]

Sitting Bull (c. 1834–1890) was one of the great chiefs who resisted white American expansionism until he was captured after destroying Custer and his men at the Battle of Little Bighorn in 1876. He was made a part of a traveling Wild West show.

Between 1877 and 1890, however, such victims were usually red, not white. News of Custer's defeat reached the East as Americans celebrated the centennial of their independence. In the words of one popular magazine, they swore revenge by the time the next anniversary arrived in 1976, when nothing would remain of the "red man but a case of flint arrow-heads, stone hatchets, and moth-eaten trappings at the Smithsonian [a museum in Washington, D.C.]." Native Americans were systematically killed, starved by the extermination of the buffalo herds on which they depended for food and other needs, or pushed into desolate reservations. General Nelson A. Miles (who, in the 1898 war, headed the U.S. Army in its fight against Spain) tracked down Sitting Bull, who had destroyed Custer's forces, and the great Indian chief became an exhibit in the popular Buffalo Bill's Wild West Show. Sitting Bull later returned to his people, but a confrontation with white authorities developed, a gun discharged accidentally, and U.S. officials quickly killed the chief and seven Sioux, while the Indian's old circus horse mistook the gunfire for the Wild West Show and did tricks. The U.S. Army then surrounded another Sioux chief, Big Foot, and some 350 followers at Wounded Knee, South Dakota, reservation in 1890. Again, an accidental gunshot apparently set off full-scale firing. The U.S. troops lost 25 men (many of them victims of their own crossfire) but killed Big Foot and 150 others, including women and children.[20]

In historian Robert M. Utley's words, "The Indian frontier of the American West vanished in the smoke of Hotchkiss shells bursting over the valley of Wounded Knee Creek."[21] With the Native Americans crushed, whites settled more land in the thirty years after 1870 than they did in the previous three hundred years. Such settlement at once formed an immensely productive landed empire and a route from the East Coast to Asian markets. The U.S. Army meanwhile used the Indian wars as training for conflicts overseas. British observers thought the 25,000-man U.S. Army and its 2,000 officers one of the world's toughest fighting forces because of its battles with the Indians. Scholar Walter L. Williams has found that of the 30 U.S. generals who fought against Philippine rebels between 1898 and 1902, 26 (or 87 percent) had earned their spurs fighting Indians. Williams has also noted that the new legal terms devised after 1870 to control the Native Americans and take away many of their rights were simply transferred to Cuban, Philippine, and Puerto Rican affairs after 1898.[22] The post-1870 Indian wars were a key link between the whites' landed expansion to 1860 and their new overseas empire taken in 1898 and after.

A Chronology of Postwar Expansion: Africa and Latin America

U.S. overseas expansion had two main characteristics after 1870: it was almost entirely interested in markets (not in land), and it moved along not one but many routes to all corners of the earth. In Africa, for example, American interests had been almost nonexistent, except for the U.S.-sponsored colonization of free African Americans in Liberia that had occurred in the 1830s and 1840s. Even in Liberia, however, Washington officials refused to recognize the new nation, which declared its independence in 1847, until 1862. The slave controversy and antiblack feelings prevented recognition of the U.S.-created colony until that time. After 1862, relations remained slight.

In the 1870s, however, Commodore Robert Shufeldt led a pioneering voyage that gained new U.S. rights to coaling stations and trade in Africa and along the Persian Gulf. In 1884, private citizens who sought markets in Africa, and diplomat John Kasson, who well understood the need of fresh markets for U.S. goods, pushed Washington officials to send a delegation (led by Kasson) to participate in the Berlin Conference. This conference was called by the German government to resolve growing problems in the Congo. In that African region, the ambitions of the Belgian king, Leopold II, seemed on a collision course with other European colonial powers. The United States only wanted—and indeed obtained—a pledge by all the powers to an "open door" so that its goods could enter the Belgian Congo on fair terms. The U.S. delegation then helped Leopold block his European rivals, although the Belgian king was enforcing one of the most brutal colonial policies in all of Africa. Kasson's work at Berlin was strongly supported by the powerful Democratic senator from Alabama, John T. Morgan. Historian Joseph A. Fry, after studying Morgan's passionate expansionism, concludes that the Alabaman believed "the Congo's throngs of unclad natives seemed to offer an unlimited market" for the South's textile industry. Morgan also saw the region "as an ideal dumping ground for the South's surplus blacks."[23]

But not even Morgan's influence was enough. The new U.S. president, Grover Cleveland, took power in 1885 and disavowed Kasson's agreement because it could possibly become an entangling alliance. Five years later, U.S. opinion against Belgium was shaped by an extraordinary man. George Washington Williams had fought in the Civil War, had been a popular preacher, editor of a major black newspaper, the first African American ever elected to the Ohio legislature, and the first major black historian in the United States. After a trip to the Congo, his *Open Letter* of 1890 detailed twelve specific charges against Leopold's brutality, including enslaving "women and children" while neither educating nor economically developing the society. But even Williams could do little more than slow the growing belief of some Americans that a rich African market awaited them. By 1890, historian Milton Plesur relates, U.S. newspapers even predicted "that the whites would in time swallow up the African Negro in the same way the North American Indian had all but disappeared."[24]

The road to Latin American markets and bases seemed clearer and was certainly a more traditional path for U.S. expansion. In 1870, President Ulysses S. Grant tried to annex Santo Domingo partly at the request of several friends who had some highly corrupt business projects in that Caribbean country. Grant also wanted to ensure that no other power could control the country. He justified annexation in part by arguing that it would help quiet racial problems at home: Santo Domingo could support "the entire colored population of the United States, should it choose to emigrate." Americans' racism had usually restrained their expansionist impulses into the Caribbean, but the president now tried to turn racism into a reason for expansionism. He ran into a buzz saw of opposition. The powerful Sumner (who before the Civil War had been an Abolitionist on the slave issue), argued that as "an Anglo-Saxon Republic" the United States must not take in "colored communities" where the "black race was predominant." Secretary of State Hamilton Fish also opposed annexation in part for racial reasons. Maria Child, for forty years a vigorous opponent of U.S. expansionism (see p. 105), fought the president with quite different arguments. Child compared Grant's grab to a pre–Civil War "filibustering project." She feared that "this Republic will sink rapidly to degeneracy and ruin if we go on thus seizing the territory of our neighbors by fraud or force."[25] Grant finally gave up his plans, but he announced in 1870 that henceforth the Monroe Doctrine contained a new principle: "Hereafter no territory on this continent shall be regarded as subject to transfer to a European power." This "nontransfer" principle had appeared as early as 1811, when President James Madison applied it to Florida. But Grant's declaration first made the principle a formal part of the Monroe Doctrine.

Another, more promising chance to seize new territory occurred in Cuba. The Cubans had begun a revolution against decaying Spanish control in 1868. Some U.S. lives and property were lost in the fighting, but the major crisis arose in 1873, when Spain seized the *Virginius*, a ship under the U.S. flag that was carrying weapons to the rebels. The Spanish executed fifty-three crew members. Cries went up in the United States for revenge—that is, for taking Cuba. But Grant's cool-headed secretary of state, Hamilton Fish, knew that the ship had been breaking the law. Fish and other officials, moreover, wanted no part of the multiracial Cuban population. When one cabinet member raised the possibility of annexing Cuba, Fish squashed the idea by noting the terrible racial problems already existing in "South Carolina and Mississippi." Spain paid an $80,000 indemnity for the lives of the crew members. By 1878, it had been able to stop the revolution, but it had been a close call. Maria Child concluded, "I do believe if we could annex the whole world, we should [then] try to get a quarrel with Saturn, in order to snatch his ring from him."[26]

U.S. attention next turned to Central America. It focused on a new grave danger: in the late 1870s, the French began building an isthmian canal in Panama (a province of Colombia). The project directly threatened the 1850 Clayton-Bulwer agreement between the United States and Great Britain for joint construction of such a passageway. More pointedly, the French enterprise endangered the growing determination of Americans to build the canal by themselves. Seward had nearly obtained such a right from Colombia in 1869, only to have the Colombian legislature reject the treaty. When the French began their digging, the U.S. government warned sharply that it would never "consent to the surrender of this control [over an isthmian canal] to any Euro-

"The Plumed Knight from Maine" (nicely caught in this portrait), James G. Blaine (1830–1893) was secretary of state twice (1881 and 1889–1892), a defeated Republican presidential candidate (1884), and—of special importance—a skilled politician who understood the needs of the new American industrial complex and preached the need for U.S.–Latin American economic ties. Blaine foresaw U.S. relations with the Latin nations much as Seward foresaw U.S. relations with Asia in the twentieth century.

pean power or combination of powers." Secretary of State James G. Blaine entered office in 1881 and opened talks about building a canal in Nicaragua—as if the 1850 treaty did not exist. For most Americans the Clayton-Bulwer Treaty indeed did not exist. As one phrased it, Americans refused "to be bound hand and foot" by that "covenant of national disgrace." The French effort finally failed in the 1880s, a victim of enormous engineering problems as well as of the deadly mosquito-carried yellow fever. It was only a matter of time before Americans would try on their own. Indeed, during these years U.S. military forces landed in Panama half a dozen times to restore order and protect American citizens threatened by armed uprisings against the Colombian government. The turn toward an ocean-to-ocean canal owned and operated by the United States occurred in the 1870s and 1880s, long before it was realized in Panama in 1903.[27]

Blaine personally exemplified the new U.S. approach to Latin America. A power in the Republican party (he was its presidential nominee in 1884), the "Plumed Knight from Maine" understood the needs of the fast-developing U.S. industrial system and the business leaders who built it—and who also contributed handsomely to his Republican party. As secretary of state, in 1881 he declared that his foreign policy must bring peace to, then increase U.S. trade in, Latin America. "To attain the second object the first must be accomplished," Blaine concluded. That conclusion meant more vigorous American intervention to ensure a secure marketplace. In 1890, again serving as secretary of state, Blaine spelled out his policy. His statement, which is a lesson in American history as well as diplomacy, serves as a summary of U.S. economic policy toward Latin America from 1865 until the late twentieth century:

> I wish to declare the opinion that the United States has reached a point where one of its highest duties is to enlarge the area of its foreign trade. Under the beneficent policy of [tariff] protection we have developed a volume of manufactures which, in many departments, overruns the demands of the home market. In the field of agriculture, with the immense propulsion given in it by agricultural implements, we can do far more than produce breadstuffs and provisions for our own people. . . . Our great demand is expansion. I mean expansion of trade with countries where we can find profitable exchanges. We are not seeking annexation of territory. At the same time I think we should be unwisely content if we did not seek to engage in what the younger Pitt so well termed annexation of trade.[28]

In 1889, the year before that speech, Blaine had called and then presided over the First International American Conference. He sought a customs union (a kind of vast, inter-American common market) and even a common currency to expedite U.S. exports southward. Blaine obtained neither objective, but the meeting did lead to the building of the Pan-American Highway system, linking the United States to nations in South America. The gathering also marked the beginning of the Pan-American movement that brought North and South Americans closer culturally and economically. Blaine's success helped lead, in 1890, to the first significant "reciprocity" tariff passed by the U.S. Congress. This legislation allowed certain Latin American products (especially coffee, hides, and sugar) to enter the United States freely as long as the nations that produced them allowed U.S. exports into their countries equally free from tariff restrictions. Under the 1890 reciprocity treaties, trade immediately boomed with Cuba and Brazil, among others.

Indeed, U.S. exports to Brazil rose $500,000 in three years, while imports from that country increased by an amazing $17 million. Then, in 1893, the friendly republican government in Brazil was threatened by an uprising led by promonarchical Brazilian naval units and encouraged by the British and other European powers. The U.S. administration of President Cleveland at first tried to remain neutral. But when U.S. exporters (including the Standard Oil Company) warned Cleveland that their trade could be endangered by a rebel victory, the president ordered naval units to protect U.S. shippers who wanted to unload goods in Brazilian ports. This order directly aided the government in the capital of Rio de Janeiro, because the government depended on revenue paid on the unloaded goods. Cleveland's action thus broke the back of the rebellion and protected the growing North American trade. When one rebel vessel challenged the U.S. warships escorting American merchantmen to the harbors, a U.S. warship fired a shell across the Brazilian vessel's bow and warned that any further challenge would result in the sinking of the rebel ship. The rebellion quickly ended. The grateful Brazilian government erected a statue to James Monroe, celebrated the Fourth of July, and even organized a serenade for the U.S. minister in Rio de Janeiro.[29]

Thus, the U.S. need to find more markets abroad had led to direct interference in internal Brazilian affairs. The story was less happy, but the conclusion much the same, when a rebellion threatened the pro-U.S. government in Chile during 1891. The U.S. minister, Patrick Egan, was a rambunctious Irishman who had the touch to be a successful politician in the United States but not a suave diplomat in Chile. His public support of the Chilean government led a mob to kill two U.S. sailors who were on shore leave in Valparaíso from the USS *Baltimore*. President Benjamin Harrison, a former Civil War hero, took a tougher line than even Egan and demanded an apology and indemnity. But Chile refused to pay for the mob's acts. As Harrison's anger grew, the two countries edged toward war. Some worried U.S. observers noted that Chile's navy was actually larger than the U.S. fleet, which had been allowed to rot after the Civil War. Blaine, in one of his last acts, and a new Chilean government then moved to cool the crisis. Chile finally paid an indemnity of $75,000 for the killing of the sailors.

The Chilean and Brazilian affairs displayed the new, active interventionism of the United States in Latin America. But nowhere did this vigorous policy appear more dramatically than in Venezuela during 1895–1896. For in that crisis, Washington officials challenged Great Britain, the world's leading power.

The showdown had begun long before, in the 1840s, when British policy makers claimed disputed territory lying between Venezuela and their colony of British Guiana. Little more happened, however, until the 1890s, when the British began to reassert their claim. Worried U.S. officials noted that the disputed land controlled the entry into the Orinoco, a vast waterway that could provide access to trade for a large section of South America. Rumors of rich mineral wealth in the region also appeared. President Cleveland especially focused on the British threat to the Monroe Doctrine. In 1895, he demanded that the London government of Lord Salisbury arbitrate the claim. Salisbury, one of Europe's great statesmen, was busy with Germany's threat to British interests in South Africa. He ignored Cleveland's message.

Infuriated, the president ordered his secretary of state, Richard Olney, to restate the U.S. position forcefully so that Salisbury would pay attention. Olney did so in a historic note of July 20, 1895. It claimed that the United States could enforce the Monroe Doctrine because the nation was now supreme in the Western Hemisphere. A surprised Salisbury became aware that his country and Cleveland's were rushing toward a conflict. He refused to recognize the legality of the Monroe Doctrine but did implicitly recognize Olney's spread-eagle claim that the "infinite resources [of the United States] combined with its isolated position render it master of the situation and practically invulnerable as against any or all other powers," as Olney had stated it in the note.[30] Salisbury agreed to arbitrate the dispute, and Venezuela indeed received the land controlling the Orinoco. The British prime minister finally bowed to U.S. demands because the gravest threat to his nation's interests came not in the New World, but from a rising Germany (especially the growing German fleet) and from explosive imperialistic rivalries with the French and Germans in Africa. Faced with those dangers, Salisbury shrewdly laid a foundation for Anglo-American friendship by agreeing to arbitrate the less important Venezuelan boundary.

For their part, Americans also replaced long-held British interests in Nicaragua during the 1890s. Indeed, throughout Central America—a region that London's power had shaped for half a century—U.S. companies and military power became overwhelming. By 1900, the United Fruit Company of Boston dominated Costa Rica's and Guatemala's economies. Soon, United Fruit's control of Central American affairs reached a point where the company was simply called "The Octopus." Sam "The Banana Man" Zamurray of New Orleans gained control of Honduras's economy after 1900, until that country became known as a banana republic. As early as the 1880s, a Guatemalan official recognized that the United States had become "the natural protector of the integrity of Central American territory."[31] But these moves into Central America only formed part of a larger expansionism that transformed the United States into the dominant power in the hemisphere between 1865 and 1896. Even Lord Salisbury had to admit the new extent of that power.

A Chronology of Postwar Expansion: The Pacific and Asia

When U.S. naval officers claimed the Midway Islands (so named because they were halfway between California and Japan) for the United States in 1867, they triggered a thirty-three-year surge of westward expansion over the Pacific Ocean. In 1867, Americans were trying to rebuild from the ruins of their civil war. By 1900, they had an army on the Asian mainland and had conquered a string of bases across the broad Pacific that linked that mainland to the United States.

The magnificent Hawaiian Islands were the first stop. As early as 1843, so many U.S. traders and missionaries worked there that wary British and French officials asked the United States to sign a treaty guaranteeing Hawaii's independence. The Americans not only refused, but a decade later tried to annex the islands—a move foiled by British opposition as well as by the growing division in Washington over the slavery and expansion issues. In 1867, Seward reopened the campaign to annex by shrewdly trying to seduce Hawaii into the U.S. orbit through a reciprocity treaty. Again, internal U.S. political fighting stopped Seward's move, but in 1875 Grant and Fish did negotiate such a trade treaty. The results were all that expansionists such as Seward and Grant could have desired. With the rich U.S. market at their disposal, Hawaiian planters, between 1876 and 1885, raised their sugar production from 26 million pounds to 171 million pounds. The planters utterly depended on the mainland as their exports to the United States quadrupled to $8.9 million in those ten years. By 1881, Blaine could call the islands "a part of the productive and commercial system of the American states."[32]

President Cleveland, mistakenly labeled by some historians as an antiexpansionist, worked hard to renew the reciprocity treaty in 1885. But domestic U.S. sugar interests hated Hawaiian competition and so opposed the agreement. The Hawaiians further sweetened the deal by giving the United States a lease on Pearl Harbor, an undeveloped but potentially spectacular naval base. Cleveland termed the islands "the stepping-stone to the growing trade of the Pacific." That phrase captured exactly how he and other officials saw Hawaii as a gateway to the great Asian commerce.[33] The Hawaiians, however, were soon shocked by the 1890 reciprocity treaties that allowed cheap Cuban sugar into U.S. markets. The islands' economy began sinking. By this time, the Americans who controlled the plantations also controlled the poli-

Queen Liliuokalani (1838–1917) was a determined and shrewd leader of her Hawaiian peoples. But in the early 1890s, she was unable to reverse the growing U.S. power on the islands, and in 1893 a coup, supported by the U.S. Navy, in effect ended her power despite President Cleveland's refusal to annex Hawaii at that point.

tics. They had demanded a constitution in 1887 that recognized their power. By the early 1890s, however, a strong-minded native monarch, Queen Liliuokalani, moved to neutralize the Americans' influence. Her attempt to reclaim power for the Hawaiians combined with the economic troubles to produce an American-led rebellion against her in January 1893. Washington's minister to Hawaii, John L. Stevens, actively helped by landing U.S. naval units to aid the rebels.

But now, Cleveland (just returned to the White House for a second term of 1893–1897) rejected the plea by the Americans in Hawaii for annexation. He knew the native Hawaiians had been coerced by U.S. force. Moreover, the president doubted that the U.S. Constitution could work when stretched across thousands of miles of water and imposed on such a non-Caucasian society. Cleveland also had enough problems at home. The 1893 stock-market collapse marked the lowest and most dangerous point in the twenty-five-year depression that had begun in 1873. But time was on the side of the pro-annexation group. Hawaii depended on U.S. markets. That dependence was tightened by an 1894 tariff bill restoring a favored place for the islands in the U.S. market. A new administration and new chance for a Pacific empire in 1898 finally allowed for the annexation of the islands. The annexation climaxed the expansionist drive that had begun more than half a century before.

The next stepping stone across the Pacific was Samoa. These beautiful islands, populated by Polynesians, had long served as an important stopping place for whaling vessels and traders (hence their early name, Navigators Islands). By the 1870s, their strategic location had attracted British and German attention. Into that rivalry stepped U.S. Naval Commander R. W. Meade. In 1871, Meade took the initiative to give Samoan chiefs American protection in return for their giving him a lease on the fine harbor of Pago Pago. The U.S. Senate did not accept that pact, but it ratified a similar treaty in 1878. Within a decade, the three Western powers were bitterly immersed in conflict over Samoa. By 1887, Cleveland's secretary of state, Thomas F. Bayard, asked for a conference before war possibly erupted. Bayard, a Delaware patrician with long political experience in an industrializing America, actually saw Samoa as an extension of the U.S. transcontinental railroad that carried U.S. goods to Asian markets. German Foreign Office officials angrily muttered that Bayard was extending the principles of "the Monroe Doctrine as though the Pacific Ocean were to be treated as an American lake."[34]

In 1887, Germany and Britain attempted to cut a deal over Samoa that threatened U.S. claims. Bayard refused to recognize the deal. At the same time, Germany began to bar U.S. meat imports (especially pork) on the grounds that they were tainted by a dangerous parasite. German-American relations, hardly in existence a generation before, suddenly became an intense rivalry over trade rights and access to the distant Pacific islands. The great German chancellor, Otto von Bismarck, had enough worries maintaining the new Germany that he had pieced together since 1860 through conquests and diplomacy. Wanting no war with Great Britain or the United States, in 1889 he called a conference in Berlin to discuss Samoa. Just before the meeting, a hurricane destroyed German and U.S. lives and vessels on the islands. Against this somber background, the Germans, British, and Americans agreed to divide the islands among themselves into a tripartite protectorate. They merely paid lip service to the Samoans' independence.

In 1899, the United States again found itself in a struggle with Germany and Great Britain over control of Samoan politics. British attention, however, was soon drawn off to that country's war in South Africa. London officials finally gave up all claims to Samoa. Germany and the United States then divided the islands between themselves, with the Americans retaining Pago Pago. The ending was peaceful, but, as historian Manfred Jonas observes, Germany, while giving in to U.S. claims, now viewed America as a rival. The Americans feared that German expansionism in Samoa might spread to the Caribbean. During this era, therefore, a "great transformation"[35] (as Jonas calls it) of the normally friendly U.S.-German relations began to strain the ties between Washington and Berlin. Within another generation, that strain would lead to war.

With the 1899 agreement on Samoa, the United States had added another key section in its bridge to Asia. The final destination was the Asian mainland itself, the quest of U.S. traders and missionaries for more than a century. Again, Seward had pointed the way. Since the 1840s, Americans had worked for an "open door" (that is, equality) for their trade in Asia. They did so, however, largely through "scavenger diplomacy"—coming behind the British Lion and taking from Asians whatever the Lion had left behind after its conquests. Seward dramatically changed that approach. In 1863 in Japan, and again in 1866 in Korea, the secretary of state worked alongside the British and French in their attempts to gain concessions. Thus, Seward added two new tactics to U.S. diplomacy in Asia: a willingness to use force, and a willingness to work with European powers to expand Western interests in Asia. These tactics shaped Washington's Asian diplomacy for the next eighty years.

Seward's policy, however, also created a problem—indeed, a contradiction—that bedeviled U.S. policy toward China over those next eighty years. For, in 1868, he signed with China's representative, Anson Burlingame, a treaty that allowed free immigration between the two nations. The agreement also pledged the United States not "to intervene in the domestic administration of China in regard to the construction of railroads, telegraphs, or other material internal improvements." Seward thus recognized China's control over its own internal development. But he refused to give up any claims on China's trade that might be made by the Western powers. While the United States thus recognized China's control of certain domestic affairs, it refused to recognize China as a fully sovereign country in control of its foreign commercial affairs. A month before he died in 1870, Burlingame wrote, "Let us try once, at least, to see what the Chinese will do if let alone by those who would Christianize them with gunpowder." Burlingame's hope was not to be realized. As his biographer, David L. Anderson, writes, Burlingame hoped to use the 1868 treaty to "replace coercion with cooperation" in U.S.-Chinese relations.[36] Instead, the United States merely mentioned Chinese sovereignty while working ever more closely with European powers to control Chinese affairs.

Seward especially got tough with Korea, the "Hermit Kingdom," over which China tried to claim control. Korea was strategically important, for it was at the gateway to the markets and raw materials of

Manchuria and northern China, as well as to eastern Russia itself. When the crew of the U.S. ship *General Sherman* mistakenly made its way into a Korean river, it was slaughtered by outraged Koreans. Seward quickly used his two new tactics. He prepared a U.S. naval attack, and asked the French to cooperate. But France, which had also lost citizens to Korean retaliation, refused to go along. In 1871, the Grant administration finally dispatched a fleet of five U.S. ships up the Han River. When Koreans fired on the ships, the Americans destroyed forts and killed more than two hundred people. Twelve Americans were killed, and the United States remained without any treaty with the tough Koreans. In 1876, Japan entered the scene by recognizing Korean independence from China. Korea now became a prize to be fought over by Japan and the Western powers.

The United States again took up the fight in 1882, when Commodore Robert Shufeldt forced Korea to sign a treaty opening itself to the Western world. An ardent expansionist, Shufeldt colorfully expressed his vision for American destiny in the Pacific:

> The Pacific is the ocean bride of America—China and Japan and Corea—with their innumerable islands, hanging like necklaces about them, are the bridesmaids, California is the nuptial couch, the bridal chamber, where all the wealth of the Orient will be brought to celebrate the wedding. Let us as Americans—let us determine while yet in our power, that no commercial rival or hostile flag can float with impunity over the long swell of the Pacific sea. . . . It is on this ocean that the East and the West have thus come together, reaching the point where search for Empire ceases and human power attains its climax.[37]

But the "bridesmaids"—Korea and China—were soon violated by Japan. The United States could do little about it. Americans certainly were concerned as Japanese power grew. Led by an extraordinary U.S. diplomat, Horace Allen, American interests in Korea temporarily increased. Allen, who nicely combined his Presbyterian missionary dedication with a robber-baron passion for making money, helped Americans develop Korean gold mines (perhaps the richest in Asia) and bribed authorities to obtain streetcar construction contracts.[38] But the U.S. attempt to split Korea from China backfired. Japan was the region's developing power, and it rightly saw Korea as vital to its own security.

As tension built between the rising Japanese and the declining Chinese empires, war finally erupted in 1894. Japan quickly forced China to quit Korea as well as give in to other demands. The Asian balance of power had shifted. Allen's and other U.S. enterprises were endangered by Japan. A prophetic U.S. senator, Anthony Higgins of Delaware, warned that when China "shall have arisen out of her defeat," she was likely to become the dominant military force of the globe. But most U.S. officials agreed with Secretary of State Walter Quintin Gresham in 1894: Japan was "the most civilized country" in Asia and, as such, could be trusted to respect the United States "as her best friend."[39] The friendship seemed to be reinforced strongly by trade. U.S. exports to China jumped from $3 million in 1890 to $7 million in 1896, but exports to Japan grew from $5 million to $8 million in those years. (The $22 million of imports from China in 1896 and $26 million of goods imported from Japan that year far outstripped U.S. exports to those two nations.)

The 1865-to-1896 Era: A Conclusion

The race for the riches of Asia was accelerating. The race for dominance in Latin America, however, had ended. The United States had won that contest by 1896. This historic victory and the growth of American power in Asia signaled fundamental changes in U.S. diplomacy between 1865 and 1896, changes that shaped diplomacy throughout the twentieth century.

Most notably, the friends and enemies of 1865 exchanged places by the 1890s. During the century after 1776, the United States and England had fought two wars. Another conflict threatened during and after the Civil War, when the British built several ships, including the *Alabama*, for use by the Confederacy. After the war, infuriated Americans, led by Senator Charles Sumner, demanded that London pay millions for the damages that the ships had caused—or, as some Americans indicated, the annexation of Canada, which would be equally satisfactory as payment. As Anglo-American relations grew tense in the late 1860s, President Grant, who had come to despise the pompous Sumner, maneuvered the senator off the chairmanship of the powerful Foreign Relations Committee and made a deal with England. In the 1872 Washington Treaty, the British essentially apologized for releasing the *Alabama* and agreed to pay $15.5 million in the so-called *Alabama* claims. The United States, in turn, agreed to submit other disputes to arbitration. As a result of this agreement and long-held British claims against Americans, the United States finally paid England $7.4 million. Both U.S. and Canadian citizens gained free access to the St. Lawrence, St. John, and Yukon rivers, and also to Lake Michigan.[40]

In 1893, U.S. and British diplomats settled a long-festering dispute over the killing of female seals in the Bering Sea. The slaughter was destroying herds that provided rich, highly profitable furs. The United States, moreover, claimed control over the Bering Sea itself. Washington officials finally had to drop that claim, but in 1892–1893 Russians and Japanese, as well as Canadians, agreed with the American demand to protect the seals.

With these agreements of 1872 and 1892–1893, the air cleared between London and Washington. U.S.-British relations also were built on marriages of the children of American robber barons, who sought respectability, to those of British aristocrats, who sought dollars. But of special importance, in the Venezuelan crisis of 1895–1896, the British in fact recognized U.S. dominance in the Western Hemisphere, while in Asia the two English-speaking peoples shared a common commitment to the "open door" to China. Theodore Roosevelt caught this historic turn in 1898 when he wrote a friend: "I feel very strongly that the English-speaking peoples are now closer together than for a century and a quarter . . . ; for their interests are really fundamentally the same, and they are far more closely akin, not merely in blood, but in feeling and principle, than either is akin to any other people in the world."[41]

At the same time, however, relations with Russia, a long-time U.S. ally, turned worse. The tsars and the British monarchs were rivals, especially in the Near and Far East. As U.S.-British relations warmed, U.S.-Russian relations cooled. In Asia, the Russians, lagging far behind British and American industrial development, could not survive in an open-door type of economic competition. They favored outright colonization, which was precisely the policy the open-door approach opposed. Of special importance to many Americans, the tsar launched vicious attacks on Russian Jews in the 1880s. These pogroms, which had deep roots in the nation's history, occurred just as millions of European Jews migrated to seek opportunities in the United States. The attacks also appeared as many U.S. businessmen, including Jews, suffered discrimination when they tried to do business in Russia. U.S. opinion changed radically. "Russia's ambition is sleepless and insatiable," a Baltimore newspaper editor proclaimed in 1886. "It goes ahead step by step, through intrigue, through treachery, through diplomatic mendacity," and she cares not if "her people remain poor." The powerful Louisville newspaper publisher, Henry Watterson, put it simply: the

Russian had "proven his ability to fight like the European, and to deceive like the Asiatic."[42]

This historic switch in their international friendships was mirrored at home, when Americans realized in the 1890s that they had reached a turning point in their domestic life. The 1890 Census announced that the frontier line had finally disappeared. A young University of Wisconsin historian, Frederick Jackson Turner, explored the meaning of the Census finding. He did so in perhaps the most influential essay ever written on American history. In 1893, Turner argued that the U.S. economy and politics had been vigorous and successful because of the frontier. ("Economic power," Turner stated, in fact "secures political power.") The frontier had also produced "individualism" in the American character. Turner then had to conclude with a dramatic warning: "And now, four centuries from the discovery of America, at the end of a hundred years of life under the Constitution, the frontier has gone, and with its going has closed the first period of American history."[43]

To many Americans, the question now became: What can we find to replace the frontier so our economy, politics, and individualism can remain strong? That question took on a special urgency as strikes, riots, political radicalism, and bankruptcy struck the United States during the economic depression of the 1890s. Turner himself argued in 1896 that the frontier's disappearance created "demands for a vigorous foreign policy . . . and for the extension of American influence to outlying islands and adjoining countries."[44]

That conclusion had already been reached by Captain Alfred Thayer Mahan, who became perhaps the most influential military strategist in U.S. history. In 1886, Mahan was a bored, middle-aged naval officer. Then in a Lima, Peru, library he read that ancient Rome's control of the sea had secured its empire. Over the next quarter-century, in a series of widely read books and in lectures at the Naval War College in Newport, Rhode Island, Mahan built on that insight into Rome to construct a global foreign policy for the United States. He assumed that American surplus production required overseas markets. In order to obtain and protect those markets, the United States needed a great navy and fueling bases as rest stops for that navy. Beginning in 1886—and especially in 1890, when the first modern U.S. battleship was commissioned (and also the year when Mahan's first great book *The Influence of Sea Power upon History, 1660–1783,* appeared)—Americans built the Great White Fleet that fought the 1898 war and formed the basis of the twentieth-century U.S. Navy. Mahan pushed hard to annex an isthmian canal area, as well as bases in the Caribbean, Hawaii, and

Alfred Thayer Mahan (1840–1914) was a friend of presidents and emperors because he knew how to use history to justify expansionism and the building of great navies. His seriousness, stiffness, discipline, and self-esteem are indicated in this portrait.

the distant Pacific to serve the fleet. He focused on the markets of Asia as the supreme prize.

To conquer that prize, he advised the United States to work with Great Britain and Japan (other seagoing powers who wanted the open door), and oppose Russia (a land-based power who opposed the open door). As a devout Christian, he believed that the seeking of this empire was "the calling of God." To do God's work, Mahan demanded a centralized government and powerful president. He blasted the democratic legacy of Thomas Jefferson, who "made a hideous mess in his own day, and yet has a progeny of backwoodsmen and planters who think what he taught a great success." Force was to be used freely, especially force in the form of large battleship fleets. The mere threat of such force, Mahan believed, prevented war. Anyway, he wrote, war had become merely "an occasional excess, from which recovery is easy."[45] Mahan enormously influenced U.S. officials, especially Presidents William McKinley and Theodore Roosevelt.

Other U.S. naval officers worked for a great navy because, in historian Peter Karsten's words, of "rank, discipline, and boredom."[46] Needing ships and action to gain personal promotion, they lobbied hard in Congress to build a new fleet with the most modern weapons. In 1883, the U.S. Navy was a pitiful collection of 90 woeful ships, 38 made of wood. Mahan and other officers, such as Mahan's mentor at the Naval War College, Stephen B. Luce, worked with Congress and such industrial giants as Bethlehem Steel and Andrew Carnegie to construct a great navy. It marked the success of the first military-industrial complex.[47] U.S. government dollars put laborers to work during the depression. Carnegie and other builders profited from highly subsidized government contracts.

The navy's officers obtained their fleet. And, in 1898, the United States moved to obtain what historian Frederick Drake calls "the empire of the seas."[48]

Notes

1. David P. Crook, *Diplomacy during the American Civil War* (New York, 1975), p. 9.
2. Arthur C. Cole, *The Irrepressible Conflict, 1850–1865* (New York, 1934), p. 345.
3. Charles A. Beard and Mary Beard, *The Rise of American Civilization,* 2 vols. (New York, 1927), II, pp. 128–129.
4. William H. Seward, *The Works of William H. Seward,* ed. George Baker, 5 vols. (Boston, 1853–1883), III, pp. 498–499.
5. Thomas C. Cochran and William Miller, *The Age of Enterprise* (New York, 1942), p. 116.
6. David M. Pletcher, "Growth and Diplomatic Adjustment," in *Economics and World Power,* ed. William H. Becker and Samuel F. Wells (New York, 1984), pp. 120–124. For the agricultural side, the pioneering account is William Appleman Williams, *The Roots of the Modern American Empire* (New York, 1969).
7. Robert V. Bruce, *1877: Year of Violence* (Indianapolis, 1959), pp. 312–314.
8. Henry Nash Smith, *Mark Twain's Fable of Progress* (New Brunswick, N.J., 1964), pp. 8–9.
9. Cochran and Miller, p. 157.
10. David Healy, *U.S. Expansionism: The Imperialist Urge in the 1890s* (Madison, Wis., 1970), p. 115.
11. John Higham, "The Reorientation of American Culture in the 1890s," in *The Origins of Modern Consciousness,* ed. John Weiss (Detroit, 1965), pp. 26, 28.

12. Ralph Dewar Bald, Jr., "The Development of Expansionist Sentiment in the United States, 1885–1895, as Reflected in Periodical Literature" (Ph.D. diss., University of Pittsburgh, 1953), 266–267.
13. Mira Wilkins, *The Emergence of the Multinational Corporation* (Cambridge, Mass., 1970), pp. 68–69, 71.
14. Ralph W. Hidy and Muriel E. Hidy, *Pioneering in Big Business, 1882–1911: A History of Standard Oil* (New York, 1955), pp. 122–154.
15. Ronald Jensen tells the story well in *The Alaska Purchase and Russian-American Relations* (Seattle, 1975); see also Foster Rhea Dulles, *Prelude to World Power: American Diplomatic History, 1860–1900* (New York, 1965), pp. 53–56, and Fred H. Harrington, *Fighting Politician: Major General N. P. Banks* (Philadelphia, 1948), pp. 182–185.
16. *U.S. Railroad and Mining Register*, 6 April 1867, in "Alaska, 1867–1869" file, Papers of William H. Seward, University of Rochester, Rochester, New York.
17. Donald M. Dozer, "Anti-Expansionism during the Johnson Administration," *Pacific Historical Review* 12 (September 1943): 255–256; Charles S. Campbell, *The Transformation of American Foreign Relations, 1865–1900* (New York, 1976), p. 17. Seward and U.S. investors nevertheless moved significantly into Mexican affairs. Their important story is well told in Thomas Schoonover, *Dollars over Dominion* (Baton Rouge, 1978), pp. 252–254, 282–283 esp.
18. A superb analysis is Walter L. Williams, "U.S. Indian Policy and the Debate over Philippine Annexation," *Journal of American History* 66 (March 1980): 816; also Robert M. Utley, *The Indian Frontier of the American West, 1846–1890* (Albuquerque, 1984), p. 14.
19. Quoted in *Washington Post Book World*, 18 November 1984, p. 14; *Washington Post*, 29 December 1986, p. A3. A classic account is Stanley Vestal's *War-Path and Council Fire* (New York, 1948) on the Plains Indians.
20. Utley, pp. 186, 201, 251–257.
21. *Ibid.*, p. 261.
22. Williams, "U.S. Indian Policy," 828; Vestal, p. xi, quotes the British expert.
23. Joseph A. Fry, "John Tyler Morgan's Southern Expansionism," *Diplomatic History* 9 (Fall 1985): 329–346.
24. *The Gilded Age, a Reappraisal*, ed. H. Wayne Morgan (Syracuse, 1963), p. 167; Williams's story is beautifully told in John Hope Franklin, *George Washington Williams, a Biography* (Chicago, 1985), esp. pp. 202–203, 234–241.
25. Alexander DeConde, *Ethnicity, Race, and American Foreign Policy* (Boston, 1992), p. 46; Edward P. Crapol, "Lydia Maria Child: Abolitionist Critic of American Foreign Policy," in *Women and American Foreign Policy*, ed. E. Crapol (Westport, Conn., 1987), p. 13.
26. Richard H. Bradford's *The Virginius Affair* (Boulder, Col., 1980) is a fine account.
27. David Pletcher, *The Awkward Years* (Columbia, Mo., 1962), p. 105; Dulles, pp. 37–38; Campbell, pp. 15–18; Robert A. Friedlander, "A Reassessment of Roosevelt's Role in the Panamanian Revolution of 1903," *Western Political Quarterly* 14 (June 1961): 538–539.
28. James G. Blaine, *Political Discussions, Legislative, Diplomatic, and Popular, 1856–1886* (Norwich, Conn., 1887), p. 411; *New York Tribune*, 30 August 1890, p. 1.
29. The story is told and footnoted in Walter LaFeber, *The New Empire* (Ithaca, N.Y., 1963), pp. 210–218.

30. Richard Olney to Thomas F. Bayard, 20 July 1895, in *Foreign Relations of the United States, 1895*, 2 vols. (Washington, D.C., 1896), I, pp. 545–562; the classic account is Dexter Perkins's *The Monroe Doctrine, 1867–1907* (Baltimore, 1937), pp. 153–168.
31. Pletcher, *Awkward Years*, pp. 35–36.
32. *Foreign Relations of the United States, 1881* (Washington, D.C., 1882), pp. 635–639; Donald M. Dozer, "Opposition to Hawaiian Reciprocity, 1876–1888," *Pacific Historical Review* 14 (June 1945): 157–183.
33. *A Compilation of the Messages and Papers of the Presidents, 1789–1897*, ed. James D. Richardson, 10 vols. (Washington, D.C., 1900), VIII, pp. 500–501.
34. Quoted in LaFeber, p. 55.
35. Manfred Jonas, *The United States and Germany* (Ithaca, N.Y. 1984), pp. 48–49.
36. David L. Anderson, "Anson Burlingame: American Architect of the Cooperative Policy in China, 1861–1871," *Diplomatic History* 1 (Summer 1977): 239–256.
37. Quoted, with excellent analysis, in Frederick G. Drake, *The Empire of the Seas: A Biography of Rear-Admiral Robert N. Shufeldt* (Honolulu, 1984), p. 116.
38. The extraordinary story of Horace Allen is superbly told in Fred H. Harrington's *God, Mammon, and the Japanese* (Madison, Wis., 1944). Harrington published a reconsideration forty-two years later: "An American View of Korean-American Relations, 1882–1905," in *One Hundred Years of Korean-American Relations, 1882–1982*, ed. Yur-Bok Lee and Wayne Patterson (University, Ala., 1986).
39. Jeffrey M. Dowart, "The Pigtail War: The American Response to the Sino-Japanese War of 1894–1895" (Ph.D. diss., University of Massachusetts, 1971), 111–112.
40. Adrian Cook's *The Alabama Claims: American Politics and Anglo-American Relations, 1865–1872* (Ithaca, N.Y., 1975) tells this story well.
41. Theodore Roosevelt, *The Letters of Theodore Roosevelt*, ed. Elting E. Morison *et al.*, 8 vols. (Cambridge, Mass., 1951–1954), II, pp. 889–890.
42. Thomas A. Bailey, *America Faces Russia* (Ithaca, N.Y. 1950), pp. 147–148.
43. Frederick Jackson Turner, *The Frontier in American History* (New York, 1947), esp. pp. 32–37.
44. Frederick Jackson Turner, "The Problem of the West," *Atlantic Monthly* 78 (September 1896): 289–297.
45. Alfred Thayer Mahan, *Letters and Papers of A. T. Mahan*, ed. Robert Seager II and Doris D. Maguire, 3 vols. (Annapolis, 1975), II, pp. 506, 662; III, pp. 80, 484; William L. Livezey, *Mahan on Sea Power* (Norman, Okla., 1947), p. 263.
46. Two books by Peter Karsten are crucial here: *The Naval Aristocracy* (New York, 1972) and *Soldiers and Society* (Westport, Conn., 1978).
47. See especially B. F. Cooling, *Gray Steel and Blue Water Navy: The Formative Years of America's Military-Industrial Complex, 1881–1917* (Hamden, Conn., 1979).
48. Drake, p. xi.

For Further Reading

Begin with the well-organized pre-1981 references in *Guide to American Foreign Relations since 1700*, ed. Richard Dean Burns (1983); the notes of this chapter and the General Bibliography at the end of this book; the up-to-date bibliography in Robert L. Beisner, *From the Old Diplomacy to the New, 1865–1900* (1986); Walter LaFeber, *The American Search for Opportunity, 1865–1913*, in *The Cambridge History of U.S. Foreign Relations*, ed. Warren Cohen (1993); and the exhaustive list of works in Charles S. Campbell's *The Transformation of American Foreign Relations, 1865–1900* (1976). The Beisner and Campbell are also most helpful and provocative overviews, as is Richard Welch, Jr., *The Presidencies of Grover Cleveland* (1988).

For the context and perspectives on the "imperialist" debate, especially helpful are *Imperialism and After: Continuities and Discontinuities*, ed. Wolfgang J. Mommsen and Jurgen Osterhammel (1986); Tony Smith, *The Pattern of Imperialism: The U.S., Great Britain and the Late Industrializing World since 1815* (1982); Eric Hobsbawm, "The Crisis of Capitalism in Historical Perspective," *Socialist Revolution* 6 (October–December 1976): 77–96, especially on 1873–1896; William H. Becker, *The Dynamics of Business-Government Relations* (1982), for a more benign view of the relationship; Joseph A. Fry, *Henry S. Sanford: Diplomacy and Business in Nineteenth-Century America* (1982), for a fine case study; Tom E. Terrill's important analysis, *The Tariff, Politics and American Foreign Policy* (1973); and Edward Crapol's readable, significant study, *America for Americans* (1973), on Anglophobia.

Ideological and cultural influences are well analyzed in Michael H. Hunt, *Ideology and U.S. Foreign Policy* (1987), especially chapter III, tying internal and external racism together; Stuart Anderson, *Race and Rapprochement: Anglo-Saxonism and Anglo-American Relations, 1895–1904* (1981); Frank A. Cassell, "The Columbian Exposition of 1893 and U.S. Diplomacy in Latin America," *Mid-America* 67 (October 1985): 109–124; Robert W. Rydell, *All the World's a Fair: Visions of Empire at American International Expositions, 1876–1916* (1985), a fascinating account; and Donald C. Bellomy, "Social Darwinism Revisited," *Perspectives in American History* New Series, I (1984): 1–129, the best analysis. The frontier's impact is also noted in Brian W. Dippie, *The Vanishing American: White Attitudes and U.S. Indian Policy* (1982).

On specific geographical areas, the Latin American problems are explored in the Anderson and Cassell accounts noted above; Craig T. Dozier, *Nicaragua's Mosquito Shore* (1985); Joseph Smith, *Unequal Giants . . . 1889–1930* on U.S.-Brazil relations; Thomas Schoonover, "Imperialism in Middle America," a superb overview, in *Eagle against Empire*, ed. Rhodri Jeffreys-Jones (1983); Joyce S. Goldberg, *The Baltimore Affair: U.S. Relations with Chile, 1891–1892* (1986), now the standard account; and James F. Vivian, "U.S. Policy during the Brazilian Naval Revolt, 1893–1894: The Case for American Neutrality," *American Neptune* 41 (October 1981), a defense of U.S. policy. For Asia, see Phillip Darby, *Three Faces of Imperialism: British and American Approaches to Asia and Africa, 1870–1970* (1987), a fine comparative study; David L. Anderson, *Imperialism and Idealism: American Diplomats in China, 1861–1898* (1986); Yur-Bok Lee, *Diplomatic Relations between the United States and Korea, 1866–1887* (1970), which is the best on the subject, and also Lee's "Establishment of a Korean Legation in the United States, 1887–1890," *Illinois Papers in Asian Studies* 3 (1983). On Africa, begin with Darby's book noted above, and also Peter Duignan and L. H. Gann, *The United States and Africa: A History* (1984).

For individual administrations, Paul S. Holbo's *Tarnished Expansion: The Alaska Scandal, the Press, and Congress, 1867–1871* (1983) is most revealing; Clifford W. Haury, "Hamilton Fish and the Conservative Tradition," in *Studies in American Diplomacy*,

1865–1945, ed. Norman Graebner (1985), an interesting interpretation; Justus D. Doenecke, *The Presidencies of James A. Garfield and Chester A. Arthur* (1981), important on Latin America and Korea especially; Michael J. Devine, *John W. Foster: Politics and Diplomacy in the Imperial Era, 1873–1917* (1981), a good analysis of a key figure; and Charles W. Calhoun, *Gilded Age Cato: The Life of Walter Q. Gresham* (1988), the standard biography.

7

Turning Point: The McKinley Years (1896–1900)

The Significance of the Late 1890s

As the twentieth century dawned, the United States stepped onto the world stage as a great power. Because of the triumphs scored between 1898 and 1900, it strode confidently now with Great Britain, France, Russia, Germany, and Japan—nations that possessed immense military strength and had used that strength for conquest. Never had a newly independent nation risen so far so fast as did the United States between 1776 and 1900.

Historians have argued not over whether the United States deserved great-power status by 1900 (all agree that it did), but whether Americans consciously intended to follow the expansionist policies after 1896 that projected them into such distant regions. Historian Ernest May believes that the United States had "greatness thrust upon it." But another scholar, Albert K. Weinberg, concludes that U.S. officials were no more passive at key moments than "is the energetic individual who decides upon, plans, and carries out the robbery of a bank."[1] The years 1896 to 1900 thus become critical for the student of U.S. foreign policy in the twentieth century. For if the nation entered the ranks of great world powers at this time, it is of central importance to know how it did so. By accident? Because of a few elite officials who pushed reluctant Americans overseas? Because of the U.S. system's domestic needs that forced that system to assume global responsibilities? The well-known saying "Just as the twig is bent, the tree's inclined" might have meaning for U.S. diplomatic history. The reasons why the United States moved outward so rapidly in the late 1890s help us understand why it grew from these roots (or twig) into a twentieth-century superpower.

McKinley and McKinleyism

Americans living in the late 1890s understood that they were witnessing a historic turn. After the triumph over Spain in 1898 brought the United States new holdings in the Caribbean and the western Pacific, Assistant Secretary of State John Bassett Moore observed that the nation had moved "from a position of comparative freedom from entanglements into the position of what is commonly called a world power. . . . Where formerly we had only commercial interests, we now have territorial and political interests as well."[2]

Moore's boss, President William McKinley, presided over these changes. McKinley won the 1896 election over the highly popular Democrat, William Jennings Bryan. The affection Americans felt for McKinley ranked with the feelings they later had toward the popular Theodore Roosevelt, Franklin D. Roosevelt, and Dwight D. Eisenhower. A gentle, soft-spoken, highly courteous man, McKinley had long been known for the love and care he had lavished on his wife, an invalid who required much of his attention. Born in Niles, Ohio, in 1843, Major McKinley had been a Civil War hero, then parlayed his reputation and uncanny political instincts into a career in the House of Representatives between 1876 and 1890. By the end of his stay, no one on Capitol Hill better understood the new industrialized America. He dominated debates on the central issues of tariffs and taxes because he had mastered the facts and understood the powerful industrialists who made the country run. Moving on to the governorship of Ohio, he maintained order in an economically depressed state while nearby regions were wracked by riots. He was not reluctant to use state forces to control strikers, but he somehow did so while keeping the good will of the labor leaders. With the help of fellow Ohioan and millionaire steel industrialist Marcus Hanna, who ran a superbly organized campaign, McKinley moved to the White House. The new president named Ohio senator John Sherman as secretary of state and then rewarded Hanna by having him appointed to the empty Senate seat. The United States thus obtained a secretary of state who was aged, sometimes incapacitated, and too often senile; but in Hanna, McKinley enjoyed a

William McKinley (1843–1901) of Ohio was the last Civil War veteran to be president (enlisting at age seventeen, he had been a hero) but the first modern American chief executive. He also appointed a modern cabinet—that is, one made up of administrators who owed allegiance to the president. He is at far left. John Hay is at McKinley's right.

trusted power broker in the Senate who followed the president's every wish.

Anyway, McKinley intended to control foreign policy himself. An accomplished negotiator and an experienced politician whose antennae could instantly detect an opponent's weakness, the president knew how to conduct back-room talks and keep secrets. His State Department depended especially on Alvey A. Adee, a long-time professional who served in the department for fifty-five years until his death in 1924. Adee personally wrote or approved nearly every outgoing message. When he once bicycled past, a Washingtonian said, "There goes our State Department now." Though hard-of-hearing, Adee seemed to have learned everything that the president needed to know about international law and diplomatic history. The closed-mouth president, deaf Adee, and senile Sherman led to the complaint that "the President says nothing, the Assistant Secretary hears nothing, and the Secretary of State knows nothing."

Controlling foreign policy in the way that he did, McKinley became not only the first twentieth-century president, but the first modern chief executive. He developed new powers, especially in maneuvering and controlling Congress, while he kept the control of foreign policy in his own hands (and used the new devices of the telephone and typewriter while doing so). McKinley expanded the Constitution's commander-in-chief powers until, without congressional permission, he used it to dispatch U.S. troops to fight in China. His action set a precedent for the "imperial presidency" of the 1960s and 1970s.

McKinley and Hanna, moreover, cleverly used the backlash caused by the 1893–1897 economic crisis that had driven the Democrats from power in 1894 and 1896. The two men built a political coalition so powerful that only one Democratic presidential nominee would be elected between 1896 and 1932. The new politics had profound influence on presidential power. As a result of the 1890s political realignment, Republicans dominated the North and Democrats controlled the South. This division meant that contests between Republicans and Democrats declined in individual states, voters grew less interested, and many (especially black people in the South) were disfranchised.[3] The president thus broke free of the hard-fought party rivalry that had marked the 1876–1896 years. He enjoyed more freedom and a more dependable political base from which to conduct foreign policy. McKinley exploited these opportunities by becoming the first chief executive to appoint a staff member who dealt with newspaper reporters and prepared press handouts that publicized the administration's case. The Ohioan was even the first president whose inaugration was put on film.

The great Kansas journalist, William Allen White, observed that McKinley survived twenty years in the jungles of Ohio politics, "where survival values combined the virtues of the serpent, the shark, and the cooing dove." White believed that the president was too much "cooing dove," "too polite," for McKinley's "Prince Albert coat was never wrinkled, his white vest front never broken. . . . He weighed out his saccharine on apothecary scales, just enough and no more for the dose that cheers but does not inebriate." White further perfectly caught McKinley's genius for handling people, especially those in Congress. After rejecting one visitor's request for a favor, the president took the carnation he always wore in his coat and told the man to "give this to your wife with my compliments and best wishes." He did it so graciously that the visitor declared, "I would rather have this flower from you for my wife than the thing I came to get."[4]

At the same time, the president understood the brute truths of politics. Historian Henry Adams watched the president closely and described "what might be called McKinleyism; the system of combinations, consolidations . . . , realized at home, and realizable abroad."[5] Under McKinley, an industrialized America moved to Americanize new parts of the world.

Two Crises, One War

McKinley took the presidential oath in March 1897 as a revolution raged just ninety miles from U.S. shores. In 1894–1895, the U.S. tariff policy had kept out Cuban sugar from mainland markets. The island went into an economic tailspin. A revolution against Spanish colonialism had broken out between 1868 and 1878. It now re-emerged with greater force. By late 1895, the rebels claimed to have established a provisional government. Support for their cause swelled in the United States, but neither Cleveland nor McKinley would recognize the revolutionaries. To do so would have released the Spanish government from its responsibility for protecting $50 million of U.S. property in Cuba. Washington officials preferred to hold Spain fully responsible for protecting U.S. lives and property, while pushing the Madrid government to give Cuba enough autonomy so that the revolutionaries would stop fighting.

Spain, however, refused to move the island toward autonomy. Its once-great, four-hundred-year-old empire had rotted away until it amounted to little more than Cuba, Puerto Rico, a few scattered islands in the Pacific, and the Philippine Islands. No government in Madrid could surrender these last holdings and expect to remain in power. The Spanish instead took a tough approach. They dispatched 150,000 soldiers, who, under the command of General Valeriano Weyler (soon nicknamed "Butcher" Weyler by U.S. newspaper editors), tried to destroy rebel support by rounding up thousands of Cubans and placing them in barbed-wire concentration camps. The revolution nevertheless continued to spread. The insurgents burned U.S. property in the hope of forcing McKinley's intervention.

Nineteenth-century Americans had little respect for Spain. They had seized its North American empire piece by piece between 1800 and 1821. The Spanish, wrote one of the first American historians, the Reverend Jedidiah Morse, are "naturally weak and effeminate," and "dedicate the greatest part of their lives to loitering and inactive pleasures." "Their character," he sniffed, "is nothing more than a grave and specious insignificance."[6] In the 1890s, leading U.S. newspapers picked up Morse's views and demanded that the more civilized Americans help Cuba. The publishers were not unselfish. Technological breakthroughs in making paper and setting type had driven newspaper prices down to a penny or two a copy. These changes opened the possibility for mass distribution and the rich advertising fee that came with such a market. Two giants of the trade, William Randolph Hearst and Joseph Pulitzer, led the struggle to gain more newspaper readers. Each man sought subscribers through sensational front-page stories, and nothing was more sensational than events in Cuba—unless, of course, it was a U.S. war against Spain. Hearst especially promoted such a conflict. Congress picked up his beat and, in 1897, pressured McKinley to recognize the rebels.

The new president was moved by neither congressional demands nor the sensationalist "yellow journal" press. He feared that U.S. recognition would lead to war, a war whose costs could drag the United States back into the economic crises from which it was finally emerging in 1897. Businessmen and conservative politicians, both Republican and Democrat, warned that such a war could be paid for only by coining more silver. But more silver would cheapen the dollar and threaten U.S. credit overseas. McKinley, moreover, opposed war because it could lead to demands for annexing Cuba. Annexation would raise constitutional problems (for example, Can the Constitution safely stretch across water to take in new states without tearing apart?). Bringing Cuba into the Union would also incorporate a multiracial society at a

José Martí (1853–1895) was the father of the Cuban revolution that erupted in 1895, but he feared U.S. intervention as much as Spanish colonialism: "And once the United States is in Cuba," he asked, "who will drive it out?" A journalist in New York during the 1880s, he returned to Cuba in early 1895 to start the final phase of the uprising but was killed a month later by Spanish troops. Half a century later, he became a great hero of Fidel Castro.

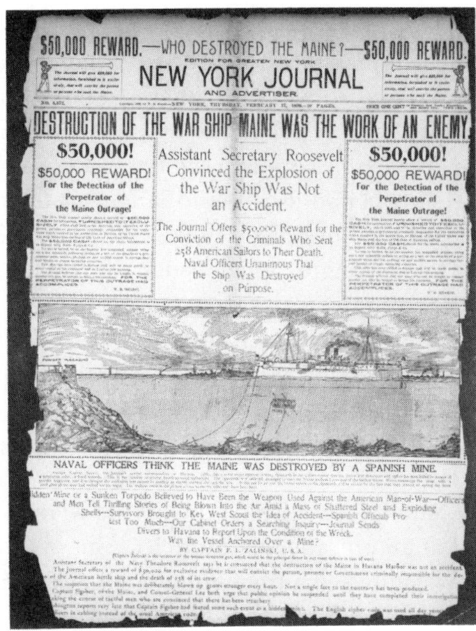

$50,000 REWARD.—WHO DESTROYED THE MAINE?—$50,000 REWARD.

EDITION FOR GREATER NEW YORK

NEW YORK JOURNAL

AND ADVERTISER.

DESTRUCTION OF THE WAR SHIP MAINE WAS THE WORK OF AN ENEMY.

$50,000!

$50,000 REWARD!

For the Detection of the Perpetrator of the Maine Outrage!

Assistant Secretary Roosevelt Convinced the Explosion of the War Ship Was Not an Accident.

The Journal Offers $50,000 Reward for the Conviction of the Criminals Who Sent 258 American Sailors to Their Death. Naval Officers Unanimous That the Ship Was Destroyed on Purpose.

$50,000!

$50,000 REWARD!

For the Detection of the Perpetrator of the Maine Outrage!

NAVAL OFFICERS THINK THE MAINE WAS DESTROYED BY A SPANISH MINE.

Hidden Mine or a Sunken Torpedo Believed to Have Been the Weapon Used Against the American Man-of-War—Officers and Men Tell Thrilling Stories of Being Blown Into the Air Amid a Mass of Shattered Steel and Exploding Shells—Survivors Brought to Key West Scout the Idea of Accident—Spanish Officials Protest Too Much—Our Cabinet Orders a Searching Inquiry—Journal Sends Divers to Havana to Report Upon the Condition of the Wreck. Was the Vessel Anchored Over a Mine?

BY CAPTAIN E. L. ZALINSKI, U. S. A.

"Yellow journalism" of the 1890s fanned the flames of war by giving Americans immediate news of foreign-policy crises, especially if that news could be sensationalized to sell more newspapers.

time when white Americans were already having problems dealing with black Americans and millions of newly arrived immigrants. McKinley, therefore, pressed Spain to grant enough reforms to undercut the revolutionaries. Madrid began to do so, even recalling "Butcher" Weyler and offering the first steps toward autonomy. The president, however, criticized the response as too little too late.

Spain had lost control. In late 1897, riots erupted in the Cuban capital of Havana. McKinley moved a warship, the *Maine*, into Havana Harbor to protect U.S. citizens and property. In early February 1898, a pro-war group in New York captured a letter in which the Spanish minister to Washington, Dupuy de Lôme, called McKinley "weak and a bidder for the admiration of the crowd." The minister also downplayed the importance of Spain's reforms. The little trust that Americans had in the Spanish evaporated. Six days later, on February 15, an explosion shook the *Maine*. Settling into the muck of Havana Harbor, the ship took more than 250 U.S. sailors to their deaths. In 1976, a thorough investigation of the tragedy concluded that the vessel had probably been destroyed by an internal explosion (perhaps in the engine room) and not by some external device set by Spanish agents.[7] In 1898, however, Americans quickly concluded that a bomb had taken those lives, and the yellow journals and congressmen screamed for war. McKinley played for time by asking for an investigation. He feared, as he told a friend, that "the country was not ready for war." Military preparations had only begun. Economic dangers still loomed. He worried about the possible results of a victory: "Who knows where this war will lead us," he told a congressional leader. "It may be more than war with Spain."[8]

When making that remark, McKinley may have had in mind a second foreign-policy crisis that emerged in March 1898. It had begun with Japan's victory over China in 1894–1895 (see p. 182). In 1897, Germany blocked Japan from grabbing further territorial spoils. Using as an excuse the murder of two German missionaries, Berlin officials demanded as indemnity from China the port of Kiaochow (now Chiao Hsien). Located at an entrance to the rich Chinese province of Manchuria, Kiaochow controlled a trade route used by an increasing number of Americans. Other European powers and Japan then clamored for important parts of China's territory. The traditional U.S. open-door policy to all of China faced extinction. Great Britain, which shared much of Washington's concern about the open door, asked McKinley for help in stopping the other Europeans. The president sympathized with the British position, but he could not help. China was too far away, Cuba too close. McKinley had to deal with revolution before he could help protect the open door. Meanwhile, worried U.S. exporters and business newspapers began chanting a warning that, in the *Journal of Commerce*'s words, the Far East crisis threatened "the future of American trade."[9]

One possible escape from the dilemma had, however, already appeared. Rebels in the Philippines had begun war against Spanish rule. The islands could become a key military base from which to protect U.S. interests in Asia. McKinley, Captain Alfred Thayer Mahan, and Assistant Secretary of the Navy Theodore Roosevelt closely watched the Philippine struggle in early 1898. On February 25, when his superior was out of the office, Roosevelt sent a series of cables that ordered U.S. naval commanders to prepare their ships for fighting. The next day, the astonished secretary of the navy, John D. Long, rushed to the White House with the news that his assistant had single-handedly tried to push the country to the brink of war. McKinley ordered that all of Roosevelt's cables be recalled—except the order to Admiral George Dewey that his Pacific fleet prepare to attack the Philippines in case of war with Spain.[10] In actuality, Dewey had earlier received orders to attack the Philippines in case of war with Spain. The president, meanwhile, had been reinforcing Dewey's squadron. McKinley later soft-soaped critics of his Philippine policy by assuring them that he had involuntarily been pushed into conquering "those darn islands," which he could not even quickly locate on a map. His statement was good politics but bad history. The president knew very well before he went to war with Spain how much the Philippine base could mean to preserving the open door in China. The crisis caused by German and Japanese grabs of China's territory left him no alternative—unless he wanted to quit the century-long U.S. quest for Asian markets. And the president had no intention of doing that.

McKinley carefully prepared his policy to deal with the Cuban and Asian crises at once. After the *Maine*'s destruction, he moved rapidly to prepare the country for war. On March 9, he acquired $50 million from Congress to begin mobilization of the army and navy. On March 17, Republican senator Redfield Proctor of Vermont, one of McKinley's close friends, returned from a visit to Cuba and electrified Americans by announcing that he had changed his anti-war stand. A strong conservative, Proctor declared that his business contacts in Cuba had told him that Spain's reforms had failed. Property was being destroyed. Conservative Cubans wanted autonomy or U.S. annexation. Proctor's fears were underlined when State Department officials in Cuba warned McKinley that unless the fighting was stopped, "there might be a revolution within a revolution."[11] This meant that the rebellion threatened to take a sharp leftward turn that could threaten conservative property holders if the revolutionaries won. McKinley thus not only had to stop the fighting, but control the revolution itself.

On March 25, the president received a telegram from a close political adviser in New York City: "Big corporations here now believe we will have war. Believe all would welcome it as a relief to suspense."[12] This cable revealed that eastern business groups, long afraid of war, now felt that battle was preferable to the fears generated by Proctor's speech and the other events of February and March. New York business leaders had concluded that the United States could safely pay for a war without having to coin silver. Many midwestern and western business groups, as well as nationwide commercial journals who were frightened over the threat to the open door in Asia, had long supported war. The business community was uniting behind McKinley's military preparations.

Between March 20 and 28, the president sent a series of demands to

Spain. The Spanish would have to pay indemnity for the *Maine*, promise not to use the *reconcentrado* policy, declare a truce, and negotiate for Cuban independence through U.S. mediation, if necessary. In the end, Spain surrendered to all the demands except the last. No Madrid government could promise Cuban independence and remain in power. Spain stalled, no doubt hoping that once the rainy season began in Cuba during early summer, McKinley would ease the pressure until the weather cleared for fighting in the autumn. But the president decided to move quickly. On April 11, he sent his message to Congress. He asked for war on the grounds that the three-year struggle on the island threatened Cuban lives, U.S. property, and tranquillity in the United States itself.

The president did not want war. But he did want results that only war could bring: protecting property in Cuba, stopping the revolution before it turned sharply to the left, restoring confidence in the U.S. business community, insulating his Republican party from Democratic charges of cowardice in safeguarding U.S. interests, and giving himself a free hand to deal with the growing Asian crisis. For these reasons, McKinley took the country into war in April 1898.

"A Splendid Little War . . ."

McKinley's war message triggered a bitter debate in Congress. Since 1895, many congressmen had supported the Cuban junto, which raised millions of dollars in the United States to support the rebels. A number of Americans invested heavily in Cuban bonds to purchase arms for the revolution. These pro-Cuban groups now insisted that McKinley recognize Cuban independence as part of the war declaration. The president instantly rejected the deal. Mistrusting the revolutionaries, he insisted on keeping his freedom of action in handling the island once the fighting ended. The Senate tried to impose the junto's policy on the president, but he blocked the measure in the House. Then, in a week of intense political infighting (during which the usually calm McKinley had to take sleeping potions so that he could rest), he forced the Senate to retreat. The president received exactly what he wanted: only a declaration of war. Theodore Roosevelt, angry because McKinley refused to rush into war, privately complained that the president had "no more backbone than a chocolate eclair" and added that the gentle Ohioan was a "white-livered cur." But as historian Paul Holbo notes, the central question by early April was not whether the country was going to war, "but who was to direct American policy."[13] The Senate fight demonstrated that the president could dominate Roosevelt, the Congress, and the powerful interests behind the Cuban junto.

Congress included in the war resolution the Teller Amendment. This provision declared that the United States was not entering the war to conquer territory. The Teller Amendment eased some consciences, but it actually aimed to protect American sugar producers from cheap Cuban sugar. (Senator Henry Teller, a Republican, came from the sugar-beet state of Colorado.) Historians later discovered, moreover, that Cuban leaders handed out $1 million in payment to lobbyists and perhaps to members of Congress who voted for the amendment. McKinley accepted the provision. He had no intention of annexing Cuba.[14] But he did want Hawaii—and quickly. The mid-Pacific islands could be vital bases for U.S. ships heading toward the Philippines. Wartime need, however, by no means explained why the United States annexed Hawaii in June 1898. The story begins earlier.

After 1893, when President Cleveland rejected requests from Americans in Hawaii for annexation, the United States paid little attention to the islands. That lack of interest dramatically disappeared in mid-1897, when McKinley received urgent messages that the Japanese were sending several warships to Hawaii. The Tokyo government was angry that its citizens who were attempting to enter the islands were being turned away. The reason for the rejection lay in numbers: in 1884, only 116 Japanese lived in Hawaii; but by 1897, their 25,000 people accounted for one-quarter of the entire population. The Japanese even outnumbered the Americans, Europeans, and native Hawaiians. If they obtained the vote, the power of the white planters who ruled the islands could be shattered. Hawaii could become a Japanese colony.

When Tokyo's two warships appeared in Hawaiian waters during early 1897, McKinley, who had long wanted to annex the islands, ordered U.S. vessels prepared for action. Captain Alfred Thayer Mahan privately warned Roosevelt in the Navy Department to be aware of "the very real present danger of war" with Japan.[15] To the delight of Roosevelt, Mahan, and other expansionists, the president sent a treaty for Hawaiian annexation to the Senate in June 1897. But he moved too quickly. The president could not line up the necessary 60 Senate votes for the two-thirds approval needed to ratify the pact. Americans wanted to think carefully before extending their Constitution that far into the Pacific. Domestic sugar producers especially assailed the pact; they feared Hawaiian sugar imports.

On May 2, 1898, a telegram reached Washington that Admiral George

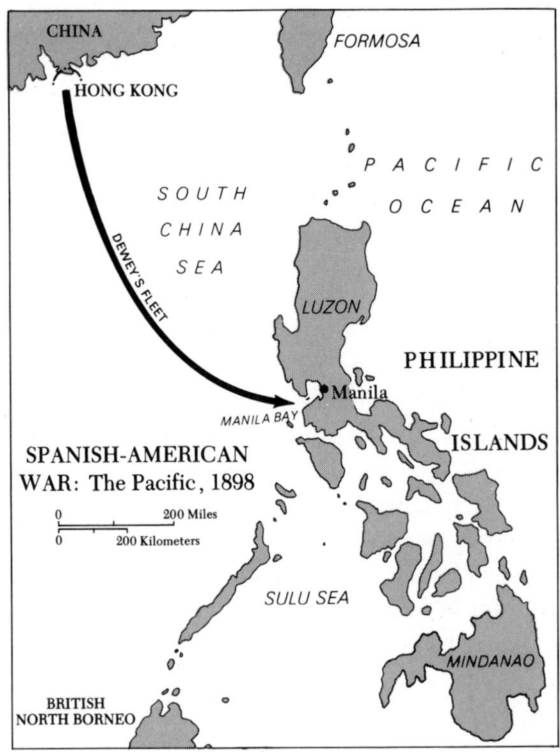

In the far west, the sailing of Dewey's fleet from Hong Kong to Manila made Americans a Pacific power. But U.S. interests had been growing in the region for a century.

Dewey's ships had destroyed the Spanish fleet in the Philippines. Two days later, McKinley again asked the Senate for Hawaiian annexation. He still did not have the needed 60 votes, so he resorted to the device of annexation through joint resolution of the House and Senate. (That same device had been used in 1846 to take Texas, see p. 108.) The majorities needed for passing the joint resolution were easily found in both houses. On August 12, 1898, Hawaii became a U.S. territory.

By then, the islands fit within a grander plan developing in McKinley's mind: "We need Hawaii just as much and a good deal more than we did California. It is manifest destiny," he had declared earlier in 1898.[16] The U.S. Minister to Siam, John A. Barrett, believed that "we need Hawaii to properly protect our cotton, flour, and richly laden ships which . . . will one day ply on the Pacific like the Spanish galleons of old," as they make themselves "masters of the Pacific seas." Mahan chimed in with his influential arguments about the need for mid-Pacific coaling stations on the route to Asia. The shortest route from California to China's markets was via the Alaskan coast. But, as historian Alan Henrikson has noted in a fascinating analysis, Mahan used Mercator, flat-world maps, not maps viewing the earth from the North and South Poles. Thus, the main U.S. Pacific base was developed at Pearl Harbor in Hawaii rather than on the more direct Alaskan–Aleutian Islands route.[17]

By early August, when Hawaii became a U.S. territory, Americans had already won the easiest conflict in their history. With the declaration of war in April, Dewey had set out from Hong Kong to engage the Spanish fleet in the Philippines. His small squadron appeared so weak that British officers at the Hong Kong Club observed sorrowfully: "A fine set of fellows, but unhappily we shall never see them again." When Dewey arrived at Manila Bay, however, he discovered seven armorless Spanish vessels. The Spanish commander was so certain of his fate that he simply moved his ships to the bay's shallowest waters so his men would not drown when their vessels were shot out from under them. Dewey then destroyed the Spanish flotilla, killing or wounding 400 men. No U.S. ship was badly hit, and only several Americans received scratches. After four hours of cannon fire, the United States had become a power in the western Pacific. "Our crews are all hoarse

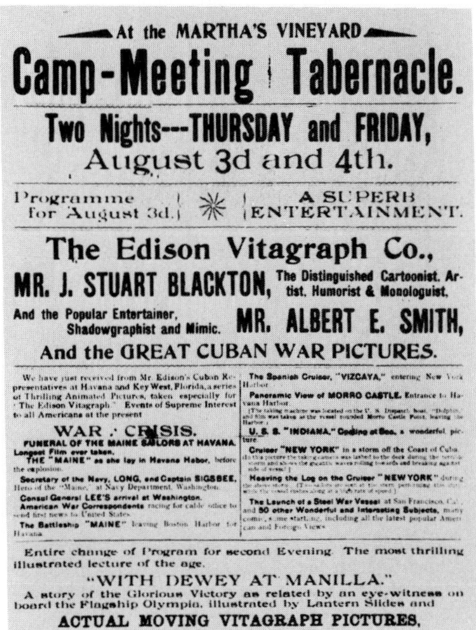

The 1898 meeting of empire, movies, and public education immediately after the "splendid little war" against Spain. Early, quite primitive motion pictures and slides brought home to Americans the thrill of the new overseas empire, as U.S. technology both won a war and then celebrated the winning.

from cheering," a U.S. official cabled Washington from Manila on May 4, "and while we suffer for cough drops and throat doctors we have no use for liniment or surgeons."

Washington officials also believed that Cuba would be captured by sea power. They, therefore, used much of the $50 million appropriated by Congress in March to prepare the navy, not the army, for action. As a result, the War Department bought few modern weapons or tropical clothing until after the fighting began. When McKinley ordered troops to prepare to invade Cuba and Puerto Rico, they had to wear heavy uniforms designed for northern climates. They ate provisions so badly prepared that one mainstay was accurately called "embalmed beef." Field weapons dated from the Civil War. As 180,000 volunteers trained to join the regular 30,000-man army, scandals rocked the War Department. Despite these disasters, in late May, General William R. Shafter began moving 16,000 troops from Tampa, Florida, to Cuba. His army traveled on 32 transports that could move no faster than 7 miles an hour. They sailed for 5½ days, much of it in well-lit vessels just off the Cuban coast, while the U.S. flagship crew enjoyed a band on deck that played ragtime.[18]

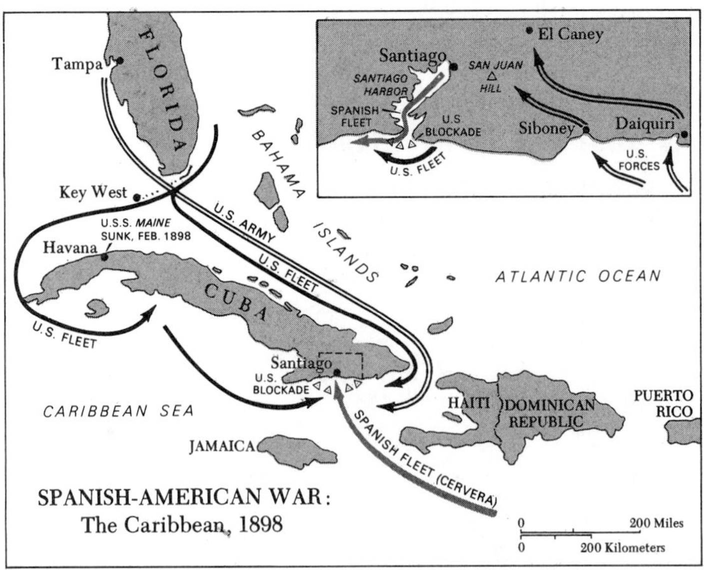

In the Caribbean, the war removed Spain from the region, made the United States the hemisphere's leading power, and opened an era of turbulent U.S.-Cuban relations.

The main U.S. fleet, including the three 10,000-ton battleships authorized in 1890, prepared to fight the Spanish fleet that was steaming across the Atlantic to Cuba. An important U.S. warship, the *Oregon*, arrived only after a highly publicized 68-day voyage from the Pacific around Cape Horn on the tip of South America to the Caribbean. It was a remarkable feat of seamanship that made Americans understand why they needed an isthmian canal cut through Central America. During the *Oregon*'s voyage, inhabitants of New York, Boston, and other coastal cities feared that their homes would be blasted by Spanish shells. They demanded protection, so McKinley sent a few broken-down Civil War coastal defense vessels, although he knew that the danger was nonexistent. The real question was whether the dilapidated Spanish squadron could even make it safely across the Atlantic. When it did, the U.S. fleet quickly cut off the four most respectable vessels in Santiago Harbor. As U.S. troops moved into Santiago by land, the Spanish ships tried to escape.[19] The twelve American vessels destroyed the entire fleet at the cost of one U.S. life. As Americans took target practice, one U.S. officer had to shout the famous order: "Don't cheer, men! Those poor devils are dying."

For nearly all Americans, the conflict gave war a good name. Fighting seemed easy and nearly cost-free. Journalist Richard Harding Davis concluded that "war as it is conducted at this end of the century is civilized."[20] No one benefited more from the conflict than Theodore Roosevelt. He left the Navy Department to organize friends (especially men he had met while living as a cowboy in South Dakota's Black Hills a decade earlier) into the "Rough Riders." Finally getting his long-sought chance to kill, TR determined to do it as a gentleman. For example, he ordered from Brooks Brothers clothiers an "ordinary Cavalry lieutenant Colonel's uniform in blue Cravenette" so that he would be properly outfitted. When he finally reached Cuba, he nearly destroyed his Rough Riders by leading them up the steep Kettle's Hill directly into hostile gunfire. Fortunately for TR, the Spanish weapons could not shoot accurately at slowly moving targets. Roosevelt emerged a national hero. He made certain his heroism was appreciated by publishing in 1899 *The Rough Riders*—a book that humorist Finley Peter Dunne ("Mr. Dooley," as he was known to newspaper readers) suggested could be entitled "Alone in Cubia."[21] But Richard Harding Davis's sarcasm at the time applied to the U.S. war effort as well as Roosevelt's: "God takes care of drunken men, sailors, and the United States."

TABLE 1

PRINCIPAL WARS IN WHICH THE UNITED STATES PARTICIPATED: U.S. MILITARY PERSONNEL SERVING AND CASUALTIES

War/conflict	*Branch of service*	*Number serving*	*Casualties*		
			Battle deaths	*Other deaths*	*Wounds not mortal*
Revolutionary War (1775–1783)	*Total*		4,435	—	6,188
	Army	—	4,044	—	6,004
	Navy	—	342	—	114
	Marines	—	49	—	70
War of 1812 (1812–1815)	*Total*	286,730	2,260	—	4,505
	Army	—	1,950	—	4,000
	Navy	—	265	—	439
	Marines	—	45	—	66
Mexican War (1846–1848)	*Total*	78,718	1,733	11,550	4,152
	Army	—	1,721	11,550	4,102
	Navy	—	1	—	3
	Marines	—	11	—	47
Civil War (Union forces only) (1861–1865)	*Total*	2,213,363	140,414	224,097	281,881
	Army	2,128,948	138,154	221,374	280,040
	Navy	—	2,112	2,411	1,710
	Marines	84,415	148	312	131
Spanish-American War (1898)	*Total*	306,760	385	2,061	1,662
	Army	280,564	369	2,061	1,594
	Navy	22,875	10	—	47
	Marines	3,321	6	—	21

Source: Department of Defense.

. . . For Control of Cuba and Puerto Rico

America's mood and future were better caught by the U.S. ambassador to France, Horace Porter. He wrote McKinley in November 1898 that European officials "express the opinion that we did in three months what the great powers of Europe had sought in vain to do for over a hundred years." These accomplishments included, Porter observed,

> having secured a chain of island posts in the Pacific, secured the Philippines, captured their trade, paved the way for a Pacific [telegraph] cable of our own, virtually taken possession of that ocean, and occupied a position at Manila . . . only a couple of days in time from the Chinese coast with no fear of Chinese or Russian armies at our back yet near enough to protect our interest in the Orient.[22]

It all seemed miraculous. At the cost of 2,900 lives (with approximately 2,500 the victims of disease, not enemy gunfire) and only $250 million, the United States became a great world power. But if Americans were dreaming big dreams, McKinley refused to be carried away. He had only certain limited diplomatic objectives. In his first public statement on possible terms of peace, McKinley wrote in June 1898 that Cuba, Puerto Rico, and a Philippine naval base had to end up in U.S. hands. By late summer, he had actually rejected the opportunity to take control of Caroline Island and the Marianas, which Spain held in the Pacific.

In Cuba, the question became whether the island should be independent, annexed, or come under informal U.S. control. McKinley quickly ruled out immediate independence. His mistrust of the Cuban revolutionaries increased. Their ill-equipped, barefoot forces proved to be superb guerrilla fighters when working alongside U.S. troops but, in American eyes, became racial inferiors and thieves of U.S. food supplies when the fighting stopped. The U.S. forces "despise" the Cubans, one journalist reported. When General Shafter was asked about possible self-government, he retorted, "Why those people are no more fit for self-government than gun-powder is for hell."[23] McKinley also refused to annex the island. That solution could bring too many unpredictable mixed races into the Union. Moreover, annexation was not needed. Because Cuba was so close to U.S. shores, it, unlike the Philippines, could be controlled informally. The United States could use the island for its own purposes, but Cubans could have the headaches of day-to-day governing.

This imaginative policy was finally formulated by McKinley and his top military commander in Cuba, General Leonard Wood. The general convened a Cuban constitutional convention in late 1900 and instructed the delegates to establish their own internal laws. Washington required, however, that they include in their new constitution certain foreign-policy provisions: (1) the United States had the right to intervene as it wished to protect Cuba's independence; (2) the Cuban debt had to be limited so that European creditors could not use it as an excuse to use force to collect it—and perhaps take Cuban territory as compensation; (3) the United States demanded a ninety-nine year lease of the naval base at Guantánamo; and (4) an extensive sanitation program was to protect the Cuban people and make the island more attractive to U.S. investors. These provisions, drawn up by McKinley and his advisers, became known as the Platt Amendment after Republican Senator Orville Platt from Connecticut formally proposed them in Congress. Furiously attacking the proposals, the Cuban delegates refused to vote on them. Wood warned that he would keep them meeting until they did vote. He knew, moreover, that the Cubans needed immediate access to the American market for their sugar. Under intense U.S. pressure, the Cuban Constitutional Convention finally accepted the Platt Amendment in 1901 by a vote of 15 to 11. "There is, of course, little or no independence left Cuba under the Platt Amendment," Wood wrote Roosevelt.[24]

The McKinley and Roosevelt administrations then overcame tough opposition from high-tariff Republicans and sugar producers to negotiate and finally ratify a reciprocity treaty in 1903. The pact thoroughly integrated the U.S. and Cuban economies. Cuba's sugar and mineral wealth moved north, as American farm and industrial products flowed south. The U.S. sugar producers lost their fight when the giant American Sugar Refining trust, which wanted cheap sugar to refine for the home market, moved into Capitol Hill and bribed the necessary number of senators.[25] U.S.-Cuban trade skyrocketed from $27 million in 1897 to over $300 million in 1917.

The United States restored order to Cuba but assumed few responsibilities. "When people ask me what I mean by stable government, I tell them money at six percent," General Wood wrote to McKinley in 1900. That kind of "order," however, proved to be dangerous. As historian Lloyd Gardner notes, the Platt Amendment built into Cuba "a revolutionary impetus," because later critics of Cuban poverty could not effectively attack the island's own government, which had little control over the economy, but had to attack the United States.[26] As early as 1906, U.S. officials had to land troops to maintain order. The Platt Amendment continued to be the basis of U.S. policy in Cuba until 1934.

McKinley also took Puerto Rico away from Spain in 1898. The conquest was a surprise. Few Americans knew or cared about that island when war began. For that reason, however, McKinley's decision to annex it (as partial indemnity from Spain for U.S. war costs) raised little debate. The Puerto Ricans were not pleased. In a rare moment of Spanish colonial wisdom, Madrid officials had given Puerto Rico a large amount of autonomy, including its own elected legislature. McKinley destroyed that autonomy. General Nelson Miles, the U.S. military commander, conquered the country without opposition, then announced that the United States intended to give "the immunities and blessings of the liberal institutions of our government." But instead of granting such blessings, Congress passed the Foraker Act of 1900, which made Puerto Rico an "unincorporated territory" subject to the whim of Congress. For one of the few times since the 1787 Ordinance (see p. 33), the United States annexed a large territory with no intention of making the inhabitants U.S. citizens. Puerto Ricans had no guaranteed rights. As one of their newspapers complained in 1901, "We are and we are not a foreign country. We are and we are not citizens of the United States. . . . The Constitution . . . applies to us and does not apply to us."[27]

The U.S. Supreme Court proved the newspaper correct when it handed down a series of judgments between 1901 and 1904. In these historic decisions, known as the Insular Cases, the Court ruled that the Foraker Act was constitutional. The United States could annex an area, make it an "unincorporated" territory, and refuse to grant its people citizenship. Thus, the Constitution did not automatically "follow the flag," as many Americans had long believed. The territory's people were at Congress's mercy. The U.S. attorney general told the Court that the government had to have such power. In the future, he prophesied, a Puerto Rico–like situation might arise in Africa or even China, given the course of U.S. expansionism. The Constitution had to be interpreted to fit that expansionism. Later, the Insular Cases did provide a legal justification for the U.S. rule of Guam and other Pacific territories.[28]

Congress, meanwhile, passed tariff legislation that integrated Puerto Rico—and especially its increasing number of sugar plantations—into the U.S. economy. In 1850, the country's landholding had been fair

A cartoonist, who captioned this work "Find the Constitution," portrays in 1901 his belief that Americans were paying a high price to acquire overseas possessions. This is from the Philadelphia North American.

and equitable when compared with other countries in the Caribbean and Central America. By 1917, the best lands had fallen into the hands of a few wealthy owners who grew crops for export. In that year, the United States finally gave Puerto Ricans citizenship through the Jones Act. In 1947, the country won the right to elect its own governor. After that, Third World and Soviet-bloc countries in the United Nations regularly proposed resolutions condemning Washington's "colonial" policy. Puerto Ricans, meanwhile, divided among a small group demanding independence, a larger faction wanting U.S. statehood, and the largest number who preferred the tax and trade preferences obtained from the United States because of their commonwealth status. But Puerto Rico remained a poor country whose people increasingly sought work in the United States. Nearly a century after the 1898 conquest, Washington officials have not been able to devise a workable policy for development.[29]

. . . And the Conquest of the Filipinos

The best-known version of how McKinley decided to annex the Philippine Islands came from the president himself, when he talked with a group of Methodist church leaders in 1899:

> I walked the floor of the White House night after night until midnight; and I am not ashamed to tell you, gentlemen, that I went down on my knees and prayed Almighty God for light and guidance more than one night. And one night it came to me in this way—. . . . (1) that we could not give [the Philippines] back to Spain—that would be cowardly and dishonorable; (2) that we could not turn them over to France or Germany—our commercial rivals in the Orient—that would be bad business and discreditable . . . ; . . . that there was nothing left to do but take them all, and educate the Filipinos, and uplift and civilize them, and by God's grace do the very best by them as our fellow-men for whom Christ also died. And then I went to bed, and went to sleep and slept soundly.[30]

It is a dramatic story, but few historians believe it. Recent scholarship reveals that the president's reasons were both more complex and fascinating. From the moment he had heard of Dewey's smashing victory in Manila Bay, the president wanted at least to annex that port for the use of U.S. commerce and warships. Indeed, he ordered troops to leave for the Philippines even before he received official word that Dewey won. It marked the first time a president had ever ordered U.S. soldiers outside the Western Hemisphere to fight. McKinley delayed deciding whether to annex all the Philippine islands, which stretched over 115,000 square miles. McKinley did not want the responsibility for governing them, especially since a strong Filipino revolutionary army, which had been effectively fighting Spain before 1898, intended to govern its own homeland. Nevertheless, as fighting continued in the summer of 1898, McKinley kept his options open: "While we are conducting war and until its conclusion we must keep all we get; when the war is over we must keep what we want."[31] On October 25, 1898, the president finally instructed the U.S. commissioners in Paris, who were negotiating peace terms, to demand all the islands. In return, the United States offered Spain $20 million.

McKinley made the decision for a number of reasons. He concluded that the Filipinos could not run their own country. Dewey had cabled him in mid-October that "the natives appear unable to govern." The problem was similar to the Cuban situation: the revolutionaries were divided among themselves, and one radical faction threatened property holdings. That difficulty led to a second reason for McKinley's decision: a civil war could allow those whom he termed "our commercial rivals in the Orient" (France, Germany, and Great Britain) to seize the islands. McKinley, moreover, had to make his decision just as the China cauldron began boiling again. Russia threatened to close Chinese ports, including Port Arthur, that were vital for U.S. commerce. Great

Britain considered quitting the open-door policy and joining the race for Chinese loot. To protect U.S. interests, the president needed a secure base. To use Manila for that purpose, however, required control of Luzon, Manila's home island. But to protect Luzon, McKinley learned, meant controlling the adjoining islands. As one U.S. army officer testified in mid-October, with "over 400 islands in the group . . . a cannon shot can be fired from one to another in many instances." Thus, the final and most important reason for McKinley's decision: to protect the naval base at Manila, he had to take all the islands.[32]

American public opinion had little to do with his decision. That opinion, as usual, was sharply divided. The *Presbyterian Banner* declared in August 1898 that the religious press, almost without exception, agreed on "the desirability of America's retaining the Philippines as a duty in the interest of human freedom and Christian progress." Three months later the same journal announced: "We have been morally compelled to become an Asiatic power. . . . America and Great Britain will see to it that China is not Russianized."[33] On the other side, many Americans, especially Democrats, feared extending the Constitution across the Pacific. Even McKinley's own cabinet was divided. His wartime secretary of state (and close friend from Ohio days), William R. Day, opposed annexation.

During a congressional campaign swing through the Midwest in October, the president decided he would test opinion on the annexation question. But he did so in an odd fashion. McKinley repeatedly brought crowds to their feet with rousing, patriotic speeches, such as one in Hastings, Iowa: "We want new markets, and as trade follows the flag, it looks very much as if we are going to have new markets." The president nevertheless seemed struck by how hard he had to work to arouse his audiences. As historian Ephraim Smith concludes, McKinley "seemed more concerned about the public's apprehension about accepting new responsibilities."[34]

Proof of that apprehension appeared on February 6, 1899, when the Senate accepted McKinley's peace treaty 57 to 27, a mere one vote more than the two-thirds needed to ratify. Until the final twenty-four hours, victory was in doubt. McKinley, aided by Republican Senate leaders, lobbied hard and distributed patronage plums with a free hand to obtain votes. Oddly, the president received unneeded last-minute help from his old Democratic opponent, William Jennings Bryan. The Democrat had fought annexation, then suddenly switched to urge Democratic senators to vote for the treaty. Bryan later argued that he wanted ratification so that the war would officially end, lives would be

Richard Jordan Gatling stands by his Gatling Gun, the parent of the machine gun. Samuel Colt and others had developed a repeating rifle before the Civil War, but Gatling's 1862 patent led to the most famous rapid-fire weapon. Not used in the Civil War, the Gatling Gun was used to quell riots in New Orleans during 1868, to kill Indians during the 1870s–1880s campaigns, and, most famously, to help win the battle of Santiago, Cuba, against Spain in 1898, and to put down the Philippine revolt.

saved, and the Philippine mistake would then be corrected through diplomacy.[35] It was, however, one of Bryan's many unrealized dreams. Of even greater importance than Bryan's turn was the news that reached Washington on the evening before the vote: Filipino rebels had attacked U.S. soldiers. The revolt against American control had begun. McKinley immediately understood that he had won: a vote against his treaty could now be seen as a vote against supporting the U.S. soldiers embattled by the Filipinos.

The insurrection marked the first of many antirevolutionary wars fought by the United States in the twentieth century. The rebels were led by Emilio Aguinaldo (a moderate who had executed the more radical opponent within the revolutionary movement, Andres Bonifacio). They had originally welcomed the U.S. force that defeated Spain. Welcome turned to hostility when they learned that the Americans intended to remain. McKinley paid little attention to Aguinaldo until the rebel declared the creation of a Philippine republic in January 1899. The war that erupted the next month continued for three years. At first, U.S. officers believed that they could subdue the barefoot opponents with 20,000 or 30,000 men. Soon, the commanders asked McKinley for 40,000, then 60,000 regulars. In all, 120,000 U.S. troops finally fought in the Philippines. Nearly 4,200 were killed and 2,800 wounded. In turn, they killed outright 15,000 rebels, and estimates run as high as 200,000 Filipinos dying from gunfire, starvation, and the effects of

U.S. troops had to fight a vicious four-year war to defeat the Filipino resistance and consolidate the American hold over Manila's valuable port, where this picture of street fighting was taken.

concentration camps into which the United States crowded civilians so that they could not help Aguinaldo's troops.[36]

Viewing the Filipinos as they had viewed Native Americans, U.S. soldiers coined the term "gooks" to describe them. These racial views allowed the war to be fought even more savagely. As a young infantryman from New York reported home: "Last night one of our boys was found shot and his stomach cut open. Immediately orders were received . . . to burn the town and kill every native in sight. . . . About 1,000 men, women, and children were reported killed. . . . I am in my glory when I can sight my gun on some dark skin and pull the trigger."[37] When rebels massacred a squad of U.S. troops, an American commander ordered the killing of every male over the age of ten—an order, fortunately, that was quickly countermanded by his superiors.

The revolution was finally quelled after McKinley moved General Arthur MacArthur to top command in 1900. The new leader (father of General Douglas MacArthur, who governed the Philippines in the 1930s and was U.S. commander in the Pacific during World War II) took a different tack. He fought the war vigorously but also offered amnesty to rebels who surrendered. MacArthur worked closely with the islands' wealthy elite, who prospered by cooperating with the Americans. In 1901, U.S. troops captured Aguinaldo. The back of the revolt was broken, although fighting continued at reduced levels until 1913. After that, U.S.-trained and -directed Filipino forces fought a continual series of wars against rebels, wars that lasted from 1913 until at least the 1990s.[38] The Philippines have never remained pacified for very long. For his part, Aguinaldo finally had revenge by collaborating with Japanese forces, who drove the United States out of the Philippines in World War II.

Warriors such as Theodore Roosevelt argued that Americans had to remain in the Philippines to develop their own character and teach the natives self-government. Democratic senator Edward Carmack from Tennessee acidly observed that Roosevelt admitted that it had taken Anglo-Saxons one thousand years to learn self-government. Thus, "we are not to hold [the islands] permanently," Carmack quipped, "we want to experiment with them for only a thousand years or so." Famed sociologist William Graham Sumner was more pointed: "We talk of civilizing lower races, but we have never done it yet. We have exterminated them." Despite such criticisms, Carmack and Sumner could not slow McKinley's and Roosevelt's policies for taking the Philippines. After all, as Assistant Secretary of the Treasury (and banker) Frank Vanderlip observed, the Philippines were to be the U.S. Hong Kong so Americans could "trade with the millions of China and Korea, French Indo-China, the Malay Peninsula and the islands of Indonesia."[39]

McKinley's Triumphs in China

In 1899–1900, the president vividly demonstrated why the Philippines were vital for his foreign policy. At long last, he was free to fight the threat to the open door in China. The crisis had begun in 1897–1898 (see p. 200). By mid-1899, the Russians and Germans threatened to colonize and close off strategic areas of China. Meanwhile, the British, French, Japanese, and Americans scrambled to protect their trade and other interests. None of the powers was primarily concerned about the Chinese themselves. As Americans, for example, pressed for greater rights in China, they closed off Chinese rights of immigration obtained in the 1868 Burlingame Treaty.

By 1882, so many Chinese had found work in the United States that Americans were fearful. In that year, Congress passed the first anti-immigration measure in U.S. history when it stopped Chinese immigration for ten years. Anti-Chinese outbreaks nevertheless spread. In 1885, a mob killed twenty-eight Chinese in Wyoming. Observers feared even worse bloodshed would occur in California, where many Asian immigrants had settled. By the 1880s and 1890s, Americans were increasingly discriminating against immigrants just as the Americans themselves were moving out into other countries such as China and the Philippines. This historic turn was dramatized in 1886, when, in magnificent ceremonies, the United States dedicated the Statue of Liberty, placed in New York City Harbor as a gift from France. Not one speech in the ceremonies mentioned the lines Emma Lazarus had written for the statue: "Give me your tired, your poor, / Your huddled masses yearning to breathe free." Instead, the speakers stressed how Americans must go forth to spread liberty throughout other lands.[40]

In China, however, Americans seemed less interested in liberty for the Chinese than the liberty to sell goods for profit and save souls for Christianity. Economically, U.S. exports to China nearly quadrupled to $15 million between 1895 and 1900.[41] The Chinese took only 1 percent to 2 percent of total U.S. exports, but Americans focused on the potential (hundreds of millions of Chinese) and that market's rapid growth since 1895. Certain industries and sections in the United States depended utterly on the China market. No producers needed it more than those making textiles. That product ranked first among exports, with petroleum second, iron and steel products third. New England textile plants had overexpanded, then were badly stung by the 1873–1897 economic depression. Some moved to the South, but, as one spokesman warned, it was better to avoid "destructive competition" at home by developing markets abroad. "We want the open door," a Georgia senator exclaimed, "and a big one at that."[42] Historian Patrick Hearden concludes that by 1899, "the New South's rapidly growing China trade promised to keep the entire American cotton industry in a healthy condition."[43]

But no group surpassed the Christian missionaries' involvement in China. It was an era of extraordinary growth: between 1870 and 1900, Americans increased their Protestant overseas missions by 500 percent. In the single decade of the 1890s, U.S. missionaries in China doubled in number to over one thousand. This great movement arose in part out of the churches' determination to defy threats to their beliefs posed by new science and Darwinian challenges. The movement also sprang from colleges, where religious revivalism on such campuses as Oberlin, Cornell, and Yale produced the Student Volunteer Movement for Foreign Missions in 1887. By 1900, the Student Volunteers, who marched under the proud banner proclaiming "The Evangelization of the World in This Generation," had chapters in nearly every Protestant college. These groups reflected the profit seeking as well as soul seeking of the late nineteenth century. Some missionaries invested in foreign land and minerals; others preached morality and profit at once by asking that saved souls wear North Carolina textiles.[44] The missionaries patriotically represented their country as well as their religion. They also became more interested in mass conversion than in the slower saving of individual sinners from the fires of hell. Thus, they looked increasingly to the U.S. government for help and protection, especially as the other foreign powers crowded into Asia. This new approach was exemplified in 1896, when the U.S. government ordered a commission to travel to the Chinese government and insist on American rights. As Professor Thomas McCormick explains, "The commission consisted of the American Consul at Tientsin, a missionary, and a naval officer—the expansionist trinity."[45]

Women, especially a rising feminist movement, became an important source of missionary expansionism both at home and abroad. In 1880, about twenty women's foreign missionary societies existed. The number doubled by 1900. By 1915, 3 million women belonged to these forty societies. Some of the groups aimed to carry abroad the values of middle-class America. As one leader wrote, "The aim of this woman's work we conceive to be *in heathen lands*— . . . in bringing the women into His Kingdom, in the creation of Christian mothers." The "fathers and brothers" were to "strike vigorous blows at the brains of heathendom, to superintend large educational and evangelistic enterprises." But "to woman belongs the quiet, patient labour in the homes of the people." Women also understood, however, how they were to bring creature comforts and new values of an industrialized America to the "heathen." As one woman declared, foreign missionary work "should appeal to every broad-minded Christian woman who is interested in education, civics, sanitation, social settlements, hospitals, good literature, the emancipation of children, the right of women to health, home and protection; and the coming of the Kingdom of our Lord." As historian Patricia R. Hill observes, by this time, it seems, the Lord's kingdom tended to come at the end of the list.[46] American goods and social values went into China with the missionaries, both male and female.

The belief grew, as Secretary of State John Hay noted in 1900, that whoever understood China "has the key to world politics for the next five centuries."[47] No one tried harder to understand, or—after Seward—contributed more to U.S. policy in China than did Hay, the author of

John Hay (1838–1905) was born in Indiana and had a distinguished career as secretary to Lincoln, an official in the Department of State, industrialist in Ohio, and U.S. ambassador to Great Britain before becoming a powerful secretary of state (1898–1905). A poet and novelist as well, Hay drafted the historic "open-door" notes of 1899–1900.

the 1899–1900 open-door notes. Nor did anyone better understand how U.S. business and politics related to policy in China. Born in Indiana in 1838, Hay went to Brown University, then used his midwestern political contacts to become Abraham Lincoln's secretary at the age of twenty-three. Hay grew to fear the mass, urbanized, industrialized society that developed after 1865. His fear multiplied when he entered the steel business in Cleveland and had to deal with the rising labor movement. He anonymously published a novel, *The Bread-Winners*, that remains one of the bitterest attacks ever made on the labor movement, especially the movement's foreign members. But he also worried that "the rich and intelligent" were so busy making money, they ignored the dangers: they "hate politics" and so "fatten themselves as sheep which could be mutton whenever the butcher was ready." Hay had no intention of becoming mutton. He supported McKinley in 1896, and the new president named him U.S. ambassador to Great Britain in 1897. Hay greatly admired England. He believed passionately that the British and Americans could save themselves and the best parts of their societies only by fighting Russia's, France's, and Germany's attempts "to divide and reduce China to a system of tributary provinces." McKinley knew Hay well and recalled him in 1898 to lead the fight for China as secretary of state.[48]

Hay's first initiative was an open-door note of 1899 that asked the other powers (especially Russia and Germany) to charge foreigners no more than their own citizens paid for shipping and railway privileges within so-called "spheres of interest" in China that each power claimed.

Hay's note also insisted that the general Chinese tariff apply to all the spheres of interest, and that China collect the duties itself. Chinese territorial integrity was to be reinforced. No other power rushed to agree with Hay's note, but none directly defied it either. Russia did not as yet believe that it had sufficient power to challenge the Americans, who were supported to some degree by Great Britain and Japan. Hay finally gained assent through an ingenious diplomatic tactic. He first gained agreement from the British and Japanese, who he knew were closest to his position, then obtained France's assent. Germany and Russia then had to agree or defy the other powers. The two nations did go along, but with considerable grumbling. With no U.S. military force in China and without making any political alliance with other powers, Hay had maneuvered them into declaring their agreement with U.S. open-door policy—a policy, as Hay neatly defined it, of "fair field and no favor" for anyone who wanted to compete in the China market. He and other knowledgeable Americans knew that with such ground rules, they could use their growing industrial power to undersell nearly any-

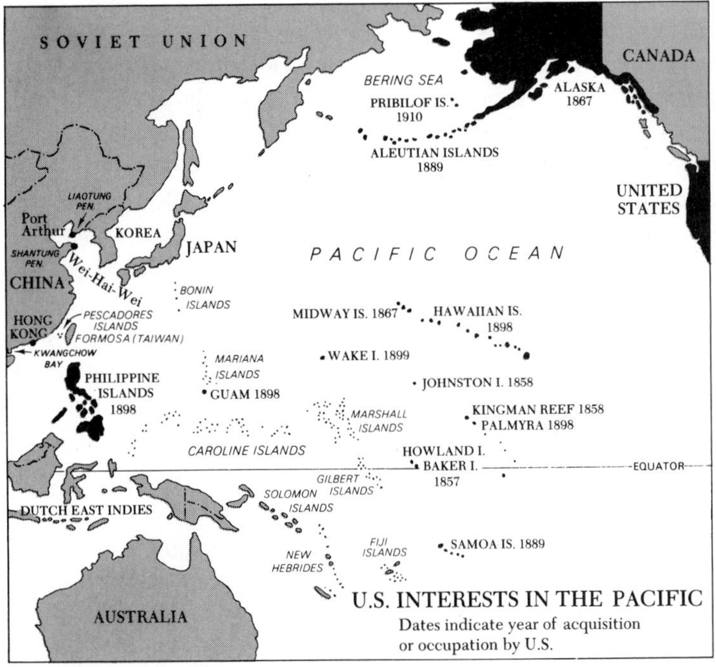

By 1900, the new U.S. economic and military interests had stepping stones for crossing the Pacific to reach Asia. The dates indicate when the United States acquired its possessions.

one and capture much of China's market. That was, indeed, another sign of the high stakes for which McKinley and Hay played: they wanted to sell to all of China, not just a sliver or a sphere they might annex.

But the Chinese themselves refused to stand still while the powers exploited them. In early 1900, the empress dowager, head of the collapsing Manchu dynasty, encouraged a radical antiforeign and militaristic society known as the Boxers to attack foreigners and their property. By May, foreign compounds in Chinese cities were besieged. On May 29, U.S. minister Edwin Conger captured the terror when he cabled Washington from the capital of Beijing (Peking): "Boxers increasing. Nine Methodist converts brutally murdered at Pachow. The movement has developed into open rebellion. Chinese government is trying but apparently is unable to surpress it. Many soldiers disloyal."[49] The foreign powers, including the United States, sent in troops to protect their citizens. It became clear, however, that Russia, Germany, and even Japan were using the Boxers as an excuse to seal off parts of China into their own spheres of interest.

After McKinley ordered 5,000 U.S. troops to move from Manila into China, Hay used the force as a bargaining chip. He tried to pressure the other powers to agree to a policy of July 3, 1900, that became known as the second open-door notes. He asked all powers to declare directly that they promised to preserve "Chinese territorial and administrative integrity." This key point had only been implied in the 1899 notes. With the powers nervously eying each other as well as the Boxers, all of them fell into line behind Hay. McKinley and his secretary of state had pulled off a remarkable victory. By 1901, Russia seemed checked. The president had greatly increased his executive power by sending thousands of U.S. troops onto the mainland of China without bothering to consult Congress. And the foreign powers maintained the Manchu dynasty as the ruler of China, although that victory was short-lived. In 1911, internal conflict again erupted, and this time the dynasty disappeared amid the beginnings of the Chinese Revolution.

Hay understood both sides of U.S. policy in China: the American need for markets both commercial and religious, and the relatively little power the United States could exert in the region. In August 1900, a crisis flared when Russia again made threatening moves. This time, the British indicated that they might join the Russians. McKinley, in the middle of a tough re-election fight against Bryan, uncharacteristically panicked. He seriously considered carving off an area of China for the United States—that is, giving up the open-door policy and joining the other colonial powers. From a sickbed in New Hampshire, Hay

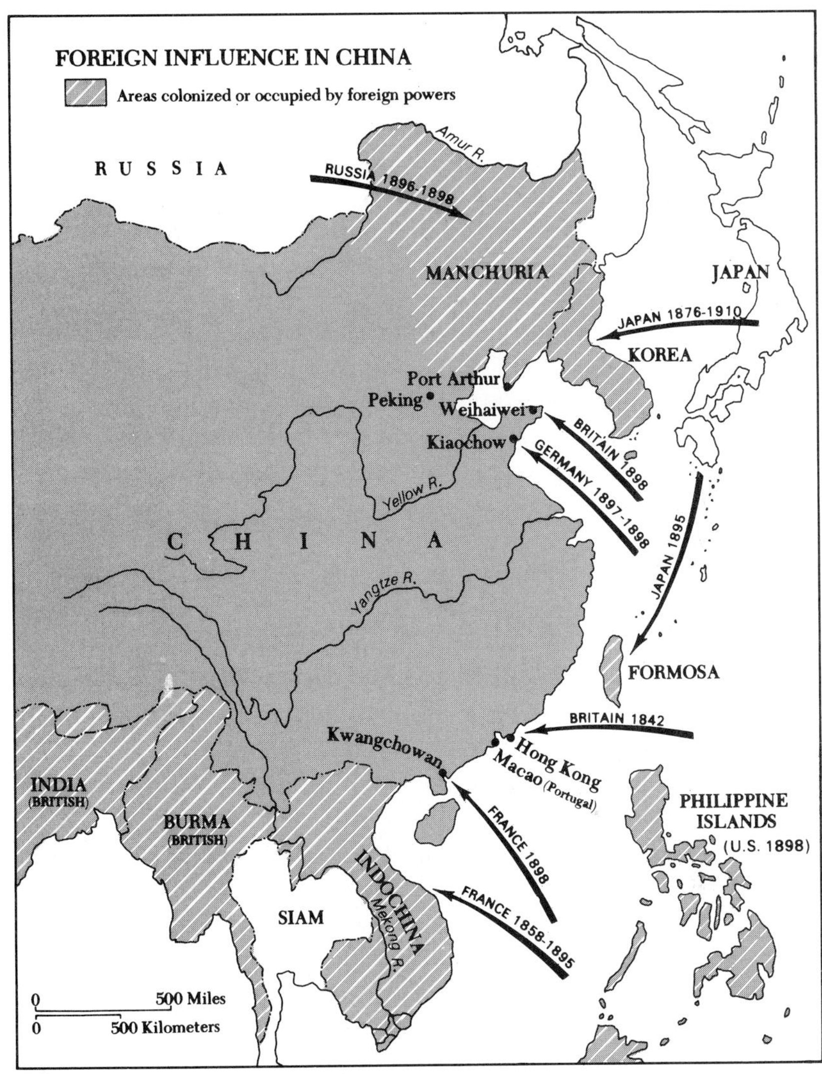

China became an object of big-power competition and colonialism—"the bone" amid the dogs, as a later U.S. official called China.

convinced the president not to surrender the open-door approach. He did so by giving McKinley a lesson in power politics:

> The inherent weakness of our position is this: we do not want to rob China ourselves, and our public opinion will not permit us to interfere, with an army, to prevent others from robbing her. Besides, we have no army. The

> talk of the papers about "our preeminent moral position giving the authority to dictate to the world" is mere flap-doodle.[50]

Hay concluded that McKinley had no alternative but to remain in China and try to keep the powers *voluntarily* lined up behind the open-door policy. This could be accomplished not through U.S. military force, but only by playing power off against power, as Hay had done in 1899 and again in 1900. The secretary of state himself weakened only once. In late 1900, the U.S. War Department insisted that the navy needed a base in China. No doubt with some embarrassment, Hay asked the Chinese for a lease at Samsah Bay. Japan, which had plans of its own for China, quickly objected by throwing Hay's policy back at him: the U.S. request violated the open-door policy. The secretary of state dropped the request.

. . . AND A FINAL TRIUMPH AT HOME

By November 1900, the crisis in China had apparently passed—and none too soon. Throughout 1899–1900, Bryan and the Democrats had planned to club McKinley's re-election hopes with the issues of the bloody Philippine campaign and the volatile China crisis. Throughout the summer of 1900, both sides hotly debated foreign policy. The Democrats termed it "the paramount issue" in the election fight.

An "anti-imperialist" movement had grown rapidly after mid-1898 to oppose McKinley's policies. This movement was led by wealthy and upper-middle-class professionals (especially lawyers), mostly from the Northeast and Midwest. But it also included an increasing number of women. Historian Judith Papachristou estimates that in the five years after 1898 tens of thousands of women became foreign-policy activists: "Never before had American women involved themselves in foreign affairs in such a way and to such an extent." When the Anti-Imperialist League began to form at a meeting in Boston's Faneuil Hall during June 1898, more than half the audience was female. Women determined to have voting rights easily identified with Filipinos who were to be governed without their consent. Some anti-imperialists, both female and male, feared that extending the Constitution to the Philippines, Puerto Rico, and even Hawaii might change the basic provisions of the document and bring into the system certain races who were considered dangerous to traditional American values. Many anti-imperialists argued that these peoples were not ready for self-government; but if the United States tried to rule them, it would turn into an imperialist power and thus destroy its own democratic values. A South Carolina senator warned against "the incorporation of a mongrel and semibarbarous population into our body politic."[51]

That warning hit home in the North as well as the South. About 150 black people were lynched each year in the United States during the early 1890s. Race riots erupted in New York City in 1900, as well as earlier in southern states. It was not the time, Bryan and other anti-imperialists argued, to try to teach democracy to Filipinos with the tips of bayonets. Henry Blake Fuller caught the spirit with his anti-imperialist poetry of 1899. He dealt with the president of the United States as follows:

> G is for Guns
> That McKinley has sent,
> To teach Filipinos
> What Jesus Christ meant.

Fuller also provided a self-portrait of McKinley's vice-presidential running mate, Theodore Roosevelt, as anti-imperialists painted it:

> I'm a cut and thrusting bronco-busting
> Megaphone of Mars,
> And it's fire I breathe and I cut my teeth
> On nails and wrought-iron bars.[52]

Such extreme rhetoric could be discounted, but McKinley could not disregard Andrew Carnegie's large bankroll which financed many anti-imperialist activities.

The president directly challenged the anti-imperialists by naming Theodore Roosevelt to the Republican ticket. No one was more identified with, or more loudly defended, U.S. expansionism. Governor of New York in 1900, Roosevelt at first did not want to be only a vice-president. ("I would rather be professor of history in some college," he wrote a friend.) But he finally gave in, rightly noting that "it was believed that I would greatly strengthen the ticket in the West, where they regard me as a fellow barbarian and like me much."[53] While McKinley remained in Washington or in his hometown of Canton, Ohio, Roosevelt spun across the country, giving as many as ten speeches a day until he finally lost his voice on the eve of the election.

He blasted the anti-imperialist arguments. Because "the Philippines are now part of American territory," the only question was whether the Democrats planned "to surrender American territory." He attacked the anti-imperialists as antiexpansionist and thus, he charged, they had deserted the ideals of their own father—Thomas Jefferson—who had taken all of Louisiana. Dealing with the Indians, TR argued, established the needed precedents for dealing with the Filipinos, who were also "savages." If whites were "morally bound to abandon the Philippines, we were also morally bound to abandon Arizona to the Apaches." Bayonets were needed because "the barbarian will yield only to force." Other Republicans mocked Democrats who urged self-government in the Philippines or Hawaii by asking when the Democrats planned to extend the Declaration of Independence to southern black people. One observer commented on "Democrats howling about Republicans shooting negroes in the Philippines and the Republicans objecting to Democrats shooting negroes in the South. This may be good politics, but it is rough on the negroes."[54]

McKinley and Roosevelt decisively won the argument. By September, the president's policy in China and TR's attacks from the stump forced Bryan to reverse his campaign strategy. The Democratic nominee dropped foreign policy and began to emphasize Republican economic policy. His decision turned out to be politically fatal. The United States had emerged from its twenty-five-year depression to bask in prosperity in 1900. McKinley ran on the slogan "Let Well Enough Alone." He defeated Bryan more decisively in 1900 than he had four years before and even captured Bryan's home state of Nebraska. In the end, many anti-imperialists, including Andrew Carnegie, found that they could not tolerate Bryan's more radical economic program (especially after he dropped foreign-policy issues) and joined McKinley.

The president had led the United States into the small, select circle of great world powers. He did so not by following those powers and conquering large colonies. Between 1870 and 1900, Great Britain added 4.7 million square miles to its empire, France 3.5 million, and Germany 1.0 million. Americans, however, added only 125,000 square miles. They wanted not land, but more markets to free them of the horrors that had resulted from the post-1873 depression. Louisville newspaper publisher and Democratic party boss Henry Watterson explained what had occurred in 1898:

> From a nation of shopkeepers we became a nation of warriors. . . . We escape the menace and the peril of socialism and agrarianism, as England escaped them, by a policy of colonization and conquest. It is true that we

> exchange domestic dangers for foreign dangers; but in every direction we multiply the opportunities of the people. We risk Caesarism certainly; but even Caesarism is preferable to anarchism.[55]

In September 1901, Watterson's "Caesar" traveled to Buffalo, New York, to explain to Americans the new world in which they lived. The president was greeted by a spectacular fireworks display that climaxed with the exclamation in the sky: "WELCOME MCKINLEY, CHIEF OF OUR NATION AND EMPIRE." As historian Edward Crapol summarizes, Americans were—finally—the equal of the British, and rapidly becoming more than equal.[56] The United States, McKinley told the Pan-American Exposition in Buffalo, now had "almost appalling" wealth. Consequently, "isolation is no longer possible or desirable." Americans had to frame new tariff and other policies to conquer world markets.

The next day, a deranged man shot and mortally wounded McKinley. That "wild man," as Marcus Hanna had called Theodore Roosevelt, suddenly became president of the United States. Once again, historian Robert Beisner notes, Americans were to test whether "a republic can prosper in a career of empire."[57] They would have to do so under the leadership of a person more flamboyant—and unpredictable—than McKinley.

Notes

1. Ernest R. May, *Imperial Democracy* (New York, 1961), p. 270; Albert K. Weinberg, *Manifest Destiny* (Baltimore, 1940), p. 273.
2. Robert L. Beisner, *From the Old Diplomacy to the New, 1865–1900* (Arlington Heights, Ill., 1986), p. 89.
3. V. O. Key, "A Theory of Critical Elections," *Journal of Politics* 17 (February 1955): 12–15.
4. William Allen White, *The Autobiography of William Allen White* (New York, 1946), p. 292; Paul Boller, Jr., *Presidential Anecdotes* (New York, 1981), p. 189.
5. Henry Adams, *The Education of Henry Adams, an Autobiography* (Boston, 1918), p. 423. The best recent study of McKinley's extensive use of presidential powers is Lewis Gould, *The Presidency of William McKinley* (Lawrence, Kans., 1980).
6. Frances Fitzgerald, "Rewriting American History," *New Yorker*, 26 February 1979, p. 66. A Latin American view of the evolving U.S.-Cuban relationship is Manuel Moreno Fraginals, "Cuban-American Relations and the Sugar Trade," in *Diplo-*

matic Claims: Latin American Historians View the United States, ed. and trans. Warren Dean (Lanham, Md., 1985).

7. *Washington Post*, 21 July 1983, p. A23.
8. L. White Busbey, *Uncle Joe Cannon* (New York, 1927), p. 187.
9. *Journal of Commerce*, 14 March 1898, p. 1.
10. Theodore Roosevelt to George Dewey, 25 February 1898, Ciphers Sent, 1888–1898, Record Group 45, National Archives, Washington, D.C.; Charles S. Campbell, *The Transformation of American Foreign Relations, 1865–1900* (New York, 1976), pp. 279–280. Campbell's is the best-detailed analysis of the entire era and has a superb bibliography.
11. Fitzhugh Lee to William R. Day, 27 November 1897, Consular, Havana, and Hyatt to William R. Day, 23 March 1898, Consular, Santiago, Record Group 59, National Archives, Washington, D.C.
12. W. C. Reick to J. R. Young, 25 March 1898, Papers of William McKinley, Library of Congress, Washington, D.C.
13. Paul S. Holbo, "Presidential Leadership in Foreign Affairs: William McKinley and the Turpie-Foraker Amendment," *American Historical Review* 72 (July 1967): 1322–1334.
14. A superb analysis of the literature on McKinley and the war is Joseph Fry, "Essay Review: William McKinley and the Coming of the Spanish-American War," *Diplomatic History* 3 (Winter 1979): 77–97; John L. Offner, *An Unwanted War* (Chapel Hill, N.C., 1992), p. 189.
15. William Michael Morgan, "The Anti-Japanese Origins of the Hawaiian Annexation Treaty of 1897," *Diplomatic History* 6 (Winter 1982): 25–34.
16. *Washington Evening Star*, 11 January 1898, p. 1; 13 January 1898, p. 4; 19 January 1898, p. 14; also William Adam Russ, Jr., *The Hawaiian Republic, 1894–1898* (Selinsgrove, Pa., 1961), p. 240.
17. Alan K. Henrikson, "Maps, Globes, and 'The Cold War,' " *Special Libraries* 65 (October–November 1974): 445–454.
18. Frank Freidel, "Dissent in the Spanish-American War," in Samuel Eliot Morison *et al., Dissent in Three American Wars* (Cambridge, Mass., 1970), pp. 74–75; the May 4 cable from Manila is in U.S. Senate Document no. 62, *A Treaty of Peace . . .*, 55th Cong., 3d sess. (Washington, D.C., 1899), p. 326.
19. Russell Weigley, *The American Way of War* (New York, 1973), pp. 183–184.
20. Frank Freidel, *The Splendid Little War* (Boston, 1958), p. 46.
21. Theodore Roosevelt, *The Letters of Theodore Roosevelt*, ed. Elting E. Morison *et al.*, 8 vols. (Cambridge, Mass., 1951–1954), II, p. 1099n.
22. Thomas J. McCormick, *The China Market* (Chicago, 1967), p. 224.
23. David F. Healy, *The United States in Cuba, 1898–1902* (Madison, 1963), pp. 34–36.
24. Leonard Wood to Theodore Roosevelt, 28 October 1901, Papers of Leonard Wood, Library of Congress, Washington, D.C.
25. Healy, pp. 204–205.
26. Lloyd Gardner, "From Containment to Liberation," in *From Colony to Empire*, ed. William Appleman Williams (New York, 1972), p. 220.
27. Richard M. Morse, "Embarrassing Colony," *New York Review of Books*, 6 December 1984, p. 17.
28. Louis Henkin, *Foreign Affairs and the Constitution* (Mineola, N.Y., 1972), pp. 268, 330.

29. The best analysis on post-1898 is now Raymond Carr, *Puerto Rico, a Colonial Experiment* (New York, 1984).
30. Lazar Ziff, *America in the 1890s* (New York, 1966), p. 221. The original account appeared after McKinley's death in the *Charleston Advocate* 68 (22 January 1903): 137–138; I am indebted to R. H. (Max) Miller for this citation.
31. H. Wayne Morgan, *America's Road to Empire: The War with Spain and Overseas Expansion* (New York, 1965), esp. chs. IV, V.
32. McCormick, pp. 168–187; Ephraim K. Smith, " 'A Question from Which We Could Not Escape': William McKinley and the Decision to Annex the Philippine Islands," *Diplomatic History* 9 (Fall 1985): 363–388; John Offner, "The U.S. and France: Ending the Spanish-American War," *Diplomatic History* 7 (Winter 1983): 1–22.
33. Julius W. Pratt, *Expansionists of 1898* (Baltimore, 1936), pp. 297–298.
34. Smith, 373.
35. William Jennings Bryan to Mrs. U. S. Wissler, 20 May 1900, Papers of William Jennings Bryan, Library of Congress, Washington, D.C. A fine discussion of this point and the context is given by Richard H. Miller in his edition of *American Imperialism in 1898* (New York, 1970), pp. 10–12.
36. Freidel, "Dissent in the Spanish-American War," p. 93.
37. A most compelling account, which includes this story, is David Haward Bain, *Sitting in Darkness: Americans in the Philippines* (Boston, 1984).
38. Russell Roth's *Muddy Glory: America's "Indian Wars" in the Philippines, 1899–1935* (West Hanover, Mass., 1981) is a good account of the post-1902 battles.
39. David Healy, *U.S. Expansionism: The Imperialist Urge in the 1890s* (Madison, 1970), pp. 237–238; Emily Rosenberg, *Spreading the American Dream* (New York, 1982), p. 43.
40. John Higham, *Strangers in the Land* (New Brunswick, N.J., 1955), pp. 14, 63.
41. U.S. Bureau of the Census, *Historical Statistics of the United States: Colonial Times to 1957* (Washington, D.C., 1960), p. 55.
42. Patrick J. Hearden, *Independence and Empire: The New South's Cotton Mill Campaign, 1865–1901* (DeKalb, Ill., 1982), pp. 127, 133.
43. *Ibid.*, p. 128.
44. Beisner, p. 83.
45. McCormick, p. 65.
46. Patricia R. Hill, *The World Their Household: The American Woman's Foreign Mission Movement and Cultural Transformation, 1870–1920* (Ann Arbor, 1985), pp. 3, 54, 112, 164; a fine case study is Joan Brumberg's *Mission for Life: The Story of the Family of Adoniram Judson . . .* (New York, 1980).
47. William Neumann, "Determinism, Destiny, and Myth in the American Image of China," in *Issues and Conflicts*, ed. George L. Anderson (Lawrence, 1959), p. 1.
48. This account is drawn from Walter LaFeber, "John Hay," in *Encyclopedia of American Biography*, ed. John A. Garraty and Jerome L. Sternstein (New York, 1974), pp. 502–503.
49. Edwin Conger to John Hay, 29 May 1900, Papers of William McKinley, Library of Congress, Washington, D.C.
50. John Hay to Alvey A. Adee, 14 September 1900, Papers of William McKinley.
51. Judith Papachristou, "American Women and Foreign Policy, 1898–1905: Exploring Gender in Diplomatic History," *Diplomatic History* 14 (Fall 1990), esp. pp. 493–500; *Congressional Record*, 55th Cong., 3d sess., 13 January 1899, p. 639.

52. Fred H. Harrington, "American Anti-Imperialism," *New England Quarterly* 10 (December 1937): 654–655.
53. Roosevelt, II, pp. 1244, 1291, 1358.
54. *Ibid.*, pp. 1404–1405; Walter L. Williams, "U.S. Indian Policy and the Debate over Philippine Annexation," *Journal of American History* 66 (March 1980): 819–826, 830–831; Martin Ridge, *Ignatius Donnelly* (Chicago, 1962), pp. 394–397.
55. Richard Hofstadter, *The Paranoid Style in American Politics and Other Essays* (New York, 1965), pp. 180–181.
56. Edward Crapol, "From Anglophobia to Fragile Rapprochement," unpublished paper in author's possession, p. 21.
57. Beisner, p. xviii.

For Further Reading

No text can hope to match the references for pre-1981 material in *Guide to American Foreign Relations since 1700*, ed. Richard Dean Burns (1983). Also consult this chapter's notes and the General Bibliography at the end of this volume. The bibliography that follows, as in all the bibliographies in this book, concentrates on post-1981 works.

Cultural influences are well explored in Stuart Anderson, *Race and Rapprochement: Anglo-Saxonism and Anglo-American Relations, 1895–1904* (1981), and Gary Marotta, "The Academic Mind and the Rise of U.S. Imperialism: Historians and Economists as Publicists for Ideas of Colonial Expansion," *American Journal of Economics and Sociology* 42 (April 1983). McKinley and the march toward war are nicely analyzed in John Offner, *An Unwanted War* (1992); Richard E. Welch, Jr., "William McKinley: Reluctant Warrior, Cautious Imperialist," in *Studies in American Diplomacy, 1865–1945*, ed. Norman Graebner (1985); Robert C. Hilderbrand, *Power and the People: Executive Management of Public Opinion in Foreign Affairs, 1897–1921* (1981), a pioneering account; Tennant McWilliams, *Hannis Taylor: The New Southerner as an American* (1978); David R. Contosta and Jessica R. Hawthorne, "Rise to World Power: Selected Letters of Whitelaw Reid, 1895–1912," in *Transactions of the American Philosophical Society* (1986), key on a major figure; Carl Parrini, "Charles A. Conant," in *Behind the Throne*, eds. T. McCormick and W. LaFeber (1993), essays in honor of Fred Harvey Harrington; and a superb study of Reid's influential newspaper in Richard Kluger, *The Paper: The Life and Death of the New York Herald Tribune* (1986). The best one-volume study of the war itself is David F. Trask, *The War with Spain in 1898* (1981).

Michael H. Hunt, "Resistance and Collaboration in the American Empire, 1898–1903: An Overview," *Pacific Historical Review* 48 (June 1979), provides interesting case studies of Cuba, China, and the Philippines; Hawaii is analyzed in Thomas J. Osborne, *Empire Can Wait: American Opposition to Hawaiian Annexation, 1893–1898* (1981), especially good on commercial interests; Cuba's revolt is seen as a prototype of later national wars for liberation in Louis A. Perez, Jr., *Cuba between Empires, 1878–1902* (1983); the Philippines are well explored in three key works: Stuart Creighton Miller, *"Benevolent Assimilation": The American Conquest of the Philippines, 1899–1903* (1983), which stresses racism; Kenton J. Clymer, *Protestant Missionaries in the Philippines, 1898–*

1916: An Inquiry into the American Colonial Mentality (1985); and *The Anti-Imperialist Reader: A Documentary History of Anti-Imperialism in the United States*, Vol. I: *From the Mexican War to the Election of 1900*, ed. Philip S. Foner and Richard C. Winchester (1984). For affairs in China, see James J. Lorence, "Organized Business and the Myth of the China Market: The American Asiatic Association, 1898–1937," in *Transactions of the American Philosophical Society* (1984); James Reed, *The Missionary Mind and American East Asia Policy* (1985); and the fascinating case study by Jane Hunter, *The Gospel of Gentility: American Women Missionaries in Turn-of-the-Century China* (1984).

New overviews include Jules R. Benjamin, *The United States and the Origins of the Cuban Revolution* (1990); Ivan Musicant, *The Banana Wars* (1990); Joseph A. Fry, *John Tyler Morgan and the Search for Southern Autonomy* (1992), a significant study of the South's expansionism; H. W. Brands, *Bound to Empire: The United States and the Philippines* (1992), a highly useful synthesis; Paul Gordon Lauren, *Power and Prejudice: The Politics and Diplomacy of Racial Discrimination* (1988); and Walter LaFeber, *The American Search for Opportunity, 1865–1913*, in *The Cambridge History of U.S. Foreign Relations*, ed. Warren Cohen (1993), which has additional bibliography.

8

The Search for Opportunity: Rough Riders and Dollar Diplomats (1901–1913)

Theodore Roosevelt and Twentieth-Century U.S. Foreign Policy

William McKinley was the first twentieth-century president, but no chief executive has better caught, exemplified, and gloried in the spirit of modern America than Theodore Roosevelt. As *Time* magazine wrote in 1979, "He was America." At the 1984 Republican convention in Dallas, a young follower of Ronald Reagan explained:

> People sometimes ask me who was the last great President. Some say Kennedy. I don't think so. . . . I say Teddy Roosevelt. He was a fighter, he was stubborn. He was almost a salesman for America. America was the greatest country in the world and he was willing to go to any lengths to prove it. And he had the qualities I was brought up on—that you do the best you can, whatever it is. . . . He *loved* life. And he loved America.[1]

No president has been more colorful. "Cowboy, crime-fighter, soldier, and explorer . . . ," David Healy writes, "he fulfilled as an adult the ambitions of every small boy."[2] Roosevelt, however, was also as complex as the nation he led. Raised in New York City by private tutors, a graduate of Harvard, having traveled abroad extensively, he came from America's aristocratic class. The author of a dozen books, an avid naturalist, a lover of art (if it was traditional), he better combined the scholar-in-politics than anyone since John Quincy Adams. But he had also been a cowboy in South Dakota's Black Hills in the 1880s (where he went to mourn after his first wife had died in childbirth), worked as a lowly ward politician amid the rank corruption of New York City, and became uncommonly popular with mass America.

An aristocrat, a scholar, and a politician, Roosevelt also loved killing. After an argument with a girl friend, the twenty-year-old vented his anger by shooting a neighbor's dog. When he killed his first buffalo in the West, Roosevelt danced wildly around the carcass while his Indian guide watched in amazement. As noted in earlier chapters, TR justified slaughtering Indians, if necessary; their life, he wrote, was only "a few degrees less meaningless, squalid, and ferocious than that of the wild beasts." But he had little more use for certain whites. In his history of New York City, he approved of the killing of thirty men who had joined antidraft riots during the Civil War. TR called the shooting an "admirable object-lesson to the remainder" of New Yorkers.[3]

Perhaps Roosevelt's inclination for war and killing was part of a common racism at the time that justified the removal of "inferior" peoples. Perhaps it arose from the belief that when a "civilized" people used force, it would be limited and improve human character: "No triumph of peace is quite so great as the supreme triumphs of war," TR believed. In this case, however, he meant war against less industrialized nations: "In the long run civilized man finds he can keep the peace only by subduing his barbarian neighbor." As for possible conflict between more "civilized" nations, however, "we have every reason . . . to believe that [wars] will grow rarer and rarer."[4] Perhaps TR's urge to subdue others simply came out of his legendary energy. France's distinguished ambassador to the United States, Jean Jules Jusserand, told Paris officials about hiking with the president through Washington's Rock Creek Park:

> At last we came to the bank of a stream, rather too wide and deep to be forded. . . . But judge of my horror when I saw the President unbutton his clothes and heard him say, "We had better strip, so as not to wet our things in the creek." Then I, too, for the honor of France removed my apparel, everything except my lavender kid gloves. . . . "With your permission, Mr. President, I will keep these on; otherwise it would be embarrassing if we should meet ladies."

Theodore Roosevelt (1858–1919), born into an elite New York family (and also having experienced the life of a cowboy in the badlands of the Dakotas), became chief executive in 1901. He loved the presidency and the exercise of the new American power around the globe as much as most Americans loved him. Understanding that the U.S. mission often required the strenuous life of military force, Roosevelt declared that "I do not like to see young Christians with shoulders that slope like champagne bottles."

Other diplomats endured much the same experience in order to talk with the president of the United States. He once entertained a formal White House luncheon by using a judo hold to throw the Swiss Minister to the floor several times. An awed British official declared that Roosevelt was a combination of "St. Vitus and St. Paul . . . a great wonder of nature."[5]

Most of all, Roosevelt used force to bring about and maintain his central objective: order. Born in 1858, he grew to manhood amid the chaos of the Civil War and the post-1873 economic depression. He feared the danger posed by both the right ("the dull purblind folly of the very rich men," the "malefactors of great wealth"), and left-wing socialist and populist movements. He understood the need for reform;

but change had to evolve slowly, preferably under the guidance of a farseeing, honest broker with an aristocratic background. Roosevelt once said that he had become a modest reformer because "I intended to be one of the governing class." Only in that position could he preserve the best of American values by maintaining order and stability. A devotion to order especially explains TR's diplomacy. His policies abroad mirrored his politics at home. He opposed those whom he believed were reactionary (as tsarist Russia and, later, Kaiser Wilhelm's Germany), because by clinging to outdated beliefs they threatened to bring about catastrophic, radical change. But Roosevelt as strongly stood against those in Russia, China, and especially Latin America who worked for revolutionary change. TR, like the America of the Progressive Era that he led, sought a middle way.

He believed in the superiority of certain races, especially the Anglo-Saxon, because, in his view, they had organized, democratized, and especially industrialized and subdued "barbarians" more effectively than had other races. Roosevelt did not have great faith in Social Darwinism. (Social Darwinism enjoyed much popularity in his era and was used then and since to help explain why "lesser" peoples had to be controlled by the more "civilized." By applying Charles Darwin's studies on the evolution of lower animals to the evolution of human society, the Social Darwinians concluded that such "superior" races as the Anglo-Saxon resulted from unrestrained competition and individualism, and that the results were scientifically inevitable.) Roosevelt believed not in the Social Darwinians' inevitability, but in free will and an individual's (especially his own) ability to change society. He did not like rampant competition and individualism, for they too often had produced economic chaos, general disorder, and revolution.[6] He, instead, believed in regulating such competition so that disorder could be avoided. Roosevelt wanted order and peace, and for that he was prepared to go to war.

TR thus personally exemplified central themes of post-1890 U.S. foreign policy—a willingness to use force to obtain order, an emphasis on a special U.S. responsibility to guarantee stability in Latin America and Asia, and a belief that Anglo-Saxon values and successes gave Americans a right to conduct such foreign policy. He also hit upon a key theme of twentieth-century U.S. foreign policy when he declared in 1905: "The United States has not the slightest desire for territorial aggrandizement at the expense of any of its southern neighbors."[7] Americans wanted no more land.

After four hundred years, their quest for territorial expansion had ended in the twentieth century. Now they needed markets abroad. As Roosevelt's brilliant secretary of state, Elihu Root, announced in 1906, Americans had "for the first time accumulated a surplus of capital beyond the requirements of internal development."[8] Statistics bore out Root's announcement. Americans had invested overseas $0.7 billion in 1897, $2.5 billion in 1908, and, by 1914, $3.5 billion. Nearly half of those amounts went into Latin America, about 23 percent into Canada, 22 percent into Europe, and 5 percent to Asia (including the Philippines). William McKinley, almost until his dying breath, had preached the need for overseas markets to absorb products from American factories and farms. Roosevelt and Root agreed, but they now added the need for capital markets as well. They also believed that imaginative leadership could use this economic power to prevent disorder and revolution. American goods and capital could create happier, more stable societies in the Caribbean and Central America—even in distant Asia. Their successors, President William Howard Taft (1909–1913) and his secretary of state, Philander C. Knox, called this policy "dollar diplomacy."

THE AMERICAN SEARCH FOR OPPORTUNITY: A NEW PRESIDENCY FOR A NEW FOREIGN POLICY

Roosevelt bragged that he used the White House " as a bully pulpit." He led Americans and made them love it. But he also inherited a position whose powers had already multiplied during the post-1860 era. Roosevelt admired Lincoln's expansion of presidential powers during the Civil War. Even without a Civil War, however, TR believed that presidents had to follow what he termed the "stewardship" theory: "Occasionally great national crises arise which call for immediate and vigorous executive action." The president must then act "upon the theory that he is the steward of the people." It is "not only [his] right but his duty to do anything that the needs of the Nation demanded unless such action was forbidden by the Constitution or the laws."[9]

In 1890, the Supreme Court had almost accidentally moved to support this theory of large presidential powers. Deciding a case *(In re Neagle)* that actually had nothing to do with foreign policy, the Court declared that the president was not limited to carrying out congressional laws and treaties. His duty included enforcing "the rights, duties, and obligations growing out of the Constitution itself, our international relations, and all the protection implied by the nature of the govern-

UNCLE SAM: "Now I can do what I please with 'em."

This cartoonist not only portrays the liberty that Uncle Sam took with the Constitution in order to control his new possessions, but catches as well some of the era's racism.

ment under the Constitution."[10] These were extraordinarily general, open-ended words, and they were obiter dicta—not binding or essential to the decision. But they were to be used later to justify the most vigorous presidential power, especially in "our international relations."

It was almost as if some members of the Supreme Court had looked into a crystal ball and had foreseen that a new foreign policy would soon require a new presidency. As late as 1897, some close observers wondered whether the Constitution could be adapted to a U.S. government that might soon have worldwide responsibilities. Captain Alfred Thayer Mahan warned that any projection of U.S. power overseas could smash up against constitutional restraints—"the lion in the path" of empire, as he vividly phrased it.[11] Apparently unfamiliar with the *Neagle* decision, Mahan believed that the ambitious president might simply have to ignore the Constitution in order to protect U.S. interests overseas. McKinley proved Mahan wrong. The president's handling of the 1898 war, the annexation of the Philippines, and the 1899–1900 China crises demonstrated the tremendous power a shrewd politician could exercise as chief executive of American foreign policy. The more Americans supported a vigorous foreign policy, the more they were going to get a vigorous presidency.

A young but already well-known political scientist best explained the effect of end-of-the-century foreign policy on presidential powers. The post-1898 "ownership of distant possessions and [the] many sharp struggles for foreign trade," Woodrow Wilson wrote in a widely used textbook, meant that "the President can never again be the mere domestic figure he has been throughout so much of our history." As the United States "has risen to first rank in power and resources," so the president "must stand always at the front of our affairs, and the office will be as big and as influential as the man who occupies it." Wilson prophesied:

> Men of ordinary physique and discretion cannot be Presidents and live, if the strain be not somehow relieved. We shall be obliged always to be picking our chief magistrates from among wise and prudent athletes—a small class.[12]

Roosevelt, the disciple of "the strenuous life," seemed perfect for the role. He believed that only the president could conduct foreign policy. Congress was too large and unwieldy. Public opinion, TR privately declared, was "the voice of the devil, or what is still worse, the voice of a fool." But he went to great lengths to ensure that public opinion was with him—or at least not against him. He, indeed, used the White House as a "bully pulpit," went on frequent speaking engagements, and carefully cultivated powerful journalists in Washington. When a New York State Supreme Court justice once tried to limit the president's power, TR dismissed him as an "amiable old fuzzy-wuzzy with sweetbread brains."[13]

More directly, Roosevelt used the president's power as commander in chief of the armed forces to dispatch U.S. troops as he saw fit in Latin America. Once when Congress refused to accept a treaty he had made, Roosevelt circumvented Congress with an "executive agreement." Such an agreement could be one of two types: authorized by congressional legislation, or—as became too common—made by a president on his own authority. A little-known device until the 1890s, presidents have used it since far more than treaties because an executive agreement is not submitted to Congress, as a treaty must be. It is an agreement between the president and another government. The real difference between the two is that treaties are binding on all parties as long as they are in force, but an executive agreement is technically binding only as long as the president who signed it is in power. That was good enough for Roosevelt. He judged (correctly) that future presidents would uphold his agreements—in part because they would want their successors to uphold their deals. Most notably, TR ignored Senate opposition by taking over the Caribbean country of Santo Domingo between 1905 and 1907. One angry congressman exclaimed that Roosevelt had "no more use for the Constitution than a tomcat has for a marriage license."[14]

But that was not entirely accurate. As a student of American history, Roosevelt had great respect for the Constitution. As a politician as well as student of his nation's history, however, he also had great respect for the need for American expansionism. And that turned out to be the problem. Americans, historian Robert Wiebe has argued, embarked on a "search for order" between 1865 and 1920. That well might have been so at home; given the long economic depression, general strikes, and social upheavals that struck the United States during those years, they understandably wanted peace and quiet. But it was not the case abroad. In their foreign policies, Americans valued a search for opportunity over the search for order. In Cuba, Hawaii, the Philippines, China, and Central America—and especially during the 1901–1913 years, in Cuba, Panama, the Dominican Republic, Nicaragua, China, and Mexico—Americans demanded opportunity for their trade, investment, and security needs. In every instance noted, the result in these countries was upheaval and, in several instances, revolution. But U.S. officials did not back off. They continued to demand economic and other rights, even if the demands climaxed in massive disorder. They valued those rights over the disorder the demands helped cause. At that point, Americans then demanded a new, more vigorous presidency to guarantee continued opportunities for their growing economic machine—and, if possible, to restore order in these foreign countries. The presidents, led by McKinley, Taft, and—most flamboyantly—Roosevelt, used military force to guarantee continued opportunity and, they hoped, order. Thus was born the twentieth-century "imperial presidency."[15]

In this new world for U.S. opportunity, Roosevelt was determined to use his considerable energy and powers to the limit. Thanks to Lincoln, the Supreme Court, McKinley, executive agreements, and the worldwide quest of Americans for opportunity, those limits stretched far. Roosevelt colorfully demonstrated Woodrow Wilson's insight: an aggressive foreign policy created a strong president. And vice versa.

East, North, and South to an Isthmian Canal

TR knew what he wanted to do with his new powers. He immediately moved to realize the American dream of a U.S.-controlled isthmian canal in Central America. First, however, he had to break the 1850 Clayton-Bulwer Treaty that made Great Britain a full partner in any canal project. Roosevelt and his first secretary of state (and close friend), John Hay, terminated that treaty. They did so while actually strengthening U.S.-British relations, despite events that tested the relationship. The tests occurred in South Africa, Alaska, and then Central America.

In South Africa, the British had become bogged down in a bloody struggle with the Boers between 1899 and 1902. The Boers (a Dutch word for "farmers") had settled at the southern tip of black Africa in 1652. The British seized the South African cape in 1795 and instantly clashed with the austere, Calvinist, isolated, and fiercely nationalistic Boers. In the 1830s, the Boers undertook the great trek north to escape British control. They created their own independent nation. Then, as diamonds and other mineral wealth were found in the 1870s, the Boers' region became a focal point for European colonial power rivalry, and the British moved in to reassert control. At that point, U.S. economic interests rapidly increased in the region. Between 1895 and the outbreak of the Boer War in 1899–1900, for example, U.S. exports to South Africa tripled to $20 million. Americans also believed that the British were more progressive and better able to "civilize" the black Africans, who represented the large majority of South Africans.

All-out war between the British and the Boers erupted in 1899. To everyone's astonishment, during "Black Week" of December, the Boer troops inflicted the worst military defeat on the powerful British forces in living memory. Most Americans, remembering 1776, sided with the Boers. But U.S. officials, while remaining officially neutral, strongly sided with the British. American bankers floated loans to pay one-fifth of England's war costs. Roosevelt and Hay were shaken by the British defeats. "It certainly does seem to me that England is on the downgrade," the president wrote privately. But he understood the need to champion Anglo-Saxon values. Roosevelt quietly supported the British and refused to send any aid to the Boers until London's armies turned the tide and won victory between 1900 and 1902. TR received few rewards for his help in South Africa. As historian Thomas Noer concludes, the United States supported Great Britain to ensure the entry of American goods through an open-door policy in South Africa, a policy that Roosevelt thought the British supported. But despite U.S. pressure and the growing interest of American blacks in South Africa after 1900, "this policy failed: British domination resulted in a decline of American economic influence and did little to improve the lot of the black African."[16]

British problems in Africa, however, did allow Roosevelt to score two victories closer to home. The first involved a disputed boundary between Alaska and Canada that became enflamed after gold was found in 1896. TR was furious at the Canadians for advancing what he considered to be an empty claim. "I'm going to be ugly," he warned his British friends. The president finally agreed to allow "six impartial jurists" to arbitrate the dispute. He showed his determination to have his way by dispatching troops to Alaska. Then he appointed three Americans who were neither "impartial" nor "jurists," but U.S. politicians who completely shared TR's views. The Canadian prime minister, Sir Wilfrid Laurier, rightly denounced the appointments as "an outrage." He named two Canadian members, and the British named their own lord chief justice—who promptly voted with the Americans and handed Roosevelt most of the land. The Canadians cried that they had been double-crossed. To the Americans and the British, however, maintaining their improving relationship was worth giving away what was a small, if valuable, slice of Canada. For not the first or last time, Canadian interests were sacrificed for the sake of U.S.-British friendship.[17]

The most significant victory over the British came after "Black Week" in South Africa. London officials reversed themselves and agreed to discuss doing away with the Clayton-Bulwer Treaty. The U.S. Senate, never reluctant to kick the British Lion as long as it was already badly wounded, pushed events along by introducing measures to build an American-owned canal regardless of the 1850 pact. In early 1900, Hay and the British ambassador to Washington signed the Hay-Pauncefote Treaty, which allowed the United States to build and own—but not fortify—an isthmian canal. The U.S. Senate indignantly rejected the treaty and told Hay to obtain the right to fortify as well. The secretary of state was furious with the Senate and especially with Democratic presidential nominee William Jennings Bryan, who led the opposition: "He struck at [the treaty] in mere ignorance and malice," Hay wrote a friend, "as an idiot might strike at a statue because he happened to have a hammer in his hand."[18] Hay nevertheless had no alternative, especially after the new president agreed with the Senate. A second Hay-Pauncefote Treaty was signed in November 1901. The United States gained the right to fortify the canal.

But where was the canal to be located? Official U.S. commissions between 1876 and 1901 recommended Nicaragua as the cheapest and most efficient route. Its rival, Panama (a province of Colombia), might have been cheaper, but the French company that owned rights to that route (Compagnie Universelle du Canal Interocéanique) demanded over

$100 million. By 1901–1902, however, as the second Hay-Pauncefote Treaty took effect, the company fell under the control of two shadowy, skilled lobbyists who changed the course of isthmian history. Philippe Bunau-Varilla was a Frenchman with extensive contacts in Panama and Washington. William Cromwell was senior partner in the influential New York law firm of Sullivan and Cromwell; he enjoyed access to powerful leaders in Washington politics and New York finance. The two men reduced their company's asking price to $40 million. Then, in June 1902, they pushed through Congress the Spooner Amendment, giving Roosevelt the right to pay $40 million to the company and purchase a six-mile zone in Panama from Colombia. The lobbying of the two men had received heaven-sent help when a Nicaraguan volcano suddenly erupted and endangered the proposed route. Bunau-Varilla quickly put a picture of the volcano (which the Nicaraguans had, unfortunately for themselves, printed on their postage stamps) on the desk of everyone in Congress.

The secretary of state negotiated the Hay-Herrán Treaty that gave Colombia $10 million plus $250,000 annually for the six-mile zone. The Colombian legislature, however, rejected the pact and demanded more money. In truth, the Colombians hoped to stall until 1904, when the French company's charter was to revert to Colombia. The Latin American country would then gain—and Bunau-Varilla and Cromwell lose—$40 million. Roosevelt blew up. All his considerable racism appeared. He refused to have those "banditti" in Latin America publicly humiliate and rob the United States. In truth, as Richard L. Lael observes in his important study of U.S.-Colombian relations, U.S. officials seemed ignorant of Colombia's deep problems as it emerged from a costly civil war, and "none of them seemed to realize, or seriously consider, the possibility that U.S. actions, as seen from Colombia, could legitimately be perceived as interventionist, dangerous, and imperialistic." Roosevelt instead spread the word that he would not be displeased if Panama revolted against Colombia. The Panamanians needed little encouragement. Since at least the 1880s, they had developed a strong nationalist movement that repeatedly tried to obtain independence. As Panama grew more restless, U.S. armed forces had become extraordinarily active. One estimate concludes that those forces had spent a total of about 200 days ashore in Panama in various forms of intervention during the second half of the nineteenth century. It was the longest U.S. occupation of any foreign area until 1898.[19]

Under Bunau-Varilla's guidance and with Washington's support, the Panamanians again revolted in November 1903. This time, the U.S.

"Man's greatest liberty with nature," the cutting of the Panama Canal, was a crucial step in building twentieth-century U.S. military and economic power. In the photo, the battleship Ohio *sails through the passageway that opened in 1914.*

warships prevented Colombian troops from landing in Panama to quell the revolt. Roosevelt recognized the new nation two days after the rebellion started. He signed a treaty giving Panama $10 million plus $250,000 a year for rights to a ten-mile-wide strip that cut the country in half. The United States fully guaranteed Panama's independence. U.S.-Colombian relations did not return to normal until a treaty gave Colombia $25 million in 1921, two years after Roosevelt's death removed the loudest objection to making the pact.

Roosevelt and Hay found ingenious excuses for their actions in November 1903. They claimed that the 1846 treaty with Colombia gave the United States the right to maintain freedom of transit across the isthmus. The treaty did so, but certainly not against Colombia, which owned Panama and with whom the United States had made the 1846 pact. Nor did the treaty require Colombia to allow a canal to be built. Another rationale for the action was offered by TR's close friend, Oscar Straus, who claimed that the 1846 treaty was "a covenant running with the land"—regardless of whether Panamanians or Colombians owned

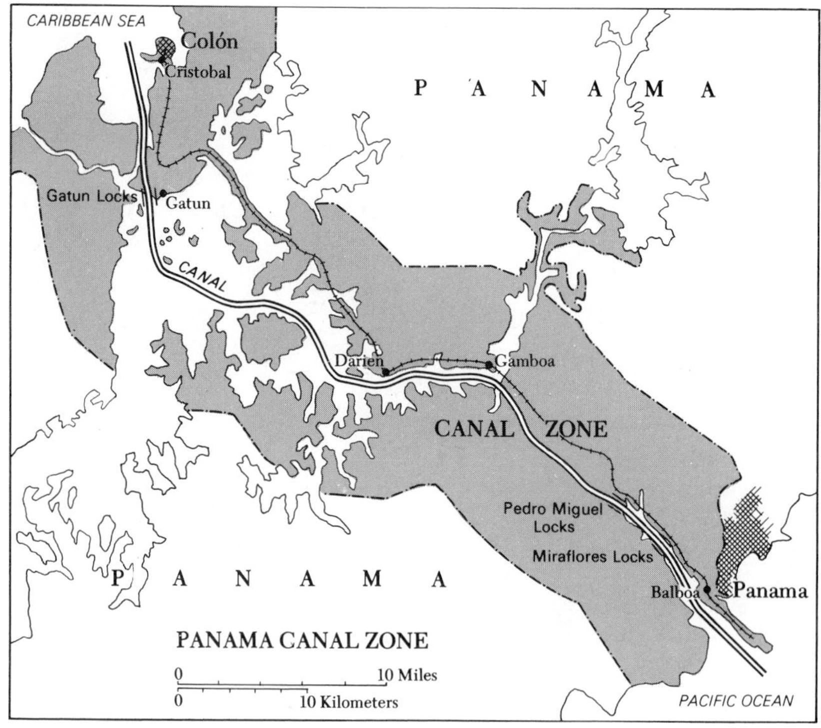

the land. A State Department lawyer dismissed Straus's interpretation with the joke that it turned out to be a "covenant running (away!) with the land." The real reasons for Roosevelt's action were his determination to build a canal and the U.S. naval power that enforced his will. As for the Panamanians, they gained independence but lost part of their country. They soon claimed title over the ten-mile-wide strip, but the United States effectively closed it off and controlled the territory. John Hay justified U.S. rights with the phrase "titular sovereignty," a claim so vague that Washington officials could not define or defend it when Panamanians demanded the return of their land (and the canal) in the 1960s and 1970s.[20]

At a cabinet meeting, TR vigorously gave his reasons for taking the canal zone, then loudly challenged his advisers: "Have I defended myself?" Elihu Root answered, "You certainly have Mr. President. You have shown that you were accused of seduction and you have conclusively proved that you were guilty of rape." Roosevelt, of course, would never admit to having doubts about his act. He had overcome Colombia's opposition. He also overcame domestic opposition. But leading newspapers, led by the *New York Times* and the Hearst journals, claimed (in Hearst's words) that the "Panama foray is nefarious. Besides being a rough-riding assault upon another republic over the shattered wreckage of international law and diplomatic usage, it is a quite unexampled instance of foul play in American politics."[21]

Most Americans, however, overwhelmingly approved Roosevelt's actions. They cared about the canal, not about the means he used to acquire it. TR made "the dirt fly," as he put it, and in 1906 paid a personal visit to witness the construction. It marked the first time a president had ever left the United States while in office. Roosevelt saw miraculous engineering feats being performed as the waterway cut through Panama's mountains and lakes. The United States was completing the biggest construction job in history. He also watched medical history being made as American scientists discovered how to find and kill the mosquito that caused malaria and yellow fever, diseases that had destroyed the French effort in the 1880s. With the opening of the canal in 1914—"the greatest liberty Man has ever taken with Nature," in the words of British ambassador James Bryce—the distance between New York and San Francisco by boat shrank from 13,615 miles to 5,300 miles. U.S. merchants and warships now moved easily between the Atlantic and Pacific oceans. And Americans grew even more sensitive about disorder in the region surrounding their canal.

A Great Departure: The Roosevelt Corollary

Long before he obtained the canal area, TR understood the importance of the most hallowed of U.S. foreign policies, the Monroe Doctrine, and how it had to be enforced. "There is a homely adage that runs 'speak softly and carry a big stick; you will go far,' " he told the Minnesota State Fair audience in 1901. "If the American nation will speak softly and yet build and keep at a pitch of the highest training a thoroughly efficient navy, the Monroe Doctrine will go far."[22]

The danger to the doctrine no longer was British expansionism. London officials were preoccupied with Africa and Europe. The danger came from two other sources. The first, Germany, was not obvious and worried mainly U.S. military planners. Modern U.S. military planning began in 1900, when McKinley established the navy's General Board. (It was created largely so that war hero Admiral Dewey could occupy himself with war games instead of running against McKinley for the presidency.) In 1903, Secretary of War Elihu Root created the

Don't forget that in the mild Dr. Jekyll there lurks the unsafe Mr. Hyde
—*Milwaukee News*

This cartoon of 1904 from the Milwaukee News—*"Don't forget that in the mild Dr. Jekyll there lurks the unsafe Mr. Hyde"—is not only critical of Roosevelt the campaigner, but also indicates why cartoonists loved to draw the always active, colorful president.*

Army General Staff. That year, an interservice planning group, the Joint Army and Navy Board, was also set up. A global foreign policy needed sophisticated military planning. In the most sensitive region, the Caribbean, the planners grew to fear the growing navy and imperial ambitions of Kaiser Wilhelm's Germany. The kaiser was getting at cross-purposes in Europe, Africa, and Asia with England, TR's closest ally. Historians later discovered that in 1899, the kaiser actually ordered plans drawn up for possible war against the United States. A lack of ships forced him to stop the planning.[23]

The second danger to the Monroe Doctrine was well known, even blatant. Frequent revolutions in the smaller Caribbean–Central American nations were an open invitation for Germany and other powers to intervene to protect their citizens—and perhaps to stay indefinitely. Much as the United States feared Soviet involvement in Latin American revolutions after 1960, so Americans feared the European presence in the area long before the Russian Revolution of 1917. At first, in 1901–1902, Roosevelt thought that the Europeans were justified in intervening to protect their citizens and property and to collect just debts, as long as they did not remain. Then in 1902–1903, Germans, French, and British took TR at his word and used force to collect debts owed to them by Venezuela.[24]

An uproar ensued in the United States. It grew when the International Court of Justice at The Hague ruled that the Europeans acted within their rights. The U.S. State Department warned Roosevelt that the ruling put "a premium on violence" and undermined the Monroe Doctrine.[25] The Europeans had been careful not only to keep the president informed of their plans, but even to indicate their recognition of the Monroe Doctrine. Roosevelt nevertheless knew he was in a tight spot. He could not tolerate major European intervention in the region, but if he opposed it, the Europeans would demand that he make the Latin Americans behave properly. "These wretched republics cause me a great deal of trouble," he lamented.[26]

His moment of decision came in 1904. In Santo Domingo, whose harbors and customshouse Americans had been eying since at least 1870, U.S. business groups came into conflict with German and French interests. The U.S. minister to Santo Domingo, William F. Powell, used the threat of Germany to convince the U.S. government to intervene directly on behalf of American bankers and shipping companies. These foreign rivalries in turn triggered internal disorders. In late 1904, TR declared that he intended to stop the threat of possible revolution. He arranged the payment of debts to Europeans by seizing the customshouses. The president announced his policy to Congress in December 1904. Reviewing major themes of post-1865 as he gave a history lesson to Congress, TR stressed his belief in the obligations—and rights—of "civilized" nations as he outlined what became known as the Roosevelt Corollary to the Monroe Doctrine:

> It is not true that the United States feels any land hunger or entertains any projects as regards the other nations of the Western Hemisphere save such as are for their welfare. All that this country desires is to see the neighboring countries stable, orderly, and prosperous. . . . Chronic wrongdoing, or an impotence which results in a general loosening of the ties of civilized society, may in America, as elsewhere, ultimately require intervention by some civilized nation, and in the Western Hemisphere the adherence of the United States to the Monroe Doctrine may force the United States, however reluctantly, in flagrant cases of such wrongdoing or impotence, to the exercise of an international police power. . . . We would interfere with [Latin Americans] only in the last resort, and then only if it became evident that their inability or unwillingness to do justice at home and abroad had violated the rights of the United States or had invited foreign aggression to the detriment of the entire body of American nations.[27]

Roosevelt's action pleased U.S. businesses in the country as well as the president, Carlos Morales, whom they supported. But many Santo Domingans disliked the idea of the United States having a blank check to interfere in their affairs. Morales finally had to sign the treaty while

This Argentine cartoon, published in a Buenos Aires newspaper in early 1905, provides a growing Latin American view of U.S. foreign policy. An Uncle Sam figure, with the head of Theodore Roosevelt, reaches throughout the hemisphere with the heavy hand of the Monroe Doctrine. Santo Domingo is depicted as the small island below Cuba and between Uncle Sam's hands.

U.S. warships protected him from his own people. That, however, turned out to be the least of TR's problems, for next the treaty was rejected by the U.S. Senate: it refused to throw an American protectorate over the restless country. Roosevelt effectively thumbed his nose at the Senate by signing an executive agreement with Morales. U.S. government agents and bankers, led by J. P. Morgan and Kuhn, Loeb and Company, took over control of Santo Domingo. They paid off the debt owed the Europeans.

Roosevelt saw his action not as imperialism, but as work that a "policeman" must do to maintain order among less civilized people. As he privately wrote a friend in 1904:

> I want to do nothing but what a policeman has to do in Santo Domingo. As for annexing the island, I have about the same desire to annex it as a gorged boa constrictor might have to swallow a porcupine wrong-end-to. . . . I have asked some of our people to go there because, after having refused for three months to do anything, the attitude of the Santo Domingans has been one of half chaotic war towards us.[28]

The gorged-boa-constrictor analogy was appropriate, given that the United States was trying to digest Hawaii, the Philippines (which TR was beginning to see as "our Achilles heel" because it was so vulnerable to such powers as Japan), Puerto Rico, Cuba, and Panama. All had been brought within the American orbit within just six years.

But a gorged boa constrictor also wants peace and quiet. Roosevelt's corollary marked a historic break from Monroe's doctrine and anticipated U.S. policy toward Latin America for the rest of the twentieth century. It did so for five reasons. First, Monroe's message had supported Latin American revolutions, but TR's opposed them. Second, Monroe had urged nonintervention in those revolts by all outside parties, including the United States. Roosevelt, however, declared that he would directly intervene to maintain "civilized" order. Third, Monroe had seen U.S. economic power acting in a traditional marketplace—that is, buying and selling according to rules set by the home country. But Roosevelt used his economic power to control that marketplace and bring it under U.S., not home-country, control. (One senator who bitterly opposed TR's action sarcastically observed that the U.S. Navy rallying cry had been that of a commander in the War of 1812: "Don't give up the ship boys"; now, however, a U.S. naval officer could cry: "We have met the enemy and they are ours. Advance the bid on Dominican bonds.")[29] Fourth, because Monroe had argued for keeping out of internal Latin American affairs, he had no need for the use of military power. But Roosevelt's policy depended on force. Between 1898 and 1920, U.S. troops entered Latin American countries no fewer than twenty times. Those nations were seen less as neighbors in the hemisphere than problems to be managed militarily. Finally, because Monroe's policy had urged abstention, Congress had no role and the president did not have to be concerned about constitutional problems with the legislature. Roosevelt, however, followed a course that constitutionally required obtaining Congress's assent (to pursue such policies, for example, as making war on foreign nations or making treaties to operate their customshouses). But he simply ignored Congress when it opposed him. His actions drew power out of the legislative branch and pulled it into the executive.

The Roosevelt Corollary opened a new era in hemispheric relations. Latin Americans fully understood. They moved to curb TR's claims. In 1907, the so-called Drago Doctrine (named after Argentina's foreign minister Luis María Drago) became accepted international law. It declared that no nation could use force to collect debts. TR strongly opposed the Drago dictum and finally acquiesced only after it was radically weakened. In 1911, the United States even expanded its new version of the Monroe Doctrine. Republican senator Henry Cabot Lodge from Massachusetts, a close friend of Roosevelt's, learned that a Japanese company was angling to buy strategic Mexican territory. The Lodge Corollary, passed in a Senate resolution, declared U.S. opposition to the sale of any strategic area to a nonhemispheric company that might be an agent for a foreign government. The Japanese firm had earlier lost interest anyway, but the State Department used the resolution to discourage similar ventures after 1911. The Monroe Doctrine resembled U.S. industry and the president's powers: it grew larger all the time.

The Fateful Triangle: The United States, China, and Japan, 1900–1908

Roosevelt fervently believed that the American future rested on events in Asia—the new Far West—as well as on those in the Western Hemisphere. He had led the fight to take the Philippines and completely supported the open-door policy. His beliefs were bolstered by his close friend, Brooks Adams. Grandson of John Quincy Adams, Brooks was a brilliant eccentric who believed that he had discovered a historical "law" proving that the world's money center had moved ever westward over a thousand years. Following the sun, it had jumped from the Mediterranean to Paris and then to London. Now, he believed, it was poised once again to bestow greatness and wealth on a people. The only question was whether it would turn west to New York, or lurch east toward Germany and Russia. Brooks Adams saw the 1898–1900 triumphs "as the moment when we won the great prize. I do believe that we may dominate the world, as no nation has dominated it in recent time."[30]

But to reach, then remain at, the peak of world power, Americans had to conquer the world's greatest market and cheapest labor supply: China. And to do that, Adams told Roosevelt, the United States had to use its vast resources—but also strong government involvement—to build the cheapest, most efficient transportation system to carry its goods to Asia. "We must have a new deal . . . , we must suppress the states, and have a centralized administration, or we shall wobble over," Adams declared. Or, as he told TR, Americans "must command the terminus in Asia—if we fail in this we shall break down."[31] The president responded in July 1903 that he agreed: "We must do our best to prevent the shutting to us of Asian markets. In order to keep the roads to these terminals we must see that they are managed primarily in the interest of the country."[32] Out of such ideas emerged laws, pushed especially by Progressives such as TR, that created new central-government agencies to regulate the railroads and make the society more efficient.

In foreign policy, such ideas led Roosevelt, Hay, and Adams to try to guarantee an open door to the China market by supporting Japan (who seemed to agree with U.S. aims) and opposing Russia's attempts to colonize Manchuria and control Korea. Secretary of State Hay believed that if TR gave the Japanese "a wink," they would "fly at the throat of Russia in a moment." When some Americans feared such a "wink" might make Japan supreme in Asia and perhaps create disorder inside Russia, Hay dismissed the critics as members "of that highly respected family, the common or barnyard ass." Roosevelt warmly supported the historic 1902 alliance between Japan and Great Britain, which further isolated Russia in the Far East. And as the rivalry between Tokyo and St. Petersburg grew hot, TR sided with Japan.

In 1904, the Japanese launched a surprise attack that destroyed most of Russia's Pacific fleet. Americans supported Japan. Leading Jewish bankers who had vivid memories of Russia's recent anti-Semitic attacks provided war loans to Tokyo. The Japanese government worked through these bankers to float the first major foreign-government loan ever offered to American investors.[33] In the bright glow of Japan's early victories and TR's Latin American triumphs in 1903–1904, few doubted his policies. One who did, however, was Henry Adams. The brother of Brooks, a close friend of the president's, and perhaps the greatest of all American historians, Henry Adams eerily prophesied in 1904 that Americans—and the world—had stumbled down the wrong road:

> Everybody is interested, and excited, and all are anti-Russian, almost to a dangerous extent [he wrote privately]. I am the only—relative—Russian afloat, and only because I am half-crazy with the fear that Russia is sailing straight into another French revolution which may upset all Europe and us too. A serious disaster to Russia might smash the whole civilized world.[34]

In 1905, Henry Adams's prophesy began to come true. Revolution erupted in Russia. The tsar smashed it, but other European monarchs grew worried. They had asked Roosevelt to try to mediate a peace, and TR agreed, in part because he feared that Japan lacked the resources to fight a long war against Russia. He called the two sides to meet at

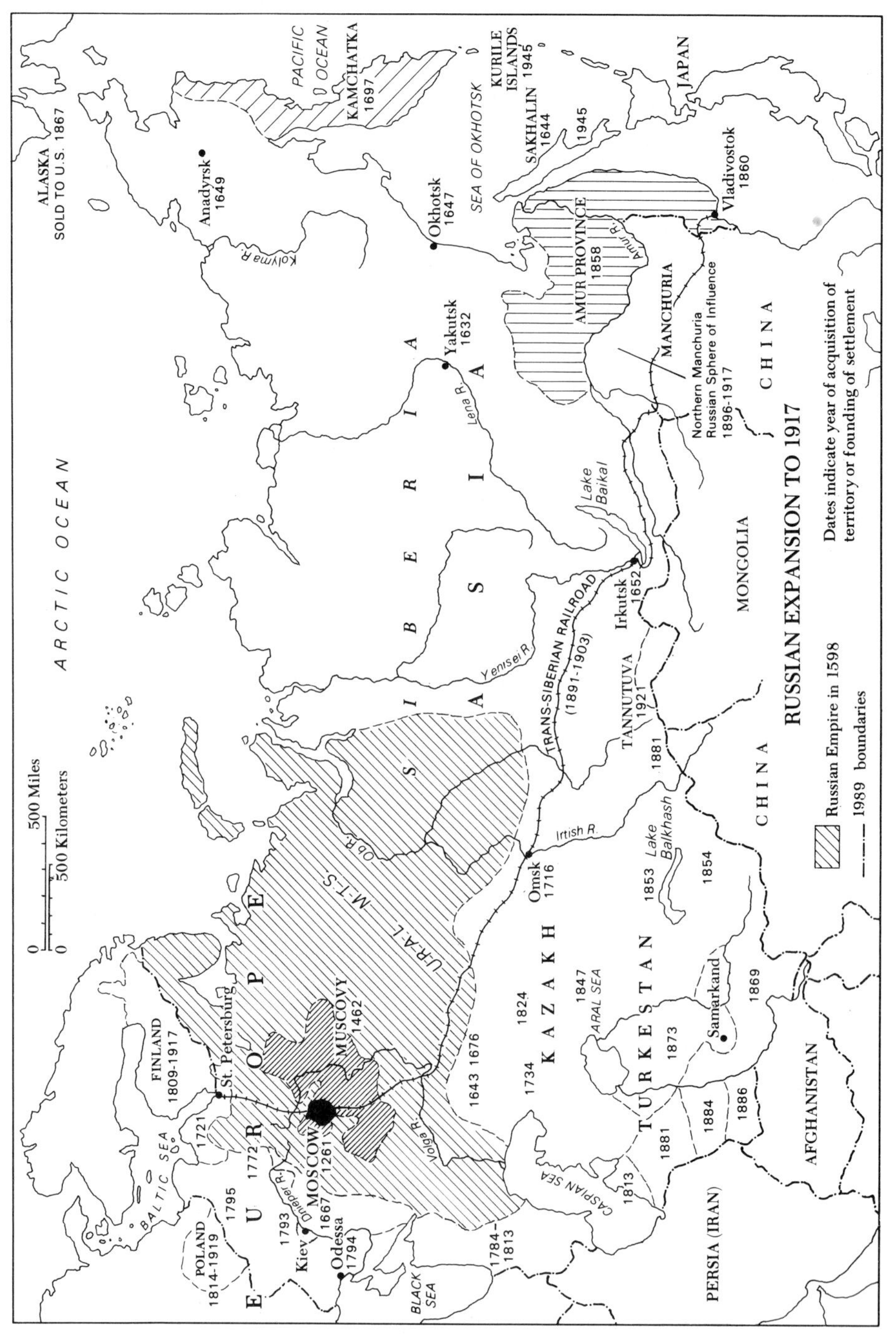

The American-Russian rivalry has deep roots. Early twentieth-century presidents mistrusted the Russians not only because of the tsars' autocratic system, but because of the history of Russian expansionism, shown on this map.

Portsmouth, New Hampshire, in late summer 1905. Although China's interests lay at the center of the talks, no Chinese were invited to participate. After the Japanese finally dropped their demand of a huge indemnity from the tsar, the two sides hammered out a peace treaty in September. Both nations agreed to respect China's territorial integrity (thus honoring the open door). But Japan emerged with controlling interest in Korea, key Chinese ports formerly belonging to Russia, the main railway in southern Manchuria, and the southern half of Sakhalin Island, formerly claimed by the tsar. The next month, Tokyo forced Korea to become a Japanese protectorate. Japan would remain in control until 1945. The Koreans appealed to TR for help, but he now refused to become involved.[35]

Instead, the president made a secret deal—the Taft-Katsura Agreement—in which Japan promised to keep hands off the Philippines, and TR recognized Tokyo's domination of Korea. He emerged from Portsmouth more anti-Russian than ever. "Bad as the Chinese are, no human being, black, yellow or white, could be as untruthful, as insincere, as arrogant—in short as untrustworthy in every way—as the Russians under their present system," he complained privately.[36]

But the Russo-Japanese War brought U.S. officials into a dangerous new world. The Chinese observed how an Asian people had humiliated a white race in conflict. Fresh antiforeign tendencies appeared when China stunned Roosevelt in 1905 by protesting U.S. immigration policy with a highly effective boycott of American goods.

A fascinating case study revealed some of the causes and results of the boycott. In the 1880s, James B. Duke learned about the invention of a machine that rolled cigarettes at high speeds. He decided—after glancing at an atlas's population chart—that only China had the population to buy so many cigarettes. By 1902, he was selling 1 billion cigarettes a year through his British-American Tobacco Company (BAT). He undercut both Chinese and Japanese competitors by using the newest technology and advanced sales techniques. When the boycott began in 1905, however, Chinese students and merchants alike targeted Duke's operation as a way of striking back at foreign control. The protestors turned BAT's advertising around by publishing posters showing a dog (which the Chinese considered a low form of life) smoking a BAT cigarette and saying, "Those who smoke American cigarettes are of my species." BAT, Standard Oil, and other U.S. firms urged TR to force the Chinese to end the boycott. But Roosevelt (who called people he deemed especially inefficient "Chinese") was bewildered by the boycott's efficiency. Finally, with its point made and pressure building, the

James Buchanan Duke (1856–1925) began working at the family's Durham, North Carolina, tobacco company in 1874. Some fifteen years later, the company controlled 50 percent of U.S. cigarette production, thanks to "Buck's" genius with machinery and marketing. He renamed it the American Tobacco Company, bought or drove off competitors, exploited the vast China market—until Chinese nationalism checked the company and the U.S. Supreme Court in 1911 dissolved Duke's monopoly. He gave generously to his hometown college, Trinity, which was renamed Duke University.

Chinese government ended the boycott. BAT quickly crushed its Chinese competitors who had appeared during the boycott, then set prices so high that by 1916 it enjoyed an 18 percent profit.[37] Three years later, in 1919, the Chinese Revolution began in earnest. The 1905 boycott, resembling the 1905 Russian revolt, had been a warning sign.

Roosevelt next had to confront a challenge from Tokyo. Japan closed off Korea to U.S. interests, then began moving into Manchuria itself. These direct threats to the open door were compounded by an uproar in the United States over Japanese immigration. In 1890, some 2,000 Japanese had lived in California. In 1900, the number reached 24,000 and the governor called the influx the "Japanese menace." The state prepared to pass an Asian exclusion bill, and in San Francisco, a city ordinance segregated Oriental children. Anti-Asian riots erupted. Fear of a U.S.-Japanese war spread. Tokyo officials were deeply angered at the discrimination, but Roosevelt could calm California only by stopping Japanese immigration. In a "gentlemen's agreement" of 1907, Japan said that it would no longer allow laborers to emigrate to the

United States provided that California stopped discriminating against Japanese.

A temporary calm set in, but TR knew that he was confronting an aggressive Japan. To show his resolve, he determined in 1907 to send the entire fleet of sixteen U.S. battleships around the world, with a special stop in Japan. Congressmen, anxious that the Japanese would sneakily attack the fleet as they had the Russian navy in 1904, threatened to withhold needed funds. Roosevelt responded that he had enough money to send the ships halfway around the world. If Congress wanted to bring them back, it could give him the funds. Congress surrendered. The fleet's visit to Japan was a huge popular success. Roosevelt, moreover, had dramatically shown the global reach of the new U.S. battle fleet.

But the trip's diplomatic effect was slight. Japan continued its pressure on Korea and Manchuria. In 1907–1908, a colorful twenty-seven-year-old U.S. consul in Manchuria, Willard Straight, set out to block Japan on his own. Raised on turn-of-century racism, Straight had turned against the Japanese after the Russo-Japanese War. "I now find myself hating the Japanese more than anything in the world," he wrote to a friend. Perhaps, he thought, it was due to the "strain of having to be polite and to seek favors from a yellow people." Straight worked with the great U.S. railroad builder, E. H. Harriman, to plan a railroad in Manchuria that would compete directly with the Japanese-held railway. The project was to be part of Harriman's round-the-world transportation scheme through which he hoped to obtain a stranglehold on global commerce. The Chinese naturally encouraged the Straight-Harriman scheme. China was following the traditional policy of playing off "barbarian against barbarian." But in 1905, the Japanese had secretly forced China to agree that no such competing rail line would be built in Manchuria. Straight, a close friend of Roosevelt's dashing daughter Alice, went to Washington to plead his case personally with the president.

Unfortunately for Straight (and the Chinese), the Japanese delegation arrived first and convinced Roosevelt (who actually needed little convincing) that it was no use challenging them. Instead of accepting the Straight-Harriman dream, TR agreed to a deal. In the Root-Takahira Agreement of 1908, he recognized Japan's pre-eminence in southern Manchuria. In return, Tokyo pledged to uphold the open door and independence of China, but carefully refused to agree to Chinese *territorial* integrity. (After all, southern Manchuria was supposedly a part of China.)[38]

In reality, Roosevelt had given up the open door in much of Manchuria. He had, however, avoided war with Japan and reached a shaky agreement with Asia's rising power. For a man who so loved war and killing, he had shown extraordinary sensitivity to the limits of U.S. power. This preacher of "the strenuous life" and the use of force against the "uncivilized" even won the Nobel Peace Prize for his efforts to end the Russo-Japanese War. In dealing with the Indians and Latin Americans, TR did use force to deal with weaker peoples. In Asia and Europe, however, he knew that the United States was outgunned. He, therefore, followed advice he had learned in the North Dakota frontier saloons: "Never draw unless you mean to shoot." Whether Roosevelt's successors in the White House could afford to follow this advice became a central question of twentieth-century American diplomacy.

TAFT, KNOX, AND DOLLAR DIPLOMACY

TR's successor in the White House between 1909 and 1913, William Howard Taft, did not follow his example in Asia. The result was near-catastrophe for both Chinese and U.S. interests. Taft's failure was not due to lack of experience. He had been Roosevelt's secretary of war, headed the commission governing the Philippines, and traveled extensively in the Far East (including one venture during which he came to know Willard Straight). Nor was the failure due initially to Taft rebelling against Roosevelt. The Rough Rider hand-picked his successor, and one wit observed that TAFT stood for "Take-Advice-From-Theodore." But their relations cooled by 1911 as they clashed over a number of issues. TR even prepared to run against Taft for the presidency in 1912. Differences over foreign policy were major reasons for the cooling.

Part of Taft's failure was due to lack of energy. He weighed 300 to 320 pounds. And since his eating increased when his policies were in trouble, by 1911–1912 he was eating a great deal. He liked playing golf, sitting on the White House front porch and listening to the "music machine" (the new phonograph), and taking naps. Taft's real love was the law and the courts—their predictability, logic, and set of rules in which he had been trained. Foreign affairs (usually neither predictable nor logical) seemed messy. Five of his nine cabinet members were lawyers. Resembling the president, they thought cautiously, believed in following precedent, and admired tradition—even as the world rapidly changed around them. Taft was no moss-backed conservative. His

William Howard Taft (1857–1930) was a distinguished lawyer and jurist, a valued assistant and adviser to Theodore Roosevelt. But, contrary to the impression left by this photo, as president between 1909 and 1913 he was a weak politician and leader, although a famous advocate of building U.S. power in Asia and Latin America through what he termed "dollar diplomacy."

administration produced the amendment to the Constitution creating the income tax; created a Department of Labor; and successfully argued a series of antitrust cases against Standard Oil, U.S. Steel, and other giants that far surpassed TR's record as a "trust buster." Aware of the legal and economic complexities of American society, Taft had no similar understanding of foreign affairs. He only clung to certain principles: the open door in Asia, order in Latin America, and the belief that enough money (dollar diplomacy) could secure both.[39]

His secretary of state, Philander C. Knox, was a much thinner version of the president. A leading Pittsburgh corporation lawyer, Knox knew little about foreign policy. A British diplomat complained that Knox thought foreign relations resembled law practice: "To him a treaty is a contract, diplomacy is litigation, and the countries interested are parties to a suit." One advantage to this approach was Taft's and Knox's reorganization of the State Department so that it worked more like a corporation. They created a neat organization chart with specialists reporting upward to the secretary of state. The specialists were arranged along separate geographical divisions (Straight became head of the Far East Division for a short time) so that they could focus on the complexities of being a great world power. Neither Knox nor some of his specialists, however, did enough homework. Many days, the secretary worked at home until late morning, spent several hours at his office, enjoyed a leisurely lunch, and then played golf much of the afternoon. During one golf match, a partner suggested that Knox should travel to China and see the growing crisis firsthand. "I'm just starting to learn this game," he replied, "and I'm not going to let anything as unimportant as China interfere." Knox soon paid for such a schedule.

He and Taft believed more constructive foreign affairs could be achieved by using the nation's rapidly growing capital resources and downplaying Roosevelt's emphasis on military force. Branded at first by critics as "dollar diplomacy," by 1912 the president himself took credit for "substituting dollars for bullets. It . . . appeals alike to idealistic humanitarian sentiments, to the dictates of sound policy and strategy, and to legitimate commercial aims."[40] Dollar diplomacy, Taft argued, could create orderly societies by helping develop the unindustrialized nations and, happily, make a nice profit for American investors.

Dollar Diplomacy in Asia

The Taft administration believed in the need to maintain the Asian open door for U.S. goods and investment. U.S. officials understood that because of this need, the Japanese and Russian domination of Manchuria had to be checked. In 1907, the old enemies had made a deal in which Russia and its Chinese Eastern Railroad effectively controlled northern Manchuria, and Japan and its South Manchurian Railroad dominated southern Manchuria. Knox, however, refused to surrender. The stakes were too high. He believed that whoever financed the Chinese railway system would be the major voice in developing all of the immense China market. Knox's most notable effort came in 1910. He tried to break the Japanese-Russian hold on Manchuria by proposing a "neutralization" scheme. All the major foreign powers, he suggested, should pool their resources, buy the railroads, then operate them in accordance with the open-door principle. The response was cold. The British and French, who increasingly needed Russia's and Japan's cooperation in protecting interests in Europe and southern Asia, pulled away. The Russians and Japanese moved closer together to fend off

Knox. On July 4, 1910, the two nations signed a fresh treaty of friendship. Seven weeks later, Japan formally annexed Korea. As historian Michael Hunt notes, "By their own standards," the Taft-Knox policy "was bankrupt." Even the once-dominant U.S. cotton textiles were replaced in Manchuria by Japanese goods.[41]

U.S. dollar diplomacy came to the same sad end in China's heartland. In that region, British, French, and German capitalists planned to build the 563-mile-long Hukwang Railway between the capital of Beijing (Peking) and the great port of Canton. Knox demanded that U.S. bankers be included. J. P. Morgan, the Rockefeller-owned National City Bank, Kuhn, Loeb, E. H. Harriman, and other U.S. investors with previous involvement in China set up a group with State Department encouragement. The Chinese government, however, pulled back. It did not want the plan reopened and Americans—and then, no doubt, Japanese and Russians—brought in. Antiforeign riots again broke out. But the collapsing Chinese government could not hold off the United States. Much as China feared, Japan and Russia next forced their way into the deal. The Chinese government signed the contract, sold bonds it could never redeem, and soon disappeared in revolution.

His hopes to become an empire-builder in Asia destroyed, Willard Straight bitterly blamed the Chinese. The power of the Manchu dynasty is gone, he wrote a friend; "he [the Manchu emperor] didn't have his wings clipped," but instead the Chinese people "just naturally pulled out the feathers, and found that it was only a jack-daw with eagles' plumage after all. . . . Verily this is a nation of skunks." Straight, however, missed the main point. Foreign demands, including U.S. demands for increased economic opportunity, had fanned antiforeign feelings in China to a boiling point and had helped create the upheaval that drove the corrupt Manchu dynasty from power in 1912. Indeed, the Manchus, who had entered China from Manchuria in 1644, and in 1909 finally claimed full power, were themselves the targets of Chinese antiforeignism. The great China Revolution was underway. (The Taft demands for an open door for foreign opportunity cast long shadows. The new Nationalist government paid interest on the Hukwang Railway bonds until 1939. In 1983, nine Americans who still held the bonds won a $41.3 million claim in an Alabama court. The infuriated Communist government in Beijing (Peking) warned President Reagan that the claim, if pushed, could severely harm U.S.-Chinese relations. The legacy of the Hay-Taft policies in Asia lived on.)[42]

Roosevelt watched Taft's bumbling with growing alarm. He suggested that his successor make the best of a terrible situation by proposing that Japan develop Manchuria in return for California's right to exclude unwanted Japanese immigrants. When Taft showed no interest, TR warned that the president must not push too hard. The only way to maintain the open door in Manchuria, he wrote, was to fight Japan, and that would require a fleet as large as Great Britain's and an army as powerful as Germany's.[43] But Taft continued to believe that he had found a better way. During 1912, Knox tried to lead U.S. bankers into a six-nation consortium that was to provide a $300 million loan to the new Chinese republic. The bankers were not enthusiastic. Knox insisted. It was a last chance to prevent other powers, and perhaps Chinese nationalism itself, from closing the door. Taft's successor, Woodrow Wilson, pulled the Americans out of the consortium in 1913. It remained to be seen whether Wilson had a better plan for propping open the door.

DOLLAR DIPLOMACY IN LATIN AMERICA AND CANADA

Revolutions also threatened in Latin America. But here, as one U.S. Navy officer boasted, the Monroe Doctrine and American force held "this hemisphere in check against Cosmic Tendencies."[44] In 1906, Secretary of State Elihu Root declared that the United States had reached the point where it both needed Latin American markets and possessed the necessary "surplus of capital beyond the requirements of internal development" to develop in the hemisphere "the peaceful prosperity of a mighty commerce." South and North Americans, he argued, were made for each other. The South had the raw materials, the North the manufacturers. The South's people were "polite, refined, cultivated"; the "North American is strenuous, intense, utilitarian." Perhaps best of all, "Where we accumulate, they spend."[45] The United States thus had other reasons than the Panama Canal to insist on order in Latin America.

In 1906, for example, TR feared that the Cubans were acquiring "a revolutionary habit." He sent in U.S. troops to oversee elections that firmly established an orderly regime. In 1906–1907, Nicaraguan dictator José Santos Zelaya intensified a long-running feud with Guatemala by invading neighboring states. Partly because Zelaya introduced the machine gun to Central Americans, record numbers of people died each day of the war. Roosevelt and the Mexican dictator, Porfirio Díaz, twice intervened to stop the carnage and, on a U.S. warship, to arrange peace terms. In 1907, the United States also helped establish a historic

Elihu Root (1845–1937) of New York was probably the nation's top corporate lawyer during the era of the robber barons, secretary of war between 1899 and 1905 (when he made reforms that, in turn, made him "the father of the modern army"), and secretary of state (1905–1909). Root well understood, and described in his speeches, how the new U.S. economic power shaped the nation's overseas needs.

institution, the Central American Court. It was charged by the Central Americans to resolve outstanding regional problems peacefully. The court worked surprisingly well until 1914–1916, when Costa Rica won a decision against the United States. The Wilson administration disregarded the decision and effectively killed the court.[46]

In several Central American countries, U.S. investors themselves had for some years maintained order. Costa Rica was the most democratic nation in the region, in part because of its more equitable landholding. In 1872, a railroad builder from Brooklyn, New York, Minor Keith—described by one journalist as "an apple-headed little man with the eyes of a fanatic"—succeeded in building a major rail system in Costa Rica. He then developed banana plantations so that the trains would have cargo. Thus began the United Fruit Company of Boston, or "The Octopus," as Central Americans came to call it. By World War I, United Fruit controlled not only the banana market, but the rail systems, shipping, banking, and governments in Costa Rica and Honduras. The Roosevelt Corollary was not needed in those countries.[47]

Other countries were not as calm, however. Haiti was temporarily pacified in 1910 by an infusion of U.S. bank loans. In several Central American nations, TR's policies seemed to have had little good effect. Taft privately complained that he needed "to have the right to knock their heads together." Nicaragua's Zelaya was the worst offender. His persistent challenges to U.S. policies climaxed when rumors spread that he was going to give a non-American power the right to build an isthmian canal. In 1909, a revolutionary movement appeared on Nicaragua's east coast. It was helped along by U.S. diplomatic officials and U.S. Marines, who landed to protect the rebels. Zelaya caught two North Americans who were trying to blow up a boatload of his troops. Despite Knox's grave warning, the dictator executed both captives. Knox and U.S. naval commanders then pressured Zelaya to resign. Several changes of government later, U.S. bankers, with Knox's encouragement, were acquiring Nicaraguan banks and railroads in return for loans that kept the government afloat.

A new president, Adolfo Díaz (who had been a clerk in an American company in Nicaragua), finally offered to make his country a U.S. protectorate in return for more loans. Angry Nicaraguans revolted. Some 2,600 U.S. troops landed in 1912 to protect Díaz. The forces remained, reduced in number, until 1925, then had to return in 1926 for another seven-year stay.[48] Modern revolutionary Nicaragua began to arise out of Knox's dollar diplomacy.

The same approach led Taft into quite another kind of problem in U.S.-Canadian relations. Those ties had been quiet since the Alaskan boundary dispute of 1902–1903. The two countries enjoyed mostly prosperous years, and, consequently, the long-present interest on both sides of the boundary in possible annexation had declined. In 1909, Taft unintentionally stirred that interest again by proposing reciprocity treaties. Correctly analyzing the needs of an industrializing United States, he hoped through the reduced tariffs to lower costs of imported raw materials. Taft made the proposal only to have the powerful high-tariff wing of the Republican party rise in revolt. Roosevelt had refused to deal with the issue ("God Almighty could not pass a tariff and win the next election," he believed). But Taft waded in, compromised with the high-tariff interests in order to obtain a bill, and was promptly branded a traitor by low-tariff politicians.

The new tariff heavily discriminated against Canadian imports. Taft and Prime Minister Wilfrid Laurier quickly moved to avoid a trade war by signing a fresh U.S.-Canadian tariff agreement. From Washington's view, the deal could serve a stunning long-range goal: integrate Canada (and, through a similar treaty, Mexico) into a vast hemispheric industrial complex controlled by the United States. Between 1901 and 1908, U.S. investment in Canada had already increased four times to nearly $750 million, mostly in minerals, lumber, and other raw materials. Historian Robert Hannigan aptly calls the emerging U.S. policy "the new continentalism." It aimed, moreover, at changing Canadian-British trade to north-south trade. Careless U.S. politicians, however, began to spell out the probable result: the annexation of Canada. Infuriated and frightened Canadian Conservatives, fully supported by the British, killed the agreement. Dollar diplomacy failed in the north as well as the Far East, although President Ronald Reagan, seventy years later, would again push the idea of "the new continentalism" for many of the same reasons.[49]

The Irony of 1900–1913

After the easy triumphs of 1898–1901, U.S. officials encountered severe setbacks in Asia and the Western Hemisphere over the next dozen years. American power nevertheless continued to push outward, even in China and Canada. The United States also became involved in European affairs, an area it had largely bypassed since 1815.

These affairs centered on European attempts to colonize more of Africa. In two episodes, U.S. officials intervened to protect what they believed were threats to an open door in Africa. The first occurred in 1904–1906 in Morocco. In that country, where France claimed a sphere of influence, Germany challenged Paris officials by recognizing Moroccan independence. As war threatened, the European powers asked Roosevelt to repeat his success as mediator at Portsmouth. He hesitated, then agreed, rationalizing that an 1880 U.S.-Moroccan trade treaty gave the United States a strong economic interest in the country. Of at least equal importance, TR feared a possible European war. He convened the Algeciras Conference in 1906 at the Spanish port city. When the meeting protected French claims, Roosevelt, who strongly favored the growing British-French alliance, was secretly pleased.

Five years later, Taft won a more resounding victory for the open door in Liberia. That African country had been colonized, and was now controlled, by descendants of black slaves from the United States. After the Civil War, the U.S. government had shown no interest in the country. In dire financial straits, Liberia's land was being seized by surrounding colonies controlled by France and Great Britain. In 1910, Taft asked Congress to provide financial help and military protection. When the Senate rejected his plea, the president—following McKinley's and Roosevelt's examples—organized financial aid through private banks. The British and French were checked. The U.S.-supported black elite continued to rule. Historian Judson M. Lyon has placed the episode in perspective: Taft's proposals for Liberia were "almost identical" to those the president offered to Nicaragua and China. As a top State Department official believed, dollar diplomacy would bring order to these nations, while "extending the Open Door to as many regions of the world as possible."[50]

Taft's luck, such as it was, ran out in 1911, when he tried to negotiate arbitration treaties with France and Great Britain. The arbitration movement had gained popularity a decade earlier as it became apparent how brutal the next conflict among industrialized powers might be. The Hague Peace Conferences of 1899 and 1907 were one result. They produced the Permanent Court of Arbitration at The Hague as well as a set of rules for fighting wars, but little on how to avoid them.[51] Roosevelt supported the 1907 conference, although he had pointedly refused to submit the Alaskan boundary question to the court. In 1911, he became deeply angry when Taft made two bilateral arbitration pacts. TR was preparing to fight Taft for the 1912 presidential nomination, so his opposition was not dispassionate. Roosevelt's friends in the Senate carved up the treaties until Taft withdrew them. Nevertheless, between 1899 and 1911, the United States for the first time signed treaties with European and other nations that provided for peaceful resolution of disputes. Twenty-two pacts went into effect under Roosevelt, another twenty-one under Woodrow Wilson.

But the arbitration movement could not grow fast enough to stop World War I or even to prevent great powers such as the United States from using force to put down revolutions. In this sense, the American entry onto the world stage between 1898 and 1914 produced a most ironic result. For just as McKinley, Roosevelt, Taft, and, later, Wilson demanded order in Latin America, Africa, Asia, and even Europe, the world began to explode into revolution. Japan's victory over a white race in 1905 helped trigger anticolonial revolts in places as far apart as Vietnam, Persia, Turkey, and China. Russia experienced an ominous uprising in 1905. Mexico erupted in 1911–1913.

An understanding of twentieth-century U.S. foreign policy requires learning one central theme: just as Americans began to claim Great

Britain's title as the globe's greatest power and, at the same time, to demand an orderly world, the globe burst into revolution. The American claim was to be realized, but the demand was never met nor the revolutions ended.

Notes

1. V. S. Naipaul, "Among the Republicans," *New York Review of Books,* 25 October 1984, p. 17.
2. David Healy, *U.S. Expansionism: The Imperialist Urge in the 1890s* (Madison, Wis., 1970), p. 110.
3. The quotes and stories are found in Edmund Morris, *The Rise of Theodore Roosevelt* (New York, 1979), the best biography of TR's life until 1901, although weak on the historical context of 1895 to 1901; see especially pp. 98, 224, 463.
4. Healy, pp. 151–153.
5. Anne H. Oman, "Past and Present," *Washington Post Weekend,* 18 January 1985, p. 6; *Time,* March 3, 1958, p. 16; Nathan Miller, *Theodore Roosevelt, A Life* (New York, 1992) p. 387.
6. David Burton, *Theodore Roosevelt: Confident Imperialist* (Philadelphia, 1969), p. 137.
7. Albert K. Weinberg, *Manifest Destiny* (Baltimore, 1940), pp. 464–465.
8. Carl P. Parrini and Martin J. Sklar, "New Thinking about the Market, 1896–1904 . . . ," *Journal of Economic History* 48 (September 1983): 559–578, analyze, in a pioneering essay, the effects of surplus capital on U.S. foreign policy, especially in Asia from 1900 to 1904.
9. Arthur M. Schlesinger, Jr., *The Imperial Presidency* (Boston, 1973), p. 83.
10. Louis Henkin, *Foreign Affairs and the Constitution* (Mineola, N.Y., 1972), p. 309.
11. Alfred Thayer Mahan, *The Interest of America in Sea Power, Present and Future* (Boston, 1898), pp. 256–257, 268.
12. Woodrow Wilson, *Constitutional Government in the United States* (New York, 1908), pp. 78–80.
13. Lawrence Martin, *The Presidents and the Prime Ministers* (Toronto, 1982), p. 58.
14. Quoted in Morris, p. 3.
15. This argument is spelled out in Walter LaFeber, *The American Search for Opportunity, 1865–1913,* in *The Cambridge History of U.S. Foreign Relations,* ed. Warren Cohen (New York, 1993).
16. Howard K. Beale, *Theodore Roosevelt and the Rise of America to World Power* (New York, 1962), pp. 85–102, discusses the turn in TR's thinking toward England; see also Stuart Anderson, "Racial Anglo-Saxonism and the American Response to the Boer War," *Diplomatic History* 2 (Summer 1978): 219–236; Thomas J. Noer, *Briton, Boer and Yankee: The U.S. and South Africa, 1870–1914* (Kent, Ohio, 1978), pp. 5–20, 135, 186.
17. Martin, pp. 58–61.

18. John Hay to William McKinley, 23 September 1900, Papers of William McKinley, Library of Congress, Washington, D.C.
19. Richard L. Lael, *Arrogant Diplomacy: U.S. Policy Toward Colombia, 1903–1922* (Wilmington, Del., 1987), esp. p. xiv; Michael L. Conniff, *Panama and the United States* (Athens, Ga., 1992), pp. 33–34.
20. Dana G. Munro, *Intervention and Dollar Diplomacy in the Caribbean, 1900–1921* (Princeton, 1964), pp. 57–58; David S. Patterson, *Toward a Warless World: The Travail of the American Peace Movement, 1887–1914* (Bloomington, Ind., 1976), pp. 124–125.
21. Richard W. Leopold, *Elihu Root and the Conservative Tradition* (Boston, 1954), p. 178; *Public Opinion* 35 (19 November 1903): 645.
22. J. Bartlett, *Familiar Quotations* (Boston, 1981), p. 687.
23. Healy, pp. 112–113.
24. Dexter Perkins, *The Monroe Doctrine, 1867–1907* (Baltimore, 1937), p. 394.
25. *Ibid.*, pp. 419–421.
26. *Ibid.*, pp. 408–409.
27. The document is available in *The Record of American Diplomacy*, ed. Ruhl J. Bartlett, 4th ed. (New York, 1964), p. 539.
28. Theodore Roosevelt, *The Letters of Theodore Roosevelt*, ed. Elting E. Morison *et al.*, 8 vols. (Cambridge, Mass., 1951–1954), IV, p. 734.
29. Perkins, p. 440.
30. Daniel Aaron, *Men of Good Hope* (New York, 1961), p. 268.
31. Brooks Adams to Theodore Roosevelt, 17 July 1903, Papers of Theodore Roosevelt, Library of Congress, Washington, D.C.
32. Theodore Roosevelt to Brooks Adams, 18 July 1903, *ibid.*
33. This loan is analyzed in Grosvenor Jones, Chief, Investment and Financial Division, Bureau of Foreign and Domestic Commerce, to Herbert Hoover, 7 August 1926, Commerce, Off. Files, Box 130, Herbert Hoover Library, West Branch, Iowa.
34. Henry Adams to Elizabeth Cameron, 10 January 1904, in Henry Adams, *Letters of Henry Adams (1892–1918)*, ed. Worthington Chauncey Ford (Boston, 1938), pp. 419–420.
35. John Edward Wiltz, "Did the United States Betray Korea in 1905?" *Pacific Historical Review* 54 (August 1985): 243–270.
36. Paul A. Varg, *The Making of a Myth: The U.S. and China, 1897–1912* (East Lansing, 1968), pp. 83–88.
37. This fascinating story is told in Sherman Cochran, "Commercial Penetration and Economic Imperialism in China . . . ," in *America's China Trade in Historical Perspective: The Chinese and American Performance*, ed. John K. Fairbank and Ernest R. May (Cambridge, Mass., 1985), pp. 190–194, esp. for the boycott.
38. Michael H. Hunt, *The Making of a Special Relationship: The United States and China to 1914* (New York, 1983), pp. 204–208.
39. These paragraphs on Taft (and the ones on Knox that follow) are drawn from three good accounts: Walter Scholes and Marie Scholes, *The Foreign Policies of the Taft Administration* (Columbia, Mo., 1970), esp. pp. 1–31; Donald F. Anderson, *William Howard Taft: A Conservative's Conception of the Presidency* (Ithaca, N.Y., 1968); James Barber, *Presidential Character* (Englewood Cliffs, N.J., 1972), pp. 174–190, which has an interesting section on Taft.

40. Quoted in Lloyd Gardner *et al.*, *The Creation of the American Empire*, 2d ed. (Chicago, 1976), p. 280.
41. Michael H. Hunt, *Frontier Defense and the Open Door: Manchuria in Chinese-American Relations, 1895–1911* (New Haven, 1973), p. 228.
42. *Ibid.*, p. 241; Straight to Calhoun, 7 November, 1911, in Papers of Willard Straight, Cornell University, Ithaca, N.Y.; *New York Times*, 20 March 1983, p. E5.
43. Henry Pringle, *Theodore Roosevelt, a Biography* (New York, 1931), pp. 684–685.
44. Richard D. Challener, *Admirals, Generals, and American Foreign Policy* (Princeton, 1973), p. 20.
45. *Foreign Relations of the United States, 1906*, 2 pts. (Washington, D.C., 1909), pt. II, pp. 1457–1461.
46. The best account is Thomas L. Karnes, *The Failure of Union: Central America, 1824–1975* (Tempe, Ariz., 1976), pp. 200–202.
47. Thomas P. McCann, *An American Company*, ed. Henry Scammell (New York, 1976), pp. 15–30; William H. Durham, *Scarcity and Survival in Central America . . .* (Stanford, 1979), pp. 115–118; Mitchell Seligson, "Agrarian Policies in Dependent Societies: Costa Rica," *Journal of Interamerican Studies* 19 (May 1977): 218–224.
48. Walter LaFeber, *Inevitable Revolutions: The United States in Central America*, 2nd ed. (New York, 1993), pp. 47–51.
49. Robert Hannigan, "Reciprocity 1911: Continentalism and American Weltpolitik," *Diplomatic History* 4 (Winter 1980): 1–18.
50. Judson M. Lyon, "Informal Imperialism: The U.S. in Liberia, 1897–1912," *Diplomatic History* 5 (Summer 1981): 221–243.
51. The standard account remains Calvin D. Davis's prize-winning *The United States and the First Hague Peace Conference* (Ithaca, N.Y., 1962), esp. pp. 54–102, on the peace movement, and 207–212, on Roosevelt and the court.

For Further Reading

Pre-1981 references are most easily found in *Guide to American Foreign Relations since 1700*, ed. Richard Dean Burns (1983). Also see the notes to this chapter and the General Bibliography at the end of this book; those references are usually not repeated here.

Fresh overviews of Roosevelt and presidential power during these years can be found in Richard H. Collin, *Theodore Roosevelt, Culture, Diplomacy, and Expansion* (1985); John Milton Cooper, Jr., *The Warrior and the Priest: Woodrow Wilson and Theodore Roosevelt* (1983); Frederick W. Marks III, "Theodore Roosevelt and the Conservative Revival," in *Studies in American Diplomacy, 1865–1945*, ed. Norman A. Graebner (1985); Kathleen Dalton, "Theodore Roosevelt and the Idea of War," *Theodore Roosevelt Association Journal* 7 (Fall 1981), an interesting cultural perspective; Lawrence Margolis, *Executive Agreements and Presidential Power* (1985), a historical framework for TR's acts in 1904–1905; George Juergens, *News from the White House: The Presidential-Press Relationship in the Progressive Era* (1981).

Three recent economic-historical analyses are pathbreaking: Paul Wolman, *Most*

Favored Nation (Chapel Hill, N.C., 1992), on the tariff battles, 1897–1912; Emily S. Rosenberg, "Foundations of U.S. International Financial Power: Gold Standard Diplomacy, 1900–1905," *Business History Review* 59 (Summer 1985); and Vivian Vale, *The American Peril* (1984), on J. P. Morgan versus Great Britain. For Latin America, Lester Langley's *The Banana Wars* (1983, 1988) is a starting point for the Caribbean–Central American region; Louis A. Pérez, Jr.'s *Cuba under the Platt Amendment, 1902–1934* (1986) is now a standard account; Thomas Schoonover's "Imperialism in Middle America," in *Eagle against Empire*, ed. Rhodri Jeffreys-Jones (1983), places the U.S. drive for an isthmian canal amid the international scramble in a pioneering essay; J. Michael Hogan's *The Panama Canal in American Politics* (1986) is excellent on Roosevelt; Terence Graham's *The "Interests of Civilization": Reaction in the United States against the Seizure of the Panama Canal Zone, 1903–1904*, Lund Studies in International History (1983), well tells a story long needed to be told; Ivan Musicant's *The Banana Wars* (1990) provides an important overview; Leslie Manigat's "The Substitution of American for French Preponderance in Haiti, 1910–1911," in *Diplomatic Claims: Latin American Historians View the United States*, ed. and trans. Warren Dean (1985), is a critical view of a critical turn. On Canadian relations, R. A. Shields's "Imperial Policy and Canadian-American Commercial Relations, 1880–1911," *Bulletin of the Institute of Historical Research* 59 (May 1986), supplements the Hannigan essay listed in the notes.

Three good overviews of U.S.-Asian relations have been recently published: Michael H. Hunt's *The Making of a Special Relationship: The U.S. and China to 1914* (1983), especially important for its analysis of the Chinese side; James C. Thomson, Jr., Peter W. Stanley, and John Curtis Perry, *Sentimental Imperialists: The American Experience in East Asia* (1981), for its controversial view of U.S. motives; and Daniel M. Crane and Thomas A. Breslin, *An Ordinary Relationship: American Opposition to Republican Revolution in China* (1986), which puts the years 1911 to 1914 within a century of U.S. opposition to revolutions. The nonofficial dimension is studied in Key Ray Chong, *Americans and Chinese Reform and Revolution, 1898–1922: The Role of Private Citizens in Diplomacy* (1984), with emphasis on Sun Yat-sen's links to Americans. Raymond A. Esthus, *Double Eagle and the Rising Sun: The Russians and Japanese at Portsmouth in 1905* (1988), should become a standard account of the conference. A good overview of the entire era is Joseph A. Fry, "In Search of an Orderly World: U.S. Imperialism, 1898–1912," in *Modern American Diplomacy*, ed. John M. Carroll and George C. Herring (1986).

9

Wilsonians, Revolutions, and War (1913–1917)

The World of Woodrow Wilson

It was Woodrow Wilson's fate to be the first U.S. president to face the full blast of twentieth-century revolutions. Wilson's responses made his policies the most influential in twentieth-century American foreign policy. "Wilsonian" became a term to describe later policies that emphasized internationalism and moralism and that were dedicated to extending democracy. Critics described them as unrealistic and especially unaware of power (by which the critics usually meant military power). Wilson's policies, however, now appear to be more complex and instructive than either his supporters or critics claimed. Many later presidents, including Lyndon Johnson, Richard Nixon, and Jimmy Carter, looked back to Wilson as the chief executive who had the largest vision of the nation's future and who had first confronted challenges that continued to plague them.

Born in Virginia in 1856, Wilson was the first native southerner to reach the White House since 1849. He had trained as a lawyer but failed miserably in his practice. The failure tended to make him mistrustful of lawyers and turned him toward an academic career. By 1912, Wilson had become a national figure. A respected political scientist and lecturer, he was president of Princeton and then the highly successful Progressive governor of New Jersey. His success came not only from his speaking ability, but also from a sharp, analytical mind that was as able to place problems in a historical context as any president's in the American experience.

A stern Calvinist, devout Presbyterian, Wilson believed he was guided by God's will. Wilson often appeared cold even to those whose support he needed. A leading Progressive journalist complained that the president's handshake was "like a ten-cent pickled mackerel in brown paper." The new chief executive even refused to attend his own inaugural dance. Privately, another Wilson sometimes appeared. This one loved vaudeville, baseball, told jokes in excellent dialect, wrote limericks, and loudly sang "Oh, You Beautiful Doll" when he courted his second wife in 1915; it now appears that he had an affair in Bermuda with a married woman during 1908. The tensions that resulted from such a background not only made him highly complex, but also caused him, starting in 1896 (when he was not yet forty), to suffer a series of small strokes. By 1916, he had to restrict his work time in the White House, and by 1919—during the critical days of the peace conference—he had to spend much time in bed recovering from flu and exhaustion.[1]

Wilson was not only a politician, but a scholar who developed policies out of an understanding of the nation's history. He knew that the large corporation was a staggering new fact of national life, but he nevertheless wanted to use government to reinforce traditional political and moral values. In his first inaugural address, Wilson repeatedly emphasized that "our duty is . . . to restore" and, again, "our work is a work of restoration." He demanded that the new corporate system be opened up so that "the little man on the make," as Wilson proudly called him, could have a chance along with the rulers of U.S. Steel. His view of history, especially his understanding that the nation's landed frontier had closed, nevertheless forced Wilson to conclude that "the days of glad expansion are gone, our life grows tense and difficult." The president had learned this directly from the great historian of the frontier, Frederick Jackson Turner. The two had met during the 1880s at Johns Hopkins University. Wilson believed that with the frontier "lost," a "new epoch will open for us."[2]

The implications for foreign policy seemed endless. U.S. producers, Wilson warned in 1912, "have expanded to such a point that they will burst their jackets if they cannot find a free outlet to the markets of the world."[3] A frontier of world markets had to be found to replace the lost landed frontier. The government, led by a strong president, must open and order those new frontiers. "The truth is that in the new order," Wilson announced, "government and business must be associated."[4]

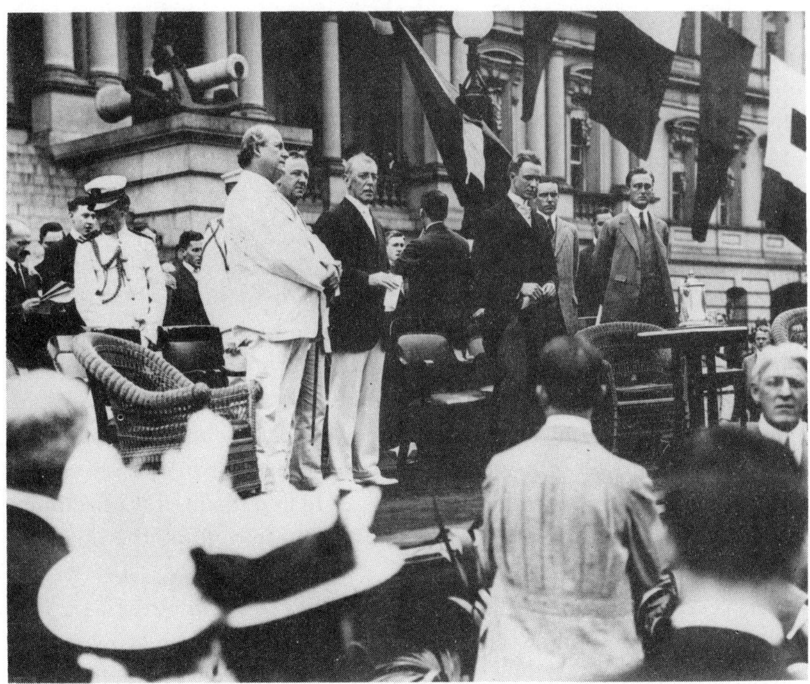

Woodrow Wilson's power as chief executive (1913–1921) arose in part from his oratorical ability. Here in white trousers, Wilson speaks in Washington during 1913 while at the far right his young assistant secretary of the navy, Franklin D. Roosevelt, and on the left his secretary of state, William Jennings Bryan, look on.

The young political scientist had been one of the first to understand the impact of the 1898 war on presidential power: "Foreign questions became leading questions again," and "in them the President was of necessity leader." Even before 1898, Wilson believed that at critical times, "the pleasure of the people" had to give way to presidential power: "He *exercises* the power, and *we obey.*"[5]

He followed this principle in the White House. At times it worked. Between 1913 and 1916, he pushed through Congress a significant series of reform measures, including the 1913 Underwood Tariff that lowered rates significantly for the first time since 1894. At other times, however (as in the 1919 fight over the peace treaty), Americans refused to "obey" the president. As a student of British politics, he admired the parliamentary system in which the prime minister, as the leader of the majority party, almost automatically was assured victory. Wilson grew short-tempered with the more cumbersome American system. Until

1918, he nevertheless dealt effectively with Congress. One reason was his decision to appear before Congress (somewhat like the British prime minister) and deliver his annual and other special messages personally. Since the time of Jefferson, who knew he was not an orator, presidents had merely sent their messages to Capitol Hill via courier. Wilson changed all that, and as he was able to whip Congress into line, he sometimes paid little attention to public opinion. Public-opinion polls did not exist. He seemed to have read newspapers unsystematically. The man in charge of the White House mail room recalled that the president apparently cared little about incoming letters. During several diplomatic crises in 1914–1916 (such as the *Sussex* episode), Wilson almost totally isolated himself, then emerged to issue a policy—often personally pecked out on his own typewriting machine. Robert Lansing, his second secretary of state, noted that Wilson's "very nature resisted outbursts of popular passion. . . . He had the faculty of remaining impervious to such influences, which so often affect the minds of lesser men."[6]

His reading of history shaped foreign policy in yet another way. Wilson feared revolutionary change. He wanted order—or at least slow reform. The president believed that the American system had prospered because it avoided radical change. In 1889, he wrote that the year marked the centennial of both the U.S. Constitution and the French Revolution. "One hundred years ago," he concluded, "we gained, and Europe lost, self-command, self-possession." A people could not be "given" democracy, Wilson argued. It required "long discipline" and "a reverence for law."[7] Thus, for example, he doubted that Filipinos were fit for self-government. American ideas and goods, however, could prepare others for democracy—and could do so while making profits:

> Lift your eyes to the horizons of business [he told a U.S. business group visiting the White House] . . . let your thoughts and your imaginations run abroad throughout the whole world, and with the inspiration of the thought that you are Americans and are meant to carry liberty and justice and the principles of humanity wherever you go, go out and sell goods that will make the world more comfortable and more happy, and convert them to the principles of America.[8]

The landed frontier had closed, but, luckily, the world frontier now spread out before Americans. With some government help, ambitious, hard-working Americans ("the little man on the make") could find opportunities abroad. The president, in leading these efforts, wanted that world to be a safe and an orderly place in which Americans could compete equally—perhaps even a place in which all people, with enough time and help, would become much like Americans.

Wilson's views were reinforced by the few foreign-policy advisers he consulted. He first named William Jennings Bryan secretary of state not because Bryan knew much about foreign policy (he did not), but for his long service to the Democratic party. Bryan agreed with Wilson's emphasis on the need to help others with U.S. goods and values. Taft's dollar diplomacy, Bryan complained, tried to "till the field of foreign investment with a pen knife; President Wilson intends to cultivate it with a spade."[9] Bryan also shared many of Wilson's traditional values, although Bryan's came from a nineteenth-century rural America that seemed quaint to some. The secretary of state was "irresistably funny," young journalist Walter Lippmann wrote, "because he moves in a world that has ceased to exist."[10] But at a critical moment in 1915, Bryan resigned as a matter of principle because he believed that Wilson was no longer truly neutral in the European war. He was replaced by Robert Lansing, a New York lawyer who was well connected (his uncle had been a secretary of state in the 1890s; his nephew, John Foster Dulles, was to occupy the office during the 1950s). Lansing was pro-British and as worried as Wilson over revolutionary outbreaks.

The president's closest adviser never held a formal office. Colonel Edward M. House, born in Texas, educated in the Northeast, and reared in smoke-filled rooms of Democratic party bosses, befriended Wilson in 1911–1912 to ride his coattails into power. Independently wealthy, he traveled abroad to talk with the powerful. House was as stealthy and secretive as a cat. One official who thought he was a close friend only years later learned that House had tried to ruin him. The colonel "was an intimate," the official's son noted, "even when he was cutting a throat."[11] Wilson appreciated House's discretion as well as the colonel's large view of policy.

Much of that view appeared in a remarkable novel, *Philip Dru: Administrator*, which House published anonymously in 1912. Dru, as House portrayed him, was a West Point graduate who all Americans demanded had to assume near-dictatorial powers to save them from rich, short-sighted interests that were driving the people to revolution. By issuing brilliant decrees (note that Congress was not to be consulted), Dru saved the country and made it prosperous and happy again. He then turned to foreign policy. Here Dru and his creator began to converge. In both the novel and real life, House urged that a U.S.-British partnership had to be developed into which Germany would be

Politician, strategic thinker, and world-class flatterer, Edward M. House (1858–1938) came out of Texas politics and eastern drawing rooms to become Wilson's closest foreign-policy adviser, although he never held office. House's shrewdness and slyness come through in this portrait.

drawn. The three would then destroy the great threat to the West by driving "Russia back" (as the novel put it). Once Russia was properly contained, House believed that the three powers could then divide up, develop, and stabilize the rest of the world.[12] Such cooperation could halt the senseless fight over colonial areas as well as stop the growing militarization that threatened to bankrupt, if not destroy, Great Britain and Germany.

Wilson came to the White House with no direct experience in foreign policy. But with House close by and his own sense of history, the new president quickly developed strong, well-thought-out views to guide his decisions.

WILSON AND REVOLUTION: CHINA

In his first major diplomatic action, Wilson ditched Taft's dollar diplomacy in Asia. He pulled U.S. bankers out of the six-power consortium set up to stabilize China. Wilson withdrew not because he feared that the consortium would exploit the new Chinese republic that had arisen in 1911 from the ashes of the Manchu dynasty. Nor did he have any intention of deserting the open door. He fully understood that China was "the market to which diplomacy, if need be power, must make an open way," as he had written a decade earlier.[13]

Wilson rejected the consortium because he understood that the Russians and Japanese, who showed little regard for the open door, controlled the group. Moreover, while the United States was in the consortium, his hands would be tied. Wilson wanted to use growing U.S. economic power and go it alone in China. He also planned to bring in smaller U.S. bankers (those "little men on the make") and not depend on the few giants who had joined the original group. As historian Jerry Israel summarizes the president's policy, "Rather than a rejection of the open door goals, the American withdrawal . . . was an effort to speed up their attainment by the United States alone."[14]

The president was willing to pay a price. In a cabinet meeting, Wilson ordered that the U.S. Navy be on alert for a possible challenge from Japan, then reported one expert's advice that U.S. financial power by itself could build 10,000 miles of railroads in China. In May 1913, he recognized the new Chinese ruler, Yüan Shih-k'ai. Yüan had seized the revolution from its father, Sun Yat-sen, and then set about destroying its republicanism and making himself a monarch. Wilson never protested. He wanted only to work with any Chinese leader who promised stability and cooperation.

Fifteen months later, Wilson's dreams shattered as World War I erupted. Suddenly the British, French, Germans, and Russians—who Wilson assumed would check each other and the Japanese in China—were absorbed in Europe. Virtually alone, Japan swiftly moved to seize the exposed German colonies, including the key entry point at Shantung. Only the United States could possibly check Japanese power, but Wilson was preoccupied with European and Mexican affairs. U.S. bankers sent vast sums to both sides fighting in Europe and had none to spare for China. The president, moreover, deeply mourned when his first wife died in 1914, then quickly became involved in a passionate courtship with Edith Galt that led to marriage the next year. Willard Straight watched his hard work for the open door disappear in the wake of Japan's advance and privately cursed the president for making love, not war. Wilson seemed "somewhat similar to the white rabbit," Straight remarked to a friend, "with the sex instinct strongly developed but unwilling to protect its young."[15]

On January 18, 1915, Japan secretly pressed China to accept a document that became known as the Twenty-one Demands. Wilson found out about most of the demands, but because they largely involved areas in which Japan was already dominant, he did little. The Chinese, however, told Bryan that a final, secret set of the demands would give Japan influence in China's military and police as well as in the vital Yangtze River region of central China. When the Japanese ambassador blandly denied the accusation, Bryan believed him. But American missionaries

The president and his soon-to-be second wife, Mrs. Edith Galt, attend baseball's 1915 World Series. After Wilson's illness in 1919, she became a powerful figure who greatly influenced White House decision making.

in China and U.S. ambassador Paul Reinsch obtained evidence that Bryan had been lied to. In two tough notes in March and May 1915, Wilson told Japan to back down from the secret demands. Tokyo officials did so, but not because of U.S. pressure. Their own internal politics and British opposition forced them to retreat. Wilson had nevertheless repeated the historic U.S. commitment to Asia. As historian Noel Pugach observes, "In the historically important note of May 11, 1915, the United States declared to China and Japan that it would not recognize any agreement which impaired the right of the United States, the political or territorial integrity of China, or the Open Door."[16]

Wilson had hoped to enjoy both the open door and freedom of action in China. Now, with Japan on the loose, his policy was endangered. A century of U.S. policy in the region hung in the balance. Ambassador Reinsch urged the president to work with China against the Japanese. But Colonel House and Secretary of State Lansing (who replaced Bryan in June 1915) wanted Wilson to control Japan through cooperation—to work with, rather than fight, Tokyo. As the United States itself prepared to go to war in early 1917, Wilson believed that he had no choice.

The United States took two steps to cut a deal with Japan. First, in November 1917, the secretary of state negotiated the Lansing-Ishii Agreement. In it, the United States recognized that "territorial propinquity creates special relations between countries." This meant that the United States recognized Japanese dominance in such areas as southern Manchuria. But Japan, in turn, reaffirmed the open door. Lansing and Ambassador Kikujiro Ishii also agreed on a protocol that remained secret until 1938. It stipulated that neither side would use the war to gain privileges in China at the expense of other states. The protocol attempted to short-circuit anything more like the Twenty-one Demands.

Wilson's second step was to control Japan by repudiating his 1913 policy and, instead, creating a second consortium. The United States, Japan, Great Britain, and France would cooperate in investment projects in China. Japanese financiers could thus be more closely watched. Wilson was not coy about government-business relations. He promised "complete support" to U.S. bankers as he asked them to join the new group. That a revolutionary China might soon try to control its own affairs worried few officials in Washington.

Wilson and Revolutions: Mexico (or, Painting the Fence Post White)

Until World War I demanded his attention, Wilson was immersed in the problems of revolutions in China, Mexico, and the Caribbean region. He understood that the upheavals arose out of such internal problems as poverty, oppression, and the failure of government to protect its citizens. He also realized that foreign intervention seldom cooled revolutionary fervor; the fervor only became more intense and antiforeign. But along with these views about internal causes, he concluded that revolutions could be caused by foreign corporate and banking interests that exploited smaller nations. By checking such interests and by cleansing a country's internal politics, revolution could be avoided. No better way existed to cleanse those politics and create a legitimate government, he reasoned, than democratic elections.

Determined to help other peoples become democratic and orderly, Wilson himself became the greatest military interventionist in U.S. history. By the time he left office in 1921, he had ordered troops into Russia and half a dozen Latin American upheavals. To preserve order in some countries, Wilson learned, required military intervention. He was not unwilling to use force. Journalist Walter Lippmann recalled

Victoriano Huerta took control of the Mexican Revolution in 1912–1913, only to run into Wilson's opposition. Their feud not only shaped U.S.-Mexican relations, but led to a historic change in U.S. recognition policy.

"one metaphor [Wilson] used to like to use a great deal illustrating his idea of how a progressive attitude was really conservative. He said 'If you want to preserve a fence post, you have to keep painting it white. You can't just paint it once and leave it forever. It will rot away.' "[17]

Some people, however, had concluded that their "fence posts" no longer served a useful purpose. They wanted the posts pulled up, not repainted. The Mexicans began reaching this conclusion in 1910–1911, when they rallied to Francisco Madero's attempt to overthrow the thirty-four-year-old dictatorship of Porfirio Díaz. Many U.S. interests were not pleased. Under Díaz's regime, U.S. investment in Mexico had sky-rocketed to nearly $2 billion, much of it in rich oil wells. Americans owned 43 percent of all the property values in Mexico—10 percent more than the Mexicans themselves owned.[18] Madero overthrew Díaz (who was rapidly becoming senile) but found that he had let loose forces he could not control. A number of armed groups tried to claim power. Unable to restore order, Madero was captured by a band led by Victoriano Huerta. The U.S. ambassador to Mexico, Henry Lane Wilson, was deeply involved in pushing Madero out of power, but he declared his surprise when Huerta's men killed Madero.

At this point, Woodrow Wilson entered the White House. Huerta not only had blood on his hands, but rumors circulated that he was supported by British oil interests that had long been in bitter competition with U.S. companies. London and other capitals soon recognized

Huerta's government. Wilson, however, refused. The president objected to Huerta's use of force to gain power. He feared that if the Mexican leader remained in power, other Latin American revolutionaries would follow his example. Wilson demanded that Mexico hold democratic elections. The president thus transformed U.S. recognition policy that went back to Jefferson's time. The United States had usually recognized any government that maintained internal order and agreed to meet foreign obligations (such as debts). Wilson added a third requirement: the new government had to come to power through a process acceptable to the United States. Most governments, of course, did not have America's democratic tradition. Indeed, he did recognize certain regimes (such as China's or Peru's) that made no pretense to being democracies. The belief grew that, in Mexico, the president used his demand for democratic elections only to get rid of the Huerta regime he so disliked.

The president began supporting Huerta's enemies, especially Venustiano Carranza, who led well-armed forces. Wilson sent a personal agent, John Lind, to tell Huerta that if he held an election in which he was not a candidate, a large loan might be available from U.S. oil, railway, and copper interests in Mexico.[19] Lind, a Minnesota politician who knew little about diplomacy, did not handle his mission well. Huerta turned down the attempt to bribe him and, with British support, conducted an election he handily won. (The election was so open, moreover, that even Lind reported he had cast a ballot.) Deeply angered, Wilson began to turn the screws on Huerta. He was determined, he said, that the Mexican government "be founded on a moral basis." Sir Edward Grey, the British secretary of state for foreign affairs, privately remarked that "it would require about 200,000 soldiers to put Mexico on a 'moral basis.' " Grey stepped back, however, after Wilson assured London that British interests in Mexico would be protected.[20]

Then, on October 27, 1913, Wilson warned, in a speech at Mobile, Alabama, that exploitative foreign "concessions" were no longer to be tolerated in Latin America. Claiming that his own nation's motives were pure ("the United States will never again seek one additional foot of territory by conquest"), the president said that Americans only wanted to be "friends" of other nations on terms "of equality and honor." He would oppose "foreign interests" that tried to "dominate" Latin America and so create "a condition . . . always dangerous and apt to become intolerable."[21] As the British and other foreign governments understood, the Mobile Address was Wilson's declaration that he now would try to throw out any foreign "concessions" that in his view created "intolerable" conditions. The British also began to realize that Huerta's days were numbered.

The president's opportunity arose suddenly in April 1914, when Huerta's agents arrested seven U.S. sailors who, while on shore leave, had wandered into a forbidden area. Huerta quickly apologized, but Wilson made a series of demands to satisfy American "honor." When Huerta rejected them, Wilson appeared before Congress to ask for the use of U.S. military force against Mexico. As Congress stalled and investigated the charges, the president learned that a German ship planned to unload arms for Huerta at Vera Cruz. Wilson ordered U.S. vessels to occupy the port. Firing broke out that killed 19 Americans and over 300 Mexicans. Latin American nations intervened to help restore peace and meet Wilson's real objective: Huerta's removal. In August 1914, Carranza assumed power. Wilson had apparently won—but only apparently. An ardent nationalist, Carranza refused to bargain with Wilson. The frustrated president now turned to aiding anti-Carranza forces, including Pancho Villa.

Carranza responded with one of the most momentous acts in the revolution. He announced plans for agrarian reform and, most notably, for Mexico's claim to all its subsoil mineral rights. In a stroke, the revolution had turned sharply to the left and threatened U.S. oil companies.[22] Wilson intensified his pressure on Carranza, but the Mexican leader succeeded in destroying most of Villa's forces. The president, involved in a continual series of crises arising out of the world war, most reluctantly recognized Carranza's government *de facto* in late 1915.

Villa responded by terrorizing Arizona and New Mexico in the hope that Wilson's military retaliation would undermine Carranza. When Villa murdered seventeen Americans in Columbus, New Mexico, and eighteen U.S. engineers in Mexico itself, Wilson demanded that Carranza allow U.S. troops to track down the killers. Carranza reluctantly agreed, but imposed limits on the movements of U.S. forces. In March 1916, 6,000 men under the command of Major-General John J. ("Black Jack") Pershing rode across the border. Pershing never captured Villa, but his forces did clash with Carranza's army when it tried to restrict Pershing's men. Forty Mexican and two U.S. troops died. Wilson was trapped. He knew the mission was failing. Carranza was firmly in power. But Wilson was determined to remove Carranza, and his determination was strongly reinforced by U.S. Roman Catholics, who feared the growing anticlericalism in the revolution. In early 1917, however, Wilson realized that he would have to enter the European struggle. He pulled out Pershing's forces and began coming to terms with Carranza.

The president had tried to stabilize and democratize the Mexican Revolution. Eighty percent of the people had never had a "look-in," he declared. "I am for that 80 percent!" He believed he knew what to do: "They say the Mexicans are not fitted for self-government," he had declared in early 1914, "and to this I reply that, when properly directed, there is no people not fitted for self-government." In "properly" directing the Mexican Revolution, however, Wilson twice invaded the country and killed Mexicans. Trying to repaint the old fence post proved expensive.

Wilson and Revolutions: Central America and the Caribbean

Upon entering office, Wilson declared that he wanted "orderly processes" in Latin America as well as stability in "the markets which we must supply."[23] But frequently, maintaining order meant maintaining the *status quo*. In much of Latin America, the *status quo* meant maintaining small elites who (as had Porfirio Díaz in Mexico) worked with foreign interests and exploited their own people. Only revolution or foreign intervention could overthrow such elites. "Democracy" often meant the continued power of those elites because they controlled elections. Wilson wanted elections, real change, order, and no foreign interventions—all at once. He never discovered how to pull off such a miracle. When he then chose order, Wilson and Bryan had to send troops into Haiti, Santo Domingo, and Cuba, as well as Mexico. Latin Americans began to call the U.S. Marines "State Department troops."

In 1913, the marines already were protecting the U.S.-created government in Nicaragua (see p. 262). President Adolfo Díaz's bankrupt regime needed money quickly. Bryan, who had made his political career by attacking bankers, had a novel idea. Why not, he asked Wilson, have the U.S. government lend the money to Nicaragua? The bankers and their exorbitant claims would be bypassed, banks and railways would remain in Central American hands, and it could "prevent revolutions, promote education, and advance stable and just government." Wilson rejected the plan. Substituting government funds for private bank loans would be too "novel and radical."[24] Bryan then resorted to the bankers, who already owned 51 percent of Nicaragua's national bank and railways. The bankers loaned Díaz another $1 million in return for the rest of the railways.

Díaz next asked that Nicaraguan (by which he meant his own) stability be guaranteed by extending the Platt Amendment's principles to the country. Bryan agreed to extend the protectorate, but the U.S. Senate rejected the plan. The secretary of state did sign the Bryan-Chamorro Treaty (finally approved in 1916) that gave Washington exclusive rights to build an isthmian canal through Nicaragua. In return, Díaz's regime received $3 million. The U.S. banks, U.S. government, and U.S. Marines controlled Nicaragua.

Wilson next ordered the marines to Haiti. That country, about the size of Maryland, had defeated the French colonials in 1804 to become the world's first black republic. Between 1843 and 1915, however, twenty-two dictators ruled Haiti in a highly corrupt version of a political revolving door. The last rulers in the line worked closely with German and French interests. Wilson disliked that connection. Moreover, the United States coveted the harbor of Môle St. Nicolas. When another revolt broke out in 1914, Bryan mentioned the Monroe Doctrine, told the Germans and French to stand aside, and asked Haiti for a treaty that handed over the country's vital interests to U.S. bankers. When the Haitians refused, Bryan landed marines, who carried $500,000 from the Haitian treasury back to New York City to protect, in the secretary of state's words, "American interests which were gravely menaced." With little financial support, the Haitian government began to collapse. Bryan demanded that elections be held. The Haitians refused. He then demanded that U.S. bankers be allowed to buy out the French interests and asked Wilson to have a U.S. warship available to obtain Haiti's attention.

The Haitians, meanwhile, were turning on President Vilbrun G. Sam, who thought he had assured himself a presidency for life by slaughtering over 160 of his imprisoned political opponents. A mob pulled Sam out of his hiding place in the French legation, hacked his body into pieces, placed parts on poles, then dragged the remaining trunk of the body through the dusty streets. Intent on teaching such mobs the meaning of democracy and order, Wilson dispatched the marines. A new government signed a treaty in August 1915 that granted the United States control over the country's foreign and financial affairs, and also the right to intervene whenever Washington officials thought it necessary. The marines remained for nineteen years.

The other part of Haiti's home island, Hispaniola, is occupied by the Dominican Republic. After 1904, when U.S. officials controlled its customshouses through the grace of the Roosevelt Corollary (see p. 247), the Dominican Republic remained stable until 1911. Renewed

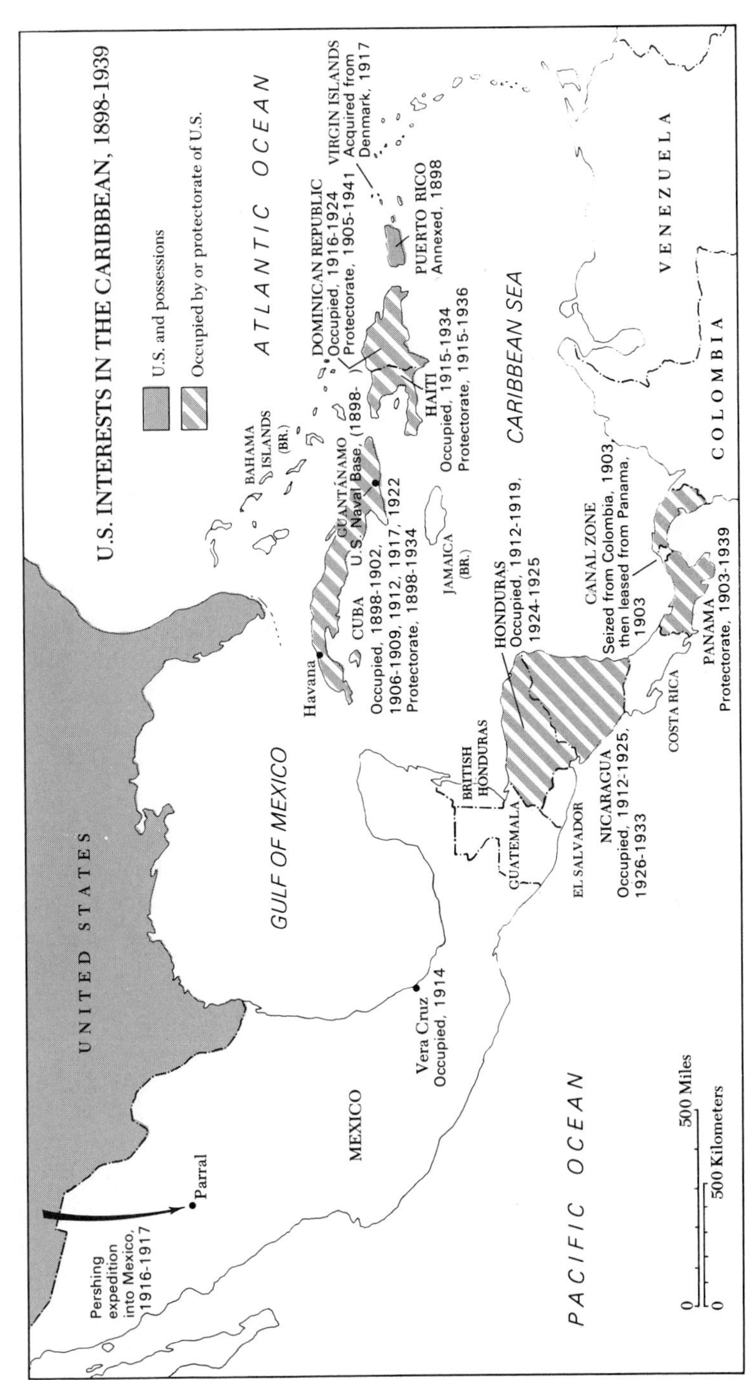

The United States was active in the Caribbean throughout the post-1890s era, but, as the dates indicate, Wilson's administration was the most active.

disorder led Wilson in 1914 to demand the usual remedy: U.S.-sponsored elections. The government agreed to elections but not to the president's next demand—that U.S. bankers oversee the country's finances. In 1916, the government threatened to default on its debt. Eager to protect strategic routes in the Caribbean as well as to stop possible instability, Wilson landed the marines in May of that year. The U.S. military tried to rule the capital city of Santo Domingo, but guerrilla warfare tore the country apart between 1917 and 1922. U.S. investors took over large sugar and real-estate holdings. Racism fueled the anti-U.S. rebellion. (In a typical incident, a black shopkeeper brushed a U.S. soldier who screamed, "Look here, you damned Negro! Don't you know that no damned Negroes are supposed to let their bodies touch the body of any Marines?") By 1922, President Warren G. Harding's administration searched for an escape from the mess. The marines pulled out in 1925. A series of dictators again took over the country's affairs. As historian Kendrick Clements summarized, "Benevolent motives, backed by seemingly unlimited force, tempted the Americans to intervene where they were not wanted and where they did not understand the situation."[25] It would not be the last time in the twentieth century, unfortunately, that such a judgment could be made.

In June 1916, Wilson prepared a message to send to Congress. "It does not lie with the American people," he wrote, "to dictate to another people what their government shall be or what use shall be made of their resources." Secretary of State Lansing read the draft, then wrote in the margin: "Haiti, S. Domingo, Nicaragua, Panama." Wilson never sent the message. He did, however, keep U.S. troops in those places.[26]

The United States and World War I: Legality versus Neutrality (1914–1916)

World War I began in August 1914. No one thought of it as a world war at first. The conflict seemed to resemble other crises that had arisen in the restless Balkans during 1908 and 1911–1913. These crises had been brought about by the slow collapse of the Austro-Hungarian and Ottoman empires. Circling the empires like vultures were two alliance systems—the Central Powers of Germany and Austria-Hungary itself, and the Entente (or Allied) powers of Great Britain, France, Russia, and, later, Italy. U.S. officials paid little attention to Balkan events. Nor, at first, did U.S. policy change in June 1914, when Archduke Francis Ferdinand of Austria was assassinated by a Serbian gunman.

When Austria tried to avenge itself against Serbia, however, Russia came to Serbia's side. Armies were mobilized, war declared, and bloodshed followed. Even then, many experts agreed with Captain Alfred Thayer Mahan's view that modern war was only an "occasional excess" from which recovery was easy. The huge arms build-up on both sides, these experts concluded, would deter either side from trying to push too hard.

By the autumn of 1914, it was clear that Mahan had been tragically wrong. As conflict expanded, all of Europe organized for war. Wilson issued a public statement urging Americans to be "neutral in fact as well as in name," "impartial in thought as well as in action." In reality, few could be neutral. Many recent Irish and German immigrants, for example, were anti-British. Many other Americans favored the Entente because of common language, the growth of economic ties, and the post-1895 warmth that cheered Anglo-American diplomats. That warmth rose considerably after British propagandists swamped the United States with stories of how the German "Huns" committed such atrocities as destroying the great library of Louvain when they invaded Belgium, killed in cold blood the famed British nurse Edith Cavell (who had, in truth, been acting as a spy), or, later, dispatched clumsy espionage agents to the United States itself.

Wilson's closest advisers quickly took sides. Colonel House had long hoped to work out U.S.-British-German cooperation. During the summer of 1914, House had been in Europe to sell these ideas to German and British leaders. As the war's shadows descended, the colonel feared that Wilson would have to choose between two evils: if the Central Powers won, German militarism would triumph; if the Allies won, then Russia could end up controlling central Europe. House chose to support the British and hoped that somehow the tsar could be held in check. Robert Lansing, then counselor in the Department of State, agreed. He was perhaps the most pro-British official in the administration's top echelons. Bryan took a more neutral position, although he was appalled by the German atrocities. Above all, the secretary of state did not want the United States to enter the war on either side.

It fell to Lansing to shape some of the first U.S. responses. When the war began, Wilson was recovering from the death of his first wife. The initial decisions, moreover, involved the U.S. response to the British naval blockade of German ports. As the administration's expert on international law, Lansing had some responsibility for drafting the proper response. By the end of 1914, he had strongly asserted U.S. neutral rights. But he had also gone far in recognizing the British right to stop

Europe divided bloodily between 1914 and 1918 as Americans (especially Wilson and House) had qualms about joining either the Central Powers or the Allies.

and search neutral (including U.S.) ships carrying munitions and other contraband (that is, weapons or other articles used to wage war) to the Central Powers. His position was good international law, but it also worked to Great Britain's advantage, especially when London officials began to expand the list of what they considered to be contraband.[27] The United States frequently protested British actions, but as Lansing later admitted, "I . . . prepared long and detailed replies" to complicate and prolong the controversies with London. Lansing hoped that as time passed, "the American people [would] perceive that German absolutism was a menace to their liberties."[28]

Lansing's tactics paid off. In February 1915, the Germans retaliated against the tightening British blockade with a submarine campaign aimed at Allied and neutral ships. The submarine (U-boat) was a shocking new weapon that brought sudden, unexpected death from the invisible depths of the Atlantic. There existed no body of international law to guide American responses to the U-boats. Wilson warned that he would hold Germany to "strict accountability" if U.S. ships were destroyed—although no one, including the president, knew exactly what this meant. The Germans took the position they had held for two years: they would call off their submarines if the British stopped trying to starve the Central Powers. Neither the British nor Wilson accepted that deal. Both believed that surface blockades were legal and traditional, but sudden submarine attacks illegal and uncivilized. In March 1915, the British passenger liner *Falaba* was sunk and one American life lost. In early May, the United States protested when one of its merchant ships was attacked and three lives lost.

Then, on May 7, a submarine sank the British liner *Lusitania.* Nearly 1,200 died, including 128 Americans. U.S. anti-German opinion grew white hot. Later investigation proved what the Germans claimed in 1915: the *Lusitania* was carrying a large cargo of munitions to Great Britain. Before it sailed, Germany had publicly warned that the ship was fair game. Wilson nevertheless prepared a note demanding that Germany pledge never again to attack a passenger liner. He insisted on the right of Americans to travel on any passenger ship they pleased. Bryan agreed on the need to protest but worried that the United States was moving slowly but surely into the Allied camp. He demanded that Wilson send an equally strong note to London protesting the British blockade. The president wavered and then, after discussing the problem with House (who was in London), refused Bryan's request. The secretary of state resigned.

"All the News That's Fit to Print."

The New York Times.

THE WEATHER

NEW YORK, SATURDAY, MAY 8, 1915—TWENTY-FOUR PAGES. ONE CENT

LUSITANIA SUNK BY A SUBMARINE, PROBABLY 1,000 DEAD;
TWICE TORPEDOED OFF IRISH COAST; SINKS IN 15 MINUTES;
AMERICANS ABOARD INCLUDED VANDERBILT AND FROHMAN;
WASHINGTON BELIEVES THAT A GRAVE CRISIS IS AT HAND

SHOCKS THE PRESIDENT

Washington Deeply Stirred by Disaster and Fears a Crisis.

BULLETINS AT WHITE HOUSE

RUMOR OF CONGRESS CALL

CAPITAL FULL OF RUMORS

Roosevelt Calls It An Act of Piracy

THE LOST CUNARD STEAMSHIP LUSITANIA

Canard Office Here Beseiged for News; Fate of 1,918 on Lusitania Long in Doubt

Loss of the Lusitania Fills London With Horror and Utter Amazement

Admiralty Puts Embargo On News Dispatches

DEATH OF FROHMAN IS FEARED IN LONDON

SOME DEAD TAKEN ASHORE

Several Hundred Survivors at Queenstown and Kinsale.

STEWARD TELLS OF DISASTER

BOATS PROMPTLY LOWERED

ATTACKED IN BROAD DAY

In his parting words, he not only questioned U.S. policy, but complained that Wilson had always allowed House to act as the real secretary of state. Louisville newspaper editor Henry Watterson expressed the popular reaction when he blasted Bryan's resignation: "Men have been shot and beheaded, even hanged, drawn, and quartered, for treason less heinous." Germany responded to Wilson's demand by apologizing for the *Lusitania* sinking and offering an indemnity. But the episode marked a turning point. Wilson had now decided to separate, openly and formally, British and German sea warfare. His demands of Germany were not to be related to his policies toward Great Britain's blockade. Bryan's resignation removed the most neutral member of the cabinet. Robert Lansing moved up to be secretary of state.[29]

In August 1915, a German submarine commander sank the British liner *Arabic* and killed two Americans. Berlin immediately disavowed the attack and apologized for the commander's action. Lansing warned that if Germany did not promise to stop attacking passenger liners (unless the passenger ships tried to escape or attack the subs), the United States "would certainly declare war." The kaiser's government finally made such a promise in the so-called "*Arabic* pledge." Merchant ships were not covered by the pledge; but in due time, Wilson would also have to close that loophole if he hoped to protect U.S. rights to travel and sell to both belligerents.

Wilson's decided tilt toward the Allies became especially notable when he had to decide whether U.S. bankers should be allowed to grant credits and loans to the belligerents. The stakes were high, for they involved nothing less than the health of the American economy. When the war began in mid-1914, the economy was entering a severe slump. The two key exports, wheat and cotton, depended on British and German markets. As the war demand shot upward, especially for these exports, the Allies and Central Powers discovered that they were quickly exhausting their cash reserves. They needed financial help, preferably loans from the Americans, who were—as Jefferson had put it a century before—"fattening upon the follies" of Europeans.

The administration at first decided against allowing loans. As Bryan declared, "Money is the worst of all contrabands because it commands everything else." But without money, the Europeans could not buy, and without their buying, the United States faced economic bad times. Wilson and Bryan decided to compromise. They quietly allowed bankers to offer credits (a transaction limited to a bank's own resources, in which the borrower usually uses the money only to buy specified goods).

They would not allow the bankers to float loans—that is, to offer securities on the public market to raise huge amounts of dollars to lend to the belligerents. The Americans who subscribed to the loans would then have to rely on British (or German) securities for repayment, a dependence that could make the lender exceptionally interested in having his or her borrower win the war.

By mid-1915, however, the bank credits proved inadequate to finance the multiplying trade in food and munitions. U.S exports by mid-1915 had more than doubled since mid-1914. The Allies and the Central Powers alike appealed for outright loans. After agonizing over the decision for a month, Wilson quietly reversed himself in September 1915 and allowed loans to be floated. (Bryan, it will be remembered, had resigned three months earlier.) The president changed his mind not only because he believed that both Germany and the Allies would have equal access to U.S. money markets, but above all because—as his secretary of the Treasury wrote—"our foreign commerce is just as essential to our prosperity as our domestic commerce."[30]

It turned out to be a pivotal decision. Bankers immediately floated the first Allied loan for $500 million. Although the amount was found only with difficulty, it opened the floodgates. The Allies, with their stronger links to U.S. banks, borrowed $2.5 billion over the next two years. (These loans were secured by British investments in American companies.) The Central Powers received less than one-tenth that amount. War-related U.S. exports doubled in the last half of 1915 to $2 billion (with most going to England and France), then doubled once more in 1916. Again, as Wilson's first major biographer observed, the president's decision to allow loans retreated from a position of " 'the true spirit of neutrality' to one based upon 'strict legality.' "[31] The decision also helped transform the United States from being one of the world's greatest debtors (it owed the world about $3.7 billion in 1914) to a creditor of $3.8 billion by the end of the war. This huge, quick movement of money between 1914 and 1918 helped turn the United States into the world's economic superpower of the twentieth century.

Wilson's dilemma was intense. He understood how U.S. submarine and financial policies were pushing him into the Allied camp. He certainly did not want a total German victory, but neither did he want an Allied triumph that destroyed the European balance of power and left Russia astride much of the continent. From the start of the conflict, he believed that he alone was in the best position to mediate a fair settlement and stop the bloodshed. Like a virtuoso, House played on Wilson's vision of himself as the great peacemaker. He convinced the president to allow him to act as Wilson's agent in Europe.

In early 1915, House sailed across the Atlantic to try to mediate an end to the war. He believed that a proper settlement would include German payment of reparations for invading Belgium and a general European disarmament. But it was too late. Too much blood had already been shed. The war aims on both sides had escalated. The Allies, moreover, had been negotiating secret treaties with Italy and Japan in which those powers promised to help the French and British in return for territory after the war. The stakes for victory were rising even as an entire generation of young Europeans was being slaughtered.

House, who seldom hid his pro-Allied biases, signed the so-called House-Grey Memorandum in February 1916 with British foreign secretary Sir Edward Grey. It attempted to seduce the Allies to a peace conference by promising that if they accepted, and if Germany refused to accept terms the Allies liked, the United States would then join the war with the Allies. When House reported his deal back to Washington, Wilson inserted the condition that Americans would "probably" join the war. Grey then rejected the proposal. He believed that it would be only a matter of time before Wilson would enter the war on London's side anyway.

The president was beginning to fear the same thing. In 1915, Wilson responded to this concern with his "preparedness campaign." Camps were set up to train American males for possible combat. Naval appropriation measures were readied. Wilson gave speeches warning his listeners that the nation had to be prepared to defend itself. Theodore Roosevelt, who had damned the president's every move because he would not take the nation into war against Germany, finally found a Wilsonian act he liked. TR justified preparedness on the grounds that it would firm the fiber of American men, especially the apparently more effete northeasterners, who responded to the call with unusual enthusiasm. Wilson, however, had other objectives. Although he wanted to counter Roosevelt's growing criticism, the president also wanted to show Germany that he meant business, as well as appease growing anti-German sentiment in the United States. Perhaps most important, he wanted to begin building military power so that he would have a strong base from which to mediate an end to the conflict. When he sat down at the peace conference, he hoped to have military leverage against both sides. In reality, as historian John W. Coogan concludes, Wilson, by late 1915, "had become a partner, and not always a silent partner, in the Allied economic campaign to strangle Germany."[32]

The Battle Cry of Peace, *one of the first movie spectaculars, was hugely popular in 1915–1916 and helped shape the debate over the preparedness campaign and U.S. neutrality. It was powerfully pro-war: foreign invaders (thinly disguised Germans) destroy New York City and Washington, kill the pacifists, and lead the women to commit suicide before they are ravaged. Theodore Roosevelt and Admiral George Dewey, among many others, strongly recommended the film. It was based on a book by Hudson Maxim, a munitions-maker and inventor of the Maxim Gun. As the picture shows, Maxim also starred in the film.*

The Decisions for War (1916–1917)

On March 24, 1916, a German U-boat sank the French passenger liner *Sussex* and injured several Americans. Lansing and House urged that this violation of the *Arabic* pledge be met with a severing of diplomatic relations. Wilson refused. The president continued to believe that only as the great neutral could he end the war and establish a just peace. He did, however, take one more step toward Lansing's position by sending a note to Berlin demanding that the submarines not attack merchant ships (as well as passenger liners). If Berlin officials would not agree, Wilson threatened, the United States would sever relations. After intense internal debate, the Germans agreed, but they implied that Wilson must put equal pressure on the British blockade. Angry at the response, the president again separated the two issues. Berlin's *Sussex* pledge nevertheless gave the initiative—a diplomatic "blank check"—

to the Germans. If they decided that it was in their interest to launch an all-out submarine attack to win the war, Wilson would have little alternative but to join the conflict. He had lost even more of his freedom of action.

The president realized that his room for maneuver had rapidly shrunk. In the summer of 1916, he tried to balance his policies by vigorously protesting against Great Britain's interception of U.S. mail and its blatant discrimination against some 800 American companies that had dealt with the Central Powers. On the other hand, when both the House of Representatives and the Senate threatened to pass the McLemore Resolution, which prohibited Americans from traveling on belligerent ships, Wilson pulled out all stops to defeat the measure. The president refused to give in on the thorny neutral-rights issue. He insisted on the rights of U.S. citizens to move on the high seas as they wished. Because of Britain's control of those seas, however, his victory also required increased U.S.-Allied cooperation.

Wilson's hopes for creating a stable and open postwar world received their greatest jolt in May 1916, when the Allies met secretly in Paris to plan economic policies. They clearly foresaw that after the war, the United States would be the world's strongest and most competitive economic power. The British, French, Russians, and Italians, therefore, drafted a program to seal themselves off from the effects of that power. The Allies planned to use government subsidies, higher tariffs, and controlled markets to fight U.S. competition. Wilson and Lansing were stunned when they learned of the Paris economic conference. The president concluded that "our businessmen ought to organize their wits in such a way as to take possession of foreign markets." He told one business group that he very much favored the "righteous conquest of foreign markets."[33]

Clearly, however, White House pep rallies were not enough. The U.S. government would have to enter the contest by directly helping the business community to neutralize the weapons developed by the Paris conference. Wilson approached the problem from two directions. In the long run, he planned to insist on a peace that provided open marketplaces, competition, and the minimum of government involvement. In such an arena, he knew that U.S. business could more than hold its own. But this meant that it was all the more important that he attend the peace conference. More immediately, he sponsored legislation to allow U.S. business to gear up for the "righteous conquest." The Webb-Pomerene Act freed corporations from anti-trust laws, thus allowing them to combine legally to conquer foreign markets. The Edge

Act removed government restraints so that U.S. banks could rapidly set up overseas operations. Wilson thus refused to join the Allies in using government power to close off and protect markets. Instead, he aimed to release government controls so that U.S. businesses could more efficiently compete abroad. But he still needed to get to the peace conference to ensure that world markets remained open.[34]

By the autumn of 1916, the president had become so determined to beat down British maritime and economic power that he sponsored a huge appropriations bill to enlarge the navy. He aimed at nothing less than the world's greatest fleet within a decade. "Let us build a navy bigger than [Great Britain's] and do what we please," he told House in September.[35] At the same time, however, the United States continued to be drawn to the British side. The Allies were now spending $10 million a day in the United States for war goods. "There is a moral obligation laid up on us to keep out of this war if possible," Wilson believed. "By the same token there is a moral obligation laid up on us to keep free the courses of our commerce and our finance." The president was snared in an ugly trap.

When the Democrats nominated him for a second term in 1916, they coined the slogan "He Kept Us Out of War." Wilson knew, however, that the days of peace were probably numbered. In his acceptance speech, he grimly announced that Americans could not long remain neutral in a war-torn world. He began to discuss a postwar "universal association of nations" (an idea mentioned earlier by such Republicans as Roosevelt, Taft, and Lodge). Such an association could establish a just world and protect U.S. interests. After he defeated Republican nominee Charles Evans Hughes in the 1916 elections, Wilson made one more attempt to mediate an end to the war. Both the Allies and Central Powers finally rejected his offer. Each side had now enlarged its war aims—for territory, bases, indemnities—that only a total victory could provide. Wilson's hopes of acting as a neutral, honest broker had been dashed.

In January 1917, Germany decided to launch all-out submarine warfare. The debate had raged in Berlin since the *Sussex* crisis. Now the kaiser was convinced by his advisers that only a military victory could obtain his war aims of new territory, a neutral Belgium, naval bases in the Atlantic and Pacific, and perhaps even war indemnities from the Allies. The moment seemed right: war-torn Russia bloodily stumbled toward collapse, and German armies seemed on the point of victory on the eastern front. Now was the time to put full pressure on the West as well. The German naval command boasted that "England will lie on the ground in six months, before a single American has set foot on the continent." Civilian advisers were not so optimistic. Berlin military experts believed that, in any case, Americans could hardly do more to help the Allied side than they were already doing.[36]

Wilson realized that the United States was about to enter the war. But he remained torn between his belief that only as a neutral could he mediate a just peace and his fear that only if the United States became a belligerent could he be assured of a seat at the peace table. It was a terrible dilemma. On January 22, 1917, he appeared on Capitol Hill to announce U.S. postwar objectives. Wilson tried to cut through his growing dilemmas by pleading for "peace without victory"—that is, a peace in which neither side could dictate terms to the other. Equally important, he announced that the postwar settlement must protect U.S. interests. He directly attacked the old European balance of power that had failed to prevent the war and now, he feared, threatened to undermine the peace: "There must be not a balance of power, but a community of power; not organized rivalries, but an organized common peace."

Such a peace, he continued, had to include certain principles: (1) self-determination for all nations, large or small; (2) freedom of the seas—"the *sine qua non* of peace, equality and cooperation," as Wilson called it when he lashed out at both British and German maritime practices; (3) no more "entangling alliances" that created "competitions of power" instead of an open world. "These are American principles, American policies," the president declared. He thus announced that the United States was entering the blood-soaked conflict not out of the goodness of its heart, not out of mere idealism, but to protect its own self-interest. He drove this point home: "I am proposing as it were, that the nations should with one accord adopt the doctrine of President Monroe as the doctrine of the world: that no nation should seek to extend its polity over any other nation or people."[37]

The speech marked Wilson's last attempt as a neutral to define peace terms that he believed necessary for both U.S. interests and "every enlightened community." But the war-shocked Europeans could no longer afford to be so enlightened. One important British observer, Sir George Otto Trevelyan, privately dismissed the president's appeal: "The man is surely the quintessence of a prig." How dare he, Trevelyan argued, come in after three years of "this terrible effort" and ask both sides to put down their arms and meekly agree to American principles. French author Anatole France compared Wilson's "peace without victory" to "bread without yeast" or "a camel without humps" or "a town without brothel . . . in brief, an insipid thing" that would be "fetid, ignominious, obscene, fistulous, hemorrhoidal."[38] Germany responded by beginning total submarine warfare on February 1, 1917. All ships in war zones were now fair game. Two days later, Wilson broke diplomatic relations with Berlin.

But even as U.S. merchant ships were torpedoed in February and early March 1917, Wilson refused to walk his last mile to war. He knew that a strong anti-war group in Congress, led by powerful Progressives such as Republican senators Robert La Follette from Wisconsin and William Borah from Idaho, posed an obstacle. On the other hand, he did not want to appear to be giving in to his bitterest critics, Theodore Roosevelt and Henry Cabot Lodge, who had urged war since 1915. (Even after Wilson asked for war, TR dismissed the president's foreign policy as "nauseous hypocrisy.")

More important, Wilson worried that U.S. involvement in Europe would allow Japan to run wild in Asia. He told Lansing that " 'white civilization' and its domination in the world rested largely on our ability to keep this country intact."[39] The secretary of state, who wanted war, began to devise tactics to keep the Japanese in check so that Wilson could fight Europeans in better conscience (see p. 277). Above all, the president feared that becoming a belligerent would ruin his chance to broker a "peace without victory." On February 2, he told his cabinet that "probably greater justice would be done if the conflict ended in a draw." He feared that joining the Allies meant "the destruction of the German nation"[40] and the creation of a dangerous political vacuum in the middle of Europe.

By early March, however, Wilson knew he had no alternative. U.S. merchant ships were being sunk. On March 1, the news broke that British intelligence had intercepted the Zimmermann telegram. In the cable, dated January 16, the German foreign minister asked Mexico to ally with Berlin in return for getting back the Texas-to-California region after the United States was defeated. Wilson did not take the telegram too seriously (fortunately for him, neither did Mexico), but the British scored a major propaganda victory. Despite the telegram, however, the Senate killed Wilson's request of March 1 to arm U.S. merchant ships. He went ahead and armed them anyway on the basis of an almost forgotten eighteenth-century law.

On March 15, the Russian front nearly collapsed, and the tsar, Nicholas II, abdicated his throne. A more liberal provisional government took power. Americans were elated, not least because the new regime promised (foolishly, as it soon turned out) to continue to fight

Germany. The United States was the first government to recognize the new regime. Roosevelt, that caustic critic of things Russian, now told a New York audience that "Russia, the hereditary friend of this country," had chosen "enlightened freedom." Wilson even announced that Russia was "a fit partner" because it had been "always in fact democratic at heart." The liberal journal *New Republic*, long a critic of the autocratic tsar, went into rapture: "The war which started as a clash of empires in the Balkans will dissolve into democratic revolution the world over."[41] As historian Peter G. Filene writes, "Americans . . . imposed American terms" on Russia, which was, "in effect, to be a Slavic version of the United States."[42]

The dramatic turn in Russia did not convince Wilson to go to war on behalf of "democratic revolution." It did allow him, however, to argue that now all Allies were "fit" partners for Americans. On March 18, three U.S. ships were torpedoed and went to the bottom of the Atlantic. On March 20, Wilson met with his cabinet to make the decision for war. Public pressure had little to do with the decision. Most important, the president concluded that U.S. rights on the high seas had to be protected and that only by becoming a full belligerent could he attain his great objective: to be a full participant at the postwar peace conference. As he told the famed Progressive reformer Jane Addams (who opposed going to war), he had to fight or otherwise be content, when the peace conference gathered, merely to "shout" at the participants "through a crack in the door."[43]

On April 2, 1917, he asked Congress to declare war. Despite strong opposition from Borah and Republican congresswoman Jeanette Rankin of Montana, on April 6 the war resolution was approved by the Senate 82 to 6 and by the House 373 to 50. Most of the opposition came from the Midwest and the Rocky Mountain states, especially areas with heavy German immigrant populations. But Borah spoke for many when he declared: "I join no crusade; I seek or accept no alliances."

Wilson had learned that in such a conflict, the United States could no longer be both neutral and prosperous. Nor could it be neutral and hope to have a decisive voice in constructing the postwar peace. To practice peace, he had to wage war. Tragic choices had to be made. And they had to be made amid bloodshed and chaos that not even the wildest imagination had conceived in 1914. "We are living and shall live all our lives now in a revolutionary world," pro-Wilson journalist Walter Lippmann declared. In that world, Wilson led Americans onto the charred fields of Europe, where 50,000 would die so that the president could try to replace revolution with a democratic world based on

Jeanette Rankin (1880–1973) was a suffragist and then the first woman member of Congress in 1917. Raised on a Montana ranch, she voted against war in 1917, lost her election campaign because of her pacifism in 1918, then was re-elected in time to vote against war again in 1941—the only person who cast a vote against entering each world war.

American principles. It was a gamble for the highest stakes. The brilliant anti-war voice of Randolph Bourne cut to the core of Wilson's dilemma: "If the war is too strong for you to prevent, how is it going to be weak enough for you to control and mold to your liberal purposes?"[44]

Notes

1. Edwin A. Weinstein, *Woodrow Wilson: A Medical and Psychological Biography* (Princeton, 1981); Paul F. Boller, Jr., *Presidential Anecdotes* (New York, 1981), p. 218.
2. David W. Noble, *The Progressive Mind, 1890–1917* (Chicago, 1970), p. 171.
3. William Diamond, *The Economic Thought of Woodrow Wilson* (Baltimore, 1943), pp. 132–133.

4. William Appleman Williams, *The Contours of American History* (Cleveland, 1961), p. 410.
5. Woodrow Wilson, *The Public Papers of Woodrow Wilson,* ed. Arthur S. Link *et al.* (Princeton, 1966–), VII, p. 352, italics in original; Woodrow Wilson, *Constitutional Government in the United States* (New York, 1908), pp. 58–59.
6. Robert Lansing, *War Memoirs of Robert Lansing, Secretary of State* (Indianapolis, 1935), p. 349.
7. Wilson, *Constitutional Government,* pp. 52–53; Lloyd Gardner, "The Cold War," manuscript, in the author's possession, has quote on 1889.
8. Diamond, pp. 136–139.
9. Lloyd Gardner, "A Progressive Foreign Policy, 1900–1921," in *From Colony to Empire,* ed. William Appleman Williams (New York, 1972), p. 225.
10. Paolo E. Coletta, *William Jennings Bryan* (Lincoln, Neb., 1964), p. 93.
11. Arthur Link, *Wilson,* 5 vols. (Princeton, 1947–), II, p. 95.
12. N. Gordon Levin, Jr., *Woodrow Wilson and World Politics* (New York, 1968), pp. 24–25, 37–38; [Colonel Edward M. House], *Philip Dru, Administrator: A Story of Tomorrow, 1920–1935* (New York, 1912), pp. 275–276.
13. Diamond, p. 133.
14. Jerry Israel, *Progressivism and the Open Door: America and China, 1905–1921* (Pittsburgh, 1971), p. 108.
15. Willard Straight to Henry P. Fletcher, 24 February 1916, Papers of Willard Straight, Cornell University Library, Ithaca, New York; excellent background for the U.S.-China relationship is in Daniel M. Crane and Thomas A. Breslin, *An Ordinary Relationship: American Opposition to Republican Revolution in China* (Miami, 1986), pp. 163–177.
16. James Reed, *The Missionary Mind and American East Asian Policy, 1911–1915* (Cambridge, Mass., 1983), is now a standard account; also, Link, III, pp. 269–270, 275–278, 280–285; Noel H. Pugach, *Paul S. Reinsch, Open Door Diplomat in Action* (Millwood, N.Y., 1979) p. 157.
17. Walter Lippmann Oral History, Columbia University Oral History Project, New York, p. 35.
18. Howard F. Cline, *The United States and Mexico,* 3d ed. (Cambridge, Mass., 1963), pp. 117–123, 130–134; Lloyd Gardner *et al., The Creation of the American Empire,* 2d ed. (Chicago, 1976), p. 305.
19. Cline, pp. 144–146.
20. Peter Calvert, *The Mexican Revolution, 1910–1914* (Cambridge, Eng., 1968), p. 238.
21. *The Record of American Diplomacy,* ed. Ruhl J. Bartlett, 4th ed. (New York, 1964), pp. 540–541.
22. Lloyd C. Gardner, *Safe for Democracy* (New York, 1984), pp. 65–68. Mark T. Gilderhaus provides an important interpretation in "Wilson, Carranza, and the Monroe Doctrine: A Question in Regional Organization," *Diplomatic History* 7 (Spring 1983): 103–115.
23. Raymond Leslie Buell, "The United States and Central American Stability," *Foreign Policy Reports* 7 (8 July 1931): 177; Diamond, p. 151.
24. Wilson *Papers,* ed. Link *et al.,* XXVIII, p. 48; Diamond, p. 153.
25. Bruce J. Calder, *The Impact of Intervention: The Dominican Republic during the U.S. Occupation of 1916–1924* (Austin, Tex., 1984), is especially important on the anti-

U.S. guerrilla war; Kendrick Clements, *The Presidency of Woodrow Wilson* (Lawrence, Kans., 1992), p. 106.

26. Diamond, p. 154n.
27. Link, III, pp. 105–129.
28. Lansing, p. 112.
29. Two excellent analyses are Link, III, pp. 390–401, and Ernest R. May, *World War and American Isolation, 1914–1917* (Cambridge, Mass., 1959), chs. 6–7.
30. Diamond, p. 156; Link, III, pp. 62–64, 133–136, 606–625.
31. Ray Stannard Baker, *Woodrow Wilson: Life and Letters*, 8 vols. (Garden City, N.Y., 1935–1939), V, p. 187.
32. John W. Coogan, *The End of Neutrality: The U.S., Britain, and Maritime Rights, 1899–1915* (Ithaca, 1981), p. 193; John Garry Clifford, *The Citizen Soldiers* (Bloomington, Ind., 1972); Michael Pearlman, *To Make Democracy Safe for America* (Urbana, Ill., 1984). Clifford's and Pearlman's accounts are standard on prepardness.
33. Lloyd Gardner, "Commercial Preparedness, 1914–1921," manuscript (1966), in the author's possession.
34. Carl P. Parrini, *Heir to Empire: United States Economic Diplomacy, 1916–1923* (Pittsburgh, 1969), pp. 15–39.
35. Link, IV, p. 337.
36. May, ch. 18.
37. Link, V, pp. 265–274.
38. *Ibid.*, pp. 273–274.
39. Entry of 4 February 1917, in Diaries of Robert Lansing, Box #2 (Microfilm ed., reel #1).
40. Edward H. Buehrig, *Woodrow Wilson and the Balance of Power* (Bloomington, Ind., 1955), p. 144.
41. Christopher Lasch, *The New Radicalism in America, 1889–1963* (New York, 1965), pp. 198–199.
42. Peter G. Filene, *Americans and the Soviet Experiment, 1917–1933* (Cambridge, Mass., 1967), pp. 10, 12–14.
43. Link, V, ch. 9, has the full account. A fine brief discussion of the context is Lawrence E. Gelfand, "The Mystique of Wilsonian Statecraft," *Diplomatic History* 7 (Spring 1983): 87–101.
44. Ronald Steel, "Revolting Times," *Reviews in American History* 13 (December 1985): 588; David Green, *Shaping Political Consciousness* (Ithaca, N.Y., 1987), p. 83.

For Further Reading

Start with the well-indexed pre-1981 references in *Guide to American Foreign Relations since 1700*, ed. Richard Dean Burns (1983), and consult the notes to this chapter and the General Bibliography at the end of this book; these references are not usually repeated below. Good recent sources are David R. Woodward and Robert F. Maddox, *America and World War I: A Selected Annotated Bibliography of English-Language Sources* (1985), and Kendrick A. Clements, *Woodrow Wilson: World Statesman* (1987).

On Wilson, start with Kendrick Clements, *The Presidency of Woodrow Wilson* (1992); Akira Iriye, *The Globalizing of America, 1914–1945* in *The Cambridge History of U.S. Foreign Relations*, ed. Warren Cohen (1993). *Woodrow Wilson and a Revolutionary World, 1913–1921*, ed. Arthur S. Link (1982), has superb essays written by experts on the era, especially in regard to Mexico, Russia, Poland, and collective security. Link's magisterial *The Public Papers of Woodrow Wilson* (1966–) is nearly completed; while Link and Robert C. Hilderbrand have edited a special volume, *The Public Papers of Woodrow Wilson*, Vol. 50: *The Complete Press Conferences* (1985). Important documents, a fine introductory essay, and an excellent bibliographic essay are in *Wilson and Revolutions: 1913–1921*, ed. Lloyd C. Gardner (1982). Important interpretations are in Frederick S. Calhoun, *Power and Principle: Armed Intervention in Wilsonian Foreign Policy* (1986), a useful overview; Lloyd Ambrosius, "Woodrow Wilson and the Quest for Orderly Progress," in *Studies in American Diplomacy, 1865–1945*, ed. Norman A. Graebner (1985); Norman A. Graebner, *America as a World Power: A Realist Appraisal from Wilson to Reagan* (1984); Michael H. Hunt, *Ideology and U.S. Foreign Policy* (1987), for placing Wilson in the context of a U.S. ideology and an antirevolutionary framework; William H. Becker, *The Dynamics of Business-Government Relations: Industry and Exports* (1982), which de-emphasizes the role of government, as opposed to the thesis found in Burton I. Kaufman, *Efficiency and Expansion: Foreign Trade Organization in the Wilson Administration 1913–1921* (1974), a pathbreaking study. Wilson's particular genius is featured in Robert C. Hilderbrand, *Power and the People: Executive Management of Public Opinion in Foreign Affairs, 1897–1921* (1982). See Ernest C. Bolt, Jr., *Ballots before Bullets* (1977), on the war-referendum idea. Important studies of film include Michael T. Eisenberg, *War on Film* (1981); and Craig W. Campbell, *Reel America and World War I* (1985).

Specific studies on the entry into the war have recently included Melvin Small, "Woodrow Wilson and U.S. Intervention in World War I," in *Modern American Diplomacy*, ed. John M. Carroll and George C. Herring (1986); John W. Coogan, *The End of Neutrality: The U.S., Britain, and Maritime Rights, 1899–1915* (1981); Kendrick A. Clements, *William Jennings Bryan: Missionary Isolationist* (1982), using Bryan to point up larger themes in U.S. diplomacy; Paolo E. Coletta, "A Question of Alternatives: Wilson, Bryan, Lansing, and America's Intervention in World War I," *Nebraska History* 63 (Spring 1982), by Bryan's biographer; and Kathleen Burk, *Britain, America and the Sinews of War, 1914–1918* (1985), which uses J. P. Morgan as a focal point of the U.S.-British competition. The anti-war groups are superbly studied by Charles DeBenedetti, *The Peace Reform in American History* (1985), which sees World War I as a turning point; Sandi E. Cooper, *Patriotic Pacifism . . . 1815–1914* (1992); and *Peace Heroes in Twentieth-Century America*, ed. Charles DeBenedetti (1986), especially the chapters on Jane Addams and Eugene Debs.

In addition to the Calhoun book, noted above, the following are important for Wilson's interventionism in Latin America: Lester Langley, *The Banana Wars* (1983), with a helpful bibliography; Brenda Gayle Plummer, *Haiti and the United States: The Psychological Moment* (1992), now the standard overview; Lester Langley, *Mexico and the United States* (1991); Friedrich Katz, *The Secret War in Mexico: Europe, the U.S. and the Mexican Revolution* (1981), an exhaustive account; Berta Ulloa, "Tampico and Vera Cruz," in *Diplomatic Claims: Latin American Historians View the United States*, ed. and trans. Warren Dean (1985); Bruce J. Calder, *The Impact of Intervention: The Dominican Republic during the U.S. Occupation of 1916–1924* (1984); David Healy, "Admiral William B. Caperton," in *Behind the Throne*, eds. T. McCormick and W. LaFeber (1993), essays in honor of Fred Harvey Harrington; and, for a rather stunning contemporary view, Hiram Bingham, *The Monroe Doctrine, an Obsolete Shibboleth* (1913).

The relations with China are studied in Daniel M. Crane and Thomas A. Breslin, *An Ordinary Relationship: American Opposition to Republican Revolution in China* (1986); John Allphin Moore, Jr., "From Reaction to Multilateral Agreement: The Expansion of America's Open Door Policy in China, 1899–1922," *Prologue* 15 (Spring 1983); and most of the accounts listed in the second paragraph of this bibliography.

10

Victors without Peace (1917–1920)

Wilson's Approach to War and Peace

President Wilson, as he informed Congress in his war message of April 2, 1917, intended to smash the "autocratic governments backed by organized force which is controlled wholly by their [the autocrats'] will, not by the will of the people." He emphasized, "We have no quarrel with the German people. We have no feeling towards them but one of sympathy and friendship."[1]

It seemed an odd way to go to war—that is, to express "friendship" for the people Americans were about to kill in large numbers. The words, nevertheless, fit Wilson's approach to the conflict. He believed that once the kaiser and other "autocrats" were destroyed, the "people" of Germany (and elsewhere) would create happier, democratic governments. Thus, he urged Americans to fight "to make the world safe for democracy." Once the "autocrats" disappeared, the mass of people would want to be democratic. Then, as he phrased it in his January 22, 1917, speech, the world could be rebuilt on "American principles."

There was idealism here, certainly, but also realism. Indeed, Wilson has become the most influential architect of twentieth-century U.S. foreign policy in part because he so eloquently clothed the bleak skeleton of U.S. self-interest in the attractive garb of idealism. Nothing, after all, could be more self-interested for Americans than to have the rest of the world act according to their principles. But the president also understood that Americans had little choice. They could no longer withdraw from world affairs. "Neutrality is no longer feasible or desirable" for the United States, he declared in his war message, "where the peace of the world is involved and the freedom of its peoples." The nation had learned this lesson the hard way between 1914 and 1917, when it mistakenly believed that it could have both neutrality and the freedom to sell anywhere it pleased. Wilson consequently hoped to make the competition play the game according to American rules. Making the "world safe for democracy" was the necessary first step.

The president, however, well understood the hurdles in his way. Most important, his closest allies disagreed with him. They wanted total victory, not "peace without victory," as he had asked. They made no distinction between the German people and their rulers. The French, who were losing one out of every two of their young men between the ages of fifteen and thirty to German machine guns, wanted vengeance. They saw little difference between the Germans who shot the weapons and the officials who gave the orders. Nor did the British intend to recognize "American principles" if one of them was freedom of the seas. London officials placed their trust in their great fleet, not in American principles. They and the French, moreover, depended on their far-flung colonial empires in Africa and Asia too much to agree to "democracy." The two European powers were not destroying an entire generation of their young men to give democracy to their imperial holdings in India or Indochina. Outspoken Americans such as Theodore Roosevelt and Henry Cabot Lodge wanted total Allied victory and total German defeat. Then, they argued, the victors could create a peace that suited them. They assumed that American and Allied war aims would be much the same. Wilson fought such views. He believed that such an approach could only produce more colonialism, more autocracy, and more wars.

The president, therefore, swept the United States into war not as an "Allied" power, but as an "Associated" power. He was doing what little he could to separate himself from the European conservatives who wanted total victory and a division of the spoils. When the president discovered that one U.S. government agency was trying to whip up war spirit by using slogans that included "Our Allies," Wilson sharply ordered the phrase changed to "our Associates . . . because we have no allies."[2]

Over There: The Western Front

The president's military policy fit this diplomatic approach. Wilson and his top military officials, led by General John J. ("Black Jack") Pershing, refused throughout 1917–1918 to allow the American Expeditionary Forces (AEF) in Europe to be integrated into Allied armies. Wilson insisted that they remain separate and under U.S. command. American armies were to be used for American, not necessarily British and French, war aims. One exception turned out to be the 200,000 African Americans who went to Europe. U.S. officers segregated and discriminated against them, to the displeasure of both the French and the black Americans. Finally, a large number of these troops were sent to fight with French forces, and they compiled a brilliant war record.

General John J. Pershing (1860–1948) led American troops in the bloody trench warfare of 1917–1918. A veteran of Indian wars and the war of 1898, and the leader of the U.S. military march into Mexico in 1916, Pershing quickly developed the American Expeditionary Force to fight on the western front. He became the nation's first general of the armies, a position that Wilson created to honor him.

Wilson insisted that U.S. forces fight on the single front of western Europe. The Allies also had to carry on campaigns in the east, where Russian troops fought with waning enthusiasm, and in Italy. Wilson cared little at first about these two fronts. In his view, they involved European imperial quarrels. He asked for a declaration of war against Austria-Hungary only in late 1917, after the Russian front had finally collapsed. Congress never did declare war against Bulgaria and Turkey, Germany's other two allies. Wilson wanted to focus on the kaiser's divisions, teach him not to sink U.S. ships, then create a democratic Germany.

The western European front, moreover, was closest to the United States and easiest for U.S. troops to reach. It was, however, a front on which British and French armies were approaching a critical point by early 1917. The carnage of trench warfare had long since become unfathomable. One young Frenchman had been unable to report for duty in August 1914 because of illness. By Christmas 1914, he was the only person still alive from his school class of twenty-seven boys. In early 1917, the British and French launched one more major offensive in the teeth of German machine guns and artillery to break through the kaiser's defenses before the Americans arrived. By late summer, the Allies had suffered 1 million casualties in this single offensive—which completely failed. Generals waited for fresh American troops to sacrifice on the battlefields. "We want men, men, men," French marshal Joseph Joffre proclaimed.

Wilson was able to place only half a million Americans under arms in 1917. U.S. officials aimed at a 2-million-man army but felt that they would need eighteen months to equip it. The Allies did not have that much time. Starvation was haunting France and Russia. Both eastern and western fronts were weakening. Under great pressure, a U.S. command under General Pershing was quickly set up in Europe during May 1917. By December, 200,000 Americans were in Europe but still in training. Nevertheless, they had to go into battle. The eastern front had collapsed, and, as the new Soviet government seized power, Russian armies evaporated. In the south, the Italians suffered a disastrous defeat at Kobarid (i.e., Caporetto), a village in Yugoslavia (later made famous by Ernest Hemingway in his novel, *A Farewell to Arms*), and were in headlong retreat toward Venice.

German commanders moved their troops from these collapsed fronts to France, where they launched a major assault on Allied positions in March 1918. By April, each side had suffered a quarter of a million casualties, but the kaiser's forces were just 40 miles from Paris. In

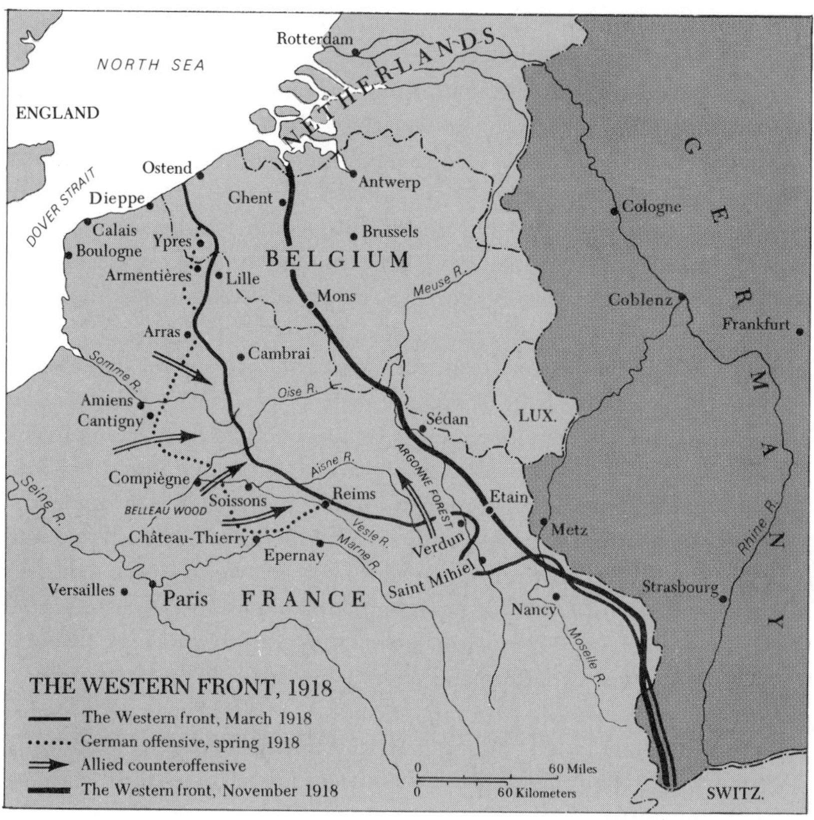

May, the Americans entered combat in force. Their successful counterattacks were critical in turning back the Germans along the Marne River. Allied armies, moving along a broad front, were now spearheaded by a new weapon—the tank—which at last gave troops mobility and some protection. By September, 600,000 American troops launched a decisive campaign that broke through German lines. The U.S. and Allied armies continued to roll until the Germans asked for peace on November 11. The offensive was the largest military effort in U.S. history. Overall, during about a year of heavy fighting, 53,402 Americans had been killed, 204,000 wounded. Over 57,000 died from disease, especially from the 1918 influenza epidemic that ravaged Europe and the United States.[3]

U.S. naval policy also was fit into Wilson's broader diplomatic aims. The navy's mission was to carry troops to Europe and defeat German armies. To accomplish this mission, the command emphasized smaller, submarine-hunting ships that could efficiently work together in "convoys" (a new idea) that accompanied troopships through U-boat–infested waters. This policy flew in the face of traditional military beliefs, formulated by Mahan and other naval planners since the 1890s, that the navy should depend on huge battleships capable of winning major battles by destroying the opponent's surface fleet. The core problem in 1917 was not the German battleship fleet, but submarines. On the Atlantic, unlike in European trenches, Americans worked more closely with the British to establish the convoy system. The U.S. assembly lines, meanwhile, performed miracles. Philadelphia's Hog Island could produce a 7,500-ton ship every seventy-two hours, although, as historian Warren Kimball notes, "its most long-lasting significance may be the addition of a new word . . . —'hogie,' describing a sandwich popular among the Hog Island workers."[4]

Certainly, much of the prewar American planning turned out to be useless, given Wilson's diplomatic objectives. As late as 1915, U.S. war plans included invading Canada and protecting New York City from British naval attack. Americans had mostly prepared to fight defensively.[5] In 1917–1918, they instead had to ship huge armies across thousands of miles of dangerous water so that they could go on the offensive and make the world safe for democracy.

Over There: In Soviet Russia

When Wilson inserted that famous phrase "make the world safe for democracy" in his 1917 war message, Colonel House objected. He feared some people might take it literally: "It looked too much like inciting revolution."[6] Some Russians did, indeed, incite revolution, but it had little to do with Wilson's message. Instead, the immediate cause of the Russian government's collapse in early 1917 was the breakdown of its war effort and the collapse of its ruling elite. The country could no longer marshal the resources needed to fight a three-year all-out war. Tsar Nicholas II, a weak, besieged man, retreated into seclusion, where not even his military commanders could reach him. The Duma (Parliament) demanded that the tsar surrender his power so that a more popular and liberal government could wage the war. The tsar—or, more accurately, his strong-willed wife—refused. They were then swept from power by bread riots and an army mutiny. In July 1918, revolutionary forces executed them and their children.

The Duma established a provisional government that, by July 1917, was led by Aleksandr Kerensky, a moderate socialist. Wilson and Lansing liked Kerensky because he insisted on fighting Germany despite the continued disintegration of Russian armies. The whirl of revolutionary politics worried and confused U.S. officials. They received infrequent help from their ambassador to Russia, David R. Francis, an elderly Missouri politician who had no diplomatic experience but, according to rumor, considerable romantic experience with a beautiful woman who was a suspected German spy.

In mid-1917, Wilson decided to send a special mission to Russia. It was led by Elihu Root, Roosevelt's former secretary of state and a strong conservative who found little to like in the chaos and dirt of revolution. His major pleasure came from a case of Haig & Haig Scotch Whisky that he had had the foresight to take on the journey. When Kerensky pleaded for more money, Root responded tartly, "No fight, no loan." Kerensky's fighting days, however, were quickly winding down. After reading Root's report, Secretary of State Lansing feared the worst. Kerensky, Lansing believed, was caving in to "the radical element." The secretary wanted to help Russia, if possible, but concluded that it was heading straight into a "hideous state of disorder," comparable to the great French Revolution.[7]

Kerensky's regime was finally destroyed when one of his own generals tried to overthrow him. The Russian army had so decomposed, however, that its soldiers would not obey the general. At that point, on October 24 (according to the old Russian calendar, November 7 according to the new), the Bolsheviks, or radical socialists, seized power. They were led by V. I. Lenin. Months earlier, the Germans had allowed him to cross their lines when he was on a train traveling from Switzerland to Russia. German officials bet that if he gained power, Lenin would effectively take Russia out of the war. The Bolshevik leader and his military commander, Leon Trotsky, first consolidated their power by destroying the moderate socialists. Kerensky escaped, living much of the next half-century in Stanford, California.

The Bolsheviks destroyed landed estates and distributed the land to peasants, nationalized banks, placed factories under the workers' control, and, in an all-out attack on the church, confiscated its property. To Wilson's discomfort, Lenin published the Allies' secret treaties of 1915 that parceled out the conquests of war. Wilson had tried to ignore these agreements because they undercut his own plans for an open postwar world shaped by self-determination. The president grew even more alarmed as the Bolsheviks called for world revolution and mass opposition to fighting the war.

Wilson suddenly found himself trapped. The French and British conservatives, with their colonialism and secret treaties, were on one side. Now Lenin was on the other. The Russian leader, moreover, offered a radical program that directly challenged Wilson's liberal agenda and threatened to end the war effort, especially on the eastern front. The president's closest advisers were divided over how to escape the trap. Lansing believed that Lenin and Trotsky were "German agents" who had to be destroyed by force. Colonel House, however, wanted Wilson to try to keep the new Soviet regime in the war—and undercut Lenin's growing appeal to Europe's war-ravaged peoples—by declaring fresh, liberal war aims. Wilson had instantly despised and feared Lenin's radical government, but, as historian N. Gordon Levin notes, the president's inability to choose between Lansing's and House's advice soon "gave a somewhat erratic quality to Wilsonian efforts to contain Russian Bolshevik influence."[8]

The president confided to House that he really wanted to tell the Russians to "go to hell," but he initially accepted the colonel's advice to woo the Russians and the wobbling European liberals.[9] The result was the Fourteen Points speech to Congress on January 8, 1918. The president offered a more detailed vision of a Wilsonian postwar world. But it was specially shaped to answer Lenin's demands for revolution and an end to the war without territorial annexations on either side. The points included:

1. "Open covenants of peace, openly arrived at, after which there shall be no private international understandings of any kind." This directly struck at the Allies' secret treaties.
2. "Absolute freedom of navigation upon the seas . . . alike in peace and in war."
3. A worldwide open door: "The removal, so far as possible, of all economic barriers and the establishment of an equality of trade conditions among all the nations."
4. Reduction of armaments.
5. An "adjustment of all colonial claims," with the people in colonial areas having "equal weight" in deciding their fate with the colonial powers.
6. "The evacuation of all Russian territory and such a settlement of all questions affecting Russia as will secure the best and freest co-operation of the other nations of the world in obtaining for her an unhampered and unembarrassed opportunity for the independent determination of her own political development." Russia was to be welcomed "into the society of free nations under

institutions of her own choosing" and receive "assistance." "The treatment accorded Russia by her sister nations in the months to come will be the acid test of their good will." . . .

14. "A general association of nations must be formed under specific covenants for the purpose of affording mutual guarantees of political independence and territorial integrity to great and small states alike."

The president also demanded that Germany leave Belgian and French territory. He wanted territorial problems in Italy, the collapsing Austro-Hungarian Empire, the Turkish Empire, and "an independent Polish state" to be largely taken care of by the people in the regions—or, what he called in one case, "along clearly recognizable lines of nationality."[10] During the remainder of the war, he added thirteen more points to his plan, but the original fourteen proved to be the most important in the debate over peace terms that soon raged in Europe and the United States.

Lenin was not moved by Wilson's appeal. Looking first to his own and his country's survival, the Bolshevik was unswerving in his determination to make peace with Germany. On March 3, 1918, he signed the Treaty of Brest Litovsk, and did so despite German terms that in a moment destroyed centuries of Russian expansion. Poland, Finland, and the Baltic States were taken from the new government. Even the rich Russian breadbasket, the Ukraine, became independent. Russia had left the war—or, more accurately, had exchanged one conflict for another; for anti-Bolshevik forces, led by conservative White Russian armies, launched a civil war to overthrow Lenin's regime.

Wilson now faced another stark decision: whether to ignore the civil war or help the White armies. For the most part, the American public was savagely anti-Lenin and showed considerable confusion about Russian affairs by calling him and Trotsky "willing German tools." Russians, who had been "democratic at heart" a year before, now became mere "children" unfit for self-government. The *New York Times* reflected the frustration by predicting ninety-one times between 1917 and 1919 that the Bolsheviks must surely be ready to collapse.[11] Wilson shared the anger and frustration, but he knew that any direct attempt to overthrow Lenin would be difficult, if not impossible, especially since the Russian people would cluster around the Bolsheviks to fight foreign invaders. In April 1918, however, Japanese forces moved into Siberia. Tokyo officials claimed that they only wanted to ensure the operation of the Trans-Siberian Railroad and help anti-German forces in the region. The Japanese received support from the British and

French. The Europeans also pressured Wilson to intervene. The president turned down six such requests between January and May 1918.

The turn came in mid-1918. In May and June, 20,000 Czech soldiers, who had been fighting the Germans on the collapsed eastern front, began to move east to find transportation and fight elsewhere. When Soviet troops tried to disarm them, fighting broke out. The Czechs reached and occupied the Russian eastern port of Vladivostok, then asked the Allies for help. A State Department officer quickly saw the request as a " 'God-send.' " Lansing used it to convince the president to move into Russia. On July 6, Wilson surrendered. He agreed to send several thousand U.S. troops to Vladivostok to help the Czech soldiers and to guard Allied military stores. But Wilson also wanted it both ways: on the one hand, he announced that the forces must stay out of Russia's internal affairs and that he would have nothing to do with British or French intervention; on the other hand, the president planned to use the move as an excuse to send in a political mission that would test Lenin's "intentions."[12]

At almost the same time (July 1918), Wilson agreed to send several U.S. battalions to intervene in the northern Russian port of Murmansk. Working under British command and with British troops, this intervention was originally aimed at saving large amounts of Allied military supplies that had been landed to help the prerevolutionary Russian armies and to prevent a German takeover of the surrounding region. But the U.S. and British troops soon found themselves pressured by Soviet, not German, forces. All the while claiming that he did not want to interfere in Russia's internal affairs, Wilson intervened with U.S. troops not once, but twice—in eastern as well as in northern Russia.

In September 1918, three U.S. battalions arrived at Vladivostok. Wilson's motives were complex. He helped the Czechs, but he also moved the 10,000 U.S. soldiers into eastern Russia to watch Japanese ambitions in the region. By participating, the president believed that he could also moderate British and especially French plans to become more deeply involved in the Russian civil war. But he was clearly working with the anti-Bolshevik forces in that war himself. Wilson dispatched his army not only to help the Czechs, but to help determine internal Russian affairs—one major reason why U.S. troops remained in the country until 1920, long after Germany's surrender in November 1918. In 1918–1920, 222 Americans lost their lives in this intervention.

Wilson had ringed his intervention with many conditions so that he would not be seen as a political bedfellow of the British and French.

But at this point (January–July 1918), Wilsonian liberals and Leninist communists joined a battle that was to rage through most of the twentieth century. Lenin challenged the liberals' view of how the world worked and was to work. He argued that, contrary to Wilson's belief, socioeconomic classes could not coexist but were fated to fight to the death. To prove the evil intent of Wilson's "associates," Lenin published the secret treaties that made a mockery of self-determination. He asked for immediate self-determination, regardless of the effect on the war effort of the colonial empires. As historian Lloyd Gardner observes, Lenin had "absconded with the biggest piece of liberal theory: the principle of self-determination. Liberals were never able afterwards . . . to reclaim nationalism for their own. . . . Little wonder Wilson sweat blood over Russia."[13]

The president even began to lose young liberals in his own government. Russian experts in the State Department unsuccessfully opposed the growing antibolshevism in the administration.[14] They were led by William Christian Bullitt, a wealthy Main Line Philadelphian who was close to Colonel House. By September 1918, as the Allied intervention was clearly failing to weaken Lenin, Bullitt outlined the dilemma that would repeatedly face U.S. officials. The number of Allied troops, he argued, was not enough to overthrow the Bolsheviks, but enough to scare the Russians—perhaps, God forbid, even to drive them "into military alliance with Germany" against the Allies. What could be done? Perhaps, Bullitt wrote House, Japan should send in half a million men "to overthrow the Soviets," or, on the other hand, the United States could open relations with Lenin. The point was, he concluded, that affairs were so bad that "I do not know [what to do]. And you do not know. And the President does not know."[15]

But the president had let slip one conclusion after he heard that Lenin had made peace with Germany. The only way to deal with the kaiser, Wilson exclaimed, was "Force, Force to the utmost, Force without stint or limit, the righteous and Triumphant Force which shall make Right the law of the world, and cast every selfish dominion down in the dust."[16] It certainly was not "peace without victory." Trapped between the European conservatives who wanted to return to their 1913 world (without the German military) and the Russian Bolsheviks who rushed to create a classless world regardless of cost, Wilson tried to break free by using unilateral U.S. force, both in western Europe and in Russia. In Mexico's revolution five years earlier, Wilson had intervened twice with U.S. forces but had failed to put his own "good men" in office. Now it was to be seen whether he could succeed in another such venture—this time on a global scale, in a world torn between the "forces of order" and the "forces of movement," as Arno Mayer terms them.[17] Against his will and contrary to his intentions when he took Americans into war, Wilson had already been compelled to choose one of those sides as he traveled to the Paris peace conference of 1919.

Preparing for Paris

Despite his twists and turns forced by Lenin's challenge, Wilson knew what he wanted to accomplish at the peace conference. His general objective was to reconstruct the world along the lines of the Fourteen Points. He hoped to reach that new world through self-determination, free trade, and a league of nations that would be able to oversee and make necessary adjustments in the cumbersome mechanism of global power politics.

This neat package began to come undone as soon as the Germans approached Wilson in October 1918 and offered to surrender on the basis of the Fourteen Points. On close examination, many of the points were maddeningly general. Wilson had ordered a group of advisers, called The Inquiry, to elaborate his peace plan, but when it did produce specific proposals, the president often ignored them and went off on his own.[18] Colonel House, suddenly faced with the need to negotiate with Germany, desperately tracked down young Walter Lippmann in Paris and said: "You helped write these points. Now you must give me a precise definition of each one. I shall need it by tomorrow morning at ten o'clock."[19] Lippmann worked all night to produce a draft, but given the incredible complexity of the problems facing the victors, it was an ominous sign of how ill-prepared Wilson was to enter into tough, lengthy talks.

He had, moreover, already compromised two of the Fourteen Points. The British flatly refused to accept Point 2 on freedom of the seas. They would not endanger their fleet's ability to control their strategic water routes. Prime Minister David Lloyd George pointed out, moreover, that Wilson had fully cooperated with British maritime restrictions after the United States entered the war. The president backed down. On Point 6—the evacuation of Russia and the self-determination of its future—Wilson had failed his own "acid test" by intervening and maintaining U.S. forces in Russia.

The president hoped to overcome these problems through the force of his own personal popularity and eloquence, and also through the

This painting by Johansen, Signing of the Treaty of Versailles, *not only pictures the Big Four in front, but catches the grandeur and historical significance of an occasion that would soon become the center of a heated debate in the United States.*

new, extraordinary power of the United States. Without doubt, Wilson did emerge from the war as the world's most popular and powerful individual. When he arrived in Europe in late 1918, millions of people greeted his triumphal tour by throwing flowers in his path. But his major opponents at Paris were to be not the German diplomats, but Lloyd George of Great Britain and the crusty, aged premier of France, Georges Clemenceau. Those two victors immediately realized that Wilson had made a near-fatal mistake in the 1918 U.S. congressional elections. He had asked Americans to give him a Democratic Congress to help him make the peace. Republicans struck back by crying that he impugned their patriotism and, after all they had done for the war effort, was accusing them of being un-American. The Republicans won the election and were able to put Wilson's archenemy, Henry Cabot Lodge, in control of the Senate Foreign Relations Committee that would have to accept or reject Wilson's work at Paris. The president then compounded his defeat by naming a peace commission, which he personally headed, that included not a single senator or Republican leader. In his defiance of Lodge, in his determination to dominate the commission, Wilson made a tactical blunder. If no Republican leader was to be involved as an architect, then the Republicans felt no responsibility for protecting the structure of the peace that Wilson brought back from Paris.

Meanwhile, Lloyd George's government won re-election by one of the largest margins in British history. In Paris, Clemenceau was given an overwhelming vote of confidence in the French Chamber of Deputies. Lloyd George suspected that Theodore Roosevelt better represented American, especially congressional, views, but the prime minister had to deal with Wilson. When the president threatened to appeal over Lloyd George's head to the British people on the freedom-of-the-seas issue, the prime minister called his bluff and dared him to try. Wilson dropped the challenge. Lloyd George called the president's threat an "unloaded blunderbuss" that intimidated neither him nor Clemenceau.[20]

The president also planned to use his country's new economic power as a weapon. During the war, he had held off pressing his postwar vision on the Allies because it would have led to disputes, perhaps even a crippling of the war effort. But Wilson did not mind. As he told Colonel House in mid-1917: "When the war is over, we can force [England and France] to our way of thinking, because by that time they will be financially in our hands."[21] And they were. By 1918, the Allies owed the United States over $3.5 billion. New York City was surpassing London as the world's financial center. But Wilson could never discover how magically to turn this power against the British and French (or the Bolsheviks).

The president did not help himself when, with the war's last shot, he pulled U.S. government representatives out of all the councils that had been established during the conflict to plan and finance the Allied war effort cooperatively. True to his pledge to build an open world, he refused to make any "special arrangements" to help Europeans rebuild their countries.[22] If they wanted help, they, like everyone else, had to go to New York private banks—not to Washington. Wilson was going to get the government out of the marketplace as rapidly as possible. That decision weakened his own economic leverage against Lloyd George and Clemenceau. Moreover, Wilson (and later presidents) learned that there were certain policies that just could not be purchased. Clemenceau's determination to ensure French security by crippling Germany had no price tag attached to it. Most nations do not place a purchase price on policies that they believe are required for their survival.

Such feelings were especially rampant in Europe after the horrors it had just experienced. Eight million soldiers and sailors had died. Over 1 million French soldiers had perished. Approximately 20 million civilians had died during the war and its immediate aftermath. More than 4,000 towns had been wiped off the map of France. Great Britain had suffered 900,000 troops killed and 2 million wounded. As Lloyd George put it, "Not a shack" had been destroyed in the United States. Americans, instead, had gotten much richer, even as the Europeans sacrificed millions of men and billions in treasure. "See that little stream?" novelist F. Scott Fitzgerald had a character say as he visited the site of the bloody Somme Valley battle. "We could walk to it in two minutes. It took the British a whole month to walk to it—a whole empire walked very slowly backward a few inches a day, leaving the dead behind like a million bloody rugs."[23]

Against that background of corpses and collapsing civilization, Clemenceau determined to protect French interests not with vague Wilsonian principles, but with boundary and economic agreements that protected France and crippled Germany. The Russian Revolution increased Clemenceau's concern. Not only did Lenin's victory threaten to radicalize much of Europe, but it destroyed France's valued prewar partner, tsarist Russia. Clemenceau had to find a new alliance arrangement. Wilson, meanwhile, sought agreement to his principles for an open, democratic world. While Clemenceau was driven by centuries of French history, Wilson believed, "If I didn't feel that I was the personal instrument of God I couldn't carry on."[24] After the peace conference, Lloyd George remarked, "I think I did as well as might be expected, seated as I was between Jesus Christ and Napoleon Bonaparte."[25] If it were true, moreover, that God helps those who help themselves, then even Wilson was in trouble. He failed to think through his own policies and suffered from severe, self-inflicted political wounds as he approached the conference table.

The "Black Cloud" over Paris

Colonel House looked at war-devastated Europe, sized up the attractiveness of Lenin's message to millions of Europeans, then concluded, "We are sitting upon an open powder magazine and some day a spark may ignite it."[26] Sparks were everywhere. After the kaiser fled Germany in November 1918, the country came under a moderate Socialist government. In January 1919, Karl Liebknecht and Rosa Luxemburg tried to imitate Lenin's success. A Communist Germany was narrowly averted as right-wing troops smashed the attempted coup and killed Liebknecht and Luxemburg. Wilson had believed that Germany

Table 2

Principal Wars in Which the United States Participated: U.S. Military Personnel Serving and Casualties

War/conflict	Branch of service	Number serving	Casualties		
			Battle deaths	Other deaths	Wounds not mortal
World War I (6 Apr. 1917–11 Nov. 1918)	*Total*	4,734,991	53,402	63,114	204,002
	Army	4,057,101	50,510	55,868	193,663
	Navy	599,051	431	6,856	819
	Marines	78,839	2,461	390	9,520
World War II (7 Dec. 1941–31 Dec. 1946)	*Total*	16,112,566	291,557	113,842	670,846
	Army	11,260,000	234,874	83,400	565,861
	Navy	4,183,466	36,950	25,664	37,778
	Marines	669,100	19,733	4,778	67,207

Source: Department of Defense.

required major social change before it was ready for democracy, but communism was certainly not what he had in mind.

Radical Socialists did gain power in Hungary. In March 1919, moreover, Lenin established the Third International of the Socialist parties in an attempt to destroy the Second International, which moderate Socialists controlled. Western officials understood that the new organization was nothing less than Lenin's attempt to create a worldwide Communist party network under his control. In September, two Communist parties even appeared—with few members but much noise—in the United States.

The Big Three (i.e., Lloyd George, Clemenceau, and Wilson) had to work out a settlement amid spreading revolution. They also had to deal with the collapsing European empires in Asia, Africa, and the Middle East as nationalist leaders turned to Lenin as a model. While the victors met in Paris, Asians and Africans met in another part of the city to prepare their own demands. (One participant was young Ho Chi Minh, who between 1930 and 1969 led Vietnam against French, Japanese, and U.S. military forces to complete the task he had set upon in 1919.)

Ray Stannard Baker, Wilson's first major biographer and the president's friend, caught the picture. As the Big Three tried to reorder the world, there arose this "black cloud of the east, threatening to overwhelm and swallow up the world." Baker concluded that "Paris cannot be understood without Moscow." Lenin was never invited to the conference, but "the Bolsheviki and Bolshevism were powerful elements at every turn. Russia played a more vital part at Paris than [Germany]! For the Prussian idea had been utterly defeated, while the Russian idea was still rising in power."[27] As Lloyd George admitted, he found it nearly impossible to discuss Germany without mentioning Russia.

The French proposed to make the "black cloud" disappear through direct military action. Lloyd George objected. He had neither the finances nor the political support at home to embark on a crusade to overthrow Lenin. He confided, moreover, "I dread wild adventures in lands whose conditions are unknown, and," he added in a pointed reference to the last French army of Napoleon's that had marched on Moscow, "where nothing but catastrophe has awaited every Empire and every Army that has ever invaded them."[28] Wilson sided with Lloyd George on this point, but he refused to go along when the prime minister suggested recognizing Lenin's regime as a first step to dealing with it.

Wilson and Clemenceau only agreed to have their agents meet Lenin at the island of Prinkipo (now Büyükada), a site off the coast of Turkey, to discuss terms. The leaders in Paris chose the island so that Bolshevik diplomats could reach it without traveling through any European country in which they might spread their germs of revolution. Lenin agreed to talks and even offered to repay pre-1917 loans and give up territory if the Big Three would pledge not to interfere in Soviet affairs. He promised noninterference in other nations' domestic politics, but added that he could not control revolutionaries or propaganda in those countries. Clemenceau and Wilson disliked Lenin's response. Moreover, Russian exiles in Paris and agents of the White Russian Army lobbied hard to kill the Prinkipo talks. The meeting was never held.

Wilson, under great pressure from Colonel House and young liberals in the U.S. delegation, finally agreed to send William Bullitt to sound out Lenin in Moscow. Bullitt returned in April 1919 with terms that he believed held promise. Wilson, pleading that he was ill, refused to see him. The French ignored the young American. Bullitt and the other liberals began to move into opposition to the president. In reality, it was too late for Wilson to try to work out an agreement with Lenin. The president had chosen to try to contain Bolsheviks, not talk with them. He allowed his food administrator, Herbert Hoover, to help bring down the Hungarian Communist government by manipulating food supplies. When the Communists threatened Austria, Hoover again helped stop them by posting notices that such action would "jeopardize" Vienna's food supply.[29]

In 1920, Wilson announced that the United States would not officially recognize the Soviet government because the latter preached revolution and refused to honor international obligations. But Lenin refused to disappear. By late 1920, Trotsky's Red Army had smashed counterrevolutionary forces and had even driven into Poland before being pushed back. Lenin set up a deadly efficient secret police, the Cheka, to destroy internal opposition. Marxist-Leninist revolutionary ideology had been wedded to the power of the Russian state. The "black cloud of the east" was casting long shadows.

At Paris: The Price of the Covenant

Twenty-seven Allied and Associated nations began deliberations in Paris on January 12, 1919. The major decisions, however, were made by the most powerful: Wilson, Lloyd George, Clemenceau, and Italian Premier Orlando. This Big Four shrank to a Big Three after Orlando stalked out because of a dispute with Wilson over Italian claims.

The Big Four first tackled the question of the losers', especially Germany's, colonies. In the secret Treaty of London in 1915, the Allies had already divided many of these areas among themselves. Wilson, however, refused to agree. He urged that smaller nations be responsible for the former colonies under a League-of-Nations mandate. He ran into a stone wall of opposition from Japan (which wanted Germany's colonies in the Pacific north of the equator), Great Britain (which had its eyes on the Pacific colonies south of the equator as well as on oil-producing regions in the Middle East), and France. General Jan Christiaan Smuts of South Africa offered a compromise: the great powers would take over the colonies but under a League mandate. Wilson accepted this "mandate" principle.

Liberals quickly attacked him for allowing the victors to seize the spoils and even gain moral approval by doing it under the proposed League's banner. They also complained that Germany had nothing to say about these decisions, nor was it to be in any way compensated for these heavy losses. The policy certainly had nothing to do with self-determination. It seemed more like glorified imperialism. Even Smuts's South Africa emerged with control over the former German colony of South-West Africa. (Under the name of Namibia, the region would continue to be fought over more than half a century later.) Wilson wanted nothing for the United States, but the Allies insisted. He ended with a mandate over chaotic, starving Armenia and Constantinople in the disintegrated Ottoman Empire. Lansing estimated that it would take 50,000 U.S. troops to control this mandate. In 1920, the U.S. Senate disdainfully rejected the responsibility.

The president accepted the unfortunate mandate policy in part because he was intent on rushing on to discuss his League-of-Nations proposal. Lloyd George, Clemenceau, and most others disagreed. They urgently wanted to deal with Germany, which had been in limbo and had been threatened by a Communist takeover since the armistice two months earlier. Wilson persisted and won his point. Germany had to wait nearly four more months for a peace treaty that was written hurriedly and badly. The president, however, had convinced himself that the final treaty might, indeed, have problems, but that a properly created League of Nations could correct those problems over time.

Working largely on his own and with too little consultation with The Inquiry or other advisers, Wilson wrote out a covenant for the League in just ten days. He then left Paris on February 14, 1919, for a month of business in Washington. Wilson lobbied hard at home for his Covenant, including a lengthy, tough, give-and-take evening session with congressional leaders at the White House. He learned that the Monroe Doctrine had to be explicitly protected if the Senate were to accept the Covenant. Even then, a number of Republicans warned that they would accept the peace treaty, but not the Covenant. Wilson shot back that he intended to tie together the treaty and Covenant so tightly that the senators would have to accept both if they wanted either. On March 4, Senator Henry Cabot Lodge dropped his bombshell. He had circulated a Republican round robin, declaring the League, "as now proposed," unacceptable. Thirty-nine senators—well over the one-third needed to defeat Wilson's pact—signed Lodge's challenge.

With his hatred for Lodge refreshed, the president returned to Paris in March determined to undercut the round robin. He insisted that the Paris delegates specifically protect such U.S. interests as certain domestic issues (including immigration, tariff, and racial policies) and, above all, the Monroe Doctrine. They did so, but only after Wilson was reduced to making a series of trades that weakened both his moral authority and the principles in the Fourteen Points. He had already surrendered Point 2 (freedom of the seas) at British insistence. Perhaps, however, his most notable and costly decision was allowing Japan to remain in Shantung. Formerly under German authority, Shantung was part of China and included some 30 million Chinese. Japan was already bitter because Wilson and the European leaders had refused to agree to include a clause in the Covenant that would uphold racial equality. When Wilson also rejected their claim to Shantung, the Japanese threatened to leave both Paris and the proposed League. The president surrendered. He felt that it was more important to have Japan in the League than to uphold self-determination. It was a horrible dilemma, and his choice further alienated liberals (such as Bullitt) in the American delegation.

Wilson called Article 10 the "heart of the Covenant." It provided that each member pledge "to respect and preserve as against external aggression the territorial integrity and existing political independence of all Members of the League." This article, aiming at orderly change in the world community (and even then only when League members consented), became the center of Wilson's later struggle with the U.S. Senate. To enforce Article 10, the delegates accepted Article 16, which provided that if members were attacked, all other nations in the League would economically isolate the aggressor. The League could also recommend the use of military force.

At Paris: A "Sanitary Cordon" Instead of a "Sanitary Europe"

The president obtained his Covenant, but the more important question was what kind of a world the new League would have to oversee. The answer to that depended on how the conference dealt with the traditional center of world power, Europe, and, specifically, how it treated Germany. Wilson and Clemenceau sharply differed. The "Tiger," as Clemenceau was appropriately known, wanted to dismember Germany so that its southwestern coal and iron regions would fall under French control. He also demanded that the Germans be held guilty for all the war's destruction and be made to pay reparations—hundreds of billions of dollars of reparations—for those damages. Such incredible payments would obviously cripple Germany's economy for decades. That was just fine with most French.

Wilson warned that Clemenceau's policy could only produce a sick, unbalanced Europe and more wars. The president had no hope of obtaining his healthy, open-trading world without a healthy and viable Europe at its center. Nor could Germany be dismembered without the principle of self-determination being made a total mockery. Above all, as he had earlier warned the British, "the spirit of the Bolsheviki is lurking everywhere." Germany was Lenin's prime target: "If we humiliate the German people and drive them too far, we shall destroy all form of government, and Bolshevism will take its place. We ought not to ground them to powder or there will be nothing to build up from."[30] The struggle with Clemenceau became so consuming that in early April, Wilson became seriously ill. Exhausted, he was confined to bed with a temperature of 103 degrees. The Tiger had little compassion. As the president stood his ground, Clemenceau bitterly accused him of being "pro-German." Wilson immediately ordered his ship, the *George Washington*, to prepare to sail back to the United States. He was ready to break up the conference. Cooler heads then prevailed, both men backed down, and deals were struck.

Clemenceau gave up his demand for French annexation of much of the German Rhineland and control of the remainder. In turn, Wilson and Lloyd George agreed that French armies could occupy the Rhineland for fifteen years. Most surprisingly, Wilson signed a security treaty with France that guaranteed its borders with Germany. Against the advice of many of his advisers, he thus signed the most entangling of alliances. But it was the price he willingly paid to keep western Ger-

A cartoonist depicts a critical view of the "Tiger," Georges Clemenceau of France, who is saying that he thinks he hears a child crying. The "child" is the generation who would fight World War II. Wilson is at far right.

many in German hands. The defeated Central Powers were to be demilitarized and any necessary German military forces sharply limited. On the critical reparations issue, Germany was forced to sign a "war guilt" clause, but the total amount of payments was to be left to a reparations commission. Thus, Clemenceau won his principle, but Wilson believed the commission of experts would scale down the actual figure. The bill turned out to be $33 billion, far more than Germany was able to pay (especially after being effectively stripped of its colonies and parts of the Rhineland) but far less than Clemenceau had demanded.

With Germany's western boundaries settled, the Big Three turned to the highly sensitive question of its eastern regions—that is, the areas touching eastern and southern Europe where the distintegration of the Russian and Austro-Hungarian empires left only near-chaos. Wilson, of course, had a formula to propose. The boundaries of such new, independent nations as Poland and Czechoslovakia were to be settled by self-determination. But two problems plagued Wilson's approach. First, victors such as Japan and Italy cared more about acquiring nearby territory for their security and economic needs than about upholding vague principles. When Italy claimed a strip that was inhabited by

The victors at Versailles had pieced Europe back together after the devastation of World War I but, in doing so, sacrificed the principle of self-determination in order to create a Europe that they hoped could hold back bolshevism.

Yugoslavs (Croats), Wilson, operating on his belief that the masses were more moral than their governments, went over Italian Premier Orlando's head and appealed directly to the Italian people. For Wilson, however, this Orlando had no dawn. The Italian leader angrily walked out of Paris. The Italians not unnaturally chose their own government's position over the American president's. Wilson backed off. Orlando finally returned. After the peace conference concluded, the Italians and Yugoslavs settled the dispute themselves.

Wilson's second problem was more general. If the principle of self-determination was applied to eastern Europe, the nations might embrace bolshevism. Hungary was already coming under the control of native Communists. Wilson was forced again to choose between his principle and European security. The result was a compromised eastern Europe. Poland, for example, received special access to the Baltic Sea through Danzig, which was made a free port although it was wholly German. Only Lloyd George's and Wilson's determination prevented Clemenceau from giving Danzig to Poland directly. An area with several million Germans also came under Czechoslovakia's control so that with this region—the Sudetenland—the Czech borders could be made more secure.

France brilliantly turned these arrangements to its advantage. It negotiated a series of pacts with the new nations in eastern and southern Europe to tie them into a security system dominated by Paris. But France's paper diplomacy—making treaties with Wilson to fix Germany's western boundary and with the smaller nations to contain Germany to the east—deceived. In reality, the Big Three placed the new, weaker states of Poland and Czechoslovakia between the two outcasts, Germany and Russia. The smaller states, thus, had to carry an enormous burden: containing both Russian and German ambitions as well as acting as a buffer to prevent bolshevism from moving westward to Germany. It, indeed, turned out to be a crushing burden. These states were too weak economically and politically to carry out such a policy.

Walter Lippmann, once an ardent Wilsonian but, by 1920, bitterly disillusioned by what he had witnessed in Paris, defined the problem when he returned to the United States: the Big Three had created a "sanitary cordon" to block Germany and Russia militarily, when they should have created a "sanitary Europe."[31]

In Washington: The Defeat of the Covenant

Wilson came home determined to obtain Senate approval of his work at Paris. His determination seemed to rise as he was forced to compromise his original plans and as opposition gathered on Capitol Hill. Perhaps a majority of Americans wanted to join the League in 1919–1920. No one will ever know. It is certain, however, that two major groups of opponents awaited to attack Wilson's handiwork, and he played into their hands.

The first group of opponents earned the name "Irreconcilables." Numbering about twelve, they were led by old Progressive Republican senators such as William Borah of Idaho and Hiram Johnson of California. They opposed U.S. membership in any kind of organization resembling the League. This group especially feared being drawn in to defend the interests of such colonial powers as Great Britain and France. Instead, most Irreconcilables wanted to focus on problems at home and, when they did act abroad, to show sympathy for revolutions in Russia and China. They did not want to withdraw from the world, but, as Johnson declared, "I am opposed to American boys policing

Hiram Johnson (on the left) was a powerful Progressive Republican senator from California. William Borah of Idaho led the opposition to war in 1917 and to the Versailles Treaty in 1919–1920. Borah, also a Progressive Republican, and Johnson led the Irreconcilables, who most bitterly fought Wilson's policies—including the president's refusal to recognize the Soviet Union.

Europe and quelling riots in every new nation's back yard."[32] Refusing to guarantee the badly drawn European borders, the Irreconcilables also condemned the Covenant, especially Article 10.

They were joined in that condemnation by a second group of opponents, the "reservationists," led by Senator Henry Cabot Lodge, the powerful Republican chairman of the Foreign Relations Committee. This group included such leading figures outside the Senate as Hughes, Taft, and Hoover. Lodge and Roosevelt had grown to hate Wilson personally, especially for what they believed to be the president's weak-kneed response to the Mexican Revolution and German submarine attacks. TR suddenly died in January 1919 at age sixty (he had never recovered from the death of his son, Quentin, on a European battlefield), and Lodge redoubled his opposition to Wilson's grand plan. But the senator also objected to the peace treaties on grounds of substance.

Along with the Irreconcilables and many liberals, the reservationists hated the deal on Shantung. When Lodge's committee considered the treaty, he pointedly substituted "China" in every spot in which Wilson had put "Japan" in dealing with the former German colonies in China. Wilson was furious. American missionaries and businessmen in China were delighted. The Lodge group also continued to believe that internal U.S. issues and especially the Monroe Doctrine were not adequately protected.

Above all, the reservationists feared Article 10. It locked the United States into having to act with the weakening European colonial powers. It also threatened Congress's power to declare war. When Wilson was asked directly whether the United States would have to act automatically if the League put Article 10 into effect, he tried to wiggle free: the commitment "constitutes a very grave and solemn moral obligation. But it is a moral, not a legal obligation, and leaves our Congress absolutely free. . . . It is binding in conscience only, not in law." His response was not good enough. Most of the Senate, as well as Wilson, took a "moral obligation" seriously. Under Article 10, the United States might—as Lansing had to admit before a congressional committee—support Japan's control of Shantung against valid Chinese claims, and Congress would have to go along with this "moral obligation." The famed economist, Thorstein Veblen, condemned the provision directly: it seemed "in effect to validate existing empires." Wilson vehemently denied that Article 10 opposed revolution, but he was never able to explain why. As historian William Widenor concludes, Article 10 was "*the* obstacle to ratification," because "the nature of the obligation assumed by Member States would determine what kind of organization the League would be."[33]

Neither the Irreconcilables nor the reservationists wanted to undertake that kind of obligation. But Lodge, who was certainly more sympathetic to British and French interests than was Borah, offered a compromise. He added fourteen points of his own to modify Wilson's Covenant. They aimed at removing any automatic U.S. commitment to the League's principles. Not surprisingly, the president refused such a compromise. He decided to go to the people. In September 1919, the president embarked on a cross-country speaking tour to whip up support for the League. Frustrated with the politics of Washington, he once again resorted to speechmaking so that his cause could transcend the grimy political arena. Working day and night, the sixty-three-year-old Wilson—already in questionable health from his angry encounters with Clemenceau—delivered thirty-six formal speeches in just twenty-three days. On September 26 at Pueblo, Colorado, he suffered a paralytic stroke. The broken president immediately returned to Washington. But assisted by his strong-willed wife, who rigidly controlled access to her husband, Wilson fought every attempt to compromise with Lodge. He received little help from House, with whom Wilson had broken after arguments in Paris. Lansing soon moved over to agree with many of Lodge's reservations. Disillusioned with Wilson (Lansing said that the president's mind was as clear as a pool ball), the secretary of state, in historian Dimitri Lazo's words, "encouraged" the Senate opposition with his "sarcastic commentary" about the treaty. In February 1920, Wilson fired him.[34] Such young liberals as Bullitt and Lippmann had already left the U.S. peace delegation and now actively opposed the president.

Historian Thomas Knock has noted that Wilson tried to put together a "progressive internationalist coalition"—a group of liberals who believed in self-determination, anti-imperialism, and even democratic socialism. But by November 1919, due in part to Wilson's own actions, hope for such crucial political support lay in ruins as the Senate prepared to vote on the Covenant.[35] The fear of bolshevism had spread to the United States, especially after a bomb exploded outside the home of Attorney General A. Mitchell Palmer in June 1919. Between November 1919 and January 1920, Palmer issued 3,000 arrest warrants and deported more than 500 aliens suspected of Bolshevist sympathies. The country was gripped by the "Red Scare." Wilson was not innocent of blame. During the war, his administration had helped inflame nationalist passions by passing an espionage act and a sedition act that allowed the government to arrest newspaper editors and others who were merely suspected of being critical of the war effort. Passions were out of hand. In Collinsville, Illinois, for example, a mob had decided that a town resident was a German spy and had then seized him, wrapped him in a U.S. flag, and murdered him. When Socialist party leader Eugene V. Debs condemned the war, he was jailed. Wilson kept him in prison until 1921, when President Warren G. Harding finally pardoned Debs. The administration's propaganda committee, directed by George Creel, played to fears of conspiracy and loudly protested Lenin's treachery in making peace with Germany. With few exceptions (historian Charles A. Beard of Columbia University was one), American intellectuals joined in the crusade.

Thus, the atmosphere was already poisoned when Wilson turned to Palmer in 1919 and ordered him not "to let this country see Red." In his 1919 tour, the president tried to gather support for his cause by

Captioned "Refusing to Give the Lady a Seat," this cartoon caricatures the three leading senators who opposed Wilson's handiwork at Paris and warns about the consequences of their opposition.

arguing that "there are apostles of Lenin in our own midst" and by warning about "the poison of disorder, the poison of revolt" that may actually have entered "into the veins of this free people." Wilson was trying to make the case that only his League could provide the antidote to this "poison." But, as historian Lloyd Gardner writes, Americans most feared that "the League would mean an increase in contacts with the poison-infected areas of the world." Or as Wilson himself cried, "This thing reaches the depths of tragedy."[36]

On November 19, in this supercharged environment, the Senate defeated the treaty containing Lodge's reservations 39 to 55. On Wilson's orders not to compromise, loyal Democrats joined the Irreconcilables to vote down the measure. Over the winter, however, public pressure built for reconsideration. Lodge's own opposition moderated. He was probably moving toward a deal with the Democrats when the Irreconcilables pulled him back, and Wilson once again refused to discuss such a deal. On March 19, 1920, the Senate again voted on the treaty that contained Lodge's reservations. This time a majority was in favor (49 to 35), but the number was short of the necessary two-thirds. Twelve Irreconcilables lined up with twenty-three diehard Wilsonian

Democrats to kill the measure, which again had a series of fifteen reservations attached. In 1921, the United States officially ended its role in the war by signing separate peace treaties with Germany and Austria.

Wilson actually hoped to recover from his paralysis and win an unprecedented third term in 1920 so that he could renew and win the fight for the League. Democratic party bosses never seriously considered his candidacy, throwing him a sop only by agreeing to make the campaign a "solemn referendum" on the Covenant. A U.S. presidential election is never a referendum on a single issue, however. Both the Republican ticket, led by Senator Warren G. Harding of Ohio, and the Democrats, headed by Ohio governor James Cox (with young New Yorker Franklin D. Roosevelt as the vice-presidential nominee), fudged the League issue until voters could not tell exactly where the candidates did stand.

Harding won an overwhelming victory by 7 million votes. The problem of restoring war-torn Europe and revolutionary Asia now fell to the Republicans. The League became a secondary issue, as well it might, for the central problem in 1919–1920 and after was not the Covenant, but the specific terms of boundaries, reparations, and mandates that the Paris peace conference produced. Historian Kendrick Clements believes that it is "perfect nonsense" to assume that U.S. membership in the League could have prevented the horrors of the 1930s.[37] Those catastrophes were rooted in the 1919 peace terms, not in the Covenant. Wilson bequeathed to Harding those treaties, a policy of containing (but not formally recognizing) the Soviet Union, and a world threatened with revolution. But the broken president was convinced that he only failed in part: "The world has been made safe for democracy. . . . But democracy has not yet made the world safe against irrational revolution."[38] It was up to Harding and, as it turned out, to all of his successors to deal with this more difficult problem of "revolution," both irrational and rational.

Notes

1. *The Record of American Diplomacy*, ed. Ruhl J. Bartlett, 4th ed. (New York, 1964), pp. 456–457.
2. Dean Acheson, "The Eclipse of the State Department," *Foreign Affairs* 49 (July 1971): 598.

3. Allan R. Millett and Peter Maslowski, *For the Common Defense* (New York, 1984), pp. 344–346, 350–352, 356–358.
4. *Churchill and Roosevelt: The Complete Correspondence*, ed. Warren Kimball, 3 vols. (Princeton, 1984), I, p. 88. A useful short analysis on naval strategy is David F. Trask, "Woodrow Wilson and World War I," in *American Diplomacy in the Twentieth Century*, ed. Warren F. Kimball (St. Louis, 1980), pp. 7–10.
5. J. A. S. Grenville and George B. Young, *Politics, Strategy, and American Diplomacy, 1873–1917* (New Haven, 1966), pp. 330–336.
6. Christopher Lasch, *The New Radicalism in America, 1889–1963* (New York, 1965), pp. 200–201.
7. Robert Lansing, *War Memoirs of Robert Lansing, Secretary of State* (Indianapolis, 1935), pp. 337–338.
8. N. Gordon Levin, Jr., *Woodrow Wilson and World Politics* (New York, 1968), pp. 50–51; Lansing, pp. 343–345.
9. Edward M. Bennett, *Recognition of Russia: An American Foreign Policy Dilemma* (Waltham, Mass., 1970), p. 26.
10. *Record of American Diplomacy*, pp. 459–461.
11. Peter G. Filene, *Americans and the Soviet Experiment, 1917–1933* (Cambridge, Mass., 1967), pp. 24–25, 59.
12. Lloyd C. Gardner, *Safe for Democracy* (New York, 1984), pp. 186–191.
13. Lloyd C. Gardner, *A Covenant with Power: America and World Order from Wilson to Reagan* (New York, 1984), pp. 20–27. A noted account is George Kennan, *Russia and the West under Lenin and Stalin* (Boston, 1960), chs. 5–8.
14. Linda Killen, *The Russian Bureau: A Case Study in Wilsonian Diplomacy* (Lexington, Ky., 1983), chs. 3–4, especially tells an interesting story.
15. William C. Bullitt to Edward M. House, 20 September 1918, Papers of Colonel Edward M. House, Yale University, New Haven, Connecticut.
16. Arthur S. Link, *Woodrow Wilson: Revolution, War, and Peace* (New York, 1979), p. 85.
17. Arno Mayer's two seminal books on the subject are *Political Origins of the New Diplomacy, 1917–1918* (New Haven, 1959), and *Politics and Diplomacy of Peacemaking . . . 1918–1919* (New York, 1967).
18. The standard study is Lawrence E. Gelfand, *The Inquiry: American Preparations for Peace, 1917–1919* (New Haven, 1963).
19. Ronald Steel, *Walter Lippmann and the American Century* (New York, 1981), pp. 149–150.
20. David Lloyd George, *War Memoirs*, 6 vols. (London, 1933–1936), I, pp. 40–48.
21. William L. Langer, "Peace and the New World Order," in *Woodrow Wilson and the World of Today*, ed. Arthur P. Dudden (Philadelphia, 1957), p. 71.
22. Woodrow Wilson, *The Public Papers of Woodrow Wilson*, ed. Ray Stannard Baker and William E. Dodd, Jr., 6 vols. (New York, 1925–1927), V, p. 569; Michael J. Hogan, "The United States and the Problem of International Economic Control . . . 1918–1920," *Pacific Historical Review* 44 (February 1975): 93–94.
23. F. Scott Fitzgerald, *Tender Is the Night: A Romance* (New York, 1948), p. 117; and also Gordon A. Craig, "The Revolution in War and Diplomacy," in *World War I: A Turning Point in Modern History*, ed. Jack Roth (New York, 1967), p. 8, for the Fitzgerald reference. A fine, brief background on the war's costs is in Paul Dukes, *A History of Europe, 1648–1948* (London, 1985), pp. 362–364.

24. Felix Frankfurter, *Felix Frankfurter Reminisces* (New York, 1960), p. 161. A provocative analysis is Lloyd E. Ambrosius, "Woodrow Wilson's Health and the Treaty Fight," *International History Review* 9 (February 1987): 82.
25. Paul F. Boller, Jr., *Presidential Anecdotes* (New York, 1981), p. 220.
26. Geoffrey Barraclough, *Introduction to Contemporary History* (New York, 1964), pp. 213–214.
27. Ray Stannard Baker, *Woodrow Wilson and the World Settlement,* 3 vols. (Garden City, N.Y., 1922), I, p. 102; II, pp. 63–64.
28. Gardner, *Safe for Democracy,* p. 262.
29. Herbert C. Hoover, *The Ordeal of Woodrow Wilson* (New York, 1958), pp. 134–137, 140–141. The contradictions in Wilson's overall policy are superbly captured in Betty Miller Unterberger, "Woodrow Wilson and the Bolsheviks: The 'Acid Test' of Soviet-American Relations," *Diplomatic History* 11 (Spring 1987): esp. 87–90.
30. John L. Snell, "Document: Wilson on Germany and the Fourteen Points," *Journal of Modern History* 26 (December 1954): 366–368.
31. Walter Lippmann, "The Political Scene," in *New Republic,* "Supplement," 22 March 1919.
32. Filene, pp. 52–53.
33. Thomas J. Knock, *To End All Wars* (New York, 1992), p. 253; William C. Widenor, *Henry Cabot Lodge and the Search for an American Foreign Policy* (Berkeley, Calif., 1980), p. 338.
34. Dimitri D. Lazo, "A Question of Loyalty: Robert Lansing and the Treaty of Versailles," *Diplomatic History* 9 (Winter 1985): 52–53; also Henry W. Brands, Jr., "Unpremeditated Lansing: His Scraps," *Diplomatic History* 9 (Winter 1985): 25–33.
35. Knock, *To End All Wars,* esp. pp. 227–270.
36. Gardner, *Safe for Democracy,* pp. 258–260; Knock, *To End All Wars,* p. 245.
37. Clements is quoted in Luther Spoehr, "Films for Classroom Reviewed," *OAH Newsletter* 14 (May 1986): 17.
38. Ronald Steel, "Revolting Times," *Reviews in American History* 13 (December 1985): 591.

For Further Reading

The extensive list of pre-1981 publications can best be found in the well-annotated chapters 18 and 19 of *Guide to American Foreign Relations since 1700,* ed. Richard Dean Burns (1983). Those references and the sources in the notes to this chapter and the General Bibliography at the end of this book are not usually repeated below. Also important is David R. Woodward and Robert F. Maddox, *America and World War I: A Selected Annotated Bibliography of English-Language Sources* (1985); and Linda Kallen and Richard Lael, *Versailles and After: An Annotated Bibliography* (1983).

Useful overviews, with excellent bibliographical references, are Kendrick A. Clements, *The Presidency of Woodrow Wilson* (1992); Thomas J. Knock, *To End All Wars* (1992); and Lloyd E. Ambrosius, *Woodrow Wilson and the American Diplomatic Tradition* (1987). Important for the war at home are Charles DeBenedetti's several important books on the peace movement, especially *Peace Heroes in Twentieth-Century America* (1986), which he edited and which has good chapters on Debs and Addams; Nick Salvatore's prize-winning biography, *Eugene V. Debs* (1983); Stephen L. Vaughn, *Holding Fast the Inner Lines: Democracy, Nationalism and the Committee on Public Information* (1980). For the war abroad, Edward M. Coffman, *The War to End All Wars: The American Military Experience in World War I* (1987), is a standard by a distinguished military historian; Lester H. Brune, *The Origins of American National Security Policy: Sea Power, Air Power and Foreign Policy 1900–1941* (1981); and Gerald W. Patton, *The Black Officer in the American Military, 1915–1941* (1981), a helpful survey. Daniel Yergin's *The Prize* (1991) is a prize-winning account of the key role of oil.

Recent work on the peace settlement includes William C. Widenor, "The United States and the Versailles Peace Settlement," in *Modern American Diplomacy*, ed. John M. Carroll and George C. Herring (1986); Edwin A. Weinstein, *Woodrow Wilson: A Medical and Psychological Biography* (1981), a provocative analysis; the relevant chapters on post-1917 affairs in *Woodrow Wilson and a Revolutionary World, 1913–1921*, ed. Arthur S. Link (1982); and Arthur Link, *The Public Papers of Woodrow Wilson* (1966–), especially volume 55 on early 1919 (1987). The critical question of Germany is discussed in A. Lentin, *Lloyd George, Woodrow Wilson, and the Guilt of Germany* (1985), provocative; Klaus Schwabe, *Woodrow Wilson, Revolutionary Germany and Peacemaking, 1918–1919* (1985), provocative and exhaustive; Manfred Jonas, *The United States and Germany: A Diplomatic History* (1984), a good overview with useful bibliography. For French relations, see Henry Blumenthal, *Illusion and Reality in Franco-American Diplomacy, 1914–1945* (1986). Thomas N. Guinsburg, *The Pursuit of Isolationism in the U.S. Senate from Versailles to Pearl Harbor* (1982), is an important work on the fight in Washington. The intervention into Russia is reinterpreted by a leading scholar of that affair, Betty Miller Unterberger, "Woodrow Wilson and the Bolsheviks: The 'Acid Test' of Soviet-American Relations," *Diplomatic History* 11 (Spring 1987); and important new sources are Benjamin D. Rhodes, "A Prophet in the Russian Wilderness: The Mission of Consul Felix Cole at Archangel, 1917–1919," *Review of Politics* 46 (July 1984), and Rhodes's *The Anglo-American Winter War with Russia, 1918–1919* (1988).

More recent, important contributions include John Milton Cooper, Jr., and Charles E. Neu, eds., *The Wilson Era: Essays in Honor of Arthur S. Link* (1991), especially the Levering, Cooper, Neu, and Knock essays on 1917–1921; Betty M. Unterberger, *The United States, Revolutionary Russia and the Rise of Czechoslovakia* (1989); Christine A. White, *British and American Commercial Relations with Russia, 1918–1924* (1992); Sevan G. Terzian, "Henry Cabot Lodge and the Armenian Mandate Question, 1918–20," *Armenian Review* 44 (Autumn 1991), 23–37; and the important overview, Akira Iriye, *The Globalizing of America, 1914–1945*, in *The Cambridge History of U.S. Foreign Relations*, ed. Warren Cohen (1993).

U.S. Presidents and Secretaries of State

Presidents	*Secretaries of State*
George Washington of Virginia (1789–1797)	Robert R. Livingston of New York (1781–1783 under Continental Congress)
	John Jay of New York (1784–1789 under Continental Congress)
	Thomas Jefferson of Virginia (1789–1793)
	Edmund Randolph of Virginia (1794–1795)
John Adams of Massachusetts (1797–1801)	Timothy Pickering of Pennsylvania (1795–1800)
	John Marshall of Virginia (1800–1801)
Thomas Jefferson of Virginia (1801–1809)	James Madison of Virginia (1801–1809)
James Madison of Virginia (1809–1817)	Robert Smith of Maryland (1809–1811)
	James Monroe of Virginia (1811–1817)
James Monroe of Virginia (1817–1825)	John Quincy Adams of Massachusetts (1817–1825)
John Quincy Adams of Massachusetts (1825–1829)	Henry Clay of Kentucky (1825–1829)
Andrew Jackson of Tennessee (1829–1837)	Martin Van Buren of New York (1829–1831)
	Edward Livingston of Louisiana (1831–1833)
	Louis McLane of Delaware (1833–1834)
Martin Van Buren of New York (1837–1841)	John Forsyth of Georgia (1834–1841)

William Henry Harrison of Ohio (1841)	Daniel Webster of Massachusetts (1841–1843)
John Tyler of Virginia (1841–1845)	Abel P. Upshur of Virginia (1843–1844) John C. Calhoun of South Carolina (1844–1845)
James K. Polk of Tennessee (1845–1849)	James Buchanan of Pennsylvania (1845–1849)
Zachary Taylor of Louisiana (1849–1850)	John M. Clayton of Delaware (1849–1850)
Millard Fillmore of New York (1850–1853)	Daniel Webster of Massachusetts (1850–1852) Edward Everett of Massachusetts (1852–1853)
Franklin Pierce of New Hampshire (1853–1857)	William L. Marcy of New York (1853–1857)
James Buchanan of Pennsylvania (1857–1861)	Lewis Cass of Michigan (1857–1860) Jeremiah S. Black of Pennsylvania (1860–1861)
Abraham Lincoln of Illinois (1861–1865)	William H. Seward of New York (1861–1869)
Andrew Johnson of Tennessee (1865–1869)	
Ulysses S. Grant of Illinois (1869–1877)	Hamilton Fish of New York (1869–1877)
Rutherford B. Hayes of Ohio (1877–1881)	William M. Evarts of New York (1877–1881)
James A. Garfield of Ohio (1881)	James G. Blaine of Maine (1881)
Chester A. Arthur of New York (1881–1885)	Frederick T. Frelinghuysen of New Jersey (1881–1885)
Grover Cleveland of New York (1885–1889)	Thomas F. Bayard of Delaware (1885–1889)
Benjamin Harrison of Indiana (1889–1893)	James G. Blaine of Maine (1889–1892) John W. Foster of Indiana (1892–1893)
Grover Cleveland of New York (1893–1897)	Walter Q. Gresham of Indiana (1893–1895) Richard Olney of Massachusetts (1895–1897)
William McKinley of Ohio (1897–1901)	John Sherman of Ohio (1897–1898) William R. Day of Ohio (1898) John Hay of the District of Columbia (1898–1905)

Theodore Roosevelt of New York (1901–1909)	Elihu Root of New York (1905–1909) Robert Bacon of New York (1909)
William Howard Taft of Ohio (1909–1913)	Philander C. Knox of Pennsylvania (1909–1913)
Woodrow Wilson of New Jersey (1913–1921)	William Jennings Bryan of Nebraska (1913–1915) Robert Lansing of New York (1915–1920) Bainbridge Colby of New York (1920–1921)
Warren G. Harding of Ohio (1921–1923)	Charles Evans Hughes of New York (1921–1925)
Calvin Coolidge of Massachusetts (1923–1929)	Frank B. Kellogg of Minnesota (1925–1929)
Herbert C. Hoover of California (1929–1933)	Henry L. Stimson of New York (1929–1933)
Franklin D. Roosevelt of New York (1933–1945)	Cordell Hull of Tennessee (1933–1944) Edward R. Stettinius of Virginia (1944–1945)
Harry S. Truman of Missouri (1945–1953)	James F. Byrnes of South Carolina (1945–1947) George C. Marshall of Pennsylvania (1947–1949) Dean G. Acheson of Maryland (1949–1953)
Dwight D. Eisenhower of New York (1953–1961)	John Foster Dulles of New York (1953–1959) Christian A. Herter of Massachusetts (1959–1961)
John F. Kennedy of Massachusetts (1961–1963)	Dean Rusk of New York (1961–1969)
Lyndon B. Johnson of Texas (1963–1969)	
Richard M. Nixon of California (1969–1974)	William P. Rogers of Maryland (1969–1973)
Gerald R. Ford of Michigan (1974–1977)	Henry A. Kissinger of the District of Columbia (1973–1977)
Jimmy Carter of Georgia (1977–1981)	Cyrus R. Vance of New York (1977–1980) Edmund Muskie of Maine (1980–1981)
Ronald Reagan of California (1981–1989)	Alexander Haig of Maryland (1981–1982)

	George Shultz of California (1982–1989)
George Bush of Texas (1989–1993)	James A. Baker of Texas (1989–1993)
William Clinton of Arkansas (1993–)	Warren Christopher of California (1993–)

General Bibliography

AFGHANISTAN: Anthony Arnold, *Afghanistan* (1981); Stanley Wolpert, *Roots of Confrontation in South Asia* (1982).

AFRICA: *Africa Contemporary Record: Annual Survey and Documents* (1968–); Peter Duignan and Lewis H. Gann, *The United States and Africa* (1984); Henry F. Jackson, *From Congo to Soweto* (1982). (See also individual countries.)

ANGOLA: John A. Marcum, *The Angolan Revolution*, 2 vols. (1969, 1978). (See also AFRICA.)

ARGENTINA: Joseph Tulchin, *Argentina and the United States* (1990); Arthur P. Whitaker, *The U.S. and the Southern Cone* (1976). (See also LATIN AMERICA.)

ATLASES: Gerard Chaliand and Jean-Pierre Rageau, *Strategic Atlas* (1985); Michael Kidron and Dan Smith, *The State of the World Atlas* (1981); Harry F. Young, *Atlas of U.S. Foreign Relations* (1983).

AUSTRALIA: Glen St. John Barclay, *Friends in High Places: The Australian-American Security Relationship since 1945* (1985).

BIBLIOGRAPHY: *Guide to American Foreign Relations since 1700*, ed. Richard Dean Burns (1983); Linda Killen and Richard L. Lael, *Versailles and After: An Annotated Bibliography of American Foreign Relations, 1919–1933* (1982). (See also individual topics.)

BRAZIL: Frank D. McCann, *The Brazilian-American Alliance, 1937–1945* (1972); Robert Wesson, *The U.S. and Brazil* (1981). (See also LATIN AMERICA.)

CAMBODIA: William Shawcross, *The Quality of Mercy* (1984); William Shawcross, *Sideshow* (1979). (See also VIETNAM.)

CANADA: Charles Doran, *Forgotten Partnership* (1985); *Canada and the United States*, ed. Charles F. Doran and John H. Sigler (1985); Seymour Martin Lipset, *Continental Divide* (1990); Lawrence Martin, *Presidents and the Prime Ministers . . . 1867–1982* (1982).

CENTRAL AMERICA: John Booth and Thomas Walker, *Understanding Central America* (1993); *The Central American Crisis*, ed. Kenneth M. Coleman and George C. Herring (1991); Walter LaFeber, *Inevitable Revolutions* (1993); Thomas M. Leonard, *Central America and U.S. Policies, 1820s–1980s* (1985). Ralph L. Woodward, *Central America* (1986). (See also individual countries.)

CENTRAL INTELLIGENCE AGENCY: John Ranelagh, *The Agency* (1987); Bradley F. Smith, *The Shadow Warriors* (1983); Gregory F. Treverton, *Covert Action* (1987).

Chile: James Petras and Morris Morley, *The U.S. and Chile* (1975); William F. Sater, *Chile and the United States* (1990).

China: Warren Cohen, *America's Response to China* (1990); John K. Fairbank, *The U.S. and China* (1983); Michael H. Hunt, *The Making of a Special Relationship: The U.S. and China to 1914* (1983); Arnold Xiangze Jiang, *The U.S. and China* (1988); Michael Schaller, *The U.S. and China in the Twentieth Century* (1990).

Colombia: Richard Lael, *Arrogant Diplomacy . . . 1903–1922* (1987).

Communism: Hoover Institution, *Yearbook on International Communist Affairs* (1966–). (See also individual countries.)

Congress: John Rourke, *Congress and the Presidency in U.S. Foreign Policymaking* (1983); *Congress and American Foreign Policy*, ed. Göran Rystad (1982); *To Advise and Consent*, 2 vols., ed. Joel Silbey (1990).

Constitution: Louis Fisher, *Constitutional Conflicts between Congress and the President* (1985); Louis Henkin, *Foreign Affairs and the Constitution* (1975); Charles A. Lofgren, *Government from Reflection and Choice* (1986); John H. Sullivan, *The War Powers Resolution* (1982).

Containment: *Containment*, 2 vols., ed. Terry L. Deibel and J. L. Gaddis (1986); J. L. Gaddis, *Strategies of Containment* (1982).

Cuba: Philip S. Foner, *A History of Cuba in Its Relations with the U.S.* (1962–); Morris H. Morley, *Imperial State and Revolution* (1987); Louis A. Perez, Jr., *Cuba: An Annotated Bibliography* (1988); Louis A. Perez, Jr., *Cuba and the United States* (1990); Robert F. Smith, *The U.S. and Cuba* (1969).

Culture and Philanthrophy: Edward H. Berman, *The Influence of the Carnegie, Ford, and Rockefeller Foundations on American Foreign Policy* (1983); Morrell Heald and Lawrence S. Kaplan, *Culture and Diplomacy* (1977); Frank A. Ninkovich, *The Diplomacy of Ideas . . . 1938–1950* (1981); Ron Robin, *Enclaves of America; The Rhetoric of American Political Architecture Abroad, 1900–1965* (1992).

Department of State: Robert U. Goehlert and Elizabeth Hoffmeister, *The Department of State and American Diplomacy* (1986) [bibliography]; Barry Rubin, *Secrets of State* (1985); Richard H. Werking, *The Master Architects: Building the U.S. Foreign Service, 1890–1913* (1977).

Dictionaries: John E. Findling, *Dictionary of American Diplomatic History* (1980).

Documents: Ruhl Bartlett, *The Record of American Diplomacy* (1964); U.S. Department of State, *Foreign Relations of the United States* (1861–); U.S. Superintendent of Documents, *Monthly Catalog of U.S. Government Publications* (1895–).

Dominican Republic: Rayford W. Logan, *Haiti and the Dominican Republic* (1968).

Economics: *Economics and World Power*, ed. William H. Becker and Samuel F. Wells, Jr. (1984); Joan Edelman Spero, *The Politics of International Economic Relations*, (1981); *Economic Coercion and U.S. Foreign Policy*, ed. Sidney Weintraub (1982); Mira Wilkins, *The Emergence of the Multinational Enterprise* (1970); Mira Wilkins, *The Maturing of the Multinational Enterprise* (1974); William A. Williams, *The Tragedy of American Diplomacy* (1988).

Egypt: William J. Burns, *Economic Aid and American Policy toward Egypt, 1955–1981* (1985). (See also Middle East.)

El Salvador: Cynthia Arnson, *El Salvador* (1982); Raymond Bonner, *Weakness and Deceit* (1984); *El Salvador*, ed. Marvin E. Gettleman *et al.*, (1981); Tommie Sue Montgomery, *Revolution in El Salvador* (1982). (See also Central America.)

Encyclopedias: *Political Handbook of the World*, ed. Arthur S. Bank (1975–); *Ency-*

clopedia of American Foreign Policy, 3 vols., ed. Alexander DeConde (1978).

ETHIOPIA: David A. Korn, *Ethiopia, the U.S., and the Soviet Union* (1986). Jeffrey S. Lefebvre, *Arms for the Horn . . . 1953–1991* (1991). (See also AFRICA.)

ETHNIC GROUPS: *Ethnic Groups and U.S. Foreign Policy*, ed. Mohammed E. Ahrari (1987); Paul Findley, *They Dare to Speak Out* (1985); Edward Tivnan, *The Lobby* (1987); Stephen A. Garrett, *From Potsdam to Poland* (1986) [on Polish ethnic groups]. (See also RACE AND ETHNICITY.)

EUROPE: Richard Barnet, *The Alliance* (1984); *American Historians and the Atlantic Alliance*, ed. Lawrence Kaplan (1991); Pierre Mélandri, *Les États-Unis face à l'unification de l'Europe: 1945–1954* (1980); *The Dissolving Alliance*, ed. Richard L. Rubenstein (1987). (See also individual countries.)

EXECUTIVE AGREEMENTS: Diane Shaver Clemens, "Executive Agreements," in *Encyclopedia of American Foreign Policy*, ed. Alexander DeConde (1978); Lawrence Margolis, *Executive Agreements and Presidential Power in Foreign Policy* (1986). (See also CONSTITUTION.)

FRANCE: Frank Costigliola, *The Cold Alliance* (1992); Julian G. Hurstfield, *America and the French Nation* (1986).

GERMANY: Manfred Jonas, *U.S. and Germany* (1984); Frank Ninkovich, *Germany and the United States* (1988); *Germany and America*, ed. Hans L. Trefousse (1981).

GREAT BRITAIN: *The Special Relationship . . . since 1945*, ed. William R. Louis and Hedley Bull (1986).

GREECE: *Greek-American Relations*, ed. Theodore A. Couloumbis and John O. Iatrides (1980); Lawrence S. Wittner, *American Intervention in Greece, 1943–1949* (1982).

GRENADA: *American Intervention in Grenada*, ed. Peter M. Dunn and Bruce W. Watson (1985); Gordon K. Lewis, *Grenada* (1987).

GUATEMALA: Jim Handy, *Gift of the Devil* (1985); Richard Immerman, *The CIA in Guatemala* (1982). (See also CENTRAL AMERICA; LATIN AMERICA.)

HAITI: Tom Barry *et al.*, *The Other Side of Paradise* (1984); Brenda Gayle Plummer, *Haiti and the United States* (1992). (See also LATIN AMERICA.)

HUMAN RIGHTS: Natalie Kaufman, *Human Rights Treaties and the Senate* (1990); A. Glenn Mower, *The U.S., UN, and Human Rights* (1979); Lars Schoultz, *Human Rights and U.S. Policy toward Latin America* (1981).

IMPERIALISM: Philip Darby, *Three Faces of Imperialism . . . 1870–1970* (1987); Michael W. Doyle, *Empires* (1986); *Imperialism and After*, ed. Wolfgang J. Mommsen and Jurgen Osterhammel (1986); Vivian Triás, *Historia del imperialismo norteamericano*, 3 vols. (1975–1977).

INDIA: H. W. Brands, *India and the United States* (1990); Gary R. Hess, "Global Expansion and Regional Balances . . . ," *Pacific Historical Review* 56 (May 1975): 159–195 [a valuable bibliographical essay]; Dennis Merrill, *The United States and India . . . 1947–1962* (1990); Kilaru Ram Chandra Rao, *India, U.S. and Pakistan* (1985).

INDIANS (NATIVE AMERICANS): Brian W. Dippie, *The Vanishing American* (1982); Francis Paul Prucha, *The Indians in American Society* (1985).

INDONESIA: Michael Leifer, *Indonesia's Foreign Policy* (1983).

INTELLIGENCE: *Knowing One's Enemies*, ed. Ernest R. May (1985). (See also CENTRAL INTELLIGENCE AGENCY.)

INTERNATIONAL LAW: Calvin D. Davis, *The U.S. and the First Hague Peace Conference* (1962); Calvin D. Davis, *The U.S. and the Second Hague Peace Conference* (1976); *International Law: A Contemporary Perspective*, ed. Richard Falk *et al.* (1985); Daniel

Patrick Moynihan, *The Law of Nations* (1990); D. P. O'Connell, *The International Law of the Sea* (1982).

Iran: James A. Bill, *The Eagle and the Lion* (1988); Mark H. Lytle, *The Origins of the Iranian-American Alliance, 1941–1953* (1987); R. K. Ramazani, *The United States and Iran* (1982).

Iraq: See Middle East; Oil; Persian Gulf.

Ireland: Donald H. Akenson, *The U.S. and Ireland* (1973).

Isolationism: Wayne S. Cole, *Roosevelt and the Isolationists* (1983); Justus D. Doenecke, *Anti-Intervention: A Bibliographical Introduction to Isolationism and Pacifism from World War I to the Early Cold War* (1987); Manfred Jonas, *Isolationism in America* (1966).

Israel: Cheryl Rubenberg, *Israel and the American National Interest* (1986); David Schoenbaum, *The U.S. and Israel* (1993); (See also Middle East.)

Italy: Alexander DeConde, *Half-Bitter, Half-Sweet* (1971); H. Stuart Hughes, *The U.S. and Italy* (1979).

Japan: *The U.S. and Japan in the Postwar World,* ed. Akira Iriye and Warren Cohen (1989); Charles E. Neu, *The Troubled Encounter* (1975); William L. Neumann, *America Encounters Japan* (1963).

Korea: *One Hundred Years of Korean-American Relations,* ed. Yur-Bok Lee and W. Patterson (1986); Chae-Jin Lee and Hideo Sato, *U.S. Policy toward Japan and Korea* (1982).

Labor: Philip S. Foner, *U.S. Labor . . . and Latin America (1846–1919)* (1988); Ronald Radosh, *American Labor and U.S. Foreign Policy* (1969).

Latin America: Cole Blasier, *The Hovering Giant* (1975); Lester Langley, *America and the Americas* (1990); Lester Langley, *Americans and the Caribbean in the Twentieth Century* (1980); John T. Reid, *Spanish-American Images of the U.S., 1790–1960* (1977); Harold Molineau, *U.S. Policy toward Latin America* (1986); (See also Central America; individual countries.)

Law: See International Law.

Lebanon: Itamar Rabinovich, *The War for Lebanon* (1986). (See also Middle East.)

Liberia: Katherine Harris, *The U.S. and Liberia* (1985); Hassan B. Sisay, *Big Powers and Small Nations* (1985).

Libya: P. E. Haley, *Qaddafi and the U.S. since 1969* (1984).

Malaysia: *The United States and Malaysia,* ed. Pamela Sodhy (1988).

Manifest Destiny: Albert K. Weinberg, *Manifest Destiny* (1935).

Mexico: George W. Grayson, *The U.S. and Mexico* (1984); Lester Langley, *Mexico and the United States* (1991); W. Dirk Raat, *Mexico and the United States* (1992); Alan Riding, *Distant Neighbors* (1984); Josefine Zoraida Vazquez and Lorenzo Meyer, *The U.S. and Mexico* (1985). (See also Latin America.)

Middle East: L. Carl Brown, *International Politics and the Middle East* (1984); Thomas Bryson, *U.S.–Middle East Diplomatic Relations, 1784–1978* (1979) [an annotated bibliography]; William R. Polk, *The Arab World Today* (1991); Steven L. Spiegel, *The Other Arab-Israel Conflict* (1985); William Stivers, *America's Confrontation with Revolutionary Change in the Middle East, 1948–1983* (1986); Seth Tillman, *The U.S. in the Middle East* (1982). (See also individual countries.)

Military: Benjamin R. Beede, *Intervention and Counterinsurgency . . . 1898–1984* (1985) [annotated bibliography]; *The Wars in Vietnam, Cambodia, and Laos, 1945–1982,* ed. Richard D. Burns and Milton Leitenberg (1984) [annotated bibliography]; John Whiteclay Chambers, *To Raise an Army: The Draft Comes to America* (1987); *A Bibli-*

ography of American Naval History, ed. Paolo E. Coletta (1981); Kenneth J. Hagan and William R. Roberts, *Against All Enemies* (1986); *American Historians and the Atlantic Alliance*, ed. Lawrence Kaplan (1991); Ariel E. Levite, Bruce W. Jentleson, Larry Berman, *Foreign Military Intervention* (1992); Peter Maslowski and Richard Millett, *The Common Defense* (1984); Paul B. Stares, *The Militarization of Space* (1985).

MISSIONS: William R. Hutchison, *Errand to the World* (1987); James Reed, *The Missionary Mind and American East Asia Policy, 1911–1915* (1986).

MONROE DOCTRINE: Dexter Perkins, *A History of the Monroe Doctrine* (1963).

NETHERLANDS, THE: *A Bilateral Bicentennial: A History of Dutch-American Relations, 1782–1982*, ed. J. W. Nordholt *et al.* (1982).

NICARAGUA: Karl Bermann, *Under the Big Stick* (1986); Peter Kornbluh, *Nicaragua, the Price of Intervention* (1987); Thomas W. Walker, *Nicaragua* (1991). (See also CENTRAL AMERICA; LATIN AMERICA.)

NORWAY: Sigmund Skard, *The U.S. in Norwegian History* (1976).

NUCLEAR ARMS: Coit D. Blacker, *Reluctant Warriors* (1987); Lawrence Freedman, *The Evolution of Nuclear Strategy* (1983); Institute for Strategic Studies (London), *The Military Balance* (1959–); Ronald Powaski, *March to Armageddon* (1987); Gordon C. Schloming, *American Foreign Policy and the Nuclear Dilemma* (1987). (See also MILITARY.)

OIL: David S. Painter, *Oil and the American Century* (1986); Stephen J. Randall, *U.S. Foreign Oil Policy, 1919–1984* (1985); Michael B. Stoff, *Oil, War, and American Security* (1980); Daniel Yergin, *The Prize* (1991).

PAKISTAN: *U.S.-Pakistan Relations*, ed. Leo E. Rose and Noor A. Husain (1985); M. S. Venkataramani, *The American Role in Pakistan, 1947–1958* (1982). (See also INDIA.)

PANAMA: Michael L. Conniff, *Panama and the United States* (1992); David N. Farnsworth and James W. McKenney, *U.S.-Panama Relations, 1902–1978* (1983); George D. Moffett III, *Limits of Victory* (1985); Walter LaFeber, *The Panama Canal* (1990). (See also LATIN AMERICA.)

PEACE MOVEMENTS: *Peace Heroes in Twentieth-Century America*, ed. Charles DeBenedetti (1986); Charles DeBenedetti, *The Peace Reform in American History* (1980); Justus D. Doenecke, *Anti-Intervention* (1987) [annotated bibliography]; Lawrence S. Wittner, *Rebels Against War . . . 1933–1983* (1984).

PERSIAN GULF: *The Persian Gulf States*, ed. Alvin J. Cottrell (1980); Charles A. Kupchan, *The Persian Gulf and the West* (1987); Michael A. Palmer, *Guardians of the Gulf: A History of America's Expanding Role in the Persian Gulf, 1833–1992* (1992); *The Gulf War Reader*, ed. M. L. Sifry and C. Serf (1991). (See also MIDDLE EAST; OIL.)

PERU: Frederick B. Pike, *The U.S. and the Andean Republics* (1977). (See also LATIN AMERICA.)

PHILIPPINES: Raymond Bonner, *Waltzing with a Dictator* (1987); H. W. Brands, *Bound to Empire* (1992); *Reappraising an Empire*, ed. Peter W. Stanley (1983).

POLAND: Stephen A. Garrett, *From Potsdam to Poland* (1986); Piotr Wandycz, *The U.S. and Poland* (1980).

PRESIDENT: E. S. Corwin, *The President* (1957); Theodore Lowi, *The Personal President* (1985); Edmund Muskie *et al.*, *The President, the Congress and Foreign Policy* (1986). (See also CONGRESS; CONSTITUTION.)

PUBLIC OPINION AND THE PRESS: Bernard C. Cohen, *The Public's Impact on Foreign Policy* (1973); W. A. Dorman and Mansour Farhang, *The U.S. Press and Iran* (1987); Ralph B. Levering, *The Public and American Foreign Policy, 1918–1978* (1978).

Puerto Rico: Raymond Carr, *Puerto Rico* (1984); *Time for Decision*, ed. George Heine (1983).

Race and Ethnicity: Alexander DeConde, *Ethnicity, Race, and American Foreign Policy* (1992); Paul Gordon Lauren, *Power and Prejudice (1988).*

Russia and the Soviet Union: Michael Beschloss and Strobe Talbott, *At the Highest Levels* (1993) [covers 1988–1992]; John L. Gaddis, *Russia, the Soviet Union and the United States* (1990); Raymond L. Garthoff, *Détente and Confrontation* (1985) [covers 1969–1984]; Colin White, *Russia and America* (1988).

Saudi Arabia: Irvine H. Anderson, *Aramco, the U.S. and Saudi Arabia* (1981); Benson Lee Grayson, *Saudi-American Relations* (1982); David E. Long, *The U.S. and Saudi Arabia* (1985). (See also Middle East; Oil.)

Somolia: Jeffrey A. Lefebvre, *Arms for the Horn . . . 1953–1991* (1991).

South Africa: Thomas Borstelmann, *Apartheid's Reluctant Uncle* (1993); Christopher Coker, *The U.S. and South Africa, 1868–1985* (1986); *The Anti-Apartheid Reader*, ed. David Mermelstein (1987); Thomas J. Noer, *Cold War and Black Liberation . . . 1949–1968* (1985); Anthony Sampson, *Black and Gold* (1987). (See also Africa.)

Terrorism: Augustus Norton and Martin Greensburg, *International Terrorism* (1980) [annotated bibliography].

Thailand: Robert J. Muscat, *Thailand and the United States* (1990).

Turkey: Theodore A. Couloumbis, *The U.S., Greece and Turkey* (1983). (See also Middle East.)

United Nations: Seymour M. Finger, *American Ambassadors at the UN* (1987); Thomas M. Franck, *Nation against Nation* (1985); Evan Luard, *A History of the UN* (1982); Edmund Jan Osmanczyk, *The Encyclopedia of the UN and International Agreements* (1985); Giuseppe Schiavone, *International Organizations: A Dictionary and Directory* (1983).

Uruguay: Arthur P. Whitaker, *The U.S. and the Southern Cone* (1976). (See also Latin America.)

Venezuela: Sheldon B. Liss, *Diplomacy and Independence* (1978); Stephen G. Rabe, *The Road to OPEC: U.S. Relations with Venezuela, 1919–1976* (1982). (See also Latin America; Oil.)

Vietnam: Loren Baritz, *Backfire* (1985); *The Wars in Vietnam, Cambodia, and Laos, 1945–1982*, ed. Richard Dean Burns and Milton Leitenberg (1984) [an annotated bibliography of 6,200 entries]; Lloyd Gardner, *Approaching Vietnam* (1988); George Herring, *The Longest War* (1986); George Kahin, *Intervention* (1986); Paul M. Kattenburg, *The Vietnam Trauma in American Foreign Policy, 1945–1975* (1980); Gabriel Kolko, *Anatomy of a War* (1985); Gareth Porter, *Vietnam* (1980) [extensive documents]; Neil Sheehan, *A Bright Shining Lie: John Paul Vann and America in Vietnam* (1988); William A. Williams *et al.*, *America in Vietnam* (1985) [documents and introductions].

Acknowledgments for the First Edition

Along with the usual but ever more sincere thanks to Sandra, Scott, and Suzanne LaFeber for making the past years and the writing of this book worthwhile, I am deeply indebted to Ed Barber of W. W. Norton & Company and Gerry McCauley for the encouragement that made the book possible. The growing length of the manuscript was unforeseen, but not Ed Barber's patience, sound advice, and humor, and they made the enterprise bearable. I am also indebted to Linda Puckette and Carol Flechner of Norton for special help in preparing the manuscript for publication, and to indexer Anne Eberle.

Lloyd Gardner of Rutgers University critiqued the entire manuscript and continues to set the example as both a committed scholar and friend. Robert Divine of the University of Texas also read all the pages, as he has of much else I have drafted, and his friendship has been especially important during the past several years. The historical profession lost what it cannot afford to lose when R. H. Miller left it to join Congressman Ron Dellums's staff. Max Miller not only read all of this book, but conducted a private four-year seminar by providing detailed comments and volumes of research materials. I am much indebted to Diane Clemens of the University of California and William Widenor of the University of Illnois, both of whom gave large sections of the manuscript close and most helpful readings. Milton Leitenberg, whether in Sweden or Washington, provided important studies of his own and others on East-West relations. Despite the Carter-Reagan attempts to close off documents from scholars, there remain some to whom we owe a huge debt for their professionalism and practicing belief that a democracy can survive only when the government's actions can be examined. These persons include David Langbart of the National

Archives, David Humphrey of the Lyndon Johnson Presidential Library, and Dennis Bilger of the Harry S. Truman Presidential Library.

Eric Edelman and Dan Fried of the Department of State, and John Greer, now a lawyer, are scholars, valued friends and detached critics. The best ideas in this book are probably largely stolen from those named above or from Fred Harvey Harrington and Tom McCormick, both of the University of Wisconsin, and William Appleman Williams of Oregon State; those three are very special as scholars and friends.

Persons associated with Cornell University have, as always, been irreplaceable. Marie Underhill Noll's encouragement is even more valued now because she is also a neighbor. David Maisel, Arthur Kaminsky, Peter Schuck, Jeff Bialos, David Wechsler, Laurie Keenan, Stephen Arbogast, Dan Weil, Mark Lytle, Eric Alterman, Douglas Little, Frank Costigliola, Fred Adams, Frederick Drake, Bob Seidel, David Green, Gayle Plummer, Rich Johnston, and Kathy Harris are former students who now enjoy much success in their various professions but are never too busy to provide valuable advice and reading materials. Rick Mandel, David Jackson, Colleen Curtin, Agnes Sagan, and Jessica Wang have been imaginative research assistants. Cathy Hendley typed the final draft carefully and against deadlines. Jackie Hubble kindly helped with the typing when the deadlines were pressing. The Cornell University Libraries continue to be unsurpassed in resources and accessibility; I owe Alain Seznec, David Corson, Caroline Spicer, Janie Harris, and Martha Hsu particular thanks.

Five friends in the History Department read much of this book in various forms and provided important materials which often resulted from their own scholarship. This book is dedicated to them. They first came to Cornell to help teach the introductory American history course, and they have remained to become distinguished scholars, noted teachers, superb colleagues, and—of special importance—close friends. They and other friends who are Americanists—Margaret Washington, Stuart Blumin, Paul Gates, Fred Somkin, Dan Usner, Glenn Altschuler, Nick Salvatore, Bob Harris, and, in a special category, Ted Lowi—have made Ithaca a stimulating place in which to study American history.

Walter LaFeber
March 1988

Photo Credits

p. 13: National Portrait Gallery, Smithsonian Institution; p. 18: Courtesy American Antiquarian Society; p. 20: Bibliothèque Nationale, Paris; p. 22: New-York Historical Society, New York; p. 31: Department of State; p. 41: American Philosophical Society; p. 50: Warder Collection; p. 53: Courtesy American Antiquarian Society; p. 55: Historical Pictures Service; p. 61: Metropolitan Museum of Art; p. 62: Courtesy Department of Library Services, American Museum of Natural History; p. 66: Library of Congress; p. 74: Metropolitan Museum of Art, Gift of I.N. Phelps Stokes, Edward S. Hawes, Alice Mary Hawes, Marion Augusta Hawes, 1937 (37.14.34); p. 79: National Archives; p. 85: Pennsylvania Academy of Fine Arts; p. 106: National Portrait Gallery, Smithsonian Institution; p. 107: Library of Congress; p. 109: Metropolitan Museum of Art, Gift of I.N. Phelps Stokers, Edward S. Hawes, Alice Mary Hawes, Marion Augusta Hawes, 1937(37.14.2); p. 118: Courtesy of the New-York Historical Society, New York; p. 122: National Archives; p. 133: Chicago Historical Society; p. 138: National Archives; p. 140: National Archives; p. 147: UPI-Bettmann; p. 160: *Public Opinion*, January 17, 1901; p. 162: *Harpers Weekly*, June 22, 1878; p. 166: Granger Collection; p. 169: State Historical Society of North Dakota; p. 170: State Historical Society of North Dakota; p. 174: Library of Congress; p. 179: Public Archives of Hawaii; p. 186: Warder Collection; p. 195: National Portrait Gallery, Smithsonian Institution; p. 198: Brown Brothers; p. 199: New-York Historical Society, New York; p. 205: National Archives; p. 212: *Literary Digest*, January 26, 1901; p. 215: Smithsonian Institution Photo No. 44412; p. 216: Library of Congress; p. 220: Library of Congress; p. 234: Library of Congress; p. 237: Warder Collection; p. 243: Library of Congress; p. 246: *Public Opinion*, September 1, 1904; p. 248: *Review of Reviews*, March 1905; p. 254: Duke University Archives; p. 257: Library of Congress; p. 261: Library of Congress; p. 271: Franklin D. Roosevelt Library; p. 274: National Portrait Gallery, Smithsonian Institution; p. 276: Library of Congress; p. 278: Library of Congress; p. 287: *The New York Times;* p. 291: Museum of Modern Art, Film Stills Archive; p. 297: UPI-Bettmann; p. 304: National Archives; p. 314: National Portrait Gallery, Smithsonian Institution; p. 323: *Daily Herald;*p. 326: Warder Collection; p. 329: Library of Congress; p. 335: Department of State; p. 336: National Portrait Gallery, Smithsonian Institution; p. 339: Wide World Photos; p. 355: Historical Pictures Service; p. 356: Cesare, *Outlook;* p. 361: National Archives; p. 371: Franklin D. Roosevelt Library; p. 373: National Portrait Gallery, Smithsonian Institution; p. 380: UPI-Bettmann; p. 384: C.D. Batchelor, © 1936 New York News Inc., reprinted with permission; p. 400:

Museum of Modern Art, Film Stills Archive; p. 401: Franklin D. Roosevelt Library; p. 403: National Archives; p. 404: Franklin D. Roosevelt Library; p. 424: Franklin D. Roosevelt Library; p. 426: Franklin D. Roosevelt Library; p. 435: Franklin D. Roosevelt Library; p. 439: Franklin D. Roosevelt Library; p. 441: National Archives; p. 444: U.S. Army, courtesy of Harry S. Truman Library; p. 449: UN Photo, 149433; p. 459: Harry S. Truman Presidential Library; p. 465: Warder Collection; p. 467: United Nations; p. 472: Wide World Photos; p. 474: Library of Congress; p. 481: Department of State; p. 485: U.S. Information Agency; p. 505: Drawing by David Levine, reprinted with permission from *The New York Review of Books*, © 1964–74; p. 510: UPI-Bettmann; p. 516: United Nations; p. 527: UPI-Bettmann; p. 529: Roche in the *Buffalo Courier Express;* p. 538: UPI-Bettmann; p. 542: Journal of American History; p. 549: European Picture Service; p. 556: dpa-Bild; p. 559: Drawing by David Levine, reprinted with permission from *The New York Review of Books*, © 1964–1974; p. 565: Bastian, *San Francisco Chronicle;* p. 568: Magnum; p. 584: Wide World Photos; p. 594: AP-Wide World; p. 598: U.S. Air Force; p. 599: Cecil Stroughton; p. 605: Lyndon Baines Johnson Library, Austin, Texas; p. 615: Lyndon Baines Johnson Library, Austin, Texas; p. 616: Life Picture Service; p. 619: Lyndon Baines Johnson Library, Austin, Texas; p. 621: UPI-Bettmann; p. 624: Brooks, *Birmingham News;* p. 625: Lyndon Baines Johnson Library, Austin, Texas; p. 637: © Jules Feiffer; p. 642: *Valley News Dispatcher;* p. 648 UPI-Bettmann; p. 653: UPI-Bettmann; p. 658: Drawing by David Levine, reprinted with permission from *The New York Review of Books*, © 1964–1974; p. 666: UPI-Bettmann; p. 667: Drawing by David Levine, reprinted with permission from *The New York Review of Books*, © 1964–1974; p. 672: White House Official Photograph; p. 684: © 1977, Time, Inc., all rights reserved, reprinted by permission from *Time;* p. 689: AP Photo; p. 691: UN Photo; p. 693: ABC News, NYT Pictures; p. 705: from Herblock, *Through the Looking Glass* (W.W. Norton, 1984); p. 707: AP-Wild World; p. 710: UPI-Bettmann; p. 715: from Herblock, *Through the Looking Glass* (W.W. Norton, 1984); p. 719: Susan Moller; p. 735: UPI-Bettmann; p. 736: UPI-Bettmann; p. 750: AP-Wide World; p. 759: Reuters-Bettmann; p. 763: AP-Wide World; p. 768: AP-Wide World; p. 773: AP-Wide World; p. 775: © 1992 Raeside, *Victoria Times-Colonist;* p. 777: AP-Wide World.

Index

Italicized page numbers refer to drawings and photographs.